Old Irish Wisdom Attributed to
Aldfrith of Northumbria:

An Edition of
Bríathra Flainn Fhína maic Ossu

Medieval and Renaissance Texts and Studies

Volume 205

This plate shows page 345 from the Book of Leinster, TCD 1339 (H.2.18), the oldest manuscript containing any of the maxims edited herein. A quarter of the way down the second column (345 b 17) is the title *Senbríathra Fíthail*, a text which, I argue, is a Middle Irish conflation of Old Irish maxims attributed to Flann Fína (Aldfrith) and an Old Irish *speculum principum* known as *Tecosca Cormaic*.

Old Irish Wisdom Attributed to Aldfrith of Northumbria:

An Edition of Bríathra Flainn Fhína maic Ossu

edited and translated by

COLIN A. IRELAND

Arizona Center for Medieval and Renaissance Studies
Tempe, Arizona
1999

A grant from the
Beaver College Center for Education Abroad, Dublin,
has assisted in meeting the publication costs of this volume.

The frontispiece is reproduced courtesy of
the Board of Trinity College, Dublin.

Library of Congress Cataloging-in-Publication Data

Aldfrith, King of Northumbria, d. 705.
    [Bríathra Flainn Fhína maic Ossu. English]
    Old Irish wisdom attributed to Aldfrith of Northumbria : an edition of Bríathra
Flainn Fhína maic Ossu / edited and translated by Colin A. Ireland.
        p. cm. — (Medieval & Renaissance texts & studies ; v. 205)
    "The present edition is based on . . . three separate recensions, two of which are
attributed to Flann Fína while the third is associated with Fíthal" — Introd.
    Includes bibliographical references (p.) and index.
    ISBN 0-86698-247-7 (hardcover : alk. paper)
    1. Maxim, Irish. 2. Irish language—To 1100—Texts. I. Ireland, Colin A.,
1949– . II. Fíthal, 3rd cent. III. Title. IV. Series: Medieval & Renaissance
Texts & Studies (Series) ; v. 205.
PN6307.I7A43 1999
891.6'28102—dc21   99–34089
                                                                           CIP

This book is made to last.
It is set in Caslon,
smythe-sewn and printed on acid-free paper
to library specifications.

Printed in the United States of America

do Honóra

§ 5.20 Tosach sothcaid dagben

Table of Contents

Foreword

I undertook to edit this text as one aspect out of many in the understanding of cross-cultural links between early Ireland and Anglo-Saxon England. These maxims represent an Old Irish text attributed to King Aldfrith of Northumbria (ca. 685–705) under his Irish name Flann Fína. I feel that Anglo-Saxonists should be aware of its contents. I have endeavoured to meet the standards of an edition required by Celticists, but my aim has been to inform the general medievalist while satisfying the specialist. I hope that both Celticists and Anglo-Saxonists will find this a useful edition and informative reference work.

I wish to thank the libraries at Trinity College Dublin, the Royal Irish Academy, and the National Library of Ireland for access to their manuscript collections. The rôle of the School of Celtic Studies at the Dublin Institute for Advanced Studies may never be fully acknowledged.

I appreciate the contributions of those who attended my seminar on this text conducted at the Institute during 1988–89. The following people have, at various times, made suggestions and observations which have found their way into the edition: Liam Breatnach, Aidan Breen, Pádraig de Brún, David Dumville, Fergus Kelly, Damian McManus, Daniel Melia, Joseph Nagy, Tomás Ó Concheanainn, Jürgen Uhlich. No one named above is responsible for how I interpreted his suggestions.

I wish to express my gratitude to the editors and staff of Medieval and Renaissance Texts and Studies (MRTS) at the Arizona Center for Medieval and Renaissance Studies. Among them I found efficiency rather than caprice, candour rather than obfuscation, generosity rather than insecurity.

Sincere thanks are due to Robert Bjork, director and general editor, and Karen Lemiski, production manager. Their professionalism has made the process a pleasure. I alone am responsible for any shortcomings or infelicities that may remain.

Colin A. Ireland
Dublin, August 1999

Abbreviations

AL   *Ancient Laws of Ireland* I–VI (ed. W. N. Hancock, Thaddeus O'Mahony, Alexander Richey and Robert Atkinson, Dublin 1865–1901).

BL   British Library

CIH   *Corpus iuris hibernici* I–VI (ed. D. A. Binchy, Dublin 1978).

DIL   *(Contributions to a) Dictionary of the Irish Language* (ed. E. G. Quin et al., Dublin 1913–75).

GOI   *A Grammar of Old Irish* (R. Thurneysen, Dublin 1946, rev. ed. 1975).

Lexique   *Lexique étymologique de l'irlandais ancien* (J. Vendryes, E. Bachellery and P.-Y. Lambert, Dublin 1959–).

NLI   National Library of Ireland

NLS   National Library of Scotland

RIA   Royal Irish Academy

TC   *The Instructions of King Cormac mac Airt* [*Tecosca Cormaic*] (ed. K. Meyer, Dublin 1909).

TCD   Trinity College, Dublin

Thes.   *Thesaurus palaeohibernicus* (ed. W. Stokes and J. Strachan, Cambridge 1901–3).

Triads   *The Triads of Ireland* (ed. K. Meyer, Dublin 1906).

ZCP   *Zeitschrift für celtische Philologie*

Introduction

GENERAL BACKGROUND

Wisdom, or gnomic, literature comprises some of the oldest and most widely distributed compilations of human thought recorded. Large collections of pithy, sometimes exhortative and moralizing, observations on the nature of the world and humankind's place in it survive from civilizations as early as those of Sumeria and Egypt. Similar collections have been gathered from pre-literate cultures like those found in southern Africa and Oceania.[1] Nearly every language recorded in western Europe has preserved collections of wisdom literature.[2] It would seem that the desire to compile sententious

---

[1] For a wide-ranging historical and geographical survey of wisdom literature, see Martin L. West, ed., *Hesiod, Works & Days*, chapter 2, "Wisdom Literature" (Oxford: Clarendon Press, 1978), 3–25. For biblical, and the larger context of Near Eastern, wisdom literature, see R. B. Y. Scott, trans., *The Anchor Bible, Proverbs and Ecclesiastes* (Garden City, N.Y.: Doubleday & Company, Inc., 1965); and the *Encyclopedia of Religion* (1987), s.v. "wisdom literature".

[2] See the surveys in H. Munro Chadwick and Nora K. Chadwick, *The Growth of Literature*, vol. 1, *The Ancient Literatures of Europe*, chapter 12, "Gnomic Poetry" (Cambridge: Cambridge Univ. Press, 1932; repr. 1986), 377–403; and Patrick L. Henry, *The Early English and Celtic Lyric*, chapter 5, "The Gnomic Manner and Matter of Old English, Irish, Icelandic and Welsh" (London: George Allen & Unwin Ltd., 1966), 91–132. For an introduction to Welsh wisdom, see Kenneth H. Jackson, *Early Welsh Gnomic Poems* (Cardiff: Univ. of Wales Press, 1935). For Old English, T. A. Shippey, ed. and trans., *Poems of Wisdom and Learning in Old English* (Cambridge: D. S. Brewer; Totowa, N.J.: Rowman and Littlefield, 1976); Stanley B. Greenfield and Daniel G. Calder, *A New Critical History of Old English Literature*, chapter 11, "Lore and Wisdom" (New York and

didactic material is universal. In content these collections may be secular or religious, a learned background may be reflected in a pedantic style, while simple diction may reveal origins in folk wisdom. Some collections are notable for observations on the natural world, while others comment on humankind in its social framework. Some concentrate on the edification of the individual, of whatever social class, while others are concerned with the stability of society at large.

A wide variety of early Irish wisdom-texts survive.[3] The present edition is based on a gnomic collection consisting predominantly of terse three-word maxims which have come down in three separate recensions, two of which are attributed to Flann Fína while the third is associated with Fíthal. Flann Fína mac Ossu is the Irish name for King Aldrith son of Oswiu who ruled Anglo-Saxon Northumbria from ca. 685 to 705. His learning, piety, and efficient rule were recognized by such noted contemporaries as the English clerics Aldelm (d. 709) and Bede (d. 735), and the Irish cleric Adomnán (d. 704). His reign laid a firm foundation for the Northumbrian "Golden Age" (see pp. 52–56). Fíthal is a legendary poet and judge often associated with the equally legendary third-century king of Tara, Cormac mac Airt (see pp. 48–52).

This collection was first edited, but not translated, by Kuno Meyer under the title *Bríathra Flainn Fína maic Ossu*, "The Sayings of Flann Fína son of Oswiu".[4] The title used in the present edition is taken from one of two

---

London: New York Univ. Press, 1986), 253–79. For a view of Old English wisdom within the context of Near Eastern and biblical wisdom, see Elaine T. Hansen, *The Solomon Complex, Reading Wisdom in Old English Poetry* (Toronto: Univ. of Toronto Press, 1988). Carolyne Larrington, *A Store of Common Sense, Gnomic Theme and Style in Old Icelandic and Old English Wisdom Poetry* (Oxford: Clarendon Press, 1993) compares content and style in Old English and Icelandic wisdom. Morton W. Bloomfield and Charles W. Dunn argue that the basic role of the poet in all early societies was to carry tribal wisdom: *The Role of the Poet in Early Societies* (Cambridge: D. S. Brewer, 1989).

[3] For a list of early Irish law-texts and wisdom-texts, see Fergus Kelly, *A Guide to Early Irish Law*, Early Irish Law Series, vol. 3 (Dublin: Dublin Institute for Advanced Studies, 1988), 266–82 and 284–86 respectively. See also the interesting discussion, which mentions several early Irish wisdom-texts including the one edited here, by F. N. Robinson, "Irish Proverbs and Irish National Character," *Modern Philology* 43, no. 1 (1945): 1–10.

[4] Kuno Meyer, ed., "Bríathra Flainn Fína maic Ossu," in *Anecdota from Irish Manuscripts*, vol. 3, ed. O. J. Bergin, R. I. Best, K. Meyer, J. G. O'Keeffe (Halle: Max Niemeyer; and Dublin: Hodges, Figgis, & Co., 1910), 10–20.

manuscripts used by Meyer.[5] A related text edited, but not translated, by Rudolf Thurneysen under the title *Senbríathra Fíthail* "The Old Sayings of Fíthal"[6] contains long strings of these same maxims.[7] In addition, this latter text holds many sections in common with another wisdom-text known as *Tecosca Cormaic* "The Instructions of [King] Cormac".[8] The two texts edited by Meyer and Thurneysen were subsequently translated by Roland Smith, who treated Thurneysen's edition as the primary text, relegating those maxims not found in *Senbríathra Fíthail* to the second half of his paper.[9] In his edition of *Senbríathra Fíthail*, Thurneysen adverted to another collection of maxims, known as *Roscada Flainn Fína maic Ossu ríg Sacsan* "The Maxims of Flann Fína son of Oswiu, king of the English",[10] found in a fifteenth-century manuscript that is now bound together with the Yellow Book of Lecan.[11] This text, which is found under the same title in several other manuscripts, is very close in content, though not in order of sections and sequence of maxims, to *Bríathra Flainn Fína* as published by Kuno Meyer.

These three apparently distinct texts, which overlap with one another in varying degrees, are treated here as three diverse recensions of a gnomic collection for which it is now impossible to reconstruct the original. The recensions are referred to by letter after the major manuscript of each: Rec. N (from 23 N 10), Rec. Y (from the Yellow Book of Lecan),[12] and Rec. L (from the Book of Leinster).[13]

---

[5] See Appendix 5 below where the left column gives the text as found in RIA MS 23 N 10 and the maxims from two other manuscripts are collated with it.

[6] Rudolf Thurneysen, "Zu irischen Handschriften und Litteraturdenkmälern," in *Abhandlungen der Königlichen Gesellschaft der Wissenschaften zu Göttingen*, Philologisch-Historische Klasse n.F., vol. 14, no. 3 (Berlin: Weidmannsche Buchhandlung, 1912–13), 11–22.

[7] See Appendix 4 below for a diplomatic edition of the text as found in the Book of Leinster.

[8] Kuno Meyer, ed. and trans., *The Instructions of King Cormac mac Airt*, Todd Lecture Series, vol. 15 (Dublin: Hodges, Figgis, & Co.; London: Williams & Norgate, 1909) [= *TC*].

[9] Roland Smith, "The *Senbriathra Fithail* and Related Texts," *Revue Celtique* 45 (1928): 1–92; ("Senbríathra Fíthail") 4–61, ("Bríathra Flainn Fína") 61–92.

[10] See Appendix 3 below for a diplomatic edition of the *Roscada*.

[11] The manuscript now called the Yellow Book of Lecan is actually a composite of sixteen separate manuscripts bound together with what is known as the "Yellow Book of Lecan Proper".

[12] See footnote 11.

[13] For an illustration of the overlap, see Appendix 5 where the maxims in the three manuscripts just cited are collated using MS 23 N 10 as the basis for comparison.

The three-word maxims preserved in these three recensions can be divided into five groups based on the word which begins each maxim. These five words include the verbs *ad·cota* "gets, obtains" and *dligid* "deserves, merits"; the nouns *descad* "characteristic, inducement" and *tosach* "beginning, basis"; and the comparative adjective *ferr* "better". Two other sections are also edited as part of the main text. The first of these, § 2 *Ba faitech* "Be cautious," contains seven injunctions, the second, § 7 *Maith dán ecnae* "Learning is a beneficial occupation," contrasts *ecnae* "learning, acquired knowledge"[14] with *láechdacht* "the martial life, the lay life."

The purpose of this new edition is twofold. First, it gathers together all maxims represented in the three recensions — basing the order of sections and sequence of maxims on the collection as found in MS 23 N 10 — and offers a fresh translation of each maxim with an analysis of its contents. Second, it seeks to demonstrate that these maxims represent a coherent text despite the varied contexts in which they have been preserved.

Discussions of wisdom-texts often distinguish between the "human-gnome" and the "nature-gnome."[15] For example, early Welsh and Old English gnomic texts make frequent statements about the world of nature. Despite fine examples of detailed observations of nature in early Irish poetry, the "nature-gnome" is infrequent in Irish wisdom literature.[16] This is particularly true of the present text.

There is a problem of precise definition under a rubric as broad as wisdom literature. Early Irish vernacular terms for gnomic statements do not constitute a definition and their semantic range may confuse rather than clarify. For example, the manuscript titles supply the terms *bríathar* (pl. *bríathra*) "word, saying" and *roscad* (pl. *roscada*) "maxim, aphorism". The latter term is often used to describe cryptic, alliterative verse, both legal and

---

[14] *Ecnae* is often used to translate Latin *sapientia* and frequently implies divine wisdom or spiritual knowledge. See Liam Mac Mathúna, "An Introductory Survey of the Wordfield 'Knowledge' in Old and Middle Irish," in *Philologie und Sprachwissenschaft*, ed. Wolfgang Meid and Hans Schmeja, Akten der 10. Österreichischen Linguisten-Tagung (Innsbruck: Innsbrucker Beiträge zur Sprachwissenschaft, 1983): 155.

[15] See, for example, Jackson, *Early Welsh Gnomic Poems*, 1–2.

[16] See Kenneth H. Jackson, *Studies in Early Celtic Nature Poetry* (Cambridge: Cambridge Univ. Press, 1935; repr. Felinfach: Llanerch Publishers, 1995), esp. chapter 3, "Gnomic Poetry," 127–48.

non-legal.[17] In other contexts it seems to overlap semantically with *fásach* (pl. *fásaige*) in the meaning "legal precedent".[18]

Deciding which English terms to use in describing this text is also problematical. "Aphorisms", self-evident statements of observed fact, are generally lacking in our text.[19] The "precept", that is, an authoritative command or injunction,[20] is also absent from the three-word maxims — although the short § 2 *Ba faitech* is preceptual in character, it is not typical of our text as a whole. Neither is the term "proverb" appropriate to these maxims.[21] Although some of the maxims have been recorded in various genres of Irish literature, and over a long period of time, they cannot be described as metaphorical or allegorical observations from common experience. In fact, as we shall see, in both form and content this collection suggests a learned background. I prefer the English term "maxim" to designate these three-word statements, in the sense "a rule or principle of conduct; also, a precept of morality or prudence expressed in sententious form."[22]

---

[17] For a brief annotated survey on *roscad*, see Liam Breatnach, "Poets and Poetry," in *Progress in Medieval Irish Studies*, ed. Kim McCone and Katharine Simms (Maynooth: Saint Patrick's College, 1996), 70–73.

[18] Kelly, *Guide*, 196–97.

[19] Nature-gnomes are often stated as aphorisms of the type "Midnight is cold" or "Streams are wet". For these examples from Welsh poetry, see Patrick K. Ford, trans., *The Poetry of Llywarch Hen* (Berkeley and Los Angeles: Univ. of California Press, 1974), 68–69 § 11. The poem "Llym Awel" is a good example of this type of poetry in Welsh: Jenny Rowland, *Early Welsh Saga Poetry, a Study and Edition of the Englynion* (Cambridge: D. S. Brewer, 1990), 454–57 (Welsh), 501–3 (English).

[20] For an example of a collection of Modern Irish precepts, see Carl Marstrander, "Bídh Crínna," *Ériu* 5 (1911): 126–43.

[21] For literature on proverbs, see Archer Taylor, *The Proverb* (Cambridge, Mass.: Harvard Univ. Press, 1931); Lutz Röhrich and Wolfgang Mieder, *Sprichwort* (Stuttgart: Metzler, 1977); Wolfgang Mieder, *International Bibliography of Explanatory Essays on Individual Proverbs and Proverbial Expressions* (Bern: Peter Lang, 1977); Wolfgang Mieder, *Proverbs in Literature: An International Bibliography* (Bern: Peter Lang, 1978); Wolfgang Mieder, *International Proverb Scholarship: An Annotated Bibliography* (New York: Garland Press, 1982). For a recent treatment of Irish proverbs, see Liam Mac Con Iomaire, comp., *Ireland of the Proverb* (Dublin: Town House, 1988).

[22] *Oxford English Dictionary*, 2nd edition (1989), third entry s.v. "maxim".

VARIETIES OF IRISH WISDOM-TEXTS

All medieval literatures have a didactic element which may be expressed in sententious form. We do not need to limit ourselves to those texts which are typically classified under the rubric of "wisdom" to find appropriate examples. In the context of the biblical books Proverbs and Ecclesiastes, James G. Williams has stated that "Wisdom is dedicated to articulating a sense of order."[23] His definition, it seems to me, need not be restricted by chronological, geographical, social, or cultural considerations. Without having to extend Williams's definition we will see that early Irish literature provides a variety of texts with the characteristics of wisdom literature, in both Latin and in Irish, and both of a religious and of a secular nature. Since these texts are concerned with the definition of appropriate behaviour and the benefits that accrue from it, it is not surprising to find that they often encourage the same thoughts and actions, and also display similarities in vocabulary and style.

Daniel A. Binchy once stated that "Irish law was admonitory not imperative."[24] In other words, Early Irish law-tracts tend to describe precedents rather than dictate practice. They contain many didactic passages, and stylistically many legal axioms are expressed in a manner similar to that of wisdom literature.[25] Conversely, many maxims from the text edited herein are stylistically akin to concisely stated legal precedents. This is particularly apparent in the *dligid* and *ferr* series.[26]

Among the wisdom-texts found in early Irish literature is the type known as *speculum principum* "a mirror for princes". As the name implies, such texts are intended to instruct kings in the proper conduct of their affairs, often

---

[23] "Proverbs and Ecclesiastes," in *The Literary Guide to the Bible*, ed. Robert Alter and Frank Kermode (Glasgow: William Collins Sons & Co., 1987; repr. London: Fontana Press, 1989), 263.

[24] Daniel A. Binchy, "Brewing in Eighth-Century Ireland," in *Studies on Early Ireland: Essays in Honour of M. V. Duignan*, ed. B. G. Scott (Belfast: privately printed, 1981), 3.

[25] See, for example, Roland Smith, "*Cach* Formulas in the Irish Laws," *Zeitschrift für celtische Philologie* 20 (1936): 262–77 [= *ZCP*]; Roland Smith, "The Alphabet of Cuigne mac Emoin," *ZCP* 17 (1928): 45–72. (This latter text is correctly known as *Aibidil Luigne maic Éremóin*: Kelly, *Guide*, 286 § 7. See further the lists of law-texts and wisdom-texts: *Guide*, 264–86 appendices 1 and 2.)

[26] For examples from the eighth-century law-text *Di Astud Chor*, see Neil McLeod, ed., *Early Irish Contract Law*, Sydney Series in Celtic Studies, vol. 1 (Sydney: Centre for Celtic Studies, n.d. [1992]), 184–85 § 51 (*ferr*), and 186–87 § 52 (*dligid*).

with emphasis on how their behaviour affects the communities which they govern. In the ninth century, the Irishman Sedulius Scottus created such a document in Latin for the Carolingian courts.[27] The oldest of these *specula* in Irish is *Audacht Morainn* "The Testament of Morann", which was recorded by the year 700 according to its latest editor.[28] In this text, the renowned judge Morann mac Móin relates through an intermediary, Neire Núallgnáth, his instructions for proper conduct by Feradach Find Fechtnach, who is about to be made king. *Tecosca Cormaic* "The Instructions of [King] Cormac", mentioned previously in connection with *Senbríathra Fíthail*, is another Old Irish *speculum*. Cormac is a legendary third-century king who is compared for his wisdom with the biblical Solomon in later sources. In *Tecosca Cormaic* he instructs Cairpre, his son, who is about to succeed him in the kingship.[29] By their very nature *specula* reflect the hierarchical predisposition of Early Irish society and assume the viewpoint of nobility.

The collection of Old Irish *Triads*[30] is another of the better known wisdom-texts. In subject matter they range from secular to religious and from concerns of the nobility to the mundane preoccupations of ordinary persons. Fergus Kelly has pointed out that many triads are legal in origin, and some of them can be shown to be reworded directly from the laws.[31] For example, *Triads* no. 185 states *Trí mna ná dlegat díri: ben lasma cuma cipé las fái, ben gatach, ben aupthach* "Three women who are not entitled to honour-price: a woman who does not care whom she sleeps with, a thieving woman, a sorceress". It is derived directly from §44 of *Bretha Crólige*

---

[27] See Edward G. Doyle, trans., *Sedulius Scottus, On Christian Rulers and the Poems*, Medieval and Renaissance Texts and Studies, vol. 17 (Binghamton: Center for Medieval and Early Renaissance Studies, 1983).

[28] Fergus Kelly, ed., *Audacht Morainn* (Dublin: Dublin Institute for Advanced Studies, 1976), xiv, xxxiii.

[29] Other examples of Irish *specula* include Roland Smith, "On the Briatharthecosc Conculaind," *ZCP* 15 (1925): 187–92; the "Tecosc Cuscraid" included in Richard I. Best, "The Battle of Airtech," *Ériu* 8, no. 2 (1916): 170–90; a piece beginning *Diambad messe bad rí réil*, see Tadhg O'Donoghue [Tadhg Ó Donnchadha], "Advice to a Prince," *Ériu* 9 (1921–23): 43–54; and Tadhg O'Donoghue, "*Cert cech ríg co réil,*" in *Miscellany Presented to Kuno Meyer*, ed. Osborn Bergin and Carl Marstrander (Halle: Max Niemeyer, 1912), 258–77.

[30] Kuno Meyer, *The Triads of Ireland*, Todd Lecture Series, vol. 13 (Dublin: Hodges, Figgis, & Co.; London: Williams & Norgate, 1906).

[31] Kelly, *Guide*, 284–85.

"Judgements of Blood-Lying".[32] Grouping items into threes seems to have been a popular method of preserving lore and is well represented in Welsh tradition.[33] The tendency to schematize information in groups is prevalent throughout the Irish law-tracts. For example, the *Heptads* organize information into groups of seven.[34]

Since we have secular wisdom-texts written in the vernacular which concern themselves with proper conduct and its consequences for society at large, then it is only natural that similar texts were also written in Latin. These Latin texts may have been composed from either a secular or a theological point of view. A gnomic compilation called *Proverbia Grecorum* may have been current in Ireland as early as the sixth century, although the seventh century is more likely. It was once assumed to be a translation into Latin from a Greek original.[35] Another Latin text, *De duodecim abusivis saeculi*, from the first half of the seventh century, is of Irish origin. Its message is directed as much at the laity as at the clergy and addresses those of high and low social status, rich and poor, men and women, young and old.[36] The section on the iniquitous king may have influenced the Carolingian and later medieval *specula principum* tradition.[37]

---

[32] Daniel A. Binchy, *"Bretha Crólige,"* Ériu 12 (1934–38): 34 = Binchy, ed., *Corpus Iuris Hibernici*, vol. 6 (Dublin: Dublin Institute for Advanced Studies, 1978), 2298.8–10; discussed in Kelly, *Guide*, 284–85.

[33] For example, Rachel Bromwich, ed. and trans., *Trioedd Ynys Prydein*, the Welsh Triads, 2nd ed. (Cardiff: Univ. of Wales Press, 1978). For an Irish example of a single triad repeated in a variety of texts, see Patrick Sims-Williams, "Thought, Word and Deed: an Irish Triad," *Ériu* 29 (1978): 78–111.

[34] Kelly, *Guide*, 266 § 3 *et passim*.

[35] James F. Kenney, *The Sources for the Early History of Ireland: Ecclesiastical, an Introduction and Guide* (New York: Columbia Univ. Press, 1929; repr. Dublin: Pádraic Ó Táilliúir, 1979), 566 § 374i; Michael Lapidge and Richard Sharpe, *A Bibliography of Celtic-Latin Literature 400–1200*, Royal Irish Academy Dictionary of Medieval Latin from Celtic Sources, Ancillary Publications, vol. 1 (Dublin: Royal Irish Academy, 1985), 98 § 344; S. Hellman, ed., *Sedulius Scottus* (Munich: Beck'sche Verlagsbuchhandlung, 1906), 121–35; Dean Simpson, *Sedulii Scotti Collectaneum Miscellaneum*, Corpus Christianorum, Continuatio Medievalis, vol. 67 (Turnhout: Brepols, 1988), 3–10; Dean Simpson, *"The 'Proverbia Grecorum',"* Traditio 43 (1987): 1–22.

[36] Kenney, *Sources*, 281–82 § 109; Lapidge and Sharpe, *Bibliography*, 96–97 § 339; see also Francis John Byrne, "Seventh-Century Documents," *Irish Ecclesiastical Record*, n.s., 108 (1967): 173. Aidan Breen is preparing a new edition and translation of this text.

[37] For evidence that Latin learning provided good examples of the genre, see Lester K. Born, "The Perfect Prince According to the Latin Panegyrists," *Transactions of the American Philological Association* 63 (1932): 20–35.

The preoccupation with individual conduct and its social consequences is reflected in the full range of ecclesiastical texts. Some religious writings, notably homilies and monastic rules, not only show a concern for proper conduct but also display similarities in style and vocabulary with secular wisdom-texts. The seventh-century *Apgitir Chrábaid* "Alphabet of Piety"[38] is quoted often in the textual notes of this edition, both for its vocabulary and for the sentiments expressed. This text tends to break each topic down into subdivisions for mnemonic purposes. The *Heptads* use this approach in the law-tracts, and the *Triads* use it in the wisdom literature. *Apgitir Chrábaid*, however, has groups of two, three, four, on up to fifteen items or more.[39]

The "Rule of Ailbe of Emly" is an Old Irish monastic rule which has much in common stylistically with *specula*. It is presented as the advice of a venerated elder — in this case, Ailbe abbot of Emly [Imlech Ibair] — through an intermediary to Éogan mac Sáráin, a younger person about to assume a position of authority. The text begins *Apair dam fri mac Sáráin* "say for me to the son of Sárán"[40] and concludes *fri hÉogan atabera* "thou shalt say them to Éogan".[41] The advice of Morann to Feradach is presented in much the same fashion in *Audacht Morainn*. The "Rule of Ailbe" is, of course, presented as a string of precepts outlining the responsibilities of the monastic life, as well as defining the proper mental attitude necessary for that life.

This brief survey argues that, in order to understand this collection of maxims, we must examine a wide variety of early Irish texts, from secular

---

[38] Vernam E. Hull, *"Apgitir Chrábaid*, the Alphabet of Piety," *Celtica* 8 (1968): 44–89. For another translation and an attempt to view this work in its cultural contexts, see Thomas Owen Clancy and Gilbert Márkus, OP, *Iona, the Earliest Poetry of a Celtic Monastery* (Edinburgh: Edinburgh Univ. Press, 1995), 195–207.

[39] For this Irish emphasis on enumeration, in both Latin and vernacular texts, see Bernhard Bischoff, "Turning-Points in the History of Latin Exegesis in the Early Middle Ages: I. Introduction," in *Biblical Studies: the Medieval Irish Contribution*, ed. Martin McNamara (Dublin: Dominican Publications, 1976), 84-93; Charles D. Wright, "The Irish 'Enumerative Style' in Old English Homiletic Literature, Especially Vercelli Homily IX," *Cambridge Medieval Celtic Studies* 18 (1989): 29–49; and Charles D. Wright, *The Irish Tradition in Old English Literature*, Cambridge Studies in Anglo-Saxon England, vol. 6 (Cambridge: Cambridge Univ. Press, 1993), esp. chapter 2, "The 'Enumerative Style' in Ireland and Anglo-Saxon England," 49–105 *et passim*.

[40] Joseph O Neill, "The Rule of Ailbe of Emly," *Ériu* 3 (1907): 96–97.

[41] O Neill, "The Rule of Ailbe of Emly," 108–9.

law-tracts to penitentials, in addition to those traditionally included under the rubric of wisdom literature.

FORM AND AFFINITIES

The maxims are impossible to date precisely because of their stylistic simplicity. It is clear from the preservation of neuter gender and the use of the independent dative after the comparative of the adjective (§ 6 *ferr* series) that the text is Old Irish. Furthermore, some maxims have been preserved in Old Irish texts of various genres, for example, in the law-tracts *Di Astud Chor* "On the Securing of Contracts" (§ 3.3 *Dligid fír fortacht* "Truth should be supported")[42] and in *Bretha Nemed Déidenach* "The Last 'Judgments of Privileged (or Professional) Persons'" (§§ 3.3 [see previous], 3.5 *Dligid clóíne cuindrech* "Iniquity should be corrected", 3.14 *Dligid maith mórad* "Good should be exalted"),[43] in the prose narrative *Tochmarc Étaíne* "The Wooing of Étaín" (§ 4.16 *Descad serce sírsilliud* "Constant gazing is symptomatic of love"),[44] and in *Sanas Cormaic* "Cormac's Glossary" (§ 4.1 *Descad cotulta freslige* "Lying down is an inducement to sleep").[45]

Conversely, several of these Old Irish maxims reappear, often in modernized form, in later texts. For example, § 6.58 *Ferr síd sochocad* "Peace is better than a successful war" can be found in the Middle Irish narrative *Togail Troí* "The Destruction of Troy".[46] A bardic poem of the fifteenth century contains § 5.8 *Tosach féle fairsinge* "Amplitude is the basis of liberality".[47] The seventeenth-century poetic debate *Iomarbhágh na bhFileadh* "The Contention of the Bards" preserves § 6.45 *Ferr teiched tairisem* "Better

---

[42] McLeod, *Contract Law*, 186–87 § 52 and note p. 237.

[43] Edited by Edward J. Gwynn as "An Old-Irish Tract on the Privileges and Responsibilities of Poets," *Ériu* 13 (1942): 22.5–6.

[44] Osborn Bergin and Richard I. Best, "*Tochmarc Étaíne*," *Ériu* 12 (1934–38): 164 § 3.

[45] Kuno Meyer, ed., "*Sanas Cormaic*, an Old-Irish Glossary Compiled by Cormac úa Cuilennáin, King-Bishop of Cashel in the Tenth Century," in *Anecdota from Irish Manuscripts*, vol. 4, ed. O. J. Bergin, R. I. Best, K. Meyer, J. G. O'Keeffe (Halle: Max Niemeyer; Dublin: Hodges, Figgis & Co., 1912), 5 § 43.

[46] Whitley Stokes, "*Togail Troí* aus H.2.17," in *Irische Texte*, vol. 2, no. 1, ed. Whitley Stokes and Ernst Windisch (Leipzig: Hirzel, 1884), 46.1454.

[47] Lambert McKenna [Láimhbheartach Mac Cionnaith], ed., *Dioghluim Dána* (Baile Átha Cliath [Dublin]: Oifig an tSoláthair, 1938), 415 § 120.

to flee than remain" in a modernized form.[48] A variant of § 6.35 *Ferr senfiach senécraiti* "Better an old debt than an old enmity" has been frequently recorded and was even used during this century. In the modern variant *senécraite* "old enmity" is replaced by *seanfhala* "old resentment".[49]

The presence of a number of Middle Irish spellings and forms among the maxims cannot be taken as proof of later age because a certain amount of modernization has taken place with transmission. For example, at § 6.93 *Ferr becc n-érai* "Better a little than a refusal" only Rec. Y manuscripts preserve the neuter gender of the o/ā-stem adjective *becc* used as an abstract noun.

More than seventy-five percent of all three-word maxims alliterate on the same consonant, or on an initial vowel, between the second and third words. If homorganic consonants are considered to alliterate, p/b, t/d, c/g, then the frequency of alliteration increases. Its incidence also increases if we allow that there may be alliteration between the initial word and the second or third word, or with the second element of a compound.[50] However, some maxims preserved clearly and unambiguously in all three recensions prove that alliteration was not required. See, for example, § 1.34 *Ad·cota tercae léiri* "Want begets industry" and § 6.1 *Ferr dán orbu* "A skill is better than an inheritance".

Among the three-word maxims only three syntactic patterns are consistently employed: (1) verb (*ad·cota* or *dligid*) + nominative + accusative, in other words, the normal sentence pattern in Irish; (2) noun (*descad* or *tosach*) + genitive + nominative; (3) *ferr* + nominative + dative. Four of the maxims edited herein are exceptional in that they have a finite verb as their third element. The four maxims are §§ 1.1a *Ad·cota sochell roda·bíatha* "Generosity begets one that feeds it", 1.2 *Ad·cota dúthracht do·rata* "Willingness creates one who gives", 3.10 *Dligid naidm nascar* "The one who goes surety is entitled to that which is bound", 6.90 *Ferr slóg suidigther* "Better a crowd that is set in order".

---

[48] Lambert McKenna, ed., *Iomarbhágh na bhFileadh, the Contention of the Bards*, vol. 1, Irish Texts Society, vol. 20 (London: Simpkin, Marshall, Hamilton, Kent & Co., Ltd., 1918), 152 § 44a.

[49] Tadhg Ó Donnchadha used a modernized from of this maxim at the turn of the century, see Ó Donnchadha, ed., *Dánta Sheáin Uí Mhurchadha na Ráithíneach* (Baile Átha Cliath [Dublin]: Connradh na Gaedhilge, 1907), 75.

[50] See James Carney, "Linking Alliteration ('Fidrad Freccomail')," *Éigse* 18 (1980–81): 251–62.

The preceding maxims suggest that many of the maxims in our text are pithy expressions of longer sayings, perhaps extracted from the law-tracts or other learned texts. However, it is also possible that our own text served as the source of inspiration for these sentiments in other texts. Instances of similarly worded maxims from various texts are cited throughout the textual notes. A particularly clear example may be found by comparing three maxims with lines from *Tecosca Cormaic*. This latter text tends to use adjectives or nouns of agency rather than abstract nouns to convey the ideas expressed. Thus compare § 4.21 *Descad serbae burbae* "Boorishness is characteristic of bitterness" with *TC* §13.13 *serb cech borb* "every boor is bitter"; § 4.22 *Descad anéolais imresan* "Contentiousness is a mark of ignorance" with *TC* §13.18 *imresnaid cech n-aneólach* "every ignorant person is a fomenter of contention"; and §4.23 *Descad ainble anecnae* "Ignorance is a mark of shamelessness" with *TC* §13.19 *anbal cech anecnaid* "every ignoramus is shameless". It would be impossible to say which text influenced the other in such a case or, indeed, if the similarity is not merely a matter of coincidence.

No consistent pattern of linking alliteration between maxims, or of parallelism in structure or contents, is found. When coupled with the lack of end rhyme these features suggest that this text was thought of as prose by its redactors. The maxims, as preserved, do not appear to have been organized for easy memorization or for oral delivery to an audience. These features may be the result of the vagaries of transmission in the surviving manuscripts, since memorization of edifying literature was held as an ideal throughout the Middle Ages.[51]

Three maxims in Y_1 have been glossed: § 6.5 *f[err] sonaidi seoita .i. a hithiar a rec*, § 6.8b *f[err] road reraib .i. expectare*, § 6.90 *f[err] slog suidigthir ut congruum fiant*. However, the glosses in this manuscript give no hints about the age or origin of the text. Any extensive glossing occurs only in late manuscripts. $N_{3,4}$ have a glossed *ferr* section, and $Y_{8,9,10}$ have glossed *ad·cota*, *tosach*, *dligid*, and *descad* sections. Unfortunately, these late glosses are simply attempts to find synonyms and do not help elucidate obscure maxims.

---

[51] See Mary J. Carruthers, *The Book of Memory, a Study of Memory in Medieval Culture*, Cambridge Studies in Medieval Literature, vol. 10 (Cambridge: Cambridge Univ. Press, 1990), chapter 1, "Models for the Memory," 16–45. For example, variations in manuscript preservation may be the result of *memoria ad res* rather than *memoria ad verbum*, that is, remembering the sense rather than memorizing word for word, and does not necessarily have to mean that the manuscript was poorly copied: *The Book of Memory*, 87–88.

CONTENTS AND INTENT

This compilation of wisdom is difficult to characterize succinctly. In Early Irish society, sententious sayings would have been applied in context-specific situations, but from our present-day vantage point we cannot always accurately recreate which situations and what contexts.[52] One cannot be certain whether or not §§ 2 and 7, for example, were originally intended to be included among the three-word maxims. The maxims lack a frame which introduces them or explains their purpose as is often found in other wisdom-texts such as the *specula* or monastic rules cited above; nor do we find distinctive headings to differentiate each section of three-word maxims.

The best way to understand the nature and original purpose of this compilation is to examine the contents of those three-word maxims shared clearly and unambiguously by all three recensions. When the contents of the maxims held in common by all recensions are examined they reveal a predominant tone and tenor. The formal restrictions of the maxims, limited to five patterns based on the five initial words, make it unlikely that this compilation was collected and classified randomly.[53] The tone and tenor of the maxims common to all three recensions and their formal stylistic restrictions suggest that they are the product of an original redactor or, at least, of a school which attempted to promote a coherent outlook.

Perhaps the easiest way to begin to describe the nature of these maxims is to state clearly what they are not. These maxims do not constitute a *speculum* text; they do not tell how one should govern; nor are they the immediate product of the Church, for they do not convey a theological or religious message. Early Irish society was very hierarchical by nature, in both the lay and ecclesiastical spheres. This fact is clearly reflected in the lawtracts and *specula*. The Church is, and always has been, a hierarchical institution. In early Ireland Church officials were drawn from the higher eche-

---

[52] Gnomic literature can be terribly ambiguous. For a discussion of multiple meaning and usage in proverbial literature, see Barbara Kirshenblatt-Gimblett, "Toward a Theory of Proverb Meaning," *Proverbium* 22 (1973): 821–27. On the other hand, for a discussion of how Irish glossators employed such devices as paronomasia and polysemy in their varied interpretations of texts, see Morgan Thomas Davies, "Protocols of Reading in Early Irish Literature: Notes on Some Notes to *Orgain Denna Ríg* and *Amra Coluim Cille*," *Cambrian Medieval Celtic Studies* 32 (1996): 1–23.

[53] Roland Smith, speaking of Irish wisdom-texts generally, stated that "they would seem to represent the slow growth, anonymously, of popular proverbial literature, added to from generation to generation, and finally collected and classified by an industrious scribe": "Fithal and Flann Fína," *Revue Celtique* 47 (1930): 33.

lons of society and they tended to see their role as supporting the divine
sanction of the nobility. The maxims do not appear to have been compiled
for a socially high-ranking audience by specifically addressing its concerns.
In fact, some maxims may be interpreted as being in sympathy with the
lower classes and those without legal franchise.[54]

As in most early medieval societies, what constituted appropriate behaviour was often public in nature. This was as true in secular as in religious
spheres. For example, notions of personal honour are as concerned with
public perception as with any internalized ethical code. Hospitality and
generosity, which were terribly important to the early Irish, are very public
virtues.[55] The fear of a curse, the act of a cleric, and satire, the weapon of
a poet, also suggests a public as opposed to a private sense of morality.[56]
Early Irish penitentials show that the Church was often as concerned with
public as with private expressions of repentance.

The Latin term *pudor* in the sense "avoidance of shame, desire of approval" might appropriately be applied to the types of public morality cited
above. But *pudor* can also mean "decency, propriety, a sense of right" and in
these latter meanings imply an internalized, private ethical or moral code.
The early Church, while concerned with public displays of morality, was
busy trying to inculcate an internalized code of morality which would result
in an altered standard of appropriate behaviour. Although there was a public
aspect to enforcement of behaviour by the Church there was also an
increasing degree of individual conscience. Patrick Sims-Williams has argued
that the prevalence of the Irish triad "thought, word and deed" shows the
emphasis the Church placed on the need for introspection with regard to in-
tentional elements of behaviour.[57] In the context of the penitentials, Allen
Frantzen has noted how the Church stressed "interiority", that is, it was
attempting to affect the individual's "frame of mind, his self-awareness."[58]
The maxims edited here, unlike the penitentials, have no overt religious

---

[54] Donncha[dh] Ó Corráin stated, "Irish literature, which is aristocratic to the core,
supplies very little information about the lower classes and is universally contemptuous of
them": *Ireland before the Normans*, The Gill History of Ireland, vol. 2 (Dublin: Gill and
Macmillan Ltd., 1972), 48.

[55] See, for example, Philip O'Leary, "Contention at Feasts in Early Irish Literature,"
Éigse 20 (1984): 115–27.

[56] See Tomás Ó Cathasaigh, "Curse and Satire," *Éigse* 21 (1986): 10–15.

[57] Sims-Williams, "Thought, Word and Deed," 110.

[58] Allen J. Frantzen, *The Literature of Penance in Anglo-Saxon England* (New Brunswick, N.J.: Rutgers Univ. Press, 1983), 9 *et passim*.

message. However, they encourage a reflective — one might say introspective — approach in everyday affairs.[59]

The following discussion of the contents of the maxims will cite only those which are found in all three recensions based on the assumption that they are most likely to reflect the intent of an original compilation.

Keeping in mind the definition that "Wisdom is dedicated to articulating a sense of order", it can be noted that these maxims encourage considerate behaviour and temperate emotions in interpersonal relationships.

§ 1.7 *Ad·cota miscais airbiri* "Hatred engenders reproach."

§ 1.33 *Ad·cota imresan imned* "Contention causes anxiety."

§ 5.2 *Tosach augrai athchomsán* "Reproach is the beginning of a quarrel."

Conciliation and consensus are urged as methods of maintaining the quality of interpersonal relationships.

§ 3.6 *Dligid augrae etargaire* "A quarrel merits mediation."

§ 6.13 *Ferr dál debiuch* "Consensus is better than discord."

An emphasis on moderation and practicality is also evident.

§ 6.63 *Ferr cíall caínchruth* "Good sense is better than fair form."

Also consistent throughout is a respect for learning and wisdom.[60]

§ 1.23 *Ad·cota gáes airmitin* "Wisdom begets respect."

§ 3.1 *Dligid ecnae airmitin* "Learning merits respect."

§ 5.1 *Tosach éolais imchomarc* "Inquiry is the beginning of knowledge."

In keeping with a respect for wisdom and learning, training and education are seen as desirable.

§ 3.18 *Dligid óc elathain* "A youth should have a skill."

§ 3.30 *Dligid mer múnad* "A fool should be instructed."

As will be seen presently, however, even wisdom and learning are not promoted as unquestioned virtues in and of themselves.

This collection of maxims, as stated earlier, is not a *speculum principum*. A

---

[59] See Carruthers, *Book of Memory*, 65-66, 71 *et passim*.

[60] Note that § 7 *Maith dán ecnae* also begins with praise for learning. See footnote 14.

comparison of this text with, for example, *Audacht Morainn* or *Tecosca Cormaic* will reveal verbal parallels and similar sentiments. Nevertheless, this text lacks any advice on how one governs. In fact, for a society as hierarchical as the early Irish, it is surprisingly free of terms for social rank. The following maxim is exceptional for its apparent concern with rank and high status.

§ 5.5 *Tosach ordain eneclann* "Honour-price is the basis of dignity."

A concern for, or perhaps warning of, the deficits of low status is also noted.

§ 1.36 *Ad·cota doíre cumgai* "Low status results in constraint."

In one of the maxims which refers explicitly to social rank we find the idea that a *fuidir*, a low-status tenant, deserves due consideration from his lord.

§ 3.8 *Dligid fuidir frithfolta* "A tenant-at-will is entitled to reciprocal services."

If this text had been compiled for a high-ranking audience one might expect to have been reminded of the *fuidir's* obligations to the lord. Instead, the tendency of this text is to reflect concern for those who are limited in their abilities effectively to conduct their own affairs.

§ 3.16 *Dligid dall dídin* "A blind person should be led."
§ 3.26 *Dligid othar a íarfaigid* "A sick person deserves to be looked after."
§ 3.32 *Dligid étnge aimsir* "The inarticulate person deserves time."

In the context of those incapable, legally or otherwise, of looking after their own affairs, one must note that the previously mentioned youth (*óc*) who deserves a skill (§ 3.18) and the fool (*mer*) who should be instructed (§ 3.30) were considered legally incapable in early Irish society and, therefore, needed the supervision of someone who enjoyed legal franchise.

The overall sentiments of the text may be characterized as being in sympathy with the moral and ethical teachings of the Church, and yet it contains no overt reference to Church teachings and no theological message. Nevertheless, the following maxim fits neatly into a religious context.

§ 5.9 *Tosach crábuid cosmailius* "Imitation is the basis of devotion."

Crábud "piety, devotion" is one of the few words used in this text that is most commonly found in a religious context. The following maxim seems more informed by Church teachings on sexual morality than by secular attitudes.

§ 1.4 *Ad·cota drús dígnae* "Lechery leads to disgrace."

Many of the virtues and ideals expressed in this text are appropriate to both secular and religious works, but do seem to reflect more readily the Church's concerns.

§ 3.3 *Dligid fír fortacht* "Truth should be supported."[61]
§ 3.4 *Dligid gó a cairiugud* "Falsehood should be rebuked."
§ 3.5 *Dligid cloíne cuindrech* "Iniquity should be corrected."
§ 3.14 *Dligid maith mórad* "Good should be exalted."[62]

Whereas some of the maxims, particularly in the *ad·cota* series, may be interpreted simply as cause-and-effect expressions of universal truth, we notice that diligence and hard work are given priority as positive characteristics.

§ 1.22 *Ad·cota accobur feidli* "Desire begets perseverance."
§ 1.34 *Ad·cota tercae léiri* "Want begets industry."
§ 5.7 *Tosach tocaid trebaire* "Prudence is the basis of good fortune."

Trebaire, translated here as "prudence", has a primary meaning of "husbandry, farming". Its semantic range, therefore, encapsulates the notion that hard work and industry are prudent courses of action. This idea that diligence and hard work are positive is confirmed by the following.

§ 6.46 *Ferr trummae dínnimi* "Rigour is better than indolence."
§ 6.47 *Ferr laubair áini* "Hard work is better than a bright wit."

The emphasis on perseverance and industry is a natural concomitant to the principle, most explicitly expressed in the law-tract *Uraicecht Becc* "The Small Primer", that a person can elevate his social status through the acquisition of wealth, the most valuable form of which is land, by the successful application of learned skills. It is stated concisely as: *i[s] sáer cid cách creanus a suíri dia dán* "everyone is privileged (*sóer*) who purchases his privileged

---

[61] This maxim is also found in the eighth-century law-tract *Di Astud Chor*: McLeod, *Contract Law*, 186–87 § 52. See footnote 42. McLeod translated this maxim as "Truth is entitled to succour".

[62] Three of these maxims, §§ 3.3, 3.5, 3.14, are also found in the Old Irish law-text *Bretha Nemed Déidenach*. See footnote 43.

status (*soíre*) through his art (*dán*)."[63] In a society where land was the chief form of wealth the following maxim comes as a surprise.

§ 6.1 *Ferr dán orbu* "A skill is better than an inheritance."

It states that the acquisition of a skilled occupation (*dán*) is preferable to inherited land (*orbae*). This maxim seems to imply that being a skilled craftsman, a member of the *áes dána*,[64] is to be preferred to being a land-owner. The notion that a person need not be socially bound by the circum-stances of his birth is supported by another maxim from *Uraicecht Becc* which reads *fearr fear a c[h]iniud* "a man is better than his kindred."[65] In other words, through the successful application of a learned skill (*dán*) one could acquire wealth and rise in social rank. In this context, one must consider the maxims which stress learning and the acquisition of skills.[66]

If it was possible to rise in social rank through the application of skills and the acquisition of wealth, then it was also possible to lose social status through indolence. The law-tracts make it clear that a person of the learned crafts who did not achieve the standards required of the grade that his father and grandfather had achieved before him could fall in social rank.[67] In this context, the maxims dealing with diligence and industry take on added significance. I have already cited a maxim which warns of the constraint of low status (*doíre*; § 1.36). The following maxims continue the warning against poverty and low status.

§ 1.32 *Ad·cota daidbre dochraiti* "Poverty leads to hardship."
§ 5.16 *Tosach doíre drochlepaid* "Bad association is the beginning of lowly status."

If crafts and skills could improve one's social standing then certainly

---

[63] Robert Atkinson, et al., ed. and trans., *Ancient Laws of Ireland*, vol. 5, *Uraicecht Becc and Certain Other Selected Brehon Law Texts* (Dublin: Alexander Thom, 1901), 14.28 = *CIH* v, 1593.15. For another translation, see Eoin Mac Neill, "Ancient Irish Law: the Law of Status or Franchise," *Proceedings of the Royal Irish Academy* 36 C (1921–24): 273.

[64] For discussions of various craftsmen and persons of learned skills, see Kelly, *Guide*, 43–67.

[65] AL v, 20.15–6 = *CIH* v, 1594.32. Note that this maxim is stylistically akin to the maxims edited here in § 6.

[66] Lines § 7.2–5 of *Maith dán ecnae* stress raising one's social standing through the acquisition of *ecnae* (see footnote 14).

[67] Liam Breatnach, ed., *Uraicecht na Ríar, the Poetic Grades in Early Irish Law*, Early Irish Law Series, vol. 2 (Dublin: Dublin Institute for Advanced Studies, 1987), 94–98.

learning and education could do the same. Examples of respect for learning have already been cited. But a docile disposition was a prerequisite for one set on the path of knowledge.

§ 5.6 *Tosach suíthi sochoisce* "Tractability is the beginning of expertise."

§ 5.10 *Tosach ecnai áilgine* "Gentleness is the beginning of wisdom."

In the context of the maxims just cited, one must recall that imitation (*cosmailius*) was noted as being the basis of devotion (*crábud*; § 5.9). Even wisdom and learning could be supplanted by the qualities of well-being and steadiness.

§ 6.57 *Ferr sobarthu suíthiu* "Well-being is better than learning."

§ 6.75 *Ferr réide rogaís* "Steadiness is better than great wisdom."

Some maxims state a preference for passivity over resentment and for knowledge over aggression and, therefore, associate wisdom with tranquility and peace.

§ 6.60 *Ferr súan serbai* "Repose is better than bitterness."

§ 6.76 *Ferr rous rúathur* "Knowledge is better than aggressiveness."

§ 6.77 *Ferr gáes gaisciud* "Wisdom is better than weapons."

A nature considerate of one's fellows is further implied by maxims that encourage a willingness to share with others. Sharing with family members is seen as superior to acquisition.

§ 6.73 *Ferr rann répiund* "Sharing is better than rending."

§ 6.78 *Ferr goire imbiud* "Filial maintenance is better than abundance."

A humble attitude toward those who possess both power and wealth is evident in the following maxims. The emphasis on humility, gratitude and acceptance of less than what is sought after all suggest that they are addressed to the middle to lower echelons of a hierarchical society.

§ 1.11 *Ad·cota becdatu caínbuidi* "Humility wins good favour."

§ 6.67 *Ferr buide dígbáil* "Gratitude is better than privation."

§ 6.93 *Ferr becc n-érai* "Better a little than a refusal."

The following is perhaps the most extreme expression of submissiveness in this hierarchical society to be found among these maxims.

§ 6.11 *Ferr mug marbad* "Better [to be] a slave than be slain."

The above maxim does not express an attitude shared by those who cultivated notions of personal honour. Slavery was common in early Ireland and
prisoners of war frequently became slaves. The maxims note the negative
effects of combat and even express explicitly pacifist sentiments.

> § 1.51 *Ad·cota cath caíniud* "Battle results in lamentation."
> § 6.58 *Ferr síd sochocad* "Peace is better than a successful war."

Despite the submissive and pacifist attitudes expressed above, the abuse of
power was a concern to be avoided as well.

> § 1.6 *Ad·cota fáiscre rofáiscre* "Repression results in greater repression."
> § 1.27 *Ad·cota bríg barainn* "Force arouses hostility."

Nevertheless, some control was seen as necessary. We find in the maxims
a preference for authority over bragging and boasting — as depicted in
heroic saga, for example — and an unwillingness to concede to lawlessness.

> § 6.30 *Ferr bríg bágaib* "Better strength than boasting."
> § 6.79 *Ferr greimm grefiul* "Control is better than chaos."

The last several maxims cited stress the prevailing concern of wisdom
literature with establishing and maintaining order.

In summary, we have a text which emphasizes considerate behaviour in
interpersonal relationships, which promotes respect for skills and learning
achieved through diligence and hard work, and which encourages humility
and non-violence. All of the above characteristics are tempered by a consistent tone of moderation.

The three-word maxims express ideals which may advise or admonish, but
which never dictate. They are not rules to be enforced through an external
authority such as the aristocracy or the Church. Although they are the
product of a hierarchical society the maxims do not adopt the view of those
at the top. In fact, they imply a sympathy with those at the middle to lower
levels of the social order and encourage those with the opportunity to strive
to move upward through the acquisition of skills and learning.

Many of the attitudes expressed in the maxims are consonant with the
teachings of the Church, yet there is no theological or religious message
propounded and no system of rewards or punishments for compliance is
proposed. These maxims represent a code of ethics which encourages interiority, that is, a private rather than public virtue. By not relying on an external authority they encourage an introspective, self-reflective attitude and
appeal to the individual conscience.

MANUSCRIPTS

I have examined thirty-three manuscripts which contain at least fragments of the text which is edited here. Other texts or fragments may emerge as more manuscripts are catalogued and old catalogues are updated. Therefore, the information presented on the facing-page table (following page 21) and in the stemmata should not be taken as comprehensive.

The manuscripts have been divided into four groups beginning with Rec. N and followed by Rec. Y and Rec. L. Manuscripts containing only fragments, and therefore not assignable to a specific recension, are referred to as Group X. Recensions are distinguished on the basis of similarities in order, number and spelling of the three-word maxims. The identification of the scribe and the date, where possible, refers only to our text in the case of composite manuscripts and manuscripts by more than one scribe.

The oldest firmly dated manuscripts in each of the three recensions (N_1, Y_1, L_1) — which are the best representatives of their respective recensions — are unlikely to be the immediate exemplars for any surviving manuscripts. It will also be shown that no surviving recension is derived from any other. All three recensions derive independently from an archetype which cannot be accurately reconstructed (see Figure 4, p. 56).

The Facing-Page Table

The manuscripts are discussed in the order in which they are listed from top to bottom on the left-hand column of the facing-page table. The number of maxims in each section is given in round brackets. For example, under *Ad·cota* the first entry reads $N_1(66)$a with the lower-case letter at the end specifying the sequence of that particular section in the manuscript.

The sections in the present edition follow the order of those in N_1 and are numbered as follows: § 1 *ad·cota*, § 2 *Ba faitech*, § 3 *dligid*, § 4 *descad*, § 5 *tosach*, § 6 *ferr*, and § 7 *Maith dán ecnae*. Two sections characteristic of Rec. Y, but also found in other recensions, § 8 *Cía fégam ránac* "Who are the keenest you have met?" and § 9 *Secht comarthai déc* "Seventeen signs" (= *TC* § 22), are edited and translated in Appendices 1 and 2 respectively. Sections held in common with *Tecosca Cormaic* are referred to by the section number in Meyer's edition: *TC* §§ 19, 22, 29, 30, 31. Three sections characteristic of the edition of *Senbríathra Fíthail* as published by Thurneysen are referred to by the numbers in his edition: *Senbríathra* §§ 10, 11, 12.

MSS	§1 Ad·cota	§2 Ba faitech	§3 Dligid	§4 Descad	§5 Tosach	§6 Ferr	§7 Maith dán ecnae
N_1	$N_1(66)a$	$N_1(7)b$	$N_1(38)c$	$N_1(23)d$	$N_1(23)e$	$N_1(87)f$†	N_1g
N_2	$N_2(65)a$	$N_2(7)b$	$N_2(37)d$	$N_2(23)e$	$N_2(23)f$	$N_2(90)g$	
N_3						$N_3(84)a$‡	N_3b
N_4						$N_4(78)a$	
Y_1	$Y_1(64)a$	$Y_1(7)c$	$Y_1(31)e$	$Y_1(24)g$	$Y_1(21)b$	$Y_1(97)f$	Y_1i
Y_2	$Y_2(64)a$	$Y_2(7)c$	$Y_2(31)e$	$Y_2(24)g$	$Y_2(21)b$	$Y_2(97)f$	Y_2i
Y_3	$Y_3(64)a$	$Y_3(6)c$	$Y_3(31)e$	$Y_3(24)g$	$Y_3(21)b$	$Y_3(95)f$	Y_3i
Y_4	$Y_4(64)a$	$Y_4(6)c$	$Y_4(31)e$	$Y_4(24)g$	$Y_4(21)b$	$Y_4(96)f$	Y_4i
Y_5	$Y_5(64)a$	$Y_5(6)c$	$Y_5(31)e$	$Y_5(24)g$	$Y_5(21)b$	$Y_5(96)f$	Y_5i
Y_6	$Y_6(63)a$	$Y_6(7)c$	$Y_6(31)e$	$Y_6(24)g$	$Y_6(21)b$	$Y_6(96)f$	Y_6i
Y_7	$Y_7(64)a$	$Y_7(7)c$	$Y_7(31)e$	$Y_7(24)g$	$Y_7(21)b$	$Y_7(96)f$	Y_7i
Y_8	$Y_8(64)a$	$Y_8(7)c$	$Y_8(30)d$	$Y_8(24)e$	$Y_8(21)b$		
Y_9	$Y_9(64)a$‡	$Y_9(7)c$	$Y_9(31)d$	$Y_9(24)e$	$Y_9(21)b$		
Y_{10}	$Y_{10}(65)a$		$Y_{10}(31)c$	$Y_{10}(21)d$	$Y_{10}(20)b$		
L_1	$L_1(32)b$	$L_1(6)c$	$L_1(27)e$		$L_1(21)a$	$L_1(45)d$	L_1m
L_2	$L_2(32)b$	$L_2(7)c$	$L_2(22)e$		$L_2(21)a$	$L_2(52)d$	L_2k
L_3	$L_3(32)b$	$L_3(6)c$	$L_3(27)e$	$L_3(27)o$‡	$L_3(21)a$	$L_3(44)d$	L_3n
L_4	$L_4(32)b$	$L_4(7)c$	$L_4(27)e$		$L_4(21)a$	$L_4(45)d$	L_4n
L_5	$L_5(31)b$	$L_5(7)c$	$L_5(27)e$		$L_5(21)a$	$L_5(47)d$	L_5n
L_6	$L_6(31)b$	$L_6(7)c$	$L_6(27)e$		$L_6(21)a$	$L_6(46)d$	L_6n
L_7	$L_7(32)b$	$L_7(7)c$	$L_7(26)e$		$L_7(21)a$	$L_7(45)d$	L_7n
L_8	$L_8(32)b$	$L_8(7)c$	$L_8(26)e$		$L_8(21)a$	$L_8(45)d$	L_8n
X_1			$X_1(16)a$			$X_1(16)c$‡	X_1b
X_2			$X_2(16)a$			$X_2(16)c$‡	X_2b
X_3			$X_3(16)a$				X_3b
X_4			$X_4(16)a$				
X_5			$X_5(16)a$				
X_6							X_6a
X_7	$X_7(13)a$						
X_8							
X_9							
X_{10}							
X_{11}							

† This section is split, ending (with §6.47) at the bottom of page 6 and resuming (with § 6.48) on the top of pa
77 (see manuscript discussion).

‡ This section is separated from those preceding or following it on this table by other material not necessari
related to the text edited here (see manuscript discussion).

§ 8 Cía fégam ránac	§ 9 Secht comarthai déc	*TC* § 29	*TC* § 30	*TC* § 31	*TC* § 19	Senbríathra § 10	Senbríathra § 11	Senbríathra § 12
N_2c								
						N_3c	N_3d	N_3e
						N_4b	N_4c	N_4d
Y_1d	Y_1h							
Y_2d	Y_2h							
Y_3d	Y_3h							
Y_4d	Y_4h							
Y_5d	Y_5h							
Y_6d	Y_6h							
Y_7d	Y_7h							
	Y_8f							
	Y_9f							
	$Y_{10}e$							
	L_1g	L_1h	L_1i	L_1f		L_1j	L_1k	L_1l
	L_2f	L_2g	L_2h	L_2i	L_2j			
	L_3f	L_3g	L_3h	L_3i	L_3j	L_3k	L_3l	L_3m
	L_4f	L_4g	L_4h	L_4i	L_4j	L_4k	L_4l	L_4m
	L_5f	L_5g	L_5h	L_5i	L_5j	L_5k	L_5l	L_5m
	L_6f	L_6g	L_6h	L_6i	L_6j	L_6k	L_6l	L_6m
	L_7f	L_7g	L_7h	L_7i	L_7j	L_7k	L_7l	L_7m
	L_8f	L_8g	L_8h	L_8i	L_8j	L_8k	L_8l	L_8m
X_8a	X_8b	X_8c						
X_9a								
	$X_{10}a$							
	$X_{11}a$							

In the following discussion maxims cited with capitalization of the initial word are from the normalized edition. Those cited without capitalization are as found in the manuscript under discussion.

Recension N

N_1 is the oldest and most important manuscript in this recension. Yet it cannot be the exemplar for any other manuscript because it omits §§ 6.88, 6.90, 6.93 which are included in $N_{2,3,4}$. The title which gives this edition its name is found in N_2. In the order of sections, and the sequence and spellings of the maxims within each section, N_2 closely resembles N_1. However, N_2 contains § 8 *Cía fégam ránac* (see Appendix 1) which is characteristic of Rec. Y. It ends with the *ferr* (90) series and so lacks § 7 *Maith dán ecnae*. N_2 cannot be a direct copy of N_1 because of the three additional maxims in the *ferr* series and the inclusion of § 8 *Cía fégam ránac*. Nevertheless, it provides reliable confirmation for several doubtful readings in N_1.

It is on the basis of the sequence and spellings in the *ferr* series that $N_{3,4}$ are included in Rec. N. The closest spelling resemblance is to N_2, although at least one reading suggests an exemplar closer to N_1 (§ 6.50 *f[err] cloth gach biudh*). N_2 leaves *gach* out of this maxim. Some maxims in $N_{3,4}$ point to an exemplar that agrees with Rec. Y (§§ 6.33 *f[err] teacht allatraigh*, 6.41 *f[err] clu caomhna*, 6.54 *f[err] cridhe giallna*). The late glosses on the *ferr* series in $N_{3,4}$ are of no help in elucidating obscure maxims.

N_1 = RIA 967 (23 N 10). Untitled. The maxims begin on parchment with the *ad·cota* series on page 5.22 and break off in the middle of the *ferr* series at § 6.47 (= *f[err] lubair aine*) at the bottom of page 6. This first section of the text is preceded by *Tecosca Cormaic* (pp. 1.1–5.21), and is followed by an acephalous copy of the *Triads* (pp. 7.1–10.z). Our text resumes on paper with § 6.48 (= *f[err] dam denmide*) at page 77.1–19, and ends with § 7 *Maith dán ecnae*. This portion of text is preceded by the article "Prull" from *Sanas Cormaic*[68] (pp. 74.7–76.z), and is followed by a colophon identifying the scribe (at

---

[68] Kuno Meyer, ed., "Sanas Cormaic, an Old-Irish Glossary Compiled by Cormac úa Cuilennáin, King-Bishop of Cashel in the Tenth Century," in *Anecdota from Irish Manuscripts*, vol. 4, ed. O. J. Bergin, R. I. Best, K. Meyer, J. G. O'Keeffe (Halle: Max Niemeyer; and Dublin: Hodges, Figgis & Co., 1912), xiii–xvii.

the bottom of p. 77). Scribe: Aodh, writing in "Baile in Chuimine" at the home of Seán Ó Maoil Chonaire, ca. 1575.

N_2 = RIA 132 (23 D 2). Title: *Briathra Floinn Fhiona meic Ossa sund.* Text begins with the *ad·cota* series on page 25.4, and ends with the *ferr* section at page 30.z. The text is preceded by *Tecosca Cormaic* (pp. 5.1–25.2). Scribe unidentified, ca. 1661.

N_3 = RIA 966 (23 N 27). Untitled. A glossed *ferr* series begins at f. 17 r 1; it is preceded by a glossed *Tecosca Cormaic* (ff. 7 v 11–16 v z) and is followed by a text beginning *Mairce don duine carus duine* (ff. 17 v 6–18 r 8).[69] On f. 18 r 9 begins § 7 *Maith dán ecnae. Senbríathra* §§ 10, 11, 12 follow (ff. 18 r 16–19 v 2). The page is concluded by sections which list "the fifteen characteristics of a good woman" and "the fifteen characteristics of a bad woman" followed by a scribal signature and date. A partially glossed *Audacht Morainn* (beg. f. 19 v 3) follows. Scribe: Domhnall Ó Duind, Carraig an Damhsa, ca. 1714.

N_4 = TCD 1391 (H.5.19)(1)(c). Untitled. A glossed *ferr* series begins on page 128.12, followed on pp. 131.1–132.10 by *Senbríathra* §§ 10, 11, 12. These sections are preceded by a glossed *Tecosca Cormaic* (pp. 97.1–128.11) and followed by a poem ascribed to Seán Ó Maoil Chonaire. Scribe: in the hand of Maurice O Gorman, eighteenth century.

N_1 cannot be the direct exemplar of any manuscript in its recension. Appendix 5 provides a diplomatic edition of N_1 collated with the overlapping sections from Y_1 and L_1. The following stemma demonstrates the interrelationship of manuscripts within Rec. N, with *n* representing the hyparchetype.

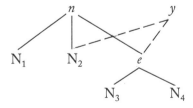

---

[69] See edition by Vernam E. Hull, "The Wise Sayings of Flann Fína (Aldfrith, King of Northumbria)," *Speculum* 4 (1929): 95–102.

Recension Y

Every manuscript in this recension gives this text the title which can be normalized as *Roscada Flainn Fína maic Ossu ríg Saxan*. Characteristic of this recension are § 8 *Cía fégam ránac* and § 9 *Secht comarthai déc* (= *TC* § 22). Five manuscripts in this recension ($Y_{2,4,5,6,7}$) are described as containing extracts from "Leabhar Droma Sneachtaigh". This is important in that it suggests a connection with the Ó Maoil Chonaire family of scribes rather than descent from the lost *Cín Dromma Snechtai* (see p. 42).

The text in Y_1 often preserves old linguistic forms and consistently provides the most reliable readings in this recension. Nevertheless, Y_1 cannot be the immediate exemplar for any other manuscript. This is shown by the occasional superior readings found in Y_2. For example, at § 1.13 *Ad·cota díbe dimmolad*, Y_1 has *dimlad*, Y_2 has *dimmoladh*; at § 3.10 *Dligid naidm nascar*, Y_1 has *maidm nascara*, Y_2 has *naidm nascar*. Y_2 thus becomes the primary confirmation for questionable readings in Y_1.

All remaining Rec. Y manuscripts descend from Y_2 itself, or something very much like it. The differences between Y_1, on the one hand, and all other Rec. Y manuscripts, on the other, can be shown at § 1.4 *Ad·cota drús dígnae*, where Y_1 has *druis digna*, and all other Rec. Y manuscripts (except for Y_{10}) have something like *druis duigna ł terge*, which includes an optional word. At § 6.81 *Ferr lín lobrai*, Y_1 has *lín lobræ*, Y_2 has *leghenn liubhra*, and all other Rec. Y readings resemble Y_2. In the two examples cited above (§§ 1.13, 3.10) of Y_2 showing superior readings to Y_1, all other Rec. Y readings agree with Y_2. Similar distinctions, usually based on spelling, between Y_1 and the other Rec. Y manuscripts can be repeated frequently.

$Y_{3,4,5,6,7}$ have run together parts of the *ad·cota* and *tosach* series in a way that shows Y_2 to be their exemplar. Y_2 is written out with two maxims per line. These lines were copied as though they had been written in parallel columns and so have mixed the order of *ad·cota* and *tosach* maxims. Manuscript readings in this group often substitute *p* for *b* and *p* for *r*. The first substitution was perhaps a deliberate attempt at archaizing; the second can only be due to mistranscription.

The last three manuscripts in this recension ($Y_{8,9,10}$) make significant omissions from the text, as can be seen on the facing-page table. They each contain glossed *ad·cota*, *tosach*, *dligid*, and *descad* series, but the glosses are late and do not help elucidate obscure maxims.

Another characteristic of this recension is the order and contents of four texts which follow immediately after § 7 *Maith dán ecnae*. The first of these

begins *Maircc don duine carus duíne* and is often ascribed to Flann Fína.[70]
This text, in turn, is followed by two shorter texts, *Dia mba trebthach, ba
trebor*[71] and *A fir féil déna trócaire co léir.* The fourth text (with the heading
Flann Fína cecinit in Y₁) begins *Ro·det i nInis find Fáil.*[72]

Y₁ = Yellow Book of Lecan, TCD 1318 (H.2.16).[73] This composite
        manuscript is made up of sections whose dates vary from 1391 to
        1572.[74] Edward Lhuyd created the compilation from manuscripts he
        collected in Ireland during 1699–1700.[75] Our text, and the four
        listed above which characteristically follow it, is contained in a
        fifteenth-century manuscript which, according to present enumera-
        tion, includes col. 217–48. To be accurate, our text is not found in
        the "Yellow Book of Lecan", but only in a later manuscript presently
        bound together with it.[76]

        Title: *Roscada Flainn Fina maic Ossa rig Sacsan insso sis* at col. 229
        a 42. Text begins with the *ad·cota* series at col. 229 b 1 and continues
        unbroken, in the order as displayed on the table, to col. 231 c z,
        ending with § 7 *Maith dán ecnae.* A fragmentary *Apgitir Chrábaid*
        ascribed to St Fursa, beginning at col. 228 b 17, precedes our text. At
        col. 232 a 1 begin the four texts which characteristically follow our
        text in this recension. Beginning at col. 234 a 3 we find a copy of
        Audacht Morain (Rec. A), which is followed by a copy of the *Triads*,
        beginning at col. 236 a 24. Scribe: Donnchadh mac Giolla na Naemh
        Uí Dhuinnín writing in Ros Broin, Co. Cork, ca. 1465.[77]

---

[70] Hull, "The Wise Sayings of Flann Fína (Aldfrith, King of Northumbria)," 95–102;
see N₃ above.

[71] Kuno Meyer, "The Duties of A Husbandman," *Ériu* 2 (1905): 172.

[72] Paul Walsh, "A Poem on Ireland," *Ériu* 8, no. 1 (1915): 64–74.

[73] See the facsimile with introduction by Robert Atkinson, *The Yellow Book of Lecan,
a Collection of Pieces (Prose and Verse) in the Irish Language* (Dublin: Royal Irish Academy,
1896).

[74] Richard I. Best, "The Yellow Book of Lecan," *Journal of Celtic Studies* 1 (1949–50):
190–92; H. P. A. Oskamp, "The Yellow Book of Lecan Proper," *Ériu* 26 (1975): 102–21.

[75] William O'Sullivan, "Ciothruadh's Yellow Book of Lecan," *Éigse* 18 (1981): 177–
81.

[76] See further Tomás Ó Concheanainn, "Scríobhaithe Leacáin Mhic Fhir Bhisigh,"
Celtica 19 (1987): 141–75.

[77] Ó Concheanainn, "Scríobhaithe Leacáin Mhic Fhir Bhisgh," 158.

$Y_2 =$ Mullingar Public Library, MS no. 1.[78] Title: *Roscadha Flaind Fina mc Ossa righ Saxan andso sis.* Text begins with the *ad·cota* series on f. 64 r a 1 and ends with § 7 *Maith dán ecnae* at f. 68 r a 15. A leaf preceding our text is missing. A copy of *Leabhar Gabhála* precedes. Following § 7 *Maith dán ecnae* we find the sequence of four texts usual in this recension. These four texts are followed by the *Triads* beginning on f. 70 v 19. The title-page — in the hand of Donncha Ó Floinn — identifies this manuscript as containing extracts from "Leabhar Droma Sneachtaigh". Scribe: according to the title-page written in 1821, Seaghan Ó Maolconaire, ca. 1560. But Tomás Ó Concheanainn noted the similarity of this hand to that in part V of Bodleian MS Rawlinson B 512, which is probably of the fifteenth century and associated with the Ó Maoil Chonaire family of scribes.[79]

$Y_3 =$ NL1 G 476. Title: *Roscada Flaind Fina mc Oss Ri Saxan.* Our text begins on page 51 a 1 and follows the order of sections as noted in the table. A copy of *Leabhar Gabhála*, beginning on page 8.11, precedes. Following § 7 *Maith dán ecnae*, which ends on page 57 b 14, we find the usual sequence of four texts. The *Triads* follow these four texts beginning on page 62 a 1. Scribe: probably Mícheál mac Peadair Uí Longáin, eighteenth century.

$Y_4 =$ RIA 697 (23 Q 9). Title: *Roscada Flaind Fina mc Oss– rig Saxan.* Our text begins on page 58 a 1 with the *ad·cota* series. A copy of *Leabhar Gabhála* precedes. Following § 7 *Maith dán ecnae*, which ends on page 65 b 13, we find the usual sequence of four texts. The *Triads* begin on page 71 a 1. The back of this manuscript, in gilt lettering, says "Extracts from Leabhar Droma Sneachtaig by J. Maolconaire, 1560". Scribe: probably Peadar Ó Longáin, nineteenth century.

$Y_5 =$ NLI G 155. Title: *Roscada Flaind Fina mc Oss righ Saxan.* Our text begins on page 95.6 with the *ad·cota* series. A copy of *Leabhar Gabhála*, beginning on page 52.2, precedes. Following § 7 *Maith dán ecnae*, which ends on page 102 a 17, we find the usual sequence of

---

[78] See the description by Pádraig de Brún, "Lámhscríbhinní Gaeilge sa Mhuileann gCearr," *Éigse* 19 (1982–83): 82–85.

[79] de Brún, "Lámhscríbhinní Gaeilge," 83 note 3. See also Breandán Ó Conchúir, *Scríobhaithe Chorcaí 1700–1850* (Baile Átha Cliath [Dublin]: An Clóchomhar, 1982), 244.

four texts. The *Triads* begin on page 107 a 1. This manuscript is also said to contain "Extracts from Leabhar Droma Sneachtaig by J. Maolchonaire 1560". Scribe: Peadar mac Mhíchíl Uí Longáin, 1845.

Y_6 = Fermoy, St Colman's College, MS 11. Title: *Roscada Flaind Fina mc Ossa righ Saxan andso sis.* Text begins on page 49 a 1 with the *ad·cota* series and ends after § 7 *Maith dán ecnae* on page 54 b 21. The usual sequence of four texts follows. The *Triads* begin on page 58.14. The title page cites as its source "Leabhar Droma Sneachtaigh re Seaghan Ó Maolchonaire". Scribe: Éamonn Ó Mathghamhna, ca. 1844.

Y_7 = RIA 595 (24 C 3). Title: *Roscada Flaind Fina mc Ossa righ Saxan andso sis.* Text begins on f. 48 r a 1 with the *ad·cota* series. An acephalous copy of *Leabhar Gabhála* precedes. Following § 7 *Maith dán ecnae*, which ends on f. 53 r b 19, we find the usual sequence of four texts. The *Triads* begin on f. 57 r 13. The title page of this manuscript refers to the "Leabhar Droma Sneachtaigh re Seaghan Ó Maolconaire". Scribe: Éamonn Ó Mathghamhna, Cork, 1840.

Y_8 = Mullingar Public Library, MS no. 2.[80] Title: *Roscadha Flaind Fina mc Ossa rig Saxan andso sis.* Text begins on page 3.1 with the *ad·cota* series, and ends on page 21.4 with § 9 *Secht comarthai déc* (= *TC* § 22). The title page precedes, and the *Triads*, beginning page 21.5, follow our text. Scribe: Sea[án] Ua Murchadha, 1756.

Y_9 = RIA 258 (23 G 25). Title: *Rosadha* [sic] *Flaind Fina mc Ossa rig Saxon andso*, preceded by the heading, *An Seanduine.* Our text begins on page 25.1 with the *ad·cota* series. From page 27.19 to the bottom of the page two unrelated quatrains intervene. On page 28.1 our text resumes with the *tosach* series and § 9 *Secht comarthai déc* completes the text on page 32.11. Our text is preceded by some unrelated quatrains, and followed, on page 32.12, by a text with the title *Ceaista Fhíthill.* Beginning on page 34.19 are notes on Irish saints; the *Triads* follow on page 37.1, also under the heading *An Seanduine.* Scribe: Mícheál Óg Ó Longáin, nineteenth century.

---

[80] de Brún, "Lámhscríbhinní Gaeilge," 86–87.

Y_{10} = Maynooth M 48. Title: *Roscadha Flainn Fína mc Ossa rígh Saxon annso*. Our text begins with the *ad·cota* series on page 357.1 and ends on page 365.z with § 9 *Secht comarthai déc*. It is preceded by some unrelated quatrains which begin on page 356.10, and is followed by a poem by Tadhg Dall Ó hUiginn which begins on page 366.1. Beginning on page 367.1 we find a copy of *Ro·det i nInis find Fáil*, this time attributed to Giolla Caomháin. Scribe: Mícheál Óg Ó Longáin, nineteenth century.

Y_1 cannot be the direct exemplar of any manuscript in its recension. The following stemma demonstrates the interrelationship between manuscripts of Rec. Y, with *y* representing the hyparchetype.

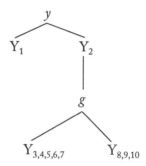

Recension L

This recension is equivalent to what Thurneysen edited as *Senbríathra Fíthail*.[81] It conflates series of three-word maxims — as well as § 2 *Ba faitech* and § 7 *Maith dán ecnae* — with sections otherwise associated with *Tecosca Cormaic* and with Cormac's legendary judge Fíthal.[82] This recension contains fewer three-word maxims than either Rec. N or Y, but nearly every maxim present in Rec. L will be found in both Rec. N and Y. Thurneysen left § 7 *Maith dán ecnae* out of his edition of *Senbríathra Fíthail*, but

---

[81] "Zu irischen Handschriften," 11–22.

[82] For a clear illustration of how this text follows, and intermingles sections from, *Tecosca Cormaic*, see Anne O'Sullivan, *The Book of Leinster, formerly Lebar na Núachongbála*, vol. 6 (Dublin: Dublin Institute for Advanced Studies, 1983), 1503–23.

in every manuscript of this recension that section immediately follows *Senbríathra* § 12 (see the table for the exceptional case of L$_2$).

L$_1$ is the oldest extant manuscript which contains these maxims. As such, it offers many old spellings and is one of three chief manuscripts used to reconstruct readings for this edition. However, despite its age, there are three reasons why L$_1$ cannot represent the exemplar for any other manuscript. First, all other manuscripts in Rec. L, except L$_1$, include *TC* § 19 within the text. Second, in L$_1$ a line (§ 2.3) is missing from the *Ba faitech* (6) series. All other manuscripts in this recension, except for L$_3$, contain seven lines. Third, in the *ferr* (45) series two maxims are missing from L$_1$ which are found in every other manuscript of Rec. L (§§ 6.60 *Ferr súan serbai*, 6.75 *Ferr réide rogaís*).

In L$_2$ the *ferr* (52) series contains five maxims not attested in any other manuscript. They are included at the end of the *ferr* series in this edition (§§ 6.98–102). L$_2$ is the only manuscript in Rec. L not to contain *Senbríathra* §§ 10, 11, 12.

The entire *descad* series is omitted from Rec. L with the exception of L$_3$ where it is appended to the *Triads*. This series contains five maxims not found in any other manuscript. They are included at the end of the *descad* series in this edition (§§ 4.25–29). Appendix 5 includes the *descad* (27) series from L$_3$ to show how similar it is to Rec. N and Y.

The first maxim in L$_{5,6}$ is § 5.12 *Tosach críne galraige* rather than the more usual § 5.2 *Tosach augrai athchomsán* in the order of Rec. L. In the catalogue description of L$_5$ (Adv. 72.1.1) by Mackinnon[83] each maxim series is described by the initial letter rather than the first word. Therefore, it is assumed that § 5.23 *araile maith mesrugud* begins the *ad·cota* series and the text is described as though all of this series began with *araile*. L$_{5,6}$ both have many spellings which suggest an exemplar that resembled L$_1$.

L$_{7,8}$ are copies of the Book of Ballymote (L$_4$).

L$_1$ = Book of Leinster, TCD 1339 (H.2.18). Title: *Senbriathra Fithail inso sis*, in smaller lettering than what surrounds it, set off by red lines top, bottom and sides, appears on page 345 b 17. Our text begins with the *tosach* (21) series on page 345 b 18 and continues unbroken, in the order displayed on the table, to the conclusion of § 7 *Maith dán ecnae* on page 346 a 43. Our text is preceded by a partial copy of

---

[83] Donald Mackinnon, *A Descriptive Catalogue of Gaelic Manuscripts in the Advocates' Library Edinburgh and Elsewhere in Scotland* (Edinburgh: Brown, 1912), 188.

Tecosca Cormaic (pp. 343 a 1–345 b 16). It is followed by a partial copy of *Audacht Morainn* (Rec. A), called *Bríathra Moraind* here (p. 346 a 44–b z). Scribe: Áed ua Crimthainn, before 1166.[84]

L₂ =   TCD 1319 (H.2.17); formerly part of the Book of Lecan, RIA 535 (23 P 2). Untitled. Our text begins with the *tosach* (21) series at f. 146 v d 15 and continues unbroken, in the order displayed on the table, to the conclusion of § 7 *Maith dán ecnae* at f. 147 v b 16. It is preceded by a partial copy of *Tecosca Cormaic* (ff. 145 v a 1–146 v d 14). It is followed by a copy of the *Triads* (ff. 147 v b 17–148 v d z). Scribe: Giolla Íosa Mac Fhir Bhisigh, ca. 1418.[85]

L₃ =   Book of Uí Mhaine, RIA 1225 (D ii 1). Untitled. Our text begins with the *tosach* (21) series at f. 131 r b 9, written as though it ran on from the end of *TC* § 18 which precedes it. It continues to the conclusion of § 7 *Maith dán ecnae* at f. 132 r a 33. Our text is preceded by a partial copy of *Tecosca Cormaic* (ff. 130 r a 14–133 r b 9) and is followed by a copy of the *Triads* (ff. 132 r a 34–133 r b 5). A *descad* (27) series is attached to the end of the *Triads* on f. 133 r b 5–19. The comment *ni d'agallaim Cormaic ₇ Cairpre co ruici sin* is written at the end of the *descad* series. Scribe: Adam Cusin, fourteenth century.[86]

L₄ =   Book of Ballymote, RIA 536 (23 P 12). Untitled. Our text begins with the *tosach* (21) series at f. 40 v b 43 and continues to the conclusion of § 7 *Maith dán ecnae* at f. 41 r b 10. The text is preceded by a partial copy of *Tecosca Cormaic* (ff. 39 v a 44–40 v b 42) and is followed by a copy of the *Triads* which begins at f. 41 r b 11 and is incomplete due to a missing folio. Scribe: Robeartus Mac Síthigh, ca. 1391.[87]

---

[84] William O'Sullivan, "Notes on the Scripts and Make-up of the Book of Leinster," *Celtica* 7 (1966): 1–31.

[85] Ó Concheanainn, "Scríobhaithe Leacáin," 145–46.

[86] William O'Sullivan, "The Book of Uí Maine formerly the Book of Ó Dubhagáin: Scripts & Structure," *Éigse* 23 (1989): 151–66. O'Sullivan (page 158) seems to suggest that the *descad* series may be in the hand of a sixteenth-century legal scribe, Uilliam mac Aodhagáin. See also Nollaig Ó Muraíle, "Leabhar Ua Maine *alias* Leabhar Uí Dhubhagáin," *Éigse* 23 (1989): 167–95.

[87] Tomás Ó Concheanainn, "The Book of Ballymote," *Celtica* 14 (1981): 15–25.

L$_5$ = NLS Adv. 72.1.1. Untitled. Our text begins with the *tosach* (21) series at f. 11 v a 49, written as though it followed directly on from *TC* § 18. It ends with § 7 *Maith dán ecnae* at f. 12 r a 53. *Tecosca Cormaic* precedes, and the *Triads* follow, our text. Scribe: Ádhamh Ó Cuirnín, ca. 1425.

L$_6$ = TCD 1349 (H.4.8). Untitled. Our text begins with the *tosach* (21) series on page 7.12 and concludes with § 7 *Maith dán ecnae* on page 12.19. It is preceded by *Tecosca Cormaic* and is followed by the *Triads*. Scribe unidentified, ca. 1700.

L$_7$ = TCD 1295 (H.2.4). Untitled. Our text begins with the *tosach* (21) series at the bottom of page 133 d 37 and continues to the end of § 7 *Maith dán ecnae* on page 136.15. *Tecosca Cormaic*, which begins on page 131.1, precedes our text, and the *Triads*, which begin on page 136.16, follow our text. Scribe: Richard Tipper, 1728.

L$_8$ = NLS G 42. Untitled. Our text begins with the *tosach* (21) series on page 228.17 and continues to the end of § 7 *Maith dán ecnae* on page 240.11. The rest of this page and the page following (p. 241) are left blank. Our text is preceded by *Tecosca Cormaic* (pp. 214–28.16) and followed by *Cáin Lánamna* (pp. 242–78). Scribe: James Wolf, nineteenth century.

As in Rec. N and Y, the oldest and most reliable manuscript of Rec. L (L$_1$) is not the immediate exemplar for any surviving manuscripts. The following stemma shows the interrelationship between manuscripts within Rec. L, with *l* representing the hyparchetype.

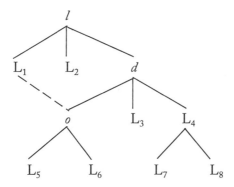

Group X (fragments)

This group of manuscripts contains only fragments. This list does not attempt to be comprehensive. I seldom list the texts which precede and follow in these manuscripts. No attempt has been made to relate these fragments to the other recensions.

The *dligid* series in $X_{1,2,3,4,5}$ does not follow the sequence of any of the three recensions, but most of the maxims are represented in them (§ 3.23 *d. athair somíad* reflects the sentiment but not the form of maxims found in the other recensions, and § 3.27 *d. econd imcoimet* is not found in Rec. L). A characteristic of the *ferr* series in $X_{1,2}$ is the use of the conjunction *ina* after the comparative of the adjective rather than the independent dative. The maxims in this series, when they coincide with maxims from our text, are found in all three recensions. However, some of the maxims have no direct counterpart which suggests that they are later accretions and, therefore, they are not included in this edition (*f[err] cara ina conmir, f. foigidne ina imrisain, f. ana ina ancis*). Only thirteen maxims are clearly legible in the *ad·cota* series in X_7. None of them is present in Rec. L. One maxim, § 1.63 *a. buille borblach*, suggests an exemplar closer to Rec. Y than to Rec. N. The § 7 *Maith dán ecnae* is never the same as those in Rec. N, Y, or L. The copy in X_6[88] differs from the three in $X_{1,2,3}$.

X_1 = BL Add. 30512. Untitled. Beginning on f. 31 v b 6 we have a short *dligid* (16) series followed by § 7 *Maith dán ecnae* ending at f. 31. v b 28 which is mixed with other gnomic sayings and *ferr* maxims. We find a short *ferr* (16) series on f. 33 r b 13–26. Scribe: Uilliam Mac an Leagha, fifteenth century.

X_2 = TCD 1285 (H.1.11). Untitled. On f.139 r 1–12 we find a short *dligid* (16) series followed by § 7 *Maith dán ecnae*. On f. 141 r 1–7 is a short *ferr* (16) series. These are the same maxims in the same order as found in X_1. Scribe: Aodh Ó Dálaigh, 1752.

X_3 = RIA 148 (23 D 9). In this manuscript on page 420.3 we find a *dligid* (16) series (written *dligair*) followed by § 7 *Maith dán*

---

[88] Stokes, in the preface to *Félire Óengusso*, cites the beginning lines of this section which show their divergence: Whitley Stokes, ed. and trans., *Félire Óengusso Céli Dé, the Martyrology of Oengus the Culdee* (London: Henry Bradshaw Society, 1905; repr. Dublin: Dublin Institute for Advanced Studies, 1984), x.

ecnae, as in $X_{1,2}$, ending on the bottom of the page. Scribe: Richard Tipper, early eighteenth century.

X_4 = RIA 154 (23 M 18). Untitled. On page 424.21–z we find the same *dligid* (16) series as found in $X_{1,2,3}$. Scribe: Seón Mac Solaimh, early eighteenth century.

X_5 = Maynooth M 13. Untitled. At page 213.9–z we find the same *dligid* (16) series found in other Group X manuscripts. Scribe: Mícheál Óg Ó Longáin, ca. 1820.

X_6 = NLI G 10. Untitled. On page 46 a 23–26 we find § 7 *Maith dán ecnae*. Scribe unidentified, sixteenth century.

X_7 = RIA 1242 (23 P 3). Untitled. On f. 14 v b 35–z we find an *ad·cota* (13) series. Scribe: Uilliam Mac an Leagha, fifteenth century.

X_8 = BL Egerton 92. Untitled. Beginning on f. 17 r a 31 we have § 8 *Cía fégam ránac* followed by § 9 *Secht comarthai déc* (= *TC* § 22) and *TC* § 29 ending on f. 17 r b 9. Scribe unidentified, 1453.

The leaf on which these paragraphs are found has a very dark edge making it impossible to record the texts fully, but enough is legible to be certain which sections they represent.

X_9 = NLI G3. Title: [*I*]*ntamail Flaind Fhina*. From f. 21 v a 14–b 15 we have § 8 *Cía fégam ránac* which has been elaborated on. Scribe unidentified, fifteenth century.

Although most of this manuscript is the work of Ádhamh Ó Cianáin, d. 1373, the folios that contain our text appear to be of the fifteenth century. The complete heading for this piece reads: [*I*]*ntamail Flaind Fhina .i. righ Saxan for* [s with a line above it in MS] *cinadaib Ereann ar a fhiarfaighidh dia mhac dhe*. It is the only one of these texts which names Flann Fína and which is presented as a dialogue between him and his son. It reproduces approximately the first twenty lines of § 8 *Cía fégam ránac*, as edited here (Appendix 1), but then elaborates on the contrast and presents Connacht, Ulster and Leinster in a negative light. The language is not Old Irish; for example, the superlative form of the adjectives do not end in -*m*.

X_{10} = NLS Adv. 72.1.7. Untitled. Beginning at f.8 v b 45 we have § 9 *Secht comarthai déc* (*drochthacrai*) (= *TC* § 22). It is the same list as found in X_{11}. This is followed, to the end of the column, by the "Seventeen signs of good-pleading (*deagtagra*)" in which only nine items are listed. Scribe unidentified, fifteenth century.

X_{11} = TCD 1432 (E.3.3). Untitled. On p. 21 b 19–28 we find a glossed § 9 *Secht comarthai déc*. Scribe unidentified, fifteenth or sixteenth century. This section is printed in *CIH* vi 2342.1–11. It begins *se comartha deg* but lists eighteen items.

DATING

The date of the text cannot be set precisely because of its stylistic simplicity. The lack of syntactic archaisms, however, is not a conclusive argument against greater age. The text conforms to Classical Old Irish of the mid-eighth to the mid-ninth centuries. Some of the maxims, as noted previously, are found in *Di Astud Chor* (§ 3.3), *Bretha Nemed Déidenach* (§§ 3.3, 3.5, 3.14), *Tochmarc Étaíne* (§ 4.16), and *Sanas Cormaic* (§ 4.1), all of which are Old Irish texts. However, the presence of these maxims in other texts does not tell us anything about their provenance or their age relative to the texts in which they are found. There is evidence for modernization of the language with transmission, seen most clearly in § 8 *Cía fégam ránac* (Appendix 1) where the N_2 version is modernized from the Old Irish of Rec. Y. Spelling is not reliable for dating purposes because so many of the manuscripts are late, but some random spellings do suggest age. There are few verbal forms by which to judge the age of composition, but those in §§ 2, 7, and 8 agree with Classical Old Irish.

Among the three-word maxims the most distinctive grammatical features for age are the preservation of neuter gender (which began to disappear in the ninth century)[89] and the use of the independent dative after the comparative adjective.[90] For the latter feature, evidence of modernization can be found in $X_{1,2}$ where the short *ferr* series in these manuscripts uses the conjunction *ina* before the thing being compared, thus eliminating the need for a distinctive dative form. Neuter gender and the independent dative are found in § 6 *ferr*, and most consistently shown in Rec. Y. The following

---

[89] Rudolf Thurneysen, *A Grammar of Old Irish*, translated by D. A. Binchy and Osborn Bergin (Dublin: Dublin Institute for Advanced Studies, 1946; revised and enlarged edition with supplement, 1975), 154 § 245 [= *GOI*].

[90] *GOI*, 160 § 251.1, 232 § 366.2.

examples are quoted from the normalized edition, with manuscripts that support the restored reading cited in parentheses.

Examples of neuter gender are:

§ 6.10 *Ferr ilar n-oscru* ($Y_{1,2}$; $N_{1,2}$; om. L).

§ 6.22 *Ferr ecnae n-anaib* ($Y_{1,2}$; N_2 = namuib; om. N_1, L).

§ 6.51 *Ferr aurlam n-adbur* ($Y_{1,2}$; $N_{1,2}$; om. L).

§ 6.93 *Ferr becc n-érai* ($Y_{1,2}$; in N and L without nasal).

Examples of the nasalization of a following dependent genitive after a neuter noun do not appear among the three-word maxims, for example, after *tosach* in § 5. Thurneysen noted that such nasalization is not consistently shown, and is more frequent in the ninth-century Milan glosses than in the earlier eighth-century Würzburg glosses.[91] Neuter gender is marked in the Rec. Y variant of § 6.20 *Ferr beccfine móraltramm* which reads, in part, *mór n-altrama*. This is an example of the o/ā-stem adjective *mór* being treated as a neuter substantive and nasalizing a following dependent genitive, showing that this variant developed in the Old Irish period.

The following are clear examples of the independent dative plural of the thing compared:

§ 6.22 *Ferr ecnae n-anaib* ($Y_{1,2}$; N_2; om. N_1, L).

§ 6.28 *Ferr bethu búadaib* ($Y_{1,2}$; $N_{1,2}$; om. L).

§ 6.30 *Ferr bríg bágaib* ($Y_{1,2}$; $N_{1,2}$; $L_{1,2}$).

§ 6.31 *Ferr duine dúilib* ($Y_{1,2}$; $N_{1,2}$; om. L).

§ 6.36 *Ferr flaith foltaib* ($Y_{1,2}$; $N_{1,2}$; om. L).

§ 6.37 *Ferr caíntórmach cintaib* ($Y_{1,2}$; $N_{1,2}$; om. L).

§ 6.42 *Ferr mac míchoraib* ($Y_{1,2}$; $N_{1,2}$; om. L).

§ 6.87 *Ferr mruig mlichtaib* ($Y_{1,2}$; N not reliable; om. L).

Some dative singular endings are distinctive enough to merit comment:

§ 6.61 *Ferr carae cormaim*; $Y_{1,2}$ and N_1 preserve the earlier dat. sg. of

---

[91] *GOI*, 148 § 237. For the importance of these sets of glosses as sources for Old Irish, see *GOI*, 4 § 5 (Würzburg) and 5 § 6 (Milan). These glosses are edited and translated in Whitley Stokes and John Strachan, ed., *Thesaurus Palaeohibernicus: a Collection of Old-Irish Glosses, Scholia, Prose, and Verse*, vol. 1 (Cambridge: Cambridge Univ. Press, 1901–3; repr. Dublin: Dublin Institute for Advanced Studies, 1975), 7–483 (Milan) and 499–712 (Würzburg) [= *Thes.*].

cuirm as n.n whereas L₁ has *coirm* dat. sg. as i-stem (*GOI*, 192 § 302).

§ 6.70 *Ferr bás bithbiniu*; *bithbiniu* (Y₁,₂) preserves the spelling of the dat. sg. of *bine* io-stem.

§ 6.83 *Ferr leth lánetiug*; *-etiug* (Y₁) preserves the dat. sg. of *etech* o.n, vb.n. of *as·toing*; the *g* is etymologically correct.

§ 6.84 *Ferr fróech forbbu*; *forbbu* (Y₁,₂) preserves the spelling of the dat. sg. of *forbbae* io.n, vb.n. of *for·ben*.

§ 6.89 *Ferr sothced séitchi*; *séitchi* (Y₁,₂) preserves the expected dat. sg. of *séitig* ī.f.

The following miscellaneous selection of features all suggest age:

§ 1.28 *Ad·cota barann bibdaid*; Y₁ preserves the unmetathesized O.Ir. form *bibdu* of this dental-stem rather than the more common Mid.Ir. form *bidba*[*id*].

§ 3.16 *Dligid dall dídin*; the word *díden* ā.f became obsolete early and was often replaced by *dítiu* n.f.

§ 6.8b *Ferr road réraib*; Y₁,₂ read *rér* for what other recensions preserve as *ríar* reflecting the change from *é* to *ía* (*GOI*, 36 § 53).

§ 6.14 *Ferr sét sous*, § 6.76 *Ferr rous rúathur*, § 6.92 *Ferr grés sous*; *rous* (Y₁, L₁) and *sous* (Y₁) suggest age, rather than the contracted forms as listed in *DIL rós, sós* (*GOI*, 71 §§ 113–14).

§ 6.16 *Ferr sothced slóg*, § 6.89 *Ferr sothced séitchi*; *sothced* (Y₁,₂) shows the unstressed *-e-* of *toceth* before becoming *-a-* of *tocad* in Classical O.Ir.

§ 6.28 *Ferr bethu búadaib*; Y₁,₂ have the clear O.Ir. spelling *bethu* nom. sg.

§ 6.47 *Ferr laubair áini*; the vocalism of the first syllable of *laubair* (Y₁) reflects its borrowing from Lat. *labor(em)* (*GOI*, 51–52 § 80c; 569 § 918).

§ 6.51 *Ferr aurlam n-adbur*; this example not only shows neuter gender but the spellings in Y₁,₂ show clearly the dat. sg. of *adbar* o.n. In addition, the spellings of Y₁,₂ for *aurlam* accurately reflect its etymology, *air-fo-lam* (*GOI*, 497–98 § 823).

§ 6.53 *Ferr coimsetu cucilchiu*; *cucilchiu* dat. sg. of the vb.n. of *con·clich* (N₁ = *cucilche*, Y₁,₂ = *cucuilgu*) suggests the io.n inflexion for verbal nouns of O.Ir. (*GOI*, 448–49 § 725).

§ 6.54 *Ferr cride gíallnai*; *gíallnae* (Y₁,₂ N₃,₄) preserves the *lln* cluster which became *ll*, the spelling of N₁,₂ and Rec. L, after Milan (*GOI*, 95 § 153e).

§ 6.84 *Ferr fróech forbbu*; *fróech* ($Y_{1,2}$) preserves the older and etymologically correct diphthong *óe*/*oí* (*GOI*, 42–43 §§ 66–67).

§ 6.87 *Ferr mruig mlichtaib*; $Y_{1,2}$, in addition to preserving the dat.
pl., preserve the initial *m-* of both words, though in transitional
form *mb-*, *mbruig mblichtaib*.

§ 6.94 *Ferr cloud cummu*; *cloud* (Y_1; L_3) preserves the older disyllabic
spelling of this word.

Old Irish forms of the copula in § 2 *Ba faitech* are preserved in some
manuscripts. *Ba*, 2sg. ipv.,[92] is preserved randomly by N_1, $L_{2,4}$. *Arnába* and
cor(o)ba, 2sg. pres. subj.,[93] are preserved randomly by N_1, $Y_{1,2}$, $L_{3,4}$. The
lines at §§ 7.16, 7.17 preserve *it*, 3pl. pres. of the copula,[94] in N_1, Y_1, L_1.
The line at § 7.19 contains *dianid*, *dia*[n] + 3sg. pres. conjunct,[95] in Y_1, L_1.

Certain forms do not conform to standard Old Irish. However, they are
few in number and are of the type that may have been introduced by scribes
at a later period. Clear datives are lacking from all manuscripts in the
following examples:

§ 6.5 *Ferr sonaide séta*[*ib*]; (N,Y, om. L), and § 6.15 *Ferr suthaine*
séta[*ib*]; (N,Y, om. L) in neither of these is a dat. pl. recorded in
any witness.

§ 6.86 *Ferr mag mórsléib*; (N,Y,L) all witnesses have *mórslíab*.

§ 6.91 *Ferr búar bréithir*; (Y only) all witnesses have *bríathar*.

Some consonantal-stem nouns show oblique forms for nominative singular, for example, § 1.28 *barann* for *barae*, § 1.66 *briugaid* for *briugu*,
§ 4.15
imcaisin for *imcaisiu*, or § 6.57 *sobarthan* for *sobarthu*. But this process has
been shown to have begun in the Old Irish period.[96] Examples of modernized forms that are not merely phonological or morphological variants are
likely to be the result of simple substitution by a scribe of a word more
familiar to him. The last three examples below may be of this latter type.
They have been allowed to stand in the normalized text, rather than substitute an older word which is not attested in any witness for them:

---

[92] *GOI*, 487 § 801.
[93] *GOI*, 488 § 802.
[94] *GOI*, 484 § 792.
[95] *GOI*, 486 § 798.
[96] Kim McCone, "The Würzburg and Milan Glosses: Our Earliest Sources of
'Middle Irish'," *Ériu* 36 (1985): 90–91.

§ 1.29 *Ad·cota biltengae mrath*; (N,Y,L), § 4.17 *Descad mraith sanas*; (N,Y,L₃) all witnesses have Mid.Ir. *brath*.

§ 1.46 *Ad·cota frithbert fúachtain*; (N,Y, om. L) all witnesses have *fúachtain* instead of older *fogal*, vb.n. of *fo·fich*.

§ 4.7 *Descad drúise dánatus*; (N,Y,L₃) *dánatus* is a later form which superseded O.Ir. *dánae*.

§ 4.19 *Descad fáilte sláinte*; (N,Y,L₃) *sláinte* is a later form which superseded O.Ir. *sláine* and *slántu*.

In a text whose form is not restricted by the requirements of verse, and which is so simple syntactically, modernization is easy to impose. For example, if the modernized N₂ copy of § 8 *Cía fégam ránac* were the only surviving version of this section we would have no reason to suspect its Old Irish origins. Nevertheless, among the three-word maxims, as well as in §§ 2 and 7, firm evidence of Old Irish origins has survived.

DESCRIPTIONS OF INDIVIDUAL SECTIONS

The text is organized so that it naturally divides into sections. The following discussion describes the contents for each section as listed across the top of the facing-page table. The descriptions of sections containing three-word maxims (§ 1 *ad·cota*, § 3 *dligid*, § 4 *descad*, § 5 *tosach*, § 6 *ferr*) will concentrate on the agreement in readings from recension to recension.

The number of maxims per section is usually indicative of recension. For example, in § 1 *ad·cota*, Rec. N manuscripts have sixty-six or sixty-five maxims, Rec. Y manuscripts average sixty-four maxims, and Rec. L manuscripts average thirty-two maxims. But the table cannot show that nearly all maxims found in Rec. L are found in both Rec. N and Rec. Y. This agreement in the contents of the maxim series means that only a minority of maxims is not found in at least two recensions. The collation of the three-word maxims in Appendix 5 clearly demonstrates this.

Correspondences from recension to recension for § 1 *ad·cota* show examples of Rec. N and Y sharing readings against L; for example, §§ 1.1, 1.37, 1.43. But one also finds examples of Rec. N and L which share readings against Y (§ 1.3); as well as examples of maxims found in Rec. N and L which are omitted from Y (§§ 1.5, 1.53). Examples also exist of maxims found in Rec. Y and L which share readings against those of Rec. N (§ 1.19), or which are omitted from N (§§ 1.67, 1.68). An example of conflation is shown in § 1.25. N₁ has *a[d·cota] bais baogal* and L₁ has *a. bais bága*, but Y₁ conflates both readings and has *a. baes bagh ɫ baegul.* On the other hand, § 1.35 shows no clear agreement among the recensions.

Sometimes § 2 *Ba faitech* contains only six, instead of the usual seven, lines. Regardless of recension, it is always § 2.3 that is omitted.

One of the most uniform sections is § 3 *dligid.* But even here, Rec. N and Y share readings against Rec. L at §§ 3.17, 3.22, and 3.23. Rec. N and L share readings against Y at §§ 3.9 (omitted), 3.15, and 3.20. Rec. Y and L share readings against N at §§ 3.7, 3.21, 3.33. Rec. N texts also contain the intrusive line § 3.2 *Ar fich gáes gail* which is paralleled elsewhere in the opening lines of *TC* § 15.[97]

Rec. L completely omits § 4 *descad,* except for the special circumstances noted in L₃. The *descad* series in L₃ is close in content and in sequence to those in Rec. N and Y. The L₃ *descad* series lacks one maxim (§ 4.5), found in both Rec. N and Y; and one maxim (§ 4.25) found only in Rec. Y. Otherwise it agrees, generally, with the readings of Rec. N and Y. In addition, it contains five maxims not found elsewhere. They are included in this edition at §§ 4.25–29. The *descad* series from L₃ is included in Appendix 5.

The greatest uniformity from recension to recension in sequence and spelling is found in § 5 *tosach.* Rec. N has a pair of maxims (§§ 5.13–14) peculiar to itself. N₁, but not N₂, has the further distinction of different readings from Rec. Y and L at §§ 5.20–21. All three recensions end the series with § 5.23 *Arailiu maith mesrugud* which, I have argued, probably represents an incorporated gloss rather than an independent maxim.

The longest section, § 6 *ferr,* shows the greatest disparity from recension to recension, even between Rec. N and Y. In some cases, it is difficult to decide whether or not we are dealing with variants or completely different maxims, for example, §§ 6.55, 6.71, 6.82. Rec. N and Y agree against Rec. L at §§ 6.61, 6.69. Rec. N and L agree against Rec. Y at §§ 6.54, 6.70. Rec. Y and L agree against Rec. N at §§ 6.35, 6.56. The following five maxims are omitted from Rec. N but are found in Rec. Y and L: §§ 6.92, 6.94–97. Maxims which differ between Rec. N and Y, and which are omitted from Rec. L altogether, include: §§ 6.4, 6.6, 6.16, 6.18, 6.20, 6.33, 6.40, 6.41, 6.48, 6.50, 6.52, 6.87, 6.88, 6.90.

The last section in most manuscripts is § 7 *Maith dán ecnae.* Thurneysen did not include this section in his edition of the *Senbríathra Fíthail,* despite the fact that it concludes nearly every manuscript in Rec. L. In N₃ and L₈

---

[97] *TC,* 26, § 15.2; and textual notes for § 3.2 below.

this section is given a separate title which ascribes it to Flann Fína.

Characteristic of Rec. Y is a section which begins with the question § 8 *Cía fégam ránac* "who are the keenest you have met?" and answers "The men of Mag Féne and wind." It names several tribal groups associated with the south of Ireland and assigns them a specific quality, not always complimentary. It is edited and translated in Appendix 1.

The sections held in common with *Tecosca Cormaic* as published by Kuno Meyer are designated by the section numbers in his edition. The only one of these sections edited here is *TC* § 22 = § 9 *Secht comarthai déc drochthacrai* "the seventeen signs of bad pleading", common to both Rec. Y and L. It is edited and translated in Appendix 2.

The following four sections, characteristic of Rec. L, are also found in *Tecosca Cormaic*. In *TC* § 29 Cairpre asks Cormac how to behave among the wise and the foolish, among friends and strangers, etc. Cormac answers him *ní ba rogáeth, ní ba robáeth* "Don't be too wise, don't be too foolish" etc., and later in the section adds the advice, "If you be too wise, one will expect (too much) of you; if you be too foolish, you will be deceived."[98]

In *TC* § 30 Cairpre asks "How shall I be?" and Cormac answers *Ba gáeth fri gáis ar ná rottogáitha nech i ngáis* "Be wise with the wise lest anyone deceive you in wisdom." The advice in this section follows the style "be proud with the proud ..., be humble with the humble ...", etc.[99]

Characteristic of *TC* § 31 are *cách* formulae of the type *Gáeth cách co reic a forbbai, báeth cách co lóg tíre* ... "Every one is wise till he comes to sell his heritage, every one is foolish till he buys land ...,". This section also contains a short list of things that are *milsem* "sweetest".[100]

The advice in *TC* § 19 begins *ní bága fri ríg, ní comrís fri báeth, ní comtéis fri díbergach* "Do not contend with a king, do not foregather with a fool, do not associate with a marauder." The advice which concludes this section reads "do not race against a wheel, nor against the cast of a spear, nor up a great height, nor against the surf of the sea, nor against danger, nor a lance ...".[101]

The three *Senbríathra* §§ 10, 11, 12 were edited by Thurneysen and trans-

---

[98] *TC*, 44–45.
[99] *TC*, 46–47.
[100] *TC*, 46–49.
[101] *TC*, 36–39.

lated by Smith under the title *Senbríathra Fíthail.*[102] These sections usually name Fíthal and are presented as a dialogue between Fíthal and his unnamed son. In *Senbríathra* § 10 Fíthal tells his son that the *indéoin trebtha* "anvil of husbandry" is a good woman, and he proceeds to tell him how to recognize her. In *Senbríathra* § 11 he answers the question *cid as dech ban?* "what is the best of women?", and in *Senbríathra* § 12, *cid as mesam ban?* "what is the worst of women?".

TITLES AND ASCRIPTIONS

The three recensions can be divided into the two which are associated by title with Flann Fína (Rec. N and Y) and the third recension (Rec. L), which is associated with Fíthal. But this division is not always clear-cut when we incorporate the evidence of sectional headings and marginal ascriptions, and is further complicated by the overlap of sections found in other texts, especially in *Tecosca Cormaic*. The titles, headings, and marginal notes suggest that the different sections were thought of as distinct units by the scribes who redacted them. These units could be placed in varying order or separated from other sections in an apparently random order without destroying their individual coherence, as shown by the various orderings and many fragments included on the facing-page table. It is difficult to decide which sections should be included among those which may have comprised an original text.

Bríathra / Roscada Flainn Fína

Rec. N and Y share the greatest similarities as evidenced by the contents for each section listed on the facing-page table and the collation of maxims in Appendix 5. Both recensions have manuscripts whose titles ascribe this collection of maxims to Flann Fína mac Ossu. All manuscripts in Rec. Y have the title which can be normalized as *Roscada Flainn Fína maic Ossu ríg Saxan* "The Maxims of Flann Fína son of Oswiu, king of the English". No reference to Fíthal is made in any Rec. Y manuscripts. However, § 9 *Secht*

---

[102] Thurneysen, "Zu irischen Handschriften," 19–21; Smith, "*Senbriathra Fithail,*" 52–60.

comarthai déc, found in all Rec. Y manuscripts, is also found in all Rec. L manuscripts, and in *Tecosca Cormaic* as TC^{103} § 22.

Rec. N is not so consistent. Only N_2 has a title, *Briathra Floinn Fhiona maic Ossa sund*, which has been normalized and used as the title for this edition. This manuscript also has the heading "Flann Fína beos" at the beginning of § 8 *Cía fégam ránac*, the section which is characteristic of Rec. Y. N_1, which forms the basis for this edition, provides no title at all, and has "Fithal dixit" in the margin at the beginning of the *tosach* series. Both N_3 and N_4 contain *Senbríathra* §§ 10, 11, 12 which are otherwise found only in Rec. L and which explicitly name Fíthal. N_3 has a title for § 7 *Maith dán ecnae* which reads *Bríathra Floinn Fiona maic Cosa anso*.

Rec. N and Y are connected by their ascriptions to Flann Fína and also by their associations with the Ó Maoil Chonaire family of scribes. N_1 was penned at the home of Seán Ó Maoil Chonaire and Y_2 is a product of an Ó Maoil Chonaire scribe. Thurneysen identified MS 23 N 10 (N_1) as being one of two manuscripts — the other being British Library MS Egerton 88 — to contain texts from a lost manuscript known as *Cín Dromma Snechtai*.[104] Five manuscripts in Rec. Y ($Y_{2,4,5,6,7}$) are described as containing extracts from the *Leabhar Droma Sneachtaigh*. Nowhere in any discussion of the *Cín Dromma Snechtai* has it ever been suggested that a text called *Bríathra / Roscada Flainn Fína* was a part of its contents. What is obviously a late tradition of the *Cín Dromma Snechtai* has no bearing on the textual history of the text edited here. But the connections of Rec. N and Y with the Ó Maoil Chonaire family of scribes, and the consequent association with the *Cín Dromma Snechtai*, help confirm that both recensions derive from a common exemplar. By the eighteenth century both N_1 and Y_2 were to be found in Co. Cork,[105] the county in which Y_1 was redacted. Future investigations into the history of scribal families in the south of Ireland may yet reveal further connections between these two recensions.

The similarities between Rec. N and Rec. Y, shown on the facing-page table

---

[103] *TC*, 40–41. See Appendix 2 below.

[104] Thurneysen discussed this lost manuscript in "Zu irischen Handschriften," 23–30; and Rudolf Thurneysen, *Die irische Helden- und Königsage bis zum siebzehnten Jahrhundert* (Halle: Max Niemeyer, 1921; repr. Hildesheim and New York: Georg Olms, 1980), 15–18. A revised view on the history and date of this manuscript has been offered by Séamus Mac Mathúna, ed. and trans., *Immram Brain, Bran's Journey to the Land of the Women* (Tübingen: Max Niemeyer, 1985), 421–69.

[105] Ó Conchúir, *Scríobhaithe Chorcaí*, 244–45.

and by the collations in Appendix 5, reveal that these two recensions derive from a collection of Old Irish maxims associated with Flann Fína mac Ossu.

Senbríathra Fíthail

Rec. L is associated with Fíthal. It contains the manuscripts used by Thurneysen in his edition of *Senbríathra Fíthail*. Only L_1, the oldest manuscript in the recension, has the title which Thurneysen used. L_1, however, cannot be the exemplar of any surviving witness to this text. No other copy in this recension has a title. In every manuscript in the recension, our text follows a fragmentary copy of *Tecosca Cormaic* after *TC* § 18; except for L_1, which follows *TC* § 19. $L_{2,5,6}$ each have the heading *Fíthal dixit* following *TC* § 18 and preceding the *tosach* series, which begins the text in this recension. In L_1, § 1 *ad·cota* and § 2 *Ba faitech* have the marginal note "Fíthal", and § 3 *dligid* has a marginal ".*F.*".

Despite the association of Rec. L with Fíthal there are several examples which show that a clear consensus was never reached as to whether this text should be ascribed to Fíthal or to Cormac. All texts in this recension contain a *TC* § 29 which is presented as advice spoken by Fíthal. In this section in L_1, Fíthal is explicitly made to address his son. However, in L_2 Fíthal addresses his advice to Cormac. In $L_{2,3,4,6,7,8}$ *TC* § 19 is preceded by *Cormac dixit fri Cairpre*, or its equivalent, on a separate line.[106] This confirms that a clear distinction has never been drawn between this recension, which is supposed to be Fíthal's advice, and the *Tecosca Cormaic*. In $L_{5,6}$ — those manuscripts which most closely resemble L_1 in spelling — *Senbríathra* §§ 10, 11, 12 are clearly separated from the preceding *TC* § 19 by a large *FINIT*, suggesting that the sections from *Tecosca Cormaic* were kept distinct by the scribes from sections which explicitly name Fíthal. The scribe of L_8 — employed to make a copy of the Book of Ballymote (L_4) — included, on a separate line, the title *Briathra Floinn Fiona mhac Cosa annso* before § 7 *Maith dán ecnae*. No other scribe in this recension attempted to separate this latter section from those that preceded it.

Meyer relied on ten manuscripts for his edition of *Tecosca Cormaic*. Four of the ten belong to Rec. L of this text ($L_{1,2,4,6}$). Meyer commented unfavourably on the versions of *Tecosca Cormaic* in each of those four manuscripts.

---

[106] At this point L_5 does not have such a line separating the sections, but it does have a reference to Cormac here.

Of L_1 (Book of Leinster) he cautioned, "In spite of its age and fine pen-
manship this MS. does not ... supply us with accurate and trustworthy
texts. The copy of *Tecosca Cormaic* contained in it has many faulty readings
...".[107] Meyer summarized L_2 (H.2.17) as "neither a complete nor a very
accurate version."[108] He noted of L_4 (Book of Ballymote) that, "Like L
[Book of Leinster], it mixes up *Tecosca Cormaic* with *Bríathra Fíthail*, passing suddenly from *Cormac dixit fri Coirpre* (p. 65a13) to *ol a mac fri Fithul*
(ib. 32). The text, though good on the whole, is never quite reliable, the
scribe often blundering in an almost incredible manner."[109] Finally, Meyer
says of L_6 (H.4.8), "This copy also has so many defects that I have but
rarely used it."[110] A fifth manuscript used by Meyer for his edition is X_{10}
(Adv. 72.1.7). The text in this manuscript breaks off with *TC* § 18, which
would indicate that the text of *Tecosca Cormaic* in X_{10} is the same text as
that which precedes all of the copies, except for L_1, of the so-called *Senbríathra Fíthail* as found in Rec. L of this edition.

Meyer found that the three best manuscripts for his edition of *Tecosca
Cormaic* were to be found among the Rec. N manuscripts. The large fragment of *Tecosca Cormaic* contained in N_1 (23 N 10), which is incorrectly
cited in Meyer's edition — it is called 23 N 17 and referred to as N^1 — he
described as "A careful and trustworthy copy on the whole."[111] Meyer
praised the copy in N_2 (23 D 2), stating that "Though written in the seven-
teenth century it contains in a remarkably neat hand both the most complete
and by far the best copy of the *Tecosca [Cormaic]*."[112] Meyer also relied on
N_3 (23 N 27). It, too, is incorrectly cited — it is called 23 N 17 and is
referred to as N^2 — but he noted that it contained "a carefully written and
heavily glossed copy of the *Tecosca [Cormaic]*".[113] The manuscript which
Meyer claimed contained the best copy of *Tecosca Cormaic*, N_2 (23 D 2), is
also the manuscript which contains the text with the title, *Bríathra Flainn
Fína*, used for this edition. N_2 is the witness which most closely resembles
N_1, the manuscript copy upon which this edition is based. The seventeenth-
century manuscript, N_2, contains one of the best witnesses for this collection

---

[107] *TC*, viii.
[108] *TC*, viii.
[109] *TC*, viii.
[110] *TC*, ix.
[111] *TC*, ix.
[112] *TC*, ix.
[113] *TC*, ix.

of Old Irish maxims and, also, what Meyer considered to be the best copy of the Old Irish *Tecosca Cormaic*.[114]

The admixture of three-word maxims and sections from *Tecosca Cormaic*, coupled with the evidence of textual titles, attributions at the head of sections, and marginal notes, supports the contention that Rec. L — the text edited by Thurneysen as *Senbríathra Fíthail* — is a deliberately conflated compilation. A new, thorough edition of *Tecosca Cormaic* would help us to understand its textual history. Since L₁ is not the immediate exemplar of any other manuscript in the recension, this conflation must have taken place before L_1 was compiled. All presently available evidence suggests that *Senbríathra Fíthail* is a selection of Old Irish maxims, elsewhere ascribed to Flann Fína mac Ossu, conflated with sections from the Old Irish *Tecosca Cormaic*. The text we now call *Senbríathra Fíthail* appears to have been redacted by an antiquarian editor working in the Middle Irish period.

AUDIENCE AND REDACTOR

Recent research has supported the argument that certain segments of early Irish society had become literate before the arrival of Christianity.[115] From the fifth-century missionaries onwards the level of literacy, in both Latin and Irish, increased.[116] By the seventh century the degree of literacy had evolved to the extent that the Irish made important contributions to the practice of punctuation, layout, and word division in the presentation of written Latin.[117] Some of the Irish conventions were passed on to the

---

[114] Meyer dates *Tecosca Cormaic* to "not later than the first half of the ninth century": *TC*, xi.

[115] The orthographic system of ogam implies a familiarity with both spoken and written Latin: Jane Stevenson, "The Beginnings of Literacy in Ireland," *Proceedings of the Royal Irish Academy* 89 C (1989): esp. 143-44. Stevenson acknowledges her debt to the work of Anthony Harvey. See especially Anthony Harvey, "Early Literacy in Ireland: the Evidence from Ogam," *Cambridge Medieval Celtic Studies* 14 (1987): 1–15.

[116] For an indication of the part St. Patrick played in the spread of literacy, see Gilbert Márkus, "What Were Patrick's Alphabets?," *Cambrian Medieval Celtic Studies* 31 (1996): 1–15. For arguments that certain stylistic features in Irish vernacular literature were developed in the sixth century under the influence of Latin poetry and rhetoric, see Johan Corthals, "Early Irish *Retoirics* and their Late Antique Background," *Cambrian Medieval Celtic Studies* 31 (1996): 17–36.

[117] M. B. Parkes, *Pause and Effect, an Introduction to the History of Punctuation in the West* (Aldershot: Scolar Press, 1992), 23–26.

continent through Anglo-Saxon intermediaries.[118] Lay literacy in the vernacular was becoming widespread during the seventh century as evinced
most graphically in secular law-tracts.[119]

However, the presence of literacy did not mean that oral culture disappeared. Orality continued in Ireland alongside literacy, most notably in
land law. Early Ireland never developed a tradition of written land charters,
beyond the immediate confines of the monasteries, as happened on the continent and in Anglo-Saxon England. This meant that transfer of land ownership was not recorded in writing, as preferred by the Church, but continued
to be a public and oral transaction.[120] Many contracts, possibly including
clientship agreements, must have been publicly and orally performed.[121]
Contractual proceedings were often, in essence, public rituals.[122]

In form, style, and content this text reflects a literate, cultured milieu. It
lacks the familiar devices like linking alliteration, end rhyme or consistent
parallelism which suggest that it was intended for easy memorization or
recitation to an audience. Bare lists subsumed under a single initial word
reflect a literate source.[123]

The preservation of lists is common in Early Irish literate culture, in both
secular and religious spheres.[124] The Irish predilection for lists is manifested in extensive genealogies,[125] in the secular tale lists,[126] and lists

---

[118] Parkes, *Pause and Effect*, 26–29.

[119] Stevenson, "Beginnings of Literacy," 161–64. And see my comments about the
seventh-century *sapientes* Cenn Fáelad and Aldfrith: Colin Ireland, "Aldfrith of Northumbria and the Learning of a *Sapiens*," in *A Celtic Florilegium, Studies in Memory of Brendan
O Hehir*, ed. Kathryn A. Klar, Eve E. Sweetser, and Claire Thomas (Lawrence, Mass.:
Celtic Studies Publications, 1996), 76.

[120] Jane Stevenson, "Literacy and Orality in Early Medieval Ireland," in *Cultural
Identity and Cultural Integration, Ireland and Europe in the Early Middle Ages*, ed. Doris
Edel (Blackrock: Four Courts Press, 1995), 12–13.

[121] Robin Chapman Stacey, *The Road to Judgment, from Custom to Court in Medieval
Ireland and Wales* (Philadelphia: Univ. of Pennsylvania Press, 1994), 32–36.

[122] Stacey, *Road to Judgment*, 32–36. See also the ritual of the handshake: McLeod,
Contract Law, 23–24.

[123] See, for example, Jack Goody, *The Domestication of the Savage Mind*, chapter 5,
"What's in a List?" (Cambridge: Cambridge Univ. Press, 1977), 74–111. Ong cites and
elaborates Goody's ideas in Walter J. Ong, *Orality and Literacy, the Technologizing of the
Word* (London and New York: Methuen, 1982), esp. 99–101, 123–26.

[124] Stevenson, "Beginnings of Literacy," 129; Stevenson, "Literacy and Orality," 18–
20.

[125] Michael A. O'Brien, ed., *Corpus Genealogiarum Hiberniae*, vol. 1 (Dublin: Dublin
Institute for Advanced Studies, 1962).

[126] Proinsias Mac Cana, *The Learned Tales of Medieval Ireland* (Dublin: Dublin

subsumed within prose narratives as we find in *Táin Bó Cúailnge* under headings like *Tochostul Fer nÉrenn* "The Muster of the Men of Ireland."[127] The list or "catalogue" incorporated within a larger narrative has a history dating back to Homer.[128] But literacy is required for a bare list to survive without a narrative frame or mnemonic devices such as rhyme, alliteration, or parallelism.[129]

Early Irish religious writing produced its share of lists including genealogies of saints.[130] The *loricae* tend to incorporate lists, the *lorica* of Laidcenn (d. 661), with its catalogue of body parts, being a particularly good example.[131] The early Irish penitentials form a literature of lists.[132] Allen Frantzen, in the context of the penitentials, noted that they suffer from "our reluctance to accept lists either as literature or as historical evidence. Lists appear to be arbitrary, even meaningless, catalogues hovering awkwardly between fiction and fact."[133] The artful employment of lists through parallelism is found in what is called the "litanic style" in Early Irish and Anglo-Saxon literature,[134] with the "enumerative style" also sharing some of the same stylistic features.[135] The creation of numbered groupings and lists based on the same initial word suggest mnemonic techniques — other than rhyme, alliteration and parallelism — employed to aid in memorizing important texts.[136]

Institute for Advanced Studies, 1980). List B, of course, is incorporated into the narrative *Airec Menman Uraird maic Coise* "The Stratagem of Urard mac Coise". For a synopsis, see *The Learned Tales of Medieval Ireland*, 33–38.

[127] Cecile O'Rahilly, ed., *Táin Bó Cúailnge, Recension I* (Dublin: Dublin Institute for Advanced Studies, 1976), 119–20 lines 3945–81 (Irish), 231–32 (English).

[128] Eric A. Havelock, *Preface to Plato* (Cambridge, Mass. and London: Belknap Press, 1963), 176–80.

[129] Havelock, *Preface to Plato*, 180.

[130] Pádraig Ó Riain, ed., *Corpus Genealogiarum Sanctorum Hiberniae* (Dublin: Dublin Institute for Advanced Studies, 1985).

[131] Michael W. Herren, ed., *The Hisperica Famina: II. Related Poems, a Critical Edition with English Translation and Philological Commentary*, Studies and Texts 85 (Toronto: Pontifical Institute of Mediaeval Studies, 1987), 76–89. For a revised edition, see David Howlett, "Five Experiments in Textual Reconstruction and Analysis," *Peritia* 9 (1995): 8–18. See also comments in Sims-Williams, "Thought, Word, Deed," 90–93.

[132] Ludwig Bieler, ed. *The Irish Penitentials*, Scriptores Latini Hiberniae, vol. 5 (Dublin: Dublin Institute for Advanced Studies, 1963).

[133] Frantzen, *Literature of Penance*, 200.

[134] Wright, *Irish Tradition*, 243–48, 262–64.

[135] Wright, *Irish Tradition*, chapter 2, "The 'Enumerative Style' in Ireland and Anglo-Saxon England," 49–105; Wright, "Irish 'Enumerative Style'," 29–49.

[136] See Carruthers, *Book of Memory*, chapter 3, "Elementary Memory Design," 80–121

Based on form and content, we can conclude that this collection of maxims is the product of an ecclesiastically educated redactor who was composing for a literate, secular audience.

Although one might think of wisdom literature as characteristically anonymous, there are many compilations which are ascribed to a known historical personage. The agreement in character between the contents of the maxims and the purported author or redactor may reveal something of the didactic intent of the collection. Even "false" ascriptions, as when the dates of the personage and the linguistic dating of the text do not agree, may help in the analysis of the contents of the text. Conversely, the text's contents may help confirm the reputation of, and cultural role played by, the purported author — even when ascribed to a legendary or mythological figure. Ascriptions, therefore, must be taken seriously.

The primary distinction to be drawn between the two personages to whom these maxims have been ascribed is that the first, Fíthal, is legendary; the second, Flann Fína mac Ossu, is historical.

Fíthal

Fíthal is the legendary third-century poet and judge of King Cormac mac Airt.[137] Only the Book of Leinster gives a title, Senbríathra Fíthail, which ascribes any of these maxims to him. Several allusions to him are made throughout Irish literature, and fragments of works attributed to him survive. A consistent biographical portrait of him is impossible to recreate. Depending on the text, he is assigned differing ancestors and progeny. He plays a passive role in most stories in which he appears. The following sketch is disjointed due to the sporadic nature of the references to him.

---

which has the sub-headings "The Numerical Grid" (page 80) and "The Alphabet and Key-Word System" (page 107). David Howlett's investigations into the structure of Latin and vernacular texts in the early Middle Ages reveals the tendency to compose texts in memorizable proportions. See, for example, D. R. Howlett, *The Celtic Latin Tradition of Biblical Style* (Blackrock: Four Courts Press, 1995).

[137] He is referred to as *fili ⁊ brethem Cormaic* "poet and judge of Cormac" in a tale called "Cormac's Dream": James Carney, "Nia son of Lugna Fer Trí," *Éigse* 2 (1940): 192. A sixteenth-century bardic poem refers to Fíthal in the context of poets: David Greene, ed., *Duanaire Mhéig Uidhir, the Poembook of Cú Chonnacht Mág Uidhir, Lord of Fermanagh 1566–1589* (Dublin: Dublin Institute for Advanced Studies, 1972), 50–51 § 17.

In the *Senbríathra Fíthail* as published by Thurneysen the three con-
cluding sections are a dialogue between Fíthal and his unnamed son in
which the son is told, first, that the "anvil of husbandry" is a good woman,
second, what is the best of women and, third, what is the worst of
women.[138] Roland Smith, in his translation of *Senbríathra* §§ 10, 11, 12,
included two sections found in several manuscripts which list "the fifteen
characteristics of a good woman" and "the fifteen characteristics of a bad
woman".[139]

In the commentary to the introduction of the *Senchas Már* Fíthal is
included along with Dubthach maccu Lugair and Morann as an example of
a *fili* who pronounced true judgements according to *recht aicnid* "the law of
nature".[140] An early law-tract attributed to Fíthal called *Aí Emnach* "Twin
Process" or "Double Process" is mentioned in legal commentaries, but has
not survived.[141] Another legal text, *Finnsruth Fíthail* "The Fair Stream of
Fíthal", still exists, at least fragmentarily, and has been discussed by Roland
Smith.[142] It deals with the methods of passing judgement and is characterized by the formula *Co bér breith* "How shall I pass judgement ...".
Binchy included this latter text among the *Nemed* school of poetico-legal
texts.[143]

According to the text "The Decision as to Cormac's Sword", the compilation of *Saltair Cormaic* — said to contain the synchronisms, pedigrees and
careers of the kings and princes of Ireland — was attended to by Fintan mac
Bóchra and Fíthal Fili.[144] "The Decision as to Cormac's Sword" is among
the most important texts in which Fíthal figures. It is Socht, Fíthal's son,
however, who plays the primary role in this story, along with Cormac

---

[138] Smith, *"Senbriathra Fithail,"* 52–60; Lisa M. Bitel, *Land of Women, Tales of Sex
and Gender from Early Ireland* (Ithaca and London: Cornell Univ. Press, 1996), 27–30.

[139] Smith, *"Senbriathra Fithail,"* 60–61; Bitel, *Land of Women*, 27–30.

[140] *AL* iii, 30.21–23 = *CIH* ii, 528.21–22.

[141] *AL* i, 26.1–2 = *CIH* v, 1655.23–24; *AL* i, 92.12–14 = *CIH* ii, 360.1–2; iv, 1439.2–
3; also Peter Smith, "Aimirgein Glúngel Tuir Tend: a Middle-Irish Poem on the
Authors and Laws of Ireland," *Peritia* 8 (1994): 129, 136 § 34.

[142] Roland Smith, "Fithal and Flann Fína," *Revue Celtique* 47 (1930): 30–38; and
Roland Smith, "Further Light on the *Finnsruth Fithail*," *Revue Celtique* 48 (1931): 325–
31.

[143] Daniel A. Binchy, *"Bretha Nemed,"* *Ériu* 17 (1955): 6.

[144] Whitley Stokes, "The Irish Ordeals, Cormac's Adventure in the Land of Promise,
and the Decision as to Cormac's Sword," in *Irische Texte*, vol. 3, no. 1, ed. Whitley
Stokes and Ernst Windisch (Leipzig: Hirzel, 1891), 199, 217 § 57.

himself and a steward named Dubdrenn. The account deals with deter-
mining ownership of a fabulous sword and the liabilities that accompany its
ownership. Fíthal's role is passive and, in fact, he refuses to argue his son's
case, commanding him, instead, to act for himself.[145] Reference to an
earlier version of this tale can be found in *Bretha Nemed Déidenach*, attesting
to the venerable age of the story.[146] This latter text also briefly cites judgements by Fíthal with regard to *ecnae, eclais, flaith, fili*.[147]

One of the few texts that reveals something of Fíthal's personality is
presented as a contentious dialogue in verse between Cormac and Fíthal.
Cormac had enjoyed a feast in Tara without inviting Fíthal, who is
described here as *féigbríathrach* "sharp-worded". Fíthal pointedly states that
Cormac feasted without him and reminds him that "Thy father never drank
without my foster-father".[148] Another epithet describing Fíthal is found in
a list of Irish authors, both legendary and historical, from the Book of
Ballymote. Here he is called *Fíthal fírgáeth láechbríathrach* "Truly-wise
warrior-worded Fíthal".[149]

The *Dindshenchas* contains another poetic reference to Fíthal. In a poem
describing the pleasures and benefits of the Fair of Carmun we have the
lines: *roisc roscada ri gail, / 's tecusca fíra Fithail* "Proverbs, maxims of might,
and truthful teachings of Fithal".[150] A Middle Irish poem on authors and
the laws, attributed to Gilla in Choimded Úa Cormaic and dated between
1050 and 1150, mentions Fíthal as an authority who lived in the time of

---

[145] Stokes, "The Irish Ordeals," 199–202, 217–21 §§ 58–80. See also Joseph Falaky
Nagy, "Sword as *Audacht*," in *Celtic Language, Celtic Culture: A Festschrift for Eric P.
Hamp*, ed. A. T. E. Matonis and Daniel F. Melia (Van Nuys, Calif.: Ford & Bailie Pub-
lishers, 1990), 131–36; John Carey, "The Testimony of the Dead," *Éigse* 26 (1992): 1–12.

[146] Gwynn, "Privileges and Responsibilities," 34.13–20, and note page 226.

[147] Gwynn, "Privileges and Responsibilities," 30.21–27. On the juxtaposition of these
four terms, see Liam Breatnach, "The First Third of *Bretha Nemed Toísech*," *Ériu* 40
(1989): 25–26.

[148] Kuno Meyer, ed., *Hibernica Minora, Being a Fragment of an Old-Irish Treatise on
the Psalter*, Anecdota Oxoniensia (Oxford: Clarendon Press, 1894), 82–83. A sixteenth-
century bardic poem apparently refers to this incident; Lambert McKenna, ed., *The Book
of O'Hara, Leabhar Í Eadhra* (Dublin: Dublin Institute for Advanced Studies, 1951), 174–
75 § 8.

[149] Whitley Stokes, "A List of Ancient Irish Authors," *ZCP* 3 (1901): 15–16. I have
normalized the text.

[150] Edward J. Gwynn, ed., *The Metrical Dindshenchas*, vol. 3, Todd Lecture Series,
vol. 10 (Dublin: Royal Irish Academy, 1913; repr. Dublin: Dublin Institute for Advanced
Studies, 1991), 20–21 lines 241–42.

Cormac and names a certain Fachtna as Fíthal's father.[151] Similarly, in a poem ascribed to a leading jurist of the late thirteenth and early fourteenth centuries, Giolla na Naomh mac Duinn Shléibhe Mhic Aodhagáin, Fíthal's instructions to his son, Flaithri, are commended as worthy of study and memorization. The lines read: *Cuimhnigh aithne Fhíothail fhéil / ar Fhlaithre ros síothaigh slóigh, / ó tharla i leabhraibh ar leith, / meabhraigh agus feith go fóill* "Keep in mind noble Fíothal's charge to Flaithre who pacified hosts, since it is found in particular books, memorise it and guard it still".[152] Unfortunately, none of the last three poems gives any indication of just what the contents of Fíthal's teachings were.

Probably the most widely known story concerning Fíthal is related by Geoffrey Keating in *Foras Feasa ar Éirinn* "A History of Ireland". In this account Fíthal's son, Flaithri, decides to test the four counsels given to him by his father before his death. The four counsels are: (1) not to foster a king's son, (2) not to share a secret with his wife, (3) not to elevate the status of a serf's son and, (4) not to entrust his sister with treasure.[153] As in the story about Cormac's sword, it is really Fíthal's son who is the main protagonist. We notice, too, in the Old Irish tale about Mac Dathó's pig, that Mac Dathó quotes similar advice attributed to Cremthann Nia Náir about not trusting women with secrets or slaves with treasure.[154] Thus we see that, although there is clear evidence from the legal tradition of a core of genuinely old materials attributed to Fíthal, the majority of surviving texts which represent his teachings deal not with law or legal procedure, but with how to assess women.[155]

It is difficult to draw a satisfactory portrait of the legendary Fíthal, although he was undeniably venerated as a poet and wise judge throughout

---

[151] Smith, "Aimirgein Glúngel Tuir Tend," 126 (Irish), 135 (English) §§ 12–13.

[152] Máirín Ní Dhonnchadha, "An Address to a Student of Law," in *Sages, Saints and Storytellers: Celtic Studies in Honour of Professor James Carney*, ed. Donnchadh Ó Corráin, Liam Breatnach and Kim McCone, Maynooth Monographs, vol. 2 (Maynooth: An Sagart, 1989), 165, 169 § 8.

[153] Patrick S. Dinneen, ed., *The History of Ireland by Geoffrey Keating, D.D.*, vol. 2, Irish Texts Society, vol. 8 (London: Irish Texts Society, 1908), 338–43; Osborn Bergin, *Stories from Keating's History of Ireland*, 3rd ed. (Dublin: Royal Irish Academy, 1930), 21–23.

[154] Rudolf Thurneysen, ed., *Scéla Mucce Meic Dathó*, Mediaeval and Modern Irish Series, vol. 6 (Dublin: Dublin Institute for Advanced Studies, 1935), 3.10–12. See Áine Ní Chróinín [Anne O'Sullivan], "The Four Counsels," *Éigse* 3 (1941–43): 67–68.

[155] See again Bitel, *Land of Women*, 27–30.

Irish cultural history. However, the sentiments of this collection of three-word maxims, as described above, and the contents of surviving texts associated with his name are not complementary. Furthermore, textual evidence supports the view that the so-called *Senbríathra Fíthail* is a deliberate conflation of the *Bríathra* (or *Roscada*) *Flainn Fína* with *Tecosca Cormaic*.

Flann Fína / Aldfrith

The identification of Flann Fína mac Ossu "Flann Fína son of Oswiu" with Aldfrith son of Oswiu is firmly established. For example, the *Annals of Tigernach* equate the two names in the entry: *Altfrith mac Ossa .i. Flann Fína la Gaedhelu, ecnaidh, rex Saxonum* "Aldfrith son of Oswiu, i.e. Flann Fína among the Irish, scholar [and] king of the English".[156] Aldfrith ruled Northumbria from ca. 685 to 705. His father, Oswiu, had ruled before him from ca. 642 to 670. For our purposes the contents of the maxims must be correlated with the reputation of King Aldfrith.

Most Irish genealogies link Flann Fína / Aldfrith, through his mother, to the Cenél nEogain branch of the northern Uí Néill.[157] His maternal grandfather, according to these genealogies, was Colmán Rímid who shared the high-kingship of Tara with Áed Sláine.[158] The *Annals of Ulster*, at his obit, assign Aldfrith the title *sapiens*, in common with Cenn Fáelad mac Ailello *sapiens*, d. 679.[159] The genealogies claim the latter as a second

---

[156] Whitley Stokes, "The Annals of Tigernach: Third Fragment," *Revue Celtique* 17 (1896): 219. David Dumville has suggested that a single entry in the *Annals of Ulster* at 733 for the death of an otherwise unknown abbot of Clonmacnoise called Flann Fíne should prevent us from making too easy an equation between Flann Fína and Aldfrith: David N. Dumville, "Two Troublesome Abbots," *Celtica* 21 (1990): 152. I have addressed the question of Aldfrith as Flann Fína in Irish sources and it is clear that when Irish sources speak of Flann Fína (mac Ossu) they refer to that son of Oswiu who ruled Northumbria at the end of the seventh century and who had a reputation for learning, that is, Aldfrith: Colin Ireland, "Aldfrith of Northumbria and the Irish Genealogies," *Celtica* 22 (1991): 64–78. I have also pointed out that the superficial similarity between the distinct words Fíne and Fína is not likely to have confused the Irish: "Aldfrith of Northumbria," 70–71 and notes 35–36.

[157] O'Brien, *Corpus Genealogiarum Hiberniae*, 135.

[158] Francis John Byrne, *Irish Kings and High-Kings* (London: B. T. Batsford Ltd., 1973), 104.

[159] Eoin Mac Neill, "A Pioneer of Nations," *Studies* 11 (1922): 13–28, 435–46; Proinsias Mac Cana, "The Three Languages and the Three Laws," *Studia Celtica* 5 (1970): 62–66. For a discussion of other seventh-century Irish *sapientes* in addition to

cousin to Flann Fína. The title *sapiens* implies that these men were ecclesiastically trained, though not necessarily clerics, and were venerated for their learning.

In addition to the text edited here, other Irish texts ascribed to Flann Fína include a religious text edited by Vernam Hull which begins *Maircc don duine carus duíne, ocus ná car Día nod car* "Woe to the man who loves mankind, and who does not love God who loves him".[160] Another is a poem which lists various regions of Ireland and describes, usually in laudatory terms, what is to be found in each. It begins *Ro·det i nInis find Fáil* and contains the lines *Fland find Fína mac Ossa / ardsuí hErend eolossa* "Fair Flann Fína son of Oswiu, chief sage of learning in Ireland".[161] Both of these texts are among the four which characteristically follow the *Roscada Flainn Fína* as described in the discussion of Rec. Y manuscripts. All texts ascribed to Flann Fína attest to the esteem accorded to him in Irish literary culture.

The *Fragmentary Annals* refer to Flann Fína as *an t-eagnaid amhra, dalta Ad[a]mnáin* "the splendid scholar, pupil of Adomnán".[162] This description is plausible, for the anonymous *Life* of St Cuthbert states that Aldfrith spent time at Iona.[163] Bede's prose *Life* of that saint, however, is vaguer and says simply that Aldfrith was in "self-imposed exile" pursuing knowledge *in insulis Scottorum*[164] or *in regionibus Scottorum*,[165] phrases which as easily suggest that Aldfrith was studying in Ireland itself. Adomnán, in his *Life* of Columba, refers to his trips to Northumbria to visit Aldfrith and calls him *Aldfridum ... amicum.*[166] We also know from Bede's *Historia Ecclesiastica* (= *HE*)[167] that on one of Adomnán's visits to Northumbria Aldfrith was

---

Cenn Fáelad and Aldfrith, see Ireland, "Aldfrith and Learning of a *Sapiens*," 63–77.

[160] Hull, "Wise Sayings of Flann Fína," 98, 100.

[161] Walsh, "Poem on Ireland," 70.

[162] Joan N. Radner, ed., *Fragmentary Annals of Ireland* (Dublin: Dublin Institute for Advanced Studies, 1978), 54.

[163] Bertram Colgrave, ed. and trans., *Two "Lives" of Saint Cuthbert, a Life by an Anonymous Monk of Lindisfarne and Bede's Prose Life* (Cambridge: Cambridge Univ. Press, 1940; repr. New York: Greenwood Press, 1969), 104.

[164] Colgrave, *Two "Lives" of Saint Cuthbert*, 236.

[165] Colgrave, *Two "Lives" of Saint Cuthbert*, 238.

[166] Alan Orr Anderson and Marjorie Ogilvie Anderson, ed. and trans., *Adomnan's Life of Columba*, revised ed. Majorie O. Anderson (Oxford: Clarendon Press, 1991), 178.

[167] The standard edition is by Bertram Colgrave and R. A. B. Mynors, ed., *Bede's Ecclesiastical History of the English People* (Oxford: Clarendon Press, 1969); but the textual

presented with a copy of the abbot's treatise on the Holy Places, *De Locis Sanctis*.[168] Aldfrith, acting as royal patron, richly rewarded Adomnán for the gift and had several copies made so that it might be disseminated throughout his kingdom (*HE* v 15).

Bede spoke highly of Aldfrith, calling him a *vir in scripturis doctissimus* (*HE* iv 26) and, elsewhere referring to *Aldfrido, viro undecumque doctissimo* (*HE* v 12). Aldfrith's reputation for scholarship and piety are thus well attested in both the Irish and English traditions. Aldfrith's father, Oswiu, and all of his uncles, including Oswald, had been raised among the Irish, perhaps at Iona itself (*HE* iii 1).[169] Bede said that Oswiu greatly admired Irish learning (*HE* iii 25). Oswald, Oswiu's brother who had ruled Northumbria ca. 634 to 642, was the English king who invited the Irish missionaries from Iona into Northumbria under Bishop Aidan. Because Oswald wanted his subjects to be converted to Christianity, and because he had a perfect command of Irish, he acted as Bishop Aidan's interpreter (*HE* iii 3). Oswald's reputation for piety is such that he is commemorated in the early ninth-century metrical martyrology *Félire Óengusso* as *ardrí Saxan sóerdae* "noble high-king of the English".[170]

Aldfrith succeeded to the Northumbrian throne in 685 after the death of his half-brother, Ecgfrith, and the near annihilation of his army by the Picts. However, in contrast to the expansionist policies of his predecessors, including Oswald and Oswiu, Bede says that Aldfrith excellently restored the demolished status of the kingdom of Northumbria, although within narrower limits (*HE* iv 26). Only the year before (684), Ecgfrith had sent an English army into Ireland which devastated Mag Breg.[171] An entry in the *Annals of Ulster* for 686 states that Adomnán returned to Ireland with sixty

---

notes are still useful in the edition by Charles Plummer, ed., *Venerabilis Baedae Opera Historica*, vol. 2 (Oxford: Clarendon Press, 1896; repr. 1975).

[168] Denis Meehan, ed., *Adamnan's "De Locis Sanctis,"* Scriptores Latini Hiberniae, vol. 3 (Dublin: Dublin Institute for Advanced Studies, 1958).

[169] For a discussion of the Northumbrian royal family's relationships with the Irish, particularly with Dál Riata, see Hermann Moisl, "The Bernician Royal Dynasty and the Irish in the Seventh Century," *Peritia* 2 (1983): 103–26.

[170] Stokes, *Félire Óengusso*, 174. For more about Oswald, see Clare Stancliffe, "Oswald, 'Most Holy and Most Victorious King of the Northumbrians'," in *Oswald, Northumbrian King to European Saint*, ed. Clare Stancliffe and Eric Cambridge (Stamford: Paul Watkins, 1995), 33–83.

[171] Byrne, *Irish Kings*, 111, 260; Daniel A. Binchy, ed., *Críth Gablach*, Mediaeval and Modern Irish Series, vol. 11 (Dublin: Dublin Institute for Advanced Studies, 1941), xiv.

freed captives who almost certainly represent prisoners taken by the English forces after Ecgfrith's foray into Ireland. Their return could only have been undertaken with the full cooperation of Aldfrith.

In addition to his benevolent and well-administered reign and his reputation for learning, Bede also suggests the extent of Aldfrith's piety by noting that he would often visit a certain monk named Dryhthelm who was famous for his vision of the after-life (*HE* v 12).[172]

This secular ruler was well enough educated to appreciate the idiosyncratic Latin writings of Bishop Aldhelm of Sherbourne, d. 709.[173] Aldhelm dedicated a lengthy, five-part *epistola* to Aldfrith.[174] The first part was an *exordium* in which Aldhelm speaks obliquely of a close spiritual relationship between the two dating back at least twenty years. The second part is a typological essay on the number 7. The third section is a work on Latin metrics, concentrating on hexameters, which displays a wide familiarity with various Latin authors. The fourth part is a collection of one hundred riddles, or *enigmata*, ostensibly to serve as metrical examples for the treatise on metrics. In the fifth, and final, section Aldhelm exhorts Aldfrith to heed the work presented to him and not to neglect his own studies, particularly of the Holy Scriptures, despite the weight of his secular responsibilities.[175]

The evidence from both Irish and English sources portrays Flann Fína / Aldfrith as an eminent ruler who represented the confluence of the two most influential families in Ireland and Britain of his day. Furthermore, we have written documentation from three of the most prestigious contemporary intellectuals and churchmen, Adomnán, Aldhelm, and Bede, attesting to his piety and earnest devotion, to the depth and scope of his education, and to the capable execution of his secular duties.

Aldfrith's reputation as the pious, learned and benevolent king of Northumbria makes plausible the ascription of these maxims to him based on their content alone.[176] Linguistic evidence of the text as preserved, however,

---

[172] For an appreciation of the larger contexts of Dryhthelm's vision, see Patrick Sims-Williams, *Religion and Literature in Western England 600–800*, Cambridge Studies in Anglo-Saxon England, vol. 3 (Cambridge: Cambridge Univ. Press, 1990), 244–45, 259–67.

[173] Andy Orchard, *The Poetic Art of Aldhelm*, Cambridge Studies in Anglo-Saxon England, vol. 8 (Cambridge: Cambridge Univ. Press, 1994).

[174] The work is addressed to "Acircius" but the identification with Aldfrith is accepted. Michael Lapidge and Michael Herren, trans., *Aldhelm, the Prose Works* (Ipswich: D. S. Brewer; and Totowa: Rowman & Littlefield, 1979), 32.

[175] Lapidge and Herren, *Aldhelm, the Prose Works*, 31–47.

[176] Contrast Roland Smith's conclusions. He stated that "The form and the whole

does not allow for such a confident assertion. Although clearly Old Irish in origin, the text contains no linguistic details which confirm a late seventh-century date. Nevertheless, the ascription of these Old Irish maxims to Flann Fína mac Ossu is a manifestation of the esteem accorded to this king of Anglo-Saxon Northumbria by subsequent Irish learned circles.

METHOD OF EDITING

The best manuscript in each of the three recensions is never the immediate exemplar of any surviving copy. No recension can be shown to be the exemplar for another, or to provide readings that are consistently superior. I show this in the following stemma, where m designates the archetype for a collection of Old Irish maxims upon which all three recensions drew. The hyparchetypes n and y most closely resembled the archetype m, but the hyparchetype l clearly drew upon the latter, i.e., archetype m, rather than upon either of the other two hyparchetypes.

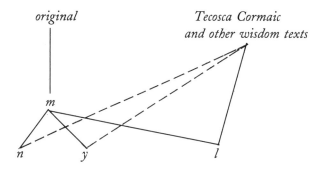

The original form, order and sequence of this text is not recoverable. M. L. West noted that collections of proverbs, commentaries, and lexica are typical examples of texts subject to rearrangement in their manuscript traditions. Such rearrangement forces us to treat each "family" as a new

tenor of the *Briathra Flainn Fína* are distinctly of the pagan tradition, and inconsonant with all we know of the Christian king Aldfrith": "The *Speculum Principum* in Early Irish Literature," *Speculum* 2 (1927): 432.

recension and often makes it impossible to reconstruct a hypothetical original text.[177] It is not possible to prove whether or not §§ 2, 7, 8, 9 — or any of the other sections displayed on the facing-page table — were originally intended to be included among the three-word maxims. I decided, therefore, to base the order of sections and sequence of maxims on the one manuscript that most concisely represents the greatest overlap of maxims from all recensions in one integrated text.

N_1 (23 N 10) contains 237 maxims out of a total 261 primary readings as edited here. (There are 292 maxims when edited variants are included.) It also contains § 2 *Ba faitech* and § 7 *Maith dán ecnae*, both of which are present in the other recensions. At the same time, this manuscript does not contain sections that are unique to itself or its recension. N_1 is the one manuscript which best represents the overlap of all three recensions. It is, therefore, the best manuscript upon which a "consensus" edition can be based. Another Recension N manuscript, N_2, not only most closely resembles N_1 and provided the title which was normalized to name this edition, but also contains what Kuno Meyer considered to be the best copy of *Tecosca Cormaic*. Recension N is most distinct from *Tecosca Cormaic*, while Recension Y manuscripts contain § 9 *Secht comarthai déc* = *TC* § 22, and Recension L represents a conflation of *Tecosca Cormaic* and lists of three-word maxims.

Y_1 also contains 237 maxims, the vast majority of which are found in N_1. Because Y_1 has many old readings, it is very helpful in reconstructing the text. But Y_1 includes § 8 *Cía fégam ránac*, which is not found in Rec. L, and § 9 *Secht comarthai déc*, which is not found in Rec. N (but is found in *Tecosca Cormaic*). An edition that included these two sections in the main text would not be representative of all recensions.

Maxims not found in N_1 have been appended to each series from other manuscripts in order to present as many maxims as possible. In this way all three-word maxims, as well as all sections associated with Flann Fína, regardless of recension, are translated and discussed as part of this edition. Any reader who so desires can reconstruct the text of *Roscada Flainn Fína mac Ossu* by referring to Appendix 3.

By appending maxims from other manuscripts to the sections as found in N_1, some maxims which are recorded only once have been edited here. Thus

---

[177] Martin L. West, *Textual Criticism and Editorial Technique, Applicable to Greek and Latin Texts* (Stuttgart: B. G. Teubner, 1973), 16–17.

five maxims from the *descad* series in L_3 are given their own listings in this edition, §§ 4.25–29; and five maxims found only in L_2 are listed as §§ 6.98–102 in the *ferr* series. Many maxims are included that are found in only one recension, though not restricted to one manuscript. One disadvantage of this system is that certain maxims which differ from recension to recension have been treated as mere variants rather than as separate maxims in their own right. When variants do occur, prominence must be given to one interpretation; other interpretations are relegated to secondary readings or to the textual notes. Therefore, one should refer frequently to the textual notes where variant readings and interpretations are discussed.

Because we are dealing with an open recension, no single manuscript was assumed to provide superior readings. Therefore, an eclectic approach was followed in choosing the best readings. The problems of dealing with an open recension prompted the decision to normalize spellings to a hypothetical standard consistent with Classical Old Irish.

Variae Lectiones

Variant readings are given from nine manuscripts: $N_{1,2,3}$, $Y_{1,2}$, $L_{1,2,3}$, X_1. So many witnesses are included because the best manuscript from each recension cannot be the exemplar for any surviving witness. In § 4 *descad* series L_3 is the only Rec. L manuscript represented. N_3 is represented only in § 6 *ferr*, and X_1 is represented sporadically in §§ 3 *dligid*, 6 *ferr*, 7 *Maith dán ecnae*.

Any manuscript readings that are not letter for letter as in the restored text are given among the variants. Marks of lenition and the letter *h* are often ignored. For example, for the edited *crod* all manuscripts read *crodh*. Similarly, where only a lenited consonant distinguishes the readings between two or more manuscripts, the varia will not differentiate which manuscript has the lenited consonant and which does not. For example, the variant reading *said(h)bre* $Y_{1,2}$ does not specify that only Y_2 has the *h*. Conversely, where an expected *h* is omitted in the manuscript, e.g., *rat* for *rath*, or where the *h* may distinguish two different words, e.g., *etech* as opposed to *éthech*, these distinctions are recorded.

In the case of variant maxims included in the edited text, all instances of the variant word are given to clarify their distribution among the manuscripts. Similarly, all examples of the possessive pronoun *a* found among the three-word maxims are recorded to clarify their inconsistent distribution among the manuscripts. Anything listed between square brackets [ ] is either very unclear or illegible. Marks of length have been ignored unless they are important in establishing the proper reading. Most abbreviations have been silently expanded; any that are potentially ambiguous have been italicized. All expansion strokes at the ends of words have been left unexpanded. Certain words in the edited text which are omitted from various manuscripts have been cited between angular brackets ‹ › in the varia in order to clarify which words are referred to.

Old Irish Wisdom Attributed to Aldfrith of Northumbria:

An Edition of Bríathra Flainn Fhína maic Ossu

1.1   Ad·cota sochell saidbres.
   1.1a   Ad·cota sochell roda·bíatha.
1.2   Ad·cota dúthracht do·rata.
1.3   Ad·cota cíall caínchruth.
1.4   Ad·cota drús dígnae.
   1.4a   Ad·cota drús déirge.
1.5   Ad·cota báes burbai.
1.6   Ad·cota fáiscre rofáiscre.
1.7   Ad·cota miscais airbiri.
1.8   Ad·cota déirge líamnai.
1.9   Ad·cota lescae fáitsini.
   1.9a   Ad·cota lescae foistini.
1.10   Ad·cota serc bríathra.
1.11   Ad·cota becdatu caínbuidi.
1.12   Ad·cota féle frithfolta.

1.1 socell N_1 : soic(h)eall N_2 L_3 : socheall Y_1 : soichell L_2 || saidbrius N_2 : said(h)bre $Y_{1,2}$ || rodabiatha L_1 : soma L_2 : robiatta L_3

1.2 dutracht N_1 : duracht L_3 || dorta Y_1 : doratha Y_2 : dorota L_1

1.3 cainc(h)ruth $N_{1,2}$ $L_{1,2}$: cruth $Y_{1,2}$: cæncruth L_3

1.4 druis $N_{1,2}$ $Y_{1,2}$ $L_{1,2,3}$: digna N_1 Y_1 $L_{1,2}$: dignæ N_2 : duigna no terghe Y_2 || derge no digna L_3 : druis dergli N_2 *only*

1.5 bais N_1 L_3 : baois N_2 : bæs L_2 : *om.* Y || burba $N_{1,2}$ $L_{1,2,3}$: *om.* Y

1.6 faiscri N_2 : fascre $Y_{1,2}$ L_1 : caiscre L_2 || rofaiscri N_2 : rof(h)ascre $Y_{1,2}$ L_1 : roaiscre L_2

1.1   Generosity engenders wealth.
  1.1a   Generosity begets one that feeds it.
1.2   Willingness creates one who gives.
1.3   Good sense results in fair form.
1.4   Lechery leads to disgrace.
  1.4a   Lechery results in abandonment.
1.5   Foolishness results in crudity.
1.6   Repression results in greater repression.
1.7   Hatred engenders reproach.
1.8   Abandonment results in slander.
1.9   Reluctance leads to [reliance on] conjecture.
  1.9a   Reluctance begets inertia.
1.10   Love begets words.
1.11   Humility wins good favour.
1.12   Decorum results in reciprocal behaviour.

1.7 maiscais N_1 : misais Y_1 : misgais L_3 || oirbhire N_2 : airb(h)ire $Y_{1,2}$ $L_{1,2,3}$

1.8 dergi N_1 *only* || liamna N_1 *only*

1.9 lesci N_1 Y_1 L_1 : leiscci N_2 : lesce Y_2 : leisci L_2 : leisce L_3 || faistine $N_{1,2}$ $Y_{1,2}$ L_2 : fatsine L_1 : faisdine L_3

1.10 sercc Y_1 : *om.* L || briatra Y_1 : *om.* L

1.11 becdata N_1 : begdata N_2 : beccdatu $Y_{1,2}$: begatu L_3 || cainbude N_1 : cænboidi N_2 : cainbuid(h)e $Y_{1,2}$ L_2 : cáinbude L_1 : cænbuide L_3

1.12 feile $N_{1,2}$ $Y_{1,2}$: *om.* L || fritfolta N_1 : frithfholta N_2 : fritholta $Y_{1,2}$: *om.* L

1.13 Ad·cota díbe dimmolad.

1.14 Ad·cota dochell cesacht.

1.15 Ad·cota gáes clotha.

1.16 Ad·cota umlae áilgini.

1.17 Ad·cota aithgne augrae.

1.18 Ad·cota santach séotu.

1.19 Ad·cota díummus dimdai.

1.20 Ad·cota cuirm carna.

   1.20a Ad·cota cuirm cornu.

1.21 Ad·cota echlach utmailli.

   1.21a Ad·cota eclach utmailli.

1.22 Ad·cota accobur feidli.

1.23 Ad·cota gáes airmitin.

1.24 Ad·cota áes allud.

1.25 Ad·cota báes báegul.

   1.25a Ad·cota báes bága.

1.26 Ad·cota briugas bronnad.

1.27 Ad·cota bríg barainn.

1.28 Ad·cota barae bibdaid.

1.29 Ad·cota biltengae mrath.

1.30 Ad·cota soithnge sídugud.

1.31 Ad·cota áine airlabrai.

1.32 Ad·cota daidbre dochraiti.

1.13 dibi Y_1 : *om.* L || dimoladh N_2 : dimlad Y_1 : *om.* L

1.14 docell N_1 : doicheall N_2 : doichell $Y_{1,2}$: *om.* L || ceisacht Y_1 : ceasacht Y_2 : *om.* L

1.15 gais N_1 Y_1 : gaois N_2 : gaiss Y_2 : *om.* L || <clotha> : *om.* L

1.16 umal N_1 : umla N_2 : hiumli Y_1 : huímli Y_2 : *om.* L || algine N_1 : ailgine N_2 $Y_{1,2}$: *om.* L

1.17 aichne N_1 : aichni $Y_{1,2}$: *om.* N_2 L || augra N_1 $Y_{1,2}$: *om.* N_2 L

1.18 sanntach N_2 Y_2 : *om.* L || seota N_1 : seoda N_2 : *om.* L

1.19 dimus N_1 $Y_{1,2}$ L_2 : diomus N_2 : diumus L_3 || tornem N_1 : toirn– N_2 || dimd(h)a $Y_{1,2}$ $L_{1,2,3}$

1.20 coirm N_1 : *om.* L || corna $N_{1,2}$: carna $Y_{1,2}$: *om.* L

1.21 echlach N_1 Y_1 : echl– N_2 : eachlach Y_2 : *om.* L || utmaille N_1 Y_2 : utmoille N_2 : *om.* L

1.22 acobar $N_{1,2}$: acobur Y_2 : ocobar L_2 : ocobur L_3 || feid(h)le N_2 $Y_{1,2}$ L_3

1.23 gæs N_1 $Y_{1,2}$: gaois N_2 : gais $L_{1,2,3}$ || airmidin N_2 L_3 : airmitiu L_1

1.24 aos N_1 : aois N_2 : æss Y_1 : aess Y_2 : *om.* L || allad(h) $N_{1,2}$: all– Y_1 : alluidh Y_2 : *om.* L

1.13 Stinginess is disparaged.

1.14 Inhospitability engenders niggardliness.

1.15 Wisdom begets fame.

1.16 Humility engenders gentleness.

1.17 Familiarity fuels strife.

1.18 A greedy person acquires possessions.

1.19 Arrogance produces disfavour.

1.20 Ale results in lechery.

    1.20a   Ale brings out the drinking horns.

1.21 A prostitute's lot is uncertainity.

    1.21a A timid person's lot is uncertainity.

1.22 Desire begets perseverance.

1.23 Wisdom begets respect.

1.24 Age acquires renown.

1.25 Foolishness results in risk.

    1.25a   Foolishness results in contention.

1.26 Hospitality invites profligacy.

1.27 Force arouses hostility.

1.28 Hostility creates an offender.

1.29 An evil tongue begets treachery.

1.30 Persuasion brings conciliation.

1.31 Perspicacity makes one a spokesman.

1.32 Poverty leads to hardship.

1.25 bais N_1 L_1 : baos N_2 : bæs $L_{2,3}$ || baogal N_1 : baog– N_2 : bagh no bægul Y_1 : bagadh no bæghul Y_2 : baga $L_{1,2,3}$

1.26 briug– N_1 : brugh– N_2 : brug(h)aid(h) $Y_{1,2}$: brugas L_1 : brudus L_2 : brughus L_3 || brond(h)ad(h) $N_{1,2}$ L_3 : bronnud L_1 : brondud L_2

1.27 barann $N_{1,2}$ Y_1 : barand Y_2 L_2 : baraind $L_{1,3}$

1.28 barann $N_{1,2}$ Y_1 : barand Y_2 : *om.* L || bidb– N_1 : biodhba N_2 : bibdu Y_1 : bidhba Y_2 : *om.* L

1.29 biltengga N_1 : biltenga N_2 $Y_{1,2}$ $L_{1,2}$: biltengtha L_3 || brath $N_{1,2}$ $Y_{1,2}$ $L_{1,2}$: bratha L_3

1.30 sotnge N_1 : soithngi N_2 : soithgne $Y_{1,2}$: *om.* L || sidug– N_1 : siodug– N_2 : sighug– $Y_{1,2}$: *om.* L

1.31 áne L_1 : anæ L_3 || irlapra N_1 : erlabra N_2 $L_{1,3}$: aurlab(h)ra $Y_{1,2}$: irlabra L_2

1.32 daidbri N_2 : daibri L_2 : daibre L_3 || dochraite N_1 L_1 : dochr–e N_2 : docraiti $Y_{1,2}$: dochmacht L_2 : docraide L_3

1.33   Ad·cota imresan imned.
1.34   Ad·cota tercae léiri.
1.35   Ad·cota soíre sáithchi.
   1.35a   Ad·cota soíre saigthigi.
1.36   Ad·cota doíre cumgai.
1.37   Ad·cota borb gnímrad.
1.38   Ad·cota flaith folabrad.
1.39   Ad·cota fírián fortacht.
1.40   Ad·cota maith a molad.
1.41   Ad·cota crodlesc legad.
1.42   Ad·cota trebad torad.
1.43   Ad·cota fergach fúasnad.
   1.43a   Ad·cota fergach frithorcuin.
1.44   Ad·cota trotach túarcuin.
1.45   Ad·cota brothchán bithnert.
1.46   Ad·cota frithbert fúachtain.
1.47   Ad·cota ferann fénnid.
1.48   Ad·cota léigend libru.
   1.48a   Ad·cota léignid libru.
1.49   Ad·cota menmnach miscais.
1.50   Ad·cota brón debthaigi.
1.51   Ad·cota cath caíniud.
1.52   Ad·cota sochlach cocorus.

1.33 imrisan N_1 : imreasain N_2 : imresin $Y_{1,2}$: imresain $L_{1,2,3}$ || imn– N_2 : imnead(h) Y_2 $L_{2,3}$

1.34 terci N_1 : terce N_2 Y_1 L_2 : teirce Y_2 : terca $L_{1,3}$ || lere N_1 : leire N_2 $Y_{1,2}$ $L_{1,2,3}$

1.35 saire N_1 $Y_{1,2}$ L_3 : saoire N_2 : sairi L_2 || sáithe N_1 : soaite N_2 : saithchi $Y_{1,2}$: soigthige $L_{1,3}$: soichlidi L_2

1.36 daire N_1 $Y_{1,2}$ L_3 : doeire N_2 : dairi L_2 || cumca N_1 : cuim(h)ge N_2 $Y_{1,2}$: cumga $L_{1,3}$: cumaigi L_2

1.37 gniomr– N_2 : gnimrudh Y_1 : gnimcha $L_{1,2,3}$

1.38 <flaith> *om.* L || folabra N_2 Y_2 : *om.* L

1.39 firen N_2 : *om.* L || furtacht N_2 : *om.* L

1.40 <maith> *om.* L || a $N_{1,2}$ $Y_{1,2}$: *om.* L || mola N_1 : *om.* L

1.41 crodhlescc N_2 : crod(h)leisc $Y_{1,2}$: *om.* L || leagad Y_2 : *om.* L

1.42 treab– N_2 : *om.* L || torudh Y_2 : *om.* L

1.33 Contention causes anxiety.

1.34 Want begets industry.

1.35 Privilege results in fulfilment.

    1.35a   Privilege pursues its [own] interests.

1.36 Low status results in constraint.

1.37 Labour is the lot of an uncouth person.

1.38 Lordship entails murmurings.

1.39 A righteous person receives support.

1.40 Good begets its own praise.

1.41 An indolent person causes waste.

1.42 Husbandry results in produce.

1.43 A wrathful person creates a disturbance.

    1.43a   A wrathful person elicits offence.

1.44 A pugnacious person gets a beating.

1.45 Pottage produces lasting strength.

1.46 Confrontation leads to injury.

1.47 A territory produces its champion.

1.48 Learning gives rise to books.

    1.48a   A scholar acquires books.

1.49 The self-assertive person is disliked.

1.50 Grief causes discord.

1.51 Battle results in lamentation.

1.52 An eminent person begets harmony.

1.43 ferg– N_1 : fercc– N_2 || fuasnad(h) $N_{1,2}$ $Y_{1,2}$ || frithorgain $L_{1,3}$: frithorcain L_2

1.44 trodach $N_{1,2}$ Y_2 troda– Y_1 : *om.* L || tuarcain N_1 : tuarcc– N_2 : tuargain $Y_{1,2}$: *om.* L

1.45 brothcain N_1 : brochan N_2 $Y_{1,2}$: *om.* L || bithnert N_2 : *om.* L

1.46 fritbert N_2 : *om.* L || fuacht– N_2 : *om.* L

1.47 feronn $N_{1,2}$: *om.* L || feindid(h) N_1 Y_2 : feind– N_2 : feinnid Y_1 : *om.* L

1.48 leigiunn N_1 : leighind N_1 : leignigh $Y_{1,2}$: *om.* L || liubr– N_1 : liubra N_2 : libra $Y_{1,2}$: *om.*
L

1.49 menmar– N_2 : *om.* L || <miscais> *om.* L

1.50 debthuighe N_1 : deabhtha N_2 : debtaighi Y_1 : debtaighe Y_2 : debthaige L_1 : debthaidi L_2
: deabthaige L_3

1.51 caine N_1 : caoin– N_2 : cainiughugh Y_2 : cóiniud L_1 : cainead(h) $L_{2,3}$

1.52 sochl– N_2 || cogarus $N_{1,2}$: cocoruss $Y_{1,2}$: cocarus $L_{2,3}$

1.53   Ad·cota imbed díchóelad.

1.54   Ad·cota miltengae breithemnas.

1.55   Ad·cota fáilte féli.

1.56   Ad·cota ségonn soíri.

1.57   Ad·cota doíre dinge.

1.58   Ad·cota crod a chaithim.

1.59   Ad·cota sáegul snímchi.

1.60   Ad·cota drochben díbe.

1.61   Ad·cota umal ordan.

1.62   Ad·cota lobar luindi.

1.63   Ad·cota buille burbai.

1.64   Ad·cota sogním soálaig.

1.65   Ad·cota bocht a bíathad.

1.66   Ad·cota briugu mugu.

   1.66a   Ad·cota briugu muige.

1.67   Ad·cota (f)laith lobrai.

   1.67a   Ad·cota (f)laith labrai.

1.68   Ad·cota étlae utmailli.

   1.68a   Ad·cota etlae utmailli.

1.69   Ad·cota cuirm clotha.

2.1   Ba faitech arnába fíachach.

2.2   Ba threbar arnába gabálach.

1.53 imed N$_1$: imet N$_2$: *om.* Y : immad L$_1$: imad L$_{2,3}$ || dicaol– N$_1$: diocaol– N$_2$: *om.* Y
   : díchoilad L$_1$: dic(h)ælad L$_{2,3}$

1.54 miltenga N$_{1,2}$: Y$_{1,2}$ L$_1$: mæltenga L$_2$: milteangtha L$_3$ || brethemnus N$_1$: bretemain N$_2$
   : braithemnacht Y$_{1,2}$: brithemnacht L$_1$: breithemnus L$_2$: breitheamnacht L$_3$

1.55 failti N$_{1,2}$ Y$_{1,2}$: *om.* L || fele N$_1$: feile N$_2$ Y$_{1,2}$: *om.* L

1.56 segaind N$_1$: segoinn N$_2$: segunn Y$_1$: seguin Y$_2$: *om.* L || saire N$_1$: saoire N$_2$: saeire
   Y$_{1,2}$: *om.* L

1.57 dair N$_1$: doeiri N$_2$: *om.* Y L || digge N$_1$: *om.* Y L

1.58 <crod> *om.* L || a N$_{1,2}$ Y$_{1,2}$: *om.* L || cait(h)em(h) N$_{1,2}$ Y$_2$: caithim Y$_1$: *om.* L

1.59 saog– N$_{1,2}$: sæg– Y$_1$: seghul Y$_2$: *om.* L || snimc(h)e N$_{1,2}$ Y$_{1,2}$: *om.* L

1.60 drocben N$_2$: drochbhean Y$_1$: *om.* L || dibi N$_1$ Y$_{1,2}$: *om.* L

1.61 humal Y$_{1,2}$: *om.* L || <ordan> *om.* L

1.62 lubair N$_2$: lobur Y$_{1,2}$: *om.* L || luinde N$_1$: luinne N$_2$ Y$_1$: lanide Y$_2$: *om.* L

1.63 builli N$_2$ Y$_1$: *om.* L || borba N$_{1,2}$: borbla– Y$_1$: borbla[c]h Y$_2$: *om.* L

1.53   An abundance ensures that things do not diminish.

1.54   Eloquence brings about adjudication.

1.55   Joy results in decorum.

1.56   One who is proficient procures privilege.

1.57   Low status incurs repression.

1.58   Wealth gets consumed.

1.59   Life entails anxiety.

1.60   A bad woman's lot is rejection.

1.61   A humble person engenders dignity.

1.62   A weak person suffers [the] vehemence [of others].

1.63   A blow begets boorishness.

1.64   A good deed leads to good behaviour.

1.65   A poor person receives his refection.

1.66   A hospitaller has slaves.

   1.66a   A hospitaller has pastures.

1.67   Liquor begets incapacity.

   1.67a   Liquor begets talkativeness.

1.68   Stealth brings about a change.

   1.68a   Renunciation brings a change [to one's life].

1.69   Ale brings fame.

2.1   Be cautious so that you may not be burdened with debts.

2.2   Be thrifty so that you may not be grasping.

1.64 sog(h)niom(h) $N_{1,2}$: *om.* L || soal– N_2 : *om.* L

1.65 <bocht> *om.* L || a $N_{1,2}$ $Y_{1,2}$: *om.* L || biat(h)ad(h) N_1 $Y_{1,2}$: biat– N_2 : *om.* L

1.66 brug(h)– $N_{1,2}$: briugaid $Y_{1,2}$: *om.* L || muig(h)e $N_{1,2}$: mughu Y_1 : mugha Y_2 : *om.* L

1.67 flaith $Y_{1,2}$ $L_{1,2,3}$: *om.* N || lubrai Y_1 : lubraighe Y_2 : labrai L_1 : labra L_2 : labraidh L_3 : *om.* N

1.68 etlai $Y_{1,2}$: etla L_1 : eclai L_2 : ealta L_3 : *om.* N || utm(h)aille $Y_{1,2}$: udmoilli L_2 : udmaille L_3 : *om.* N

1.69 coirm $L_{1,2,3}$: *om.* N Y || <clotha> *: om.* N Y

2.1 bat N_2 $Y_{1,2}$ L_1 : bad $L_{2,3}$ || fait– N_2 : fattech L_1 || flaith L_2 : faiteach L_3 || arnabat N_2 L_1 : arnarbat $Y_{1,2}$: nabad L_2 : arnarbad L_3 || fiac– N_2

2.2 bat N_2 Y_1 : b. L_1 : bad L_3 || trebur $N_{1,2}$: treab(h)ar Y_1 L_3 : trebor Y_2 : trebar $L_{1,2}$ || arnaba*tur* N_1 : arnabat N_2 $L_{1,2}$: arnarbat $Y_{1,2}$: arnarbad L_3 || turgbhal– N_2 : gabaltach Y_1 : gabhalac L_3

2.3   Ba éimid corba sercach.
2.4   Ba eslabar corba airdirc.
   2.4a   Ba eslabar corba dércach.
2.5   Ba gartaid corba sochraid.
2.6   Ba buidech corba airech.
2.7   Ba umal corba úasal.

3.1   Dligid ecnae airmitin.
3.2   Ar·fich gáes gail.
3.3   Dligid fír fortacht.
3.4   Dligid gó a cairiugud.
3.5   Dligid cloíne cuindrech.
3.6   Dligid augrae etargaire.
3.7   Dligid rath ríara.
   3.7a   Dligid rath ríarugud.
3.8   Dligid fuidir frithḟolta.
3.9   Dligid aite a ṡochraiti.
3.10   Dligid naidm nascar.
3.11   Dligid ráth a imdegail.
3.12   Dligid fíadnaise a fuigell.

2.3 bad N_1 : bat N_2 $Y_{1,2}$: *om.* $L_{1,3}$ || enigh N_1 : en– N_2 : emidh $Y_{1,2}$: hemich L_2 || gurbat N_1 : corbat N_2 $Y_{1,2}$: corbad L_2 : *om.* $L_{1,3}$ || searceach Y_2 : serccach L_2 : *om.* $L_{1,3}$

2.4 bat N_2 $Y_{1,2}$: b. L_1 : bad L_3 || heslabar N_1 : eislabur N_2 : heslabra L_2 : heaslabur L_3 || gurbat N_1 : corbat N_2 : corot Y_1 : corod Y_2 : corbot L_1 : coro $L_{2,3}$ || dercach N_1 : d–ctach N_2 : erder–c Y_1 : terderc– Y_2 : erdairc L_1 : dergthar L_2 : [dergtar] L_3

2.5 bat N_2 $Y_{1,2}$: b. L_1 : bad L_3 || gartait N_1 : gart– N_2 : gartaig(h) $Y_{1,2}$ L_3 : gairtich L_2 || gurub N_1 L_3 : corbat N_2 L_1 : corop $Y_{1,2}$: curbat L_2 || soc(h)raid(h) N_1 $L_{1,2,3}$: sochr– N_2 : sochraigh $Y_{1,2}$

2.6 bad(h) N_1 L_3 : bat N_2 $Y_{1,2}$: b. L_1 || buidach N_1 : buid– N_2 : buideach Y_1 L_3 || gurbat N_1 : corbat N_2 : corbo $Y_{1,2}$: c. L_1 : corob L_2 : gurub $L3$ || irach N_1 $Y_{1,2}$ L_1 : air– N_2 : fhaireach L_3

2.7 bat N_2 $Y_{1,2}$: b. L_1 || humal N_1 $Y_{1,2}$ $L_{2,3}$ || gurab N_1 : gorbat N_2 : corbo Y_1 : corobo Y_2 : corbot L_1 : cursat L_2 : gurbo L_3 || uas– N_2 : huassal Y_1 : huasal Y_2 L_3

3.1 ecna N_1 $L_{1,2}$: eaccna N_2 : eacnai Y_1 : ecnai Y_2 : eagna L_3 : egna X_1 || airmidin N_2 $L_{2,3}$: airmidein $Y_{1,2}$

2.3   Be obliging so that you may be loved.
2.4   Be generous so that you may be renowned.
   2.4a   Be generous so that you may be charitable.
2.5   Be hospitable so that you may appear decorous.
2.6   Be grateful so that you may experience increase.
2.7   Be humble so that you may be exalted.

3.1   Learning merits respect.
3.2   Intelligence overcomes fury.
3.3   Truth should be supported.
3.4   Falsehood should be rebuked.
3.5   Iniquity should be corrected.
3.6   A quarrel merits mediation.
3.7   A fief-payment warrants services in return.
   3.7a   A fief-payment should be ministered to.
3.8   A tenant-at-will is entitled to reciprocal services.
3.9   A teacher deserves his following.
3.10   The one who goes surety is entitled to that which is bound.
3.11   A surety should be protected.
3.12   Eyewitness evidence should be appealed to.

3.2 arfich N_1 : arfig N_2 : *om.* Y L || gais N_1 : gaois N_2 : *om.* Y L || goil N_2 : *om.* YL

3.3 furtacht N_2 Y_2 L_2 : furacht L_3

3.4 <gó> *om.* N_2 || a N_1 only || cairiug– N_1 $Y_{1,2}$ X_1 : *om.* N_2 : cairigud L_1 : coireadug L_2 : cairigiud L_3

3.5 claon N_1 : claoine N_2 : cloeine $Y_{1,2}$: clóine L_1 : claine L_2 : claeine L_3 || condrech N_1 : condr– N_2 : cundrech L_1 : cuinrech L_2

3.6 ugra $N_{1,2}$ $L_{1,2,3}$: augra $Y_{1,2}$ || ettorghoire N_2 : edairi L_2 : edargaire L_3

3.7 rat N_1 || riarug– N_1 : riar– N_2 : riara $Y_{1,2}$ $L_{1,2,3}$: riaradh X_1

3.8 fuider N_1 : fudir L_1 : fuigir L_3 : fudhair X_1 || frithfol– N_1 : friothfola N_2 : fritholta $Y_{1,2}$ $L_{1,2}$ X_1 : fritolta L_3

3.9 aiti N_1 L_2 : aide L_3 : *om.* Y || a N_1 L_1 *only* || soc(h)raidi N_1 L_2 : soc(h)raide N_2 L_3 : shochraite L_1 : *om.* Y

3.10 maidm Y_1 $L_{2,3}$ || nascur N_1 : nasccor N_2 : nascara Y_1 : nascor L_2

3.11 rat N_1 || a N_1 $Y_{1,2}$ $L_{1,3}$: *om.* N_2 L_2 || imdighail Y_2 : imdeadail L_2 : imdeaghail L_3

3.12 fiadnusi N_1 : fiadnaisi N_2 Y_1 $L_{2,3}$: fiadhnuse Y_2 || a N_1 $Y_{1,2}$ $L_{1,3}$: *om.* N_2 L_2 || fugell N_1 L_1 : fuigheall L_3

3.13   Dligid díummus dermat.
3.14   Dligid maith mórad.
3.15   Dligid díbe dimmolad.
  3.15a   Dligid díbe dínsem.
3.16   Dligid dall dídin.
3.17   Dligid airndel airfócrae.
  3.17a   Dligid airdál airfócrae.
3.18   Dligid óc elathain.
3.19   Dligid altramm imfochaid.
3.20   Dligid sen sogoiri.
  3.20a   Dligid maigister sogoiri.
3.21   Dligid foíndelach fócrae.
3.22   Dligid máthair míngoiri.
3.23   Dligid athair ógréir.
  3.23a   Dligid athair sogoiri.
3.24   Dligid aite airraim.
3.25   Dligid coibche certugud.
3.26   Dligid othar a íarfaigid.
3.27   Dligid éconn imchomét.
3.28   Dligid anidan aurchailliud.
3.29   Dligid comaithches coímchloud.

3.13 dimus N_1 : diumus N_2 : dimmus $Y_{1,2}$: *om.* L || dermit N_1 : dermut Y_2 : *om.* L
3.14 mait Y_2
3.15 dib(h)i $Y_{1,2}$ X_1 || dimolad(h) N_1 L_3 X_1 : diomaldh N_2 || dinsem Y_1 : dinsein Y_2 ||
    dimmolud L_1 : dimmolad L_2
3.16 daill N_2 || a X_1 *only* || ditin N_1 Y_1 L_1 : diden N_2 Y_2 : didean L_3
3.17 airnell N_1 : airndel N_2 : airneal $Y_{1,2}$: erdál L_1 : erdail L_2 : erdhal L_3 || aurfocra N_1 :
    urfhogra N_2 : airfocra $Y_{1,2}$: erfhócra L_1 : fhuruagra L_2 : eruagra L_3
3.18 occ N_1 : og N_2 L_3 X_1 || eladain N_1 $L_{1,2}$: eal*adh*ain N_2 : ealadhain L_3 : eladha X_1
3.19 altrom $N_{1,2}$ L_2 : altram Y_1 L_1 : altrum Y_2 L_3 X_1 || iomfoch– N_2 : imfochid $Y_{1,2}$:
    impocad L_2 : imocor L_3 : immaithigh X_1
3.20 maigister N_1 $L_{2,3}$: maighist– N_2 : magist– L_1 : maighistir X_1 : sen $Y_{1,2}$ || sog(h)aire N_1
    $Y_{1,2}$ $L_{1,3}$ X_1 : sogoire N_2 : sogairi L_2
3.21 faindel N_1 : faoindel N_2 : foendela– $Y_{1,2}$: foindelach L_1 : *om.* L_2 : fannaideac L_3 :
    fændlegach X_1 || furfocra N_1 : furfogra N_2 : fuacra $Y_{1,2}$ L_1 : *om.* L_2 : fuagra L_3 : f*u*rogra
    X_1

3.13 Arrogance deserves oblivion.

3.14 Good should be exalted.

3.15 Stinginess deserves to be disparaged.

   3.15a Stinginess should be spurned.

3.16 A blind person should be led.

3.17 A trap should carry a warning.

   3.17a A distribution should be announced.

3.18 A youth should have a skill.

3.19 Fosterage should be impugned.

3.20 An old person deserves dutiful maintenance.

   3.20a A teacher deserves dutiful maintenance.

3.21 A fugitive should be proclaimed.

3.22 A mother deserves gentle maintenance.

3.23 A father deserves to have his way fully.

   3.23a A father deserves dutiful maintenance.

3.24 A teacher merits respect.

3.25 A contract merits adjustment.

3.26 A sick person deserves to be looked after.

3.27 An incapable person should be watched over.

3.28 An impure thing should be prohibited.

3.29 The law of neighbourhood entails reciprocal dealings.

3.22 mathair N_1 : math– N_2 X_1 : m–r $Y_{1,2}$ $L_{1,3}$: *om.* L_2 || mingaire N_1 $Y_{1,2}$: miongoire N_2 : mine $L_{1,3}$ X_1 : *om.* L_2

3.23 athair N_1 $L_{1,3}$: ath– N_1 Y_1 X_1 : atair Y_2 : *om.* L_2 || a N_1 *only* || og(h)reir N_1 $Y_{1,2}$: oighreir N_2 || sogaire $L_{1,3}$: *om.* L_2 : somíad X_1

3.24 aide N_1 : [?]ite N_2 : aiti $Y_{1,2}$: *om.* L || urraim N_1 : urroim N_2 : erraim $Y_{1,2}$: *om.* L

3.25 coibchi $Y_{1,2}$: *om.* L_2 || certug– N_1 $Y_{1,2}$: certucch– N_2 : *ce*rtugud $L_{1,3}$: *om.* L_2

3.26 othur N_1 Y_1 L_1 : othor Y_2 : otha L_2 : ota L_3 || a N_1 Y_2 *only* || iarfaigi N_1 : iarf–e N_2 : fiarf–e Y_2 : fhiarfaidi L_2

3.27 econd N_1 Y_2 : othur N_2 : *om.* L : ecconn X_1 || imcomet N_1 : iomcoimhed N_2 : himcoimed Y_1 : himcoimet Y_2 : *om.* L : imcoimet X_1

3.28 ainiodan N_2 : *om.* L || urchailedh N_1 : urchaol– N_2 : aurcailiud Y_1 : aurcuil– Y_2 : *om.* L

3.29 comaitcius N_1 : comathches Y_1 : commaithces Y_2 : *om.* L || caomclodh N_1 : caomcl– N_2 : cloemclod $Y_{1,2}$: *om.* L

3.30 Dligid mer múnad.
3.31 Dligid aurdonál airfócrae.
3.32 Dligid étnge aimsir.
3.33 Dligid tóraic tuinide.
3.34 Dligid aí astud.
3.35 Dligid sommae soíri.
3.36 Dligid bés bréithir.
3.37 Dligid dóig díthech.
3.38 Dligid fír fíachu.

4.1 Descad cotulta freslige.
4.2 Descad sírechtae sírdord.
4.3 Descad díbi deog.
4.4 Descad ferge miscais.
4.5 Descad athargaib esarcon.
4.6 Descad eclae ómun.
  4.6a Descad éca ómun.
4.7 Descad drúise dánatus.
4.8 Descad trebaire túae.
4.9 Descad étrebaire rolabrae.
4.10 Descad cartha gnáthaige.
4.11 Descad coillte cesachtaige.
  4.11a Descad cailte cesachtaige.

3.30 mir N_2 : mear $L_{2,3}$ || mun– N_2 X_1 : múnud L_1
3.31 urdonail N_2 : *om.* Y L || erfocra N_1 : urfoccra N_2 : *om.* Y L
3.32 eitnge N_2 : eitgi Y_1 : eitge Y_2 L_1 : eitchi L_2 : etce L_3 || amsir N_1 Y_1 L_1 : aimser L_2 : aimiris L_3
3.33 toreic N_1 : toirec N_2 : tairic $Y_{1,2}$: tairec L_1 : *om.* L_2 : toradh L_3 || tuinid(h)e $N_{1,2}$ $Y_{1,2}$ L_3 : tunide L_1 : *om.* L_2
3.34 aoi N_2 : cú X_1 || a X_1 *only* || astad N_2 : astod L_2 : asdud L_3 : hastud X_1
3.35 sommai N_1 : soma N_2 : *om.* Y L || saire N_1 : saoire N_2 : *om.* Y L
3.36 <bés> *om.* Y L || breiter N_2 : *om.* Y L
3.37 *om.* Y L
3.38 <fír> *om.* Y L : .F. N_1 || fiacha N_2 : *om.* Y L
4.1 cod–ta N_2 : codulta Y_2 L_3 || frislige N_1 L_3 : freislighe N_2 : freislighi Y_1 : freisl– Y_2

3.30 A fool should be instructed.

3.31 A herald should proclaim.

3.32 An inarticulate person deserves time.

3.33 What one finds one is entitled to keep.

3.34 A legal case should be kept fixed.

3.35 Wealth entitles one to privilege.

3.36 'Perhaps' requires one's word.

3.37 'Probability' requires an oath of denial.

3.38 Proof demands payments due.

4.1 Lying down is an inducement to sleep.

4.2 A lasting plaint is a symptom of longing.

4.3 Drink is a catalyst for rejection.

4.4 Hatred is an inducement to anger.

4.5 An attack is an inducement to a counter-attack.

4.6 Timidity is a catalyst of fear.

   4.6a Fear is the leaven of death.

4.7 Impudence is a symptom of lechery.

4.8 Silence is a characteristic of discretion.

4.9 Excess talk is a characteristic of indiscretion.

4.10 Frequenting is symptomatic of love.

4.11 Complaint is a symptom of mistreatment.

   4.11a Niggardliness is a characteristic of meanness.

4.2 sirrechto N_1 : sirrechta N_2 : sirechta $Y_{1,2}$: sireacca L_3 || siordord N_2 : sirdorda Y_1 : sirdorda– Y_2 : sirord L_3

4.3 dibe $N_{1,2}$ L_3 || deoghmaire L_3

4.4 feirgi N_1 : f–ge N_2 : feirge Y_2 || mioscaiss N_2 : miscaiss Y_1 : romiscais L_3

4.5 aturguib N_2 : *om.* L_3 || esarcoin N_1 : esorguin N_2 : *om.* L_3

4.6 eca N_1 : ecca N_2 : ecla $Y_{1,2}$: eagla L_3 || uaman $N_{1,2}$ Y_2 : huaman Y_1 : omhan L_3

4.7 druisi $N_{1,2}$ Y_1 : druissi Y_2 : druine L_3 || danatuss N_2 : danadus L_3

4.8 treaboire N_2 : treabhaire L_3 || tuæ N_1 $Y_{1,2}$: tnuth N_2 : tuar L_3

4.9 ettreab–e N_2 : edtreabaire $Y_{1,2}$: etreabaire L_3 || rolabra $N_{1,2}$ L_3 : solabra $Y_{1,2}$

4.10 carta N_1 : carthana L_3 || gnathuige N_1 : gnath–e N_2 : gnat(h)aid(h)e $Y_{1,2}$: gnathgaire L_3

4.11 caillti $N_{1,2}$ $Y_{1,2}$: cailte L_3 || cesachtoige N_1 : cesacht–e N_2 : cessachtge Y_1 : cesar L_3

4.12 Descad gensa dímaise.
4.13 Descad baíse banchobrae.
4.14 Descad mire rogáire.
4.15 Descad sainte imcaisiu.
4.16 Descad serce sírṡilliud.
4.17 Descad mraith sanas.
4.18 Descad debtha athchomsán.
4.19 Descad fáilte sláinte.
4.20 Descad bróin bithgubae.
4.21 Descad serbae burbae.
4.22 Descad anéolais imresan.
4.23 Descad ainble anecnae.
4.24 Descad uilc úabar.
4.25 Descad romescae roól.
4.26 Descad éolais aithigid.
4.27 Descad crábuid caínbésa.
4.28 Descad frecrai fis.
4.29 Descad burbae bithfognam.

5.1 Tosach éolais imchomarc.
5.2 Tosach augrai athchomsán.
5.3 Tosach etig airliciud.
   5.3a Tosach éthig airliciud.

4.12 gensa $N_{1,2}$ $Y_{1,2}$ || dímaisi L_3 : dimaisi N_1 Y_1 : diomhaise N_2 : dimaissi Y_2 : genus L_3
4.13 baisi $N_{1,2}$ Y_2 L_3 : bæsi Y_1 || bancobra $N_{1,2}$ $Y_{1,2}$: banchomhradh L_3
4.14 rogairi Y_1
4.15 sainti N_1 $Y_{1,2}$: sainnti N_2 || imcisin N_2 : imchasaid L_3
4.16 s–ci N_2 : seirci $Y_{1,2}$: seirce L_3 || sirsill– N_1 L_3 : sirsilleadh N_2 : sirsellad Y_1 : sirsealladh Y_2
4.17 braith N_1 $Y_{1,2}$ L_3 : brat N_2 || sanuis N_1 : sanais N_2 L_3
4.18 deabt(h)a N_2 L_3 || athc(h)osan N_1 Y_1 : athcomsan N_2 : athcusan Y_2 : acmosan L_3
4.19 failti $N_{1,2}$: fælti Y_1 : fæilti Y_2 || slainti N_1 $Y_{1,2}$
4.20 bithduba N_1 : biothdubha N_2 : bithgub(h)a $Y_{1,2}$ L_3
4.21 serb– N_1 : serba N_2 L_3 : searba $Y_{1,2}$ || burba $N_{1,2}$ $Y_{1,2}$ L_3
4.22 aineoluis $N_{1,2}$: aneoluis Y_2 : aineolais L_3 || imrisain N_1 Y_1 : imreasoin N_2 : imrisin Y_2 : imreasain L_3

4.12 Lack of adornment is a sign of chastity.
4.13 The conversation of women is a catalyst for folly.
4.14 Excess laughter is a sign of madness.
4.15 Looking about is a sign of covetousness.
4.16 Constant gazing is symptomatic of love.
4.17 Whispering is a sign of treachery.
4.18 Reproach is a mark of strife.
4.19 Good health is a sign of happiness.
4.20 Constant mourning is a sign of sorrow.
4.21 Boorishness is characteristic of bitterness.
4.22 Contentiousness is a mark of ignorance.
4.23 Ignorance is a mark of shamelessness.
4.24 Pride is a catalyst for evil.
4.25 Much drinking is an inducement to much drunkenness.
4.26 Frequency leads to familiarity.
4.27 Good habits lead to piety.
4.28 Knowledge leads to an answer.
4.29 Continuous servitude leads to boorishness.

5.1   Inquiry is the beginning of knowledge.
5.2   Reproach is the beginning of a quarrel.
5.3   Lending is the beginning of refusal.
  5.3a Borrowing is the beginning of lying.

4.23 ainbli N_2 : anble Y_2 : ainfhele L_3 || ainecna N_1 : aineccna N_2 : aneacna Y_1 : anecna Y_2
   : aineacna L_3
4.24 uilcc Y_2 : *om.* N L || <úabar> : *om.* N L_3
4.25 romesce L_3 : *om.* N Y || <roól> *om.* N Y
4.26 *om.* N Y
4.27 crabaid L_3 : *om.* N Y || <caínbésa> : *om.* N Y
4.28 freagra L_3 : *om.* N Y || <fis> : *om.* N Y
4.29 burba L_3 : *om.* N Y || <bithfognam> *om.* N Y
5.1 eoluis $N_{1,2}$ Y_2 || imcomarc N_1 Y_1 L_3 : iomchom–c N_2 : iumcomharcc Y_2
5.2 ugra $N_{1,2}$: aigrai $Y_{1,2}$: acra L_2 : agrai L_3 || atchosan N_1 : athcomsan N_2 : athcusan $Y_{1,2}$
   : athchosan L_1 : achmosan $L_{2,3}$
5.3 eit– $N_{1,2}$: eithig(h) $Y_{1,2}$ L_3 : ethig L_1 : eitich L_2 || airlegad N_1 : airleag– N_2 : airliugudh
   Y_1 : airliug– Y_2 : arlicud L_1 : airliuc– L_2 : airleagudh L_3

5.4   Tosach écndaig airbire.
5.5   Tosach ordain eneclann.
5.6   Tosach suíthi sochoisce.
5.7   Tosach tocaid trebaire.
5.8   Tosach féle fairsinge.
5.9   Tosach crábuid cosmailius.
5.10 Tosach ecnai áilgine.
5.11 Tosach uilc úabarbríathar.
5.12 Tosach críne galraige.
5.13 Tosach dothcaid somescae.
5.14 Tosach sothcaid domescae.
5.15 Tosach córae caínepert.
5.16 Tosach doíre drochlepaid.
5.17 Tosach tróge toirsige.
5.18 Tosach lobrae lén.
5.19 Tosach cutmae gúforcell.
5.20 Tosach sothcaid dagben.
5.21 Tosach dothcaid drochben.
5.22 Tosach míairle malartchae.
5.23 Arailiu maith mesrugud.

5.4 ecnaig(h) N_1 Y_1 $L_{1,3}$: eccn– N_2 : ecnaid Y_2 : ecnaich L_2 || oirbire $N_{1,2}$: airbiri Y_1

5.5 eneclainn N_1 : einech N_2 : enecclann $Y_{1,2}$: enecland L_1 : enicland L_2 : eineacland L_3

5.6 saithe N_1 : saoiti N_2 : súthi L_1 : saithi L_2 || socoisgi N_2 : socoisci $Y_{1,2}$: sochaidi L_2

5.7 tocuid N_1 : tacaid $L_{2,3}$ || treaboiri N_2 : trebhuire Y_2 : treabaire L_3

5.8 feile $N_{1,2}$ Y_2 $L_{2,3}$: feili Y_1 : féli L_1 || fairsingi Y_1 L_2 : forsinge L_1

5.9 crab– N_2 Y_2 : crabaid(h) $L_{1,2,3}$ || cosma N_1 : cosmhailes N_2 : cosmailus Y_2 : cosmailis L_2

5.10 eccna N_2 : eaccnai $Y_{1,2}$: ecna L_2 : eagna L_3 || alg(h)ine N_1 $Y_{1,2}$ L_1

5.11 uaborbriathro N_1 : uab–briathor N_2 : uaborbriathar Y_1 L_1 : uaburbriatra L_3

5.12 gallruighe N_1 : gal[. . .] N_2 : gallraighi Y_1 : gallraig(h)e Y_2 $L_{1,3}$: gallraite L_2

5.13 dotchaid N_1 : dotch– N_2 : *om.* Y L || somesci N_1 : soimeiscci N_2 : *om.* Y L

5.14 sotchaid N_1 : sothch– N_2 : *om.* Y L || domesci N_1 : doimeisc[ce] N_2 : *om.* Y L

5.15 coru N_1 : cora N_2 $L_{2,3}$: corai $Y_{1,2}$ L_1 || caoineb–t N_2 : cainbert L_2 : cainbr[. . .] L_3

5.16 daire N_1 $Y_{1,2}$ L_3 : daoire N_2 : duire L_2 || drochlebaid N_1 L_2 : drochleab– N_2 :
    drochlepuid Y_2 : drochleabaidh L_3

5.4 A reproach is the beginning of slander.
5.5 Honour-price is the basis of dignity.
5.6 Tractability is the beginning of expertise.
5.7 Prudence is the basis of good fortune.
5.8 Amplitude is the basis of liberality.
5.9 Imitation is the basis of devotion.
5.10 Gentleness is the beginning of wisdom.
5.11 Vain speech is the beginning of evil.
5.12 Sickliness is the beginning of old age.
5.13 Drunkenness is the beginning of misfortune.
5.14 Soberness is the beginning of good fortune.
5.15 Gentle speech is the beginning of concord.
5.16 Bad association is the beginning of lowly status.
5.17 Weariness is the beginning of misery.
5.18 Misfortune is the beginning of infirmity.
5.19 False-witness is the beginning of a downfall.
5.20 A good wife is the beginning of good fortune.
5.21 A bad wife is the beginning of misfortune.
5.22 Prodigality is the beginning of bad management.
5.23 Conversely, moderation is good.

5.17 troig(h)e $N_{1,2}$ $Y_{1,2}$ L_3 : troide L_2 || torrsige N_1 : tuirs–e N_2 : toirrsighi Y_1 : toirrsighe Y_2 L_3 : toirrse L_2

5.18 lubra $N_{1,2}$ $L_{1,2,3}$: lubrai $Y_{1,2}$

5.19 cudma $N_{1,2}$ L_2 : cutma $Y_{1,2}$ L_1 : gudma L_3 || guf*org*heall N_2 : guforcell Y_1 : cuf–cell Y_2 : guf–ogholl L_2 : gufoirgell L_3

5.20 sodch– N_1 : sotch– N_2 : sothocaid $Y_{1,2}$: sodchaid L_1 : sochaidi L_2 : socaidh L_3 || soben N_1 : deig(h)ben N_2 L_2 : dagben $Y_{1,2}$ L_1 : daigbean L_3

5.21 dotcha N_1 : dotch– N_2 : dotacaid(h) $Y_{1,2}$: dodchaid L_1 : dochma L_2 : docaidh L_3 || doben N_1 : droichben N_2 : drochben $Y_{1,2}$ $L_{1,2}$: drochbean L_3

5.22 miarle N_1 : miairli N_2 : miarli $Y_{1,2}$ L_1 : merli L_2 : meirle L_3 || malarta N_1 $L_{2,3}$: malairtche N_2 : malartacha Y_1 : malartach Y_2 : malartcha L_1

5.23 araile N_1 Y_2 $L_{2,3}$: aroile N_2 : araili Y_1 : árrali L_1 || mesrug– N_1 $Y_{1,2}$ L_1 : measrughadh N_2 : measrudhudh L_3

6.1   Ferr dán orbu.
6.2   Ferr ledb lugu.
6.3   Ferr doairm diairm.
6.4   Ferr slán sásad.
6.5   Ferr sonaide séta[ib].
6.6   Ferr dígde dígail.
6.7   Ferr ordan angbus(?).
6.8   Ferr rath ríaraib.
   6.8a   Ferr rath ríarugud.
   6.8b   Ferr road réraib.
6.9   Ferr éolas ilur.
6.10   Ferr ilar n-oscru.
6.11   Ferr mug marbad.
6.12   Ferr essomnae airbiri.
6.13   Ferr dál debiuch.
6.14   Ferr sét sous.
6.15   Ferr suthaine séta[ib].
6.16   Ferr sothced slóg.
   6.16a   Ferr soithnge slóg.
6.17   Ferr sochraite slabrai.
6.18   Ferr bréo burbai.
6.19   Ferr briugas búar.
6.20   Ferr beccfine móraltramm.

6.1 orba $N_{1,2}$ L_3 : orbbai $Y_{1,2}$: orbba L_1 : fhorba L_2

6.2 ledp $Y_{1,2}$: leadhb L_3 || luga N_1 $Y_{1,2}$ L_2 : lugh– N_2 : luge L_1 lug[. . .] L_3

6.4 liechslansasai [written as one word] Y_1 : liech slansasai Y_2 : *om.* L

6.5 sonaighe N_1 : son–e $N_{2,3}$: sonaidi Y_1 : sonaid Y_2 : *om.* L || seota N_1 : seoid N_2 : seoda N_3 : seoita Y_1 : seoit Y_2 : *om.* L

6.6 digi N_2 : dighe N_3 : dig(h)di $Y_{1,2}$: *om.* L || dioghoil N_2 : dioghail N_3 : dighu no digail Y_1 : dighul no digail Y_2 : *om.* L

6.7 <ordan> *om.* L || angbas $Y_{1,2}$: *om.* L

6.8 rath $N_{1,2,3}$ $L_{1,2,3}$ X_1 : road $Y_{1,2}$ || riaruib N_1 : riaraibh N_2 : riar– N_3 : reraib Y_1 : rer Y_2 : riarugud $L_{1,2,3}$: ina riag– X_1

6.9 eolas N_2 Y_1 : *om.* L || ilar N_1 : iolar $N_{2,3}$: hilur Y_2 : *om.* L

6.10 iolar $N_{2,3}$: ilur Y_2 : *om.* L || naiscre N_1 : noiscre $N_{2,3}$: noiscri $Y_{1,2}$: *om.* L

6.11 mod(h) $N_{2,3}$: mog(h) $Y_{1,2}$ $L_{1,2,3}$ || marb– $N_{1,2}$

6.1   A skill is better than an inheritance.
6.2   Better a remnant than a yearning.
6.3   It is better to be poorly armed than unarmed.
6.4   Better good health than being satiated.
6.5   Good fortune is better than wealth.
6.6   Better forgiveness than vengeance.
6.7   Dignity is better than ruthlessness(?).
6.8   Better a fief-payment than [owing] services in return.
   6.8a   Better a fief-payment than having to serve.
   6.8b   Better prosperity than [owing] services in return.
6.9   Expertise is better than many [talents].
6.10   Better many [talents] than ignorance.
6.11   Better [to be] a slave than be slain.
6.12   Confidence is better than reproach.
6.13   Consensus is better than discord.
6.14   The path [of virtue] is better than learning.
6.15   A long life is better than riches.
6.16   Good fortune is better than force of numbers.
   6.16a   An eloquent person is better than force of numbers.
6.17   Friendship is better than wealth.
6.18   Better the spark [of excellence] than ignorance.
6.19   Hospitality is worth more than cattle.
6.20   Better a small kindred than a great deal of fosterage.

6.12 essomnai N_1 : esomna N_2 $Y_{1,2}$: easamuin N_3 : *om.* L || oirbiri N_1 : oirb(h)ire $N_{2,3}$: airbire Y_2 : *om.* L

6.13 dail $N_{1,2,3}$ $Y_{1,2}$ $L_{2,3}$: dala X_1 || deb– N_1 : deabhuith N_2 : deab– N_3 : debech $Y_{1,2}$ L_1 : deibech L_2 : deibeach L_3 : ina deab– X_1

6.14 sed $N_{2,3}$: *om.* L || sofis N_1 : soifios N_2 : sofhios N_3 : *om.* L

6.15 suithaine N_1 : suthaini N_2 : *om.* L || seota N_1 : seoda $N_{2,3}$: seotu $Y_{1,2}$: *om.* L

6.16 soitch– N_1 : soitce N_2 : soitnge N_3 : sothced $Y_{1,2}$: *om.* L || slog(h) $N_{1,3}$ $Y_{1,2}$: sl– N_2 : *om.* L

6.17 sochraide $N_{1,3}$: sochraidi N_2 : socraiti $Y_{1,2}$: *om.* L || slaib(h)re $N_{1,2,3}$: *om.* L

6.18 brab $N_{1,2,3}$: *om.* L || burba $N_{1,2}$: borba N_3 : borbbai $Y_{1,2}$: *om.* L

6.19 brugas N_1 $Y_{1,2}$: brugachus N_2 : *om.* L || <búar> : *om.* L

6.20 beigfini N_2 : beagfhine N_3 : *om.* L || moraltrom $N_{1,2,3}$: no mor naltrama Y_1 : no mor naltruma Y_2 : *om.* L

6.21   Ferr reconn íarcunn.

6.22   Ferr ecnae n-anaib.

6.23   Ferr uirb(?) orbu.

6.24   Ferr orbae uirb(?).

6.25   Ferr drúb déini.

6.26   Ferr déine dobeli.

6.27   Ferr dobele dochur.

6.28   Ferr bethu búadaib.

6.29   Ferr búaid pliptecht(?).

6.30   Ferr bríg bágaib.

6.31   Ferr duine dúilib.

6.32   Ferr drochthrebaire dagaicdi.

6.33   Ferr techt allatróg.

6.34   Ferr móin immattrub.

6.35   Ferr senfíach senécraiti.

6.36   Ferr flaith foltaib.

6.37   Ferr caíntórmach cintaib.

6.38   Ferr gním galraigi.

6.39   Ferr cluiche garbai.

6.40   Ferr gorad grísaib.

     6.40a   Ferr grúad grísad.

6.41   Ferr clú cáemnu.

     6.41a   Ferr clú gnímrud.

6.21 recond N_1 $Y_{1,2}$: riaconn N_2 : riacconn N_3 : *om.* L || iarconn N_1 Y_1 : iarcconn $N_{2,3}$: iarcoim Y_2 : *om.* L

6.22 eccna $N_{1,2}$ Y_1 : eagna N_3 : eccno Y_2 : *om.* L N_1 || namuib N_2 : namha N_3 : *om.* L

6.23 <uirb> *om.* L || orba $N_{1,3}$: forba N_2 : orbbai $Y_{1,2}$: *om.* L

6.24 orba $N_{1,2}$ $Y_{1,2}$: orb N_3 : *om.* L || <uirb> *om.* L

6.25 druib $N_{2,3}$: *om.* L || dene $N_{1,3}$: deine $Y_{1,2}$: *om.* L

6.26 dene $N_{1,3}$: deini N_2 : *om.* L || dobele $N_{1,2,3}$ $Y_{1,2}$: *om.* L

6.27 doibeile N_2 : *om.* N_3 L || dochar $N_{1,2}$: *om.* N_3 L

6.28 beatha N_1 : betha $N_{2,3}$: *om.* L || buaduib N_1 : buada N_2 : buadhoib N_3 : buadhaib Y_1 : buaidhaibh Y_2 : *om.* L

6.29 <búaid> *om.* L || blipecht N_1 : blipfeacht N_2 : bithblioct N_3 : *om.* L

6.30 bri N_2 || baghuidh N_1 : baguib N_2 : buad– N_3 : breaghaib L_3

6.31 duini $Y_{1,2}$: *om.* L || <dúilib> *om.* L

6.32 drochtreab–e N_2 : drocht(h)reab(h)aire N_3 Y_1 : drochtreab– Y_2 : *om.* L || dagaicde N_1 : daghoige N_2 : daghaige N_3 : degaici $Y_{1,2}$: *om.* L

6.21   Forethought is better than afterthought.

6.22   Wisdom is better than wealth.

6.23   An *uirb*(?) is better than an inheritance.

6.24   An inheritance is better than an *uirb*(?).

6.25   Better a delay than haste.

6.26   Better haste than an unfavourable situation.

6.27   Better an unfavourable situation than disadvantage.

6.28   Life is better than triumphs.

6.29   Excellence is better than *pliptecht*(?).

6.30   Better strength than boasting.

6.31   A person is better than the elements.

6.32   Poor implements are better than a fine structure.

6.33   Better possession than another state of wretchedness.

6.34   Better a bog than living hemmed in.

6.35   Better an old debt than an old enmity.

6.36   Better lordship than clientship obligations.

6.37   Fair increase is better than crimes.

6.38   Activity is better than sickliness.

6.39   Play is better than roughness.

6.40   Better a warm blush than heated passions.

6.40a   Better a blush on the cheek than an affront.

6.41   Better a good reputation than being provided for.

6.41a   Fame is better than deeds.

6.33 techta $N_{1,2}$: teacht N_3 : *om.* L || allaitr– $N_{1,2}$: allatraigh N_3 : allathrugh $Y_{1,2}$: *om.* L

6.34 <móin> [. . .] N_2 || imaitreb N_1 : iomaitreb N_2 : imaitreabh N_3 : immatreab $Y_{1,2}$: immatreb L_1 : imaitreib L_2 : imaittreabad L_3

6.35 senf(h)iacha $N_{1,3}$: seinfiacha N_2 : seinfiach Y_2 : senfheich L_2 : senfhei[t]h L_3 || senf-(h)ala $N_{1,3}$: senfola N_2 || senécraite L_1 : senacra L_2 : se[. . .]ide L_3

6.36 <flaith> *om.* L || foltuib N_1 : *om.* L

6.37 caintormaig(h) N_1 $Y_{1,2}$: coentormach N_2 : caointroma N_3 : *om.* L || cintoib N_1 : ciontaibh N_2 : cionta N_3 : caintaib(h) $Y_{1,2}$: *om.* L

6.38 gniom N_2 : *om.* N_3 L || gallruige N_1 : galr–e N_2 : gallraithi $Y_{1,2}$: *om.* N_3 L

6.39 cluithe N_2 : cluichi Y_1 : *om.* N_3 L || gairb(h)e $N_{1,2}$: *om.* N_3 L

6.40 gruad N_1 : gruaid $N_{2,3}$: gorad(h) $Y_{1,2}$: *om.* L || grisadh N_1 : griosadh $N_{2,3}$: grisaib(h) $Y_{1,2}$: *om.* L

6.41 <clú> *om.* L || gnimrad N_1 : gniomhradh N_2 || caomhna N_3 : caemna Y_1 : cæmna Y_2 : *om.* L

6.42 Ferr mac míchoraib.
6.43 Ferr tiugbae torud.
6.44 Ferr túath tinnscru.
6.45 Ferr teiched tairisem.
6.46 Ferr trummae dínnimi.
6.47 Ferr laubair áini.
6.48 Ferr dán déinmichi.
6.49 Ferr bó blíadain.
6.50 Ferr cloth cach biud.
   6.50a Ferr cloth cach búaid.
6.51 Ferr aurlam n-adbur.
6.52 Ferr lurchaire trénriuth.
6.53 Ferr coimsetu cucilchiu.
6.54 Ferr cride gíallnai.
6.55 Ferr gart grísad.
6.56 Ferr tairisiu tairngiriu.
   6.56a Ferr taircsiu tairngiriu.
6.57 Ferr sobarthu suíthiu.
6.58 Ferr síd sochocad.
6.59 Ferr soben socheníul.
6.60 Ferr súan serbai.

6.42 <mac> *om.* L || midchoruib N_1 : miodcoruib N_2 : michoirib N_3 : michoraib(h) $Y_{1,2}$: *om.* L

6.43 tig(h)ba N_1 $Y_{1,2}$ $L_{1,2}$: tiugba N_2 : diogbadh N_3 : tidhbha L_3 || torad(h) $N_{1,2,3}$ $Y_{1,2}$ $L_{2,3}$

6.44 tuat N_2 Y_2 : tuaith N_3 : tu[ath] L_3 || tindscra N_1 L_2 : tionnsccra N_2 : tionnscra N_3 : tinscra $Y_{1,2}$: tinnscra L_1 : tindsgra L_3

6.45 teich– N_1 X_1 : teic(h)ead(h) N_3 $L_{2,3}$: teithedh $Y_{1,2}$ || tairisium N_1 : toirisimh N_2 : tairisi N_3 L_2 : tairisim $Y_{1,2}$: tairisin L_3 : ina tairisi X_1

6.46 trumma N_1 L_1 : torma N_2 : troma N_3 : truma $Y_{1,2}$ L_2 : *om.* L_3 || dinime $N_{1,3}$: dinnimhe N_2 : dindime Y_2 L_2 : *om.* L_3

6.47 lubair $N_{1,2}$ L_1 : lobhar N_3 : laubar Y_1 : labur Y_2 : lubar $L_{2,3}$ || aine $N_{1,2,3}$ $Y_{1,2}$ $L_{1,2,3}$

6.48 dam(h) $N_{1,2,3}$: *om.* L || denmide N_1 : deinm–e N_2 : denmhe N_3 : *om.* L

6.49 bliaduin N_1 : bl–ain N_2 X_1 : bliadhoin N_3 : bliaghain Y_2

6.50 cloith $Y_{1,2}$: *om.* L || gach biudh N_1 : biudh N_2 : g– biudh N_3 : ca–buaidh Y_1 : can–buaidh Y_2 : *om.* L

6.51 urlam(h) $N_{1,2,3}$: *om.* L || nadb(h)air $N_{1,2}$: nadhbar N_3 : *om.* L

6.42   Better a surety than invalid contracts.

6.43   Better a survivor than increase.

6.44   Better the tribe than the bride-price.

6.45   Better to flee than remain.

6.46   Rigour is better than indolence.

6.47   Hard work is better than a bright wit.

6.48   A skill is better than idleness.

6.49   Better a cow than a year.

6.50   Fame is better than any food.

   6.50a   Fame is better than any triumph.

6.51   Preparedness is better than potentiality.

6.52   Better a foal than a strong run[ner ?].

6.53   Appropriateness is better than turbulence.

6.54   Better affection than submission.

6.55   Cordiality is better than fomenting discord.

6.56   Better trustworthiness than a promise.

   6.56a   Better an attempt than a promise.

6.57   Well-being is better than learning.

6.58   Peace is better than a successful war.

6.59   Better a good wife than an exalted family.

6.60   Repose is better than bitterness.

6.52 luchair $N_{1,2,3}$: laurchauri Y_1 : laurchuari Y_2 : *om.* L || tindrith N_1 : trenrioth $N_{2,3}$: tenrith $Y_{1,2}$: *om.* L

6.53 caimseta N_1 : caoimseda N_2 : caintsed N_3 : caimsetu $Y_{1,2}$: *om.* L || cucilche N_1 : cucailce N_2 : coccuilce N_3 : cucuilgu $Y_{1,2}$: *om.* L

6.54 cridei N_1 : craide N_2 : crid(h)i $Y_{1,2}$ L_2 : cridhiu L_3 || gialla $N_{1,2}$ $L_{1,3}$: giallna N_3 : giallu L_2

6.55 grisaib N_1 : griosadh N_2 : grios– N_3 : gressaib $Y_{1,2}$: grissadh L_3

6.56 taircsi $N_{1,2}$: tairgsi N_3 : tairisiu $Y_{1,2}$ L_1 : tairisi L_2 : *om.* L_3 || tarngire N_1 : tairrngire N_2 L_3 : tairngere N_3 Y_2 : tarrngere Y_1 : tairngire L_1 : tairngiri L_2

6.57 soburthan N_1 $Y_{1,2}$: sobartan N_2 : sobharth– N_3 : sobart(h)ain $L_{1,2,3}$: soburthon X_1 || saithe $N_{1,2}$: saoithe N_3 : suithi $Y_{1,2}$ L_2 : suithe $L_{1,3}$: ina imad X_1

6.58 sith $N_{2,3}$ $L_{2,3}$ || sochogadh N_2 : sochog[. . .] N_3 : sococodh Y_1 : sococudh Y_2 : sochacad L_2 : socagad L_3 : ina socogad X_1

6.59 soiben N_2 : [. . .] N_3 : sob– Y_1 : sobur Y_2 : sobean L_3 || soceneoil N_1 : soicenel N_2 : [. . .]c(h)inel N_3 L_3 : soc(h)iniul $Y_{1,2}$: sochenel L_2

6.60 <súan> *om.* L_1 || serb(h)a N_1 L_3 : serbad N_2 : searbha N_3 : serbae Y_1 : serbæ Y_2 : sirba L_2 : *om.* L_1

6.61 Ferr carae cormaim.
6.62 Ferr airmitiu sáith.
6.63 Ferr cíall caínchruth.
6.64 Ferr cloth cumaid.
6.65 Ferr comae coimdiud.
6.66 Ferr áithe opud.
6.67 Ferr buide dígbáil.
6.68 Ferr aire íarraid.
6.69 Ferr aicsiu aititin.
  6.69a Ferr aititiu aicsin.
6.70 Ferr bás bithbiniu.
  6.70a Ferr bás bithainim.
6.71 Ferr anae fognam.
6.72 Ferr astud aimiris.
6.73 Ferr rann répiund.
6.74 Ferr rath rolgad.
6.75 Ferr réide rogaís.
6.76 Ferr rous rúathur.
6.77 Ferr gáes gaisciud.
6.78 Ferr goire imbiud.
6.79 Ferr greimm grefiul.

6.61 cara $N_{1,2,3}$ $Y_{1,2}$ $L_{1,2,3}$ X_1 || cormaim $N_{1,2}$ $Y_{1,2}$: corma[. . .] N_3 : coirm $L_{1,2,3}$: ina cuirm X_1 : *also* ina conmir X_1

6.62 airmiti N_1 : airmidi N_2 : airmidiu $Y_{1,2}$: *om.* N_3 L || saite N_1 : *om.* N_3 L

6.63 caincruth N_1 $Y_{1,2}$ L_2 : caoncruth N_2 : caoinchruth N_3 : caencruth L_3 : ina cæmcruth X_1

6.64 cloith Y_1 : *om.* L || comhuidh N_3 : cubaidh Y_1 : cubuidh Y_2 : *om.* L

6.65 comaid N_1 : cum– N_2 : comhuidh N_3 : coma $Y_{1,2}$ $L_{1,3}$: cuma L_2 || coimd– N_2 : coimdigh N_3 L_3 : coemdiud $Y_{1,2}$: coimtid L_1 : comthid L_2

6.66 it(h)e $N_{1,2}$ L_3 X_1 : *om.* N_3 : ai[c]hi Y_1 : aithi Y_2 : athe $L_{1,2}$ || obad(h) N_1 $L_{2,3}$: ob– N_2 : *om.* N_3 : aopudh $Y_{1,2}$: opad L_1 : ina cobadh X_1

6.67 buithe N_3 : buidi Y_1 X_1 : bude L_1 : buigi L_2 || dibail N_1 : dioghbhail $N_{2,3}$: ina dighb– X_1

6.68 airiaraid [written as one word] L_2 : are L_3 : fairi X_1 || iarr– N_2 : iaraid(h) N_3 Y_1 X_1 : iaruidh Y_2 : *also* ina iar– X_1

6.69 aicsi $N_{1,2,3}$ $Y_{1,2}$ || aititiu L_1 : aiti L_2 : aiditiu L_3 : aitidin N_1 : aititiud N_2 : aididiugha N_3 : aititin $Y_{1,2}$ || acsin L_1 : tuicsi L_2 : aigsin L_3

6.70 bass Y_2 || bithainim(h) $N_{1,2,3}$ $L_{2,3}$: bithbiniu $Y_{1,2}$: bithanim L_1

6.61 A friend is better than ale.

6.62 Better [to have] respect than one's fill.

6.63 Good sense is better than fair form.

6.64 Better a good reputation than grief.

6.65 Better [to agree to] terms than [suffer] confiscation.

6.66 Sharp words are better than a refusal.

6.67 Gratitude is better than privation.

6.68 Increase is better than a fosterage-fee.

6.69 Better to see than to consent.

   6.69a Better to consent than to see.

6.70 Death [for the criminal] is better than persistent crime.

   6.70a Death is better than a lasting blemish.

6.71 Wealth is better than rendering service.

6.72 Certainty is better than doubt.

6.73 Sharing is better than rending.

6.74 Better a boon than great concession.

6.75 Steadiness is better than great wisdom.

6.76 Knowledge is better than aggressiveness.

6.77 Wisdom is better than weapons.

6.78 Filial maintenance is better than abundance.

6.79 Control is better than chaos.

6.71 ana $N_{1,2}$ $L_{1,2,3}$ X_1 : [. . .] N_3 : anæ $Y_{1,2}$ || urfognum N_1 : urf(h)og(h)nam(h) $N_{2,3}$: auognam $Y_{1,2}$: foglaim L_2 : ina ancis X_1

6.72 asda N_1 : astad(h) $N_{2,3}$: asdadh L_3 || aimiris N_1 Y_1 L_3 : aimirse N_2 : am(h)iris N_3 Y_2 : amaires L_1 : amurus L_2

6.73 roind N_1 $L_{2,3}$: roinn N_2 : rand L_1 || rebaind N_1 : reb– N_2 : reabainne N_3 : repinn $Y_{1,2}$: repind L_1 : rebad $L_{2,3}$

6.74 rat N_2 : *om.* L || rolag– N_2 : rolgud $Y_{1,2}$: *om.* L

6.75 reidhi N_2 : redhe Y_1 : *om.* L_1 : reigi L_2 : reige X_1 || roghaois $N_{2,3}$: rogæs Y_1 : rogoes Y_2 : *om.* L_1 : rogair L_2 : ina rogaos X_1

6.76 rus $N_{1,2,3}$: ruus $Y_{1,2}$: rois L_2 || ruat(h)har $N_{1,2,3}$ Y_2 L_2 : ruthar L_3

6.77 gais N_1 $L_{1,2,3}$: gaeis N_2 : gaois N_3 : gæs Y_1 : goes Y_2 || gaisced $N_{1,3}$ L_2 : gaiscc– N_2 : gascudh Y_1 : gaiscudh Y_2 : gasced L_1 : gaisgedh L_3

6.78 gaire $N_{1,2,3}$ $Y_{1,2}$ $L_{1,2,3}$ || imad(h) N_1 Y_2 $L_{2,3}$: iomad $N_{2,3}$: immudh Y_1 : immad L_1

6.79 greim $N_{1,2,3}$ $Y_{1,2}$ L_3 : gremm L_1 : grem L_2 || grefel $N_{1,2}$ L_2 : grifel N_3 : crephul Y_1 : crapul Y_2 : *gref*el L_1 : greifheal L_3

6.80   Ferr lúaithe dígáirsi.
6.81   Ferr lín lobrai.
   6.81a   Ferr lén lobrai.
6.82   Ferr léire laimthinchi.
6.83   Ferr leth lánetiug.
6.84   Ferr fróech forbbu.
6.85   Ferr dúthracht dligiud.
6.86   Ferr mag mórsléib.
6.87   Ferr mruig mlichtaib.
6.88   Ferr fír frithoíb.
   6.88a   Ferr fír fertaib.
6.89   Ferr sothced séitchi.
6.90   Ferr slóg suidigther.
6.91   Ferr búar bréithir.
6.92   Ferr grés sous.
6.93   Ferr becc n-érai.
6.94   Ferr cloud cummu.
6.95   Ferr ré ráthaib.
6.96   Ferr búaine áini.
6.97   Ferr drochdán dílmaini.
6.98   Ferr engnam eniuch.
6.99   Ferr degmuirn dúthchus.

6.80 luithe N_1 : loice N_2 : loithe N_3 : luaithi $Y_{1,2}$ L_2 : luathi L_1 || digraisi L_2

6.81 lin (*no e above line*) N_1 : lin $N_{2,3}$ Y_1 : leghenn Y_2 : *om.* L || lubra $N_{1,3}$: lubræ N_2 : lobræ Y_1 : liubhra Y_2 : *om.* L

6.82 lere $Y_{1,2}$: leri L_2 || laimnide N_1 : laimtnighe N_2 : lainmhidhe N_3 : laimnithi $Y_{1,2}$: lamide L_1 : laimdidi L_2 : laimidhe L_3

6.83 leath N_3 : let Y_2 : *om.* L || lanetech N_1 : laineiteach $N_{2,3}$: lanethiug Y_1 : lanetiug– Y_2 : *om.* L

6.84 fraech N_1 : fræch N_2 : fraoch N_3 : *om.* L || forbæ N_1 : forba $N_{2,3}$: *om.* L

6.85 dutracht N_1 : dathracht Y_2 : *om.* L || dlig(h)ed(h) $N_{1,2}$: dligheadh N_3 : dlig– $Y_{1,2}$: *om.* L

6.86 mad(h) N_1 Y_2 || morsliab(h) $N_{1,3}$ $Y_{1,2}$ $L_{1,2}$: moirsliab(h) N_2 L_3

6.87 mbruithe N_1 : mbrughaidh N_2 : mbrugh N_3 : mbruig $Y_{1,2}$: *om.* L || mblichtai N_1 : mbliocht $N_{2,3}$: mbli[cht]aib Y_1 : mblichtaib Y_2 : *om.* L

6.88 fior $N_{2,3}$: *om.* N_1 L || fertuib N_2 : feartoibh N_3 : frithaib(h) $Y_{1,2}$: *om.* N_1 L

6.80 Promptness is better than impetuosity.
6.81 Better a full complement than incapacity.
  6.81a Better a setback than incapacity.
6.82 Diligence is better than audacity.
6.83 Half is better than a complete refusal.
6.84 Better the heather than fighting.
6.85 Willingness is better than being under obligation.
6.86 Better an open plain than a moorland.
6.87 Better farmland than milk-yield [from it].
6.88 Better truth than its antithesis.
  6.88a Proof is better than grave mounds.
6.89 Good fortune is better than a consort.
6.90 Better a crowd that is set in order.
6.91 Cattle are better than a promise.
6.92 A craft is better than learning.
6.93 Better a little than a refusal.
6.94 Change is better than destruction.
6.95 A respite is better than securities.
6.96 Constancy is better than a bright wit.
6.97 A lowly craft is better than idleness.
6.98 Better skill than honour.
6.99 Enthusiasm is better than inherent ability.

6.89 sothced $Y_{1,2}$: *om.* N L || <séitchi> *om.* N L

6.90 <slóg> *om.* N_1 L || suid*iu*gadh N_2 : suidhiughadh N_3 : suidigt(h)ir $Y_{1,2}$: *om.* N_1 L

6.91 <búar> *om.* N L || briathar $Y_{1,2}$: *om.* N L

6.92 gress $Y_{1,2}$: *om.* N || souss $Y_{1,2}$: soos L_1 : *om.* N

6.93 beg $N_{2,3}$: *om.* N_1 : bec $L_{1,2}$ X_1 : beag L_3 || era N_2 $L_{1,3}$: eura N_3 : *om.* N_1 : erai L_2 : ina era X_1

6.94 cloudh Y_1 L_3 : clough Y_2 : colud L_1 : cloth L_2 : *om.* N || cuma $Y_{1,2}$ $L_{1,3}$: cumma L_2 : *om.* N

6.95 ren L_3 : *om.* N || <ráthaib> *om.* N

6.96 buane $Y_{1,2}$ L_1 : *om.* L_3 N || ane $Y_{1,2}$ L_1 : aine L_2 : *om.* L_3 N

6.97 <drochdán> *om.* N || dilmaine Y_1 $L_{1,2,3}$: dilmuine Y_2 : *om.* N

6.98 engnum enech L_2 *only*

6.99 degnurm duchas L_2 *only*

6.100 Ferr anae iluch.

6.101 Ferr gres múcnaid.

6.102 Ferr rosc dígbud.

7.1   Maith dán ecnae.

7.2   Do·gní ríg di bocht.

7.3   Do·gní ánsruth di esirt.

7.4   Do·gní sochenél di docheníul.

7.5   Do·gní gáeth di báeth.

7.6   Maith a thosach.

7.7   Ferr a deired.

7.8   Airmitnech isin cenntur.

7.9   Lógmar isin alltur.

7.10 Ní derchoíntech fri deired,

7.11 .i. fri tabairt nime dó.

7.12 Doilig dán láechdacht.

7.13 Ní airdirc,

7.14 ⁊ is dérgnae a duí.

7.15 Gnímach duthain a suí.

6.100 ana ilach L$_2$ *only*

6.101 gres mucnaid L$_2$ *only*

6.102 rosc digbad L$_2$ *only*

7.1 <maith> *om.* N$_2$ Y$_{1,2}$ L$_1$ || <dán> *om.* N$_2$ || ecna N$_1$ L$_1$: *om.* N$_2$: eagna N$_3$: eccna Y$_{1,2}$
: eacna L$_2$: eagnai L$_3$: maith dán egna X$_1$

7.2 doni N$_{1,3}$ Y$_{1,2}$ L$_3$: *om.* N$_2$ || ri N$_{1,3}$: *om.* N$_2$ || do N$_{1,3}$ Y$_{1,2}$ L$_{1,2,3}$: *om.* N$_2$ || <bocht> *om.*
N$_2$

7.3 doni N$_1$ Y$_{1,2}$ L$_3$: *om.* N$_2$: ⁊ L$_2$ || ansruith N$_3$: *om.* N$_2$: anadh Y$_{1,2}$: anrath L$_1$: anrad(h)
L$_{2,3}$ || do N$_1$ Y$_{1,2}$ L$_{1,2,3}$: d' N$_3$: *om.* N$_2$ || eisirt N$_1$: *om.* N$_2$: eseart N$_3$: esseirt Y$_1$:
eisseirt Y$_2$: essirt L$_1$: esert L$_2$: eiseart L$_3$

7.4 do N$_3$: *om.* N$_2$: doni Y$_2$ L$_3$: d– L$_1$: ⁊ L$_2$ || sochinel N$_{1,3}$: *om.* N$_2$: soc(h)enel Y$_1$ L$_1$:
socineol Y$_2$: soichinel L$_3$ || do N$_{1,3}$ Y$_{1,2}$ L$_{1,2,3}$: *om.* N$_2$ || d(h)oc(h)inel N$_{1,3}$ L$_3$: *om.* N$_2$
: doc(h)en*iu*l Y$_1$ L$_1$: docineol Y$_2$: dochenel L$_2$

7.5 doni Y$_2$ L$_3$: *om.* N$_2$: d– L$_1$: ⁊ L$_2$ || gæth N$_1$ Y$_1$ L$_{1,2,3}$: *om.* N$_2$: gaoth N$_3$ || do N$_{1,3}$ Y$_{1,2}$
L$_{1,2,3}$: *om.* N$_2$ || bæth N$_1$ Y$_{1,2}$ L$_{1,2,3}$: *om.* N$_2$: bhaoth N$_3$

7.6 <maith> *om.* N$_2$ || <a> *om.* N$_2$ || t(h)ossach Y$_{1,2}$ L$_{1,2}$

7.7 fearr N$_3$ Y$_1$ L$_3$: *om.* N$_2$: maith L$_2$ || <a> *om.* N$_2$ || dered N$_1$ L$_{1,2}$: *om.* N$_2$: dereadh L$_3$
: ferr dan forba X$_1$

6.100 Prosperity is better than exultation.

6.101 Better an effort than being repressed.

6.102 Better to incite than to stifle.

7.1   Learning is a beneficial occupation.

7.2   It makes a king of a poor person.

7.3   It makes an accomplished person of a landless one.

7.4   It makes an exalted family of a lowly one.

7.5   It makes a wise person of a fool.

7.6   Its commencement is good.

7.7   Its end is better.

7.8   It is respected in this world.

7.9   It is precious in the next.

7.10   It is not despairing concerning the end,

7.11   i.e. bestowing heaven upon him.

7.12   The martial life is a distressful occupation.

7.13   It is not renowned,

7.14   and its unskilled practitioner is undistinguished.

7.15   Its expert is toiling [and] transitory.

7.8 airmitin N_1 : *om.* N_2 : airmhidneach N_3 : airmidnech L_2 : airbidneach L_3 || hisin Y_1 : *om.* N_2 : isa L_3 || cennt– N_1 : *om.* N_2 : ccentar N_3 : cendtur Y_2 : chentur L_1 : ceantar L_3

7.9 log(h)mur N_1 Y_2 L_3 : *om.* N_2 : lodmar L_2 || isi[. .] Y_2 : issind L_1 : isan L_3 : *om.* N_2 || altur N_1 L_1 : *om.* N_2 : alltar N_3 L_3 : nalltur Y_2 L_2

7.10 [ní] Y_2 : *om.* N_2 || derc(h)aintech N_1 $Y_{1,2}$: *om.* N_2 : dercaointech N_3 : dærchain L_2 : dercainteach L_3 || <fri> *om.* N_2 || a dheired N_3 : *om.* N_2 : deireadh $Y_{1,2}$: dered L_1 : dead L_2 : dereadh L_3

7.11 <.i. fri> *om.* N_2 || tabairt N_1 : *om.* N_2 || foglaim L_2 : neime Y_2 : *om.* N_2 : nimi L_2 || <dó> *om.* N_2 L_2 : don anmoin N_3 : don anmain L_3

7.12 doil– N_1 : dolig L_1 : *om.* N_2 || <dán> *om.* N_2 || læchdacht N_1 Y_1 $L_{1,2,3}$: *om.* N_2 : læchtacht Y_2 : doilig dán læchact X_1

7.13 <ní> *om.* N_2 || horrderc N_1 : *om.* N_2 : hoirrdherc N_3 : herdairce $Y_{1,2}$: erdairc L_1 : hairrdirc L_2 : hairrddirc L_3

7.14 <ɔ> *om.* N_2 || <is> *om.* $N_{1,2}$ || dergna N_1 $Y_{1,2}$ $L_{1,3}$: *om.* N_2 : dercnaigh N_2 : dergnai L_2 || a d(h)ai N_1 L_3 : *om.* N_2 : a dhaigh N_3 : a diu L_2

7.15 gniom– N_3 : *om.* N_2 : gnimuch L_1 || <duthain> *om.* N_2 || a sai N_1 L_2 : *om.* N_2 : a saoi N_3 : a ssai L_3

7.16   It tregtaig a bí.

     7.16a   It étradaig a bí.

7.17   It ifernaig a mairb.

7.18   Ní·timnai athair dia mac.

     7.18a   Nír·thimna athair dia mac.

7.19   Mairg dán láechdacht,

     7.19a   Mairg dianid dán láechdacht.

7.20   mani·tair aithrige mór.

7.16 <it> *om.* N_2 || .i. N_3 : itreg L_2 : a L_3 : tregdaid N_1 : *om.* N_2 : treagd– N_3 : tregtaidh Y_1 : tregaidh Y_2 : etradaig L_1 : daithi L_2 : tedradhaigh L_3 || a bi $N_{1,3}$ $Y_{1,2}$ $L_{1,3}$: *om.* N_2 : a mbai L_2 : ni suthain a mbi X_1

7.17 <it> *om.* N_2 L_2 : a N_3 : at L_3 || ifernaig N_1 : *om.* N_2 : hiofern N_3 : ifernnaigh $Y_{1,2}$: iffernaig L_1 : iferdaich L_2 : ifearnaigh L_3 || a mmairb L_1 : *om.* N_2 : ifernnaig a mairbh X_1

7.18 ni t(h)imain N_1 $L_{2,3}$: *om.* N_2 : ni thiomain N_3 : ni timnai Y_1 : nimtimnai Y_2 : nir thimna L_1 || ath– Y_1 : *om.* N_2 || da mac L_1 : *om.* N_2 : ni thimuin athar dia mac X_1

7.16 Its living [practitioners] are pierced through.

   7.16a   Its living are lustful.

7.17 Its dead are bound for hell.

7.18 A father does not bequeath [it] to his son.

   7.18a   Let not a father bequeath [it] to his son.

7.19 The martial life is a woeful occupation,

   7.19a   Woe to him whose occupation is the martial life.

7.20 unless a great repentance should be achieved.

7.19 mairg dan N_1 : *om.* N_2 : maircc darab dan N_3 : mairg dianid dan Y_1 L_1 : mairg dianadh dan Y_2 : is mairg dan dan [m] L_2 : mairg dianadh dan in L_3 || laoechdacht N_1 : *om.* N_2 : laochdacht N_3 : læchdacht Y_1 $L_{1,2,3}$: læchtacht Y_2 : mairg dianad dan læchact X_1

7.20 muna thair N_1 : muna ttair N_3 : *om.* N_2 Y L || aithrighe moir N_1 : aithr–e N_3 : *om.* N_2 Y L

Notes

§ 1 AD·COTA

§ 1 The O.Ir. verb *ad·cota* has the basic meaning "gets, obtains". Sjoestedt-Jonval has cited an example from the glosses where it has the meaning "to have" ("Études sur le temps et l'aspect," 231–32). This latter meaning is a logical outcome of the resultative/potential sense of this verb discussed by McCone (*Early Irish Verb*, 127–30). The potentiality inherent in its semantics is displayed by the development of the prototonic stem ·*éta* into Mid.Ir. *fétaid* "is able, can", which yields Mod.Ir. *féadann* (*Early Irish Verb*, 198). The resultative/potential sense makes the dictionary meanings of "gets, obtains, procures" inadequate for translating many of these maxims. Smith uniformly translated *ad·cota* as "begets". I have relied on a far greater variety in translating this word — "entails, engenders, results in, leads to" etc. — than for any other initial word among the maxims.

1.1 There is an alternation between *saidbres* (Rec. N) and *saidbre* (Rec. Y). For the third word L$_2$ has the form *soma* which should be understood as the alliterating synonym *sommae* "wealth". For the third word L$_{1,3,4}$ preserve finite verbal forms. L$_1$ has the version *Ad·cota sochell roda·biatha* and I have followed Gwynn who translated it as "Generosity begets one that feeds it" ("Senbriathra Fithail," 268). The form is 3sg. pres. subj. of *bíathaid* "feeds, nourishes, supports", with the legal sense of "provides refection for". The Class C infixed pronoun -*da*- can be either 3sg. f. or 3pl. Gwynn translated the maxim with the 3sg. f. pronoun evidently referring back to *sochell*. It is also possible to think of *sochell* as a self-perpetuating phenomenon. That is, we can translate it as "He gets generosity who feeds it". If we choose to translate the infixed pronoun as 3pl. then L_1 offers us a definition of sorts for someone who has the quality of *sochell*, "one who feeds them". $L_{3,4}$ have the form *robiatta* (= *ro·bíatha*?) without a pronoun. Compare §§ 1.14 *Ad·cota dochell cesacht*, 1.32 *Ad·cota daidbre dochraiti*, and 1.65 *Ad·cota bocht a bíathad*.

1.2 This maxim has a finite verbal form as its third element. The form is the suppletive 3sg. pres. subj. of *do·beir* "gives, places" (*GOI*, 469 § 759 IIb). Gwynn translated this maxim as "Good-will begets one that gives" ("Senbriathra Fithail," 268). It is also possible to translate as "He gets [his] desire who gives". A good example of the juxtaposition of *dúthracht* and *do·rata* comes from an O.Ir. homily: *Dorata in talam a toirthiu (?), dorata int aier a bróinu, dorata a mmuir a íascrada (?) ... do cách ... asa dúthracht domelam; dorata Día a chétchutrummae dó* translated as "May the earth give its fruits; may the air give its showers; may the sea give its fishes ... to everyone ... whose goodwill we enjoy; may God give him a hundred fold ..." (Strachan, "Old Irish Homily," 5, 9). In *Triads* no. 225 *dúthracht* is listed as one of "three welcomes of the ale-house" which Meyer translated as "kindliness".

1.3 Rec. Y witnesses read *cruth* rather than *caínchruth*. The prefixed adjective *caín* "fine, fair" is frequently used in this text, §§ 1.11, 4.27, 5.15, 6.37, 6.50a, 6.63. The diphthong of *caín* has been explained as due to borrowing from Britannic (*Lexique* C 16), and the adjective *cain* "good, fair", without a diphthong, must be considered as a possible variant here (*Lexique* C 15). Contrast § 6.63 *Ferr cíall caínchruth* which makes a definite value judgement preferring "good sense" to "good appearance". Compounds of *cíall* are found at §§ 1.1, 1.14.

1.4 Several of the manuscripts show variations of this maxim. $L_{3,4}$ read *ad*[*·cota*] *druis derge no digna*, Y_2 reads *acotta druis duigna no terghe* and N_2 has the additional maxim *atc. druis dergli*. Thus a possible variant with *déirge* "forsaking, quitting, desertion, abandonment", or possibly *derge* "redness, flushing, intensity, fervour", is represented in every recension. Compare § 1.8 *Ad·cota déirge líamnai*. Questions of sexual morality are frequently addressed in the wisdom literature. One *speculum* poem contains the line *adaltras coilles cach clú* "adultery which damages each reputation" (O'Donoghue, "Advice to a Prince," 50 § 35). *Triads* no. 193 lists the three signs of *drúis* as *bág, imresain, condailbe* "boasting, contending, partiality". At *Triads* no. 83 we find listed among "the three deaf things of the world" *cosc mná báithe do drúis* "keeping a wanton woman from lechery".

1.5 This maxim does not appear in Rec. Y. *Triads* no. 82 lists *Trí buirb an betha* "three rude ones (*borb*) of the world". *TC* § 32.6 includes within the "code of ridicule" among the Irish a *fer báeth borb brasbríathrach* "a silly, crude, big-worded man".

1.6 This example is the only citation for *fáiscre* in *DIL*, which, as it notes, O'Clery glosses as *foiréigean* "violence". O'Clery quotes this maxim with the explanation that *anté do ní foiréigean dligheadh sé ro eigean do dhénamh air* "he who does violence deserves to have violence done to him" (Miller, "O'Clery's Glossary," 414). *DIL* lists *fáiscre* with a long *a*. It is evidently an io-stem neuter vb.n. (*GOI*, 449 § 725). If the *a* is short it could be derived from *fo·feiscren, fo·faiscren* "decays, fails(?)". However, *feiscre* (*feiscred*) io.n "shrinking, contracting", is the vb.n. for this verb, derived in Lewis and Pedersen from **fo-ess-crin-* (*Comparative Grammar*, 354 § 528). If we are to accept the *a* as long, it may have developed by analogy with the semantically similar verb *fáiscid* "presses, squeezes", vb.n. *fáscud*. On the other hand, the meanings of "repression, oppression" could be explained by deriving *fáiscre* from the verbal stem *fáisc-* and a suffix like *-r(a)e*, as found in *bélre, godrae* (O'Brien, "Varia IV," 157). These latter words, however, are derived from a noun and an adjective respectively, not from verbal stems. *DIL* translates this maxim as "Coercion engenders tyranny" (s.v. *fáiscre*).

1.8 This maxim is found only in N_1. *Líamain*, a late vb.n. of *líid* "charges, accuses", often implies an accusation of sexual misconduct. I have treated it as a fem. i-stem. See § 1.4 and notes for variants with *déirge*.

1.9 *Lescae* (*leisce*) means not only "laziness" but implies an unwillingness to act. It seems improbable that the last word is *foistine* "state of rest, sojourning", despite the fact that in this text there is ample evidence for the use of *ai* for *oi* (*gaire* for *goire*, see §§ 3.20, 3.22, 6.78). *Lescae* nearly always implies a negative quality, but *foistine*, in an abstract sense, conveys the positive notion of "composure, equanimity". There are many examples of *fáitsine* "prophesying, augury" with metathesis of *s* and *t*, especially in Mid.Ir. I have extrapolated a meaning of "guess, surmise, conjecture" for *fáitsine* based on a similar saying found in the *Aibidil: airdmesach cech lesc* "every lazy person is calculating" (Smith, "Alphabet of Cuigne," 66 § 56). *Airdmes* u,[m], is a vb.n. formation from **air-di-mid-* (Pender, "K. Meyers Nachträge," 330). It has the meaning "act of estimating, calculating" and is also recorded in the sense of "foretelling" (*DIL* A 188.76–78). See also the glossary entry *airdmhes .i. nélladóirecht* "cloud-divination, nephelomancy" (Pearson, "Medieval Glossary," 62). Compare *do·midethar* "weighs, measures, estimates" in the meaning "guesses, solves a riddle" (Breatnach, "Varia IV," 195). I have, therefore, postulated a similar semantic range for *fáitsine* in what is otherwise a very obscure maxim. See § 1.41 for a compound of *lesc*.

1.10 This maxim, which is not found in Rec. L, is ambiguous despite its apparent simplicity. *Serc* can mean "love", both sacred and profane, as well as the object of love, whether a person or thing. *Bríathar* "word, utterance, saying" extends to more specific meanings like "promise, pledge" or "blessing". This maxim is perhaps meant to echo the biblical *ex abundantia enim cordis os loquitur* "from the abundance of the heart the mouth speaks" (Luke 6:45; Matthew 12:34).

1.11 T. F. O'Rahilly described the semantics of *buide* as meaning not so much "thanks" as "goodwill", specifically the goodwill of another towards you as a result of your own actions. *Buide* may imply that one curries favour or goodwill by being subservient or ingratiating ("Tuillim Buide," 206). *TC* § 30.5 reads *ba becda fri becdataid a ndéntar do thol* "be humble with the humble when your will is being done". For examples which stress humility, see §§ 1.16 *Ad·cota umlae áilgini*, 1.61 *Ad·cota umal ordan*, § 2.7 *Ba umal corba úasal*.

1.12 This maxim is not found in Rec. L. Binchy explained *frithfolad* as a counter-obligation; it is what is owed in return ("Irish History and Law," 23–30). For example, *Audacht Morainn* states *nach frithfoluth rodn·dligther to·rata* "let him give any reciprocal service which is due from him" (Kelly, *Audacht*, 10 § 30 line 78). I take this maxim to mean that proper behaviour on the part of one person merits similar behaviour on the part of those he comes in contact with.

1.13 This maxim is not found in Rec. L. While this maxim states simply that one thing results from the other, another maxim, § 3.15 *Dligid díbe dimmolud*, implies a value judgement, "Stinginess deserves to be disparaged". See other examples of *díbe* at §§ 1.60, 4.3.

1.14 This maxim is not found in Rec. L. Contrast this maxim with § 1.1. In *Audacht Morainn* we find the line *to·léci dochell do clothaib* "Inhospitality yields to hospitality", with the variant reading for *clothaib* in NLS MS Adv. 72.1.42 being *tsoicill* [i.e., *sochell*] ⁊ *clotha* (Kelly, *Audacht*, 16 § 54f line 123).

1.15 This maxim is not found in Rec. L. Compare § 1.23 *Ad·cota gáes airmitin*. *Cloth* is usually plural in early texts, as it is here. For other examples of *cloth*, see § 1.69 where it is plural, and §§ 6.50, 6.64 where it is singular (but see discussions).

1.16 This maxim is not found in Rec. L. Compare § 1.11 and note for other examples of *umlae* and *umal*. One gnomic poem contains the line *eochair ecna umla* "humility unlocks wisdom" (Meyer, "Mitteilungen [1908]," 270 § 1).

1.17 This maxim is not found in Rec. L. I have restored *aithgne* "recognition, getting to know", which is often attested as *aichne*, rather than following Smith who restored *aithne* "depositing, entrusting for safe keeping" (*"Senbriathra Fithail,"* 63). Although his suggestion makes good sense, *aithne* is not attested as *aichne*. However, in defence of Smith's interpretation, *Triads* no. 249 lists *aithne* "giving a thing into keeping" as one of the "three dark things of the world". As I have listed it, this maxim is an Old Irish equivalent of the modern English saying "Familiarity breeds contempt".

1.18 This maxim is not found in Rec. L. Using similar words Broccán's *Hymn* says of St Brigit *nīpu for sēotu santach* "She was not greedy for treasures" (*Thes.* ii, 328.1).

1.19 In Rec. N the variant reading for *dimdae* is *toirnem*, a Mid.Ir. development of *tairniud* "lowering, abating, reducing". *Ad·cota díummus toirnem* is similar to the line in Rec. A of *Audacht Morainn* which reads *dligid cach diumsach tairniud* (Kelly, *Audacht*, 65 § 34c line 114 = Thurneysen, "Morands Fürstenspiegel," 84 § 34c). Compare § 3.13 *Dligid díummus dermat*. One *speculum* poem has the line *tairnem na diumsa ro dlecht* "the humbling of pride is proper" (O'Donoghue, "Advice to a Prince," 45 § 5). *TC* § 3.23, in answer to the question "what is best for the good of a tribe", lists *fianna cen díummus* "warrior bands without arrogance". In the law-tract on clientship, *Cáin Aigillne*, we have the line *ecubus cach ndiumus domidider mamu* "without conscience is every prideful one who despises obligations" (*AL* ii, 320.2 = *CIH* ii, 496.31 = Thurneysen, "Aus dem irischen Recht I," 386 § 51). Smith compared this maxim and its variants to the English proverb "Pride goeth before a fall" (*"Senbriathra Fithail,"* 11).

1.20 Each recension supports a different and defensible reading for this maxim (§ 1.69 may be a variant). The primary reading must be considered in the light of maxims which are concerned with sexual mores, §§ 1.4, 1.8, 1.21, 1.60, 4.7, 4.12. *Carna* [?< Lat. *caro* "flesh"] implies "lust, lechery". The law-tract *Di Astud Chirt ⁊ Dligid* states that the *fedb* "widow", *ainder* "non-virgin", and *bé carna* "prostitute" may receive the same *díre* "honour-price" as a maiden if they do penance for, and further refrain from, their multiple cohabitations (*AL* v, 448.1–3 = *CIH* i, 230.14–15, 24; Power, "Classes of Women," 108). An entry in O'Davoren states *bé charna .i. merdrech, ar dia ndech in ben co cuicir is bé charna* "*bé carna* i.e., a prostitute, for if a woman goes with five men she is a *bé carna*" (Stokes, "O'Davoren's Glossary," 231 § 213; discussed in Power, "Classes of Women," 108). In *Senbríathra* § 12 the answer to the question "What is the worst kind of woman?" is *bé carna* [L₁ = *bé chairn*, L₃,₄ = *be cairn*, N₃ = *be charna*] (Smith, "*Senbriathra Fithail*," 58). The use of *cairn* instead of *carna* is elucidated by the etymological gloss included in O'Davoren (Stokes, "O'Davoren's Glossary," 231 § 213). See Smith's discussion for additional details ("*Senbriathra Fithail*," 58).

It is also possible to read *carna* in its literal sense as "meat" and interpret the maxim as meaning that food follows drink. Such a reading is supported by a quatrain which describes the "dues of summer's end". The first line of the quatrain reads *carna, cuirm, cnoimes, cadla* "meat, ale, nutmast, tripe" (Meyer, *Hibernica Minora*, 49).

Rec. N offers the variant *Ad·cota cuirm cornu* which Smith dismisses as a corruption possibly introduced by a Christian scribe opposed to the pagan love of drinking. However, the early penitentials and monastic rules make it clear that drinking was frequently indulged in by monks and clerics. For example, an O.Ir. penitential states that any monk who eats and drinks beer until he vomits must do thirty days penance (Bieler, *Penitentials*, 261 § 15). St Brigit is credited with the miracle of creating enough ale from one sack of malt for all the churches to celebrate Easter (Ó hAodha, *Bethu Brigte*, 7, 24–25 § 21). In the "Teaching of Máel Ruain" Dublitir, contrary to Máel Ruain's teaching, allows his monks to drink ale and claims that his monks will enter heaven along with Máel Ruain's (Gwynn, *Rule of Tallaght*, 24–25 § 40).

A proverb for an uncompleted task similar to our maxim was once current in saga. The proverb reads *ro budh c[h]uirm gan chorna* "it would be [like] ale without drinking horns" (Jackson, *Cath Maighe Léna*, 55.1408–9). The variant *Ad·cota cuirm cornu* might therefore imply the natural order of things which follow one from the other.

1.21 As presented, the readings for this maxim are from Rec. N and Y, with the variant given at 1.21a supported by the reading *eclai* from L₂ (discussed below). *Echlach* is attested in the meaning "prostitute" or "concubine". It was unlawful to pay an excessive "bride-price" (*coibche*; see discussion at § 3.25) for an *echlach* (*AL* iv, 56.28–31 = *CIH* i, 221.18–19; Power, "Classes of Women," 100). *Echlach* is often interchangeable with *merdrech* (<Lat. *meretrix*; see in connection with *bé carna*, § 1.20). The *echlach* had very little protection, or right of compensation, under the law.

Power noted that she "had no claim, when the connexion ended, to the profit arising from work done by her while it lasted" ("Classes of Women," 101 and discussion 99–103).

An alternative interpretation is supported by the glosses from $Y_{8,9}$ which read *dlighe teachtaire deithneas no luas* "a messenger should have speed or quickness". Evidence for *echlach* "messenger" from *Táin Bó Cúailnge* suggests that this meaning is a late development. C. O'Rahilly noted that, although *echlach* is used thirty-five times with the meaning "messenger" in the Book of Leinster version, it is not used at all in the earlier Rec. I of the *Táin* ("Marcach," 32). *Utmaille* also appears more often in the wisdom-texts with a meaning of "unsteadiness, uncertainty" rather than a meaning expressing overt physical movement. For example, at *TC* § 25.5 "the worst form of arguing before an assembly" is *ái utmaille* "an unsteady arguing". We also find among the "seventeen signs of bad pleading" *utmaille tacrai* "an unsteady argument" or "shifting one's plead-ing" (*TC* § 22.15 = *CIH* vi, 2342.5 = § 9.14 in Appendix 2).

It would be tempting to give the primary reading as *eclach* <*ecal*, as is done in § 1.21a, and which is suggested by L_2 = *eclai*. This reading is supported by the maxim from the *Aibidil* which reads *udmall cach n-ecol* "Every timid person is uneasy" (Smith, "Alphabet of Cuigne," 65 § 54). The sentiment of that maxim is repeated in *TC* § 15.13 *úathmar cech ecal* "every timid person is easily frightened".

Most manuscripts in Rec. L have a maxim with a reading like *etlae / étlae* which would at first appear to be a variant of this maxim. But Rec. Y also contains a maxim with such a reading; so it is treated at the end of this section, at § 1.68, with maxims not found in N_1.

1.22 *Accobur* can carry negative connotations like "greed, lust" as well as the more positive connotations of "desire". In the context of "those things combined in holiness" in *Apgitir Chrábaid* we find the phrase *accobur co fedli* "desire with perseverance" (Hull, "Alphabet of Piety," 58 § 1 line 1). See the note for § 4.13 for a further discussion of *accobur*.

1.23 Compare §§ 1.15 *Ad·cota gáes clotha* and 3.1 *Dligid ecnae airmitin*.

1.24 This maxim is not found in Rec. L. Compare § 3.20 *Dligid sen sogoiri*.

1.25 I have followed the reading of Rec. N here. Rec. L readings are based on *bág* "boast, threat, contest", and Rec. Y offers a choice: Y_1 reads *a[d·cota] bagh no bægul. Báes* "folly, levity" also means "lack of judgement" which results in legal incapacity. *Báegul* "dangerous or hazardous condi-tion" also implies an error in judgement for which the person making the error is legally liable (Binchy, "*Bretha Crólige*," 60). In the *Aibidil* we find the similar saying *cach baíth a báegul* "to every fool his danger" (Smith, "Alphabet of Cuigne," 52 § 32). A legal maxim from *Bretha Étgid* reads *cach breithemain a báegul* "to every judge his legal liability" (*AL* iii, 304.4 = *CIH* i, 292.33 = Smith, "Alphabet of Cuigne," 46 § 1). *Bág* also makes good sense in this context, and would suggest a disparaging attitude towards the traditional picture of heroic martial exploits as depicted in many early sagas.

1.26 *Briugas* means both the function of a *briugu* as dispenser of hospitality, and also "riches, abundance". *Bronnad* has two primary meanings: (1) "destroying, consuming, using up" and (2) "bestowing, giving gifts". Both meanings make sense here. In O'Davoren *briugu* is glossed by *umad* (Stokes, "O'Davoren's Glossary," 248 § 325), and *briugas* is glossed by *imat* (229 § 196) and *umat* (239 § 266), all variants of O.Ir. *imbed* "abundance, excess". O'Davoren also quotes a variant of this maxim as follows: *briuga .i. umad,* [*ut est*] *adcoda briuga bronna*[*d*] (Stokes, "O'Davoren's Glossary," 248 § 325). The practice which anthropologists call "potlatch", whereby the bestower of a gift puts the receiver under obligation to him and can expect some form of reciprocation, seems to be at work here. One's prestige increases with the amount given, not with the amount received. This ritualized giving could reach the point of overt destruction of property. This concept of "potlatch" seems to be encapsulated in the two primary meanings of *bronnad*. The tale *Esnada Tige Buchet* describes what happens to a hospitaller when his generosity is abused (Stokes, "Buchet's House," 18–39; Greene, *Fingal Rónáin*, 27–44). For further examples of *briugas*, or derived words, see §§ 1.66, 6.19.

1.27 This maxim expresses a cautious attitude toward force. It should be read in conjunction with § 1.28. *TC* § 1.29–30 lists among those things "which are best for a king": *drong claidebbémnech ar choimét cacha túaithe, forrána dar crícha* "a sword-beating troop for the protection of each tribe, [and] assaults across borders". This text is less aggressive, but the power of authority is seen as positive in §§ 6.70 *Ferr bás bithbiniu,* 6.79 *Ferr greimm grefiul* (see discussions).

1.28 This maxim is absent from Rec. L; nevertheless, it makes a couplet with the preceding maxim. All manuscripts in Rec. N and Y have Mid.Ir. *barann,* an oblique form of O.Ir. *barae* n.f. Such oblique forms for nom. sg. are already noted in the Glosses (McCone, "Würzburg and Milan Glosses," 91).

1.29 This maxim is ambiguous. *Bil* is explained as "good" in O'Clery (Miller, "O'Clery's Glossary," 372), and in *Sanas Cormaic* we find the entry *bilt*[*h*]*engthach .i. a bellingis* (Meyer, "*Sanas Cormaic*," 16 § 174). On the other hand, O'Davoren glosses *bil* as "bad, evil" and cites this maxim (Stokes, "O'Davoren's Glossary," 230 § 206). Confusion between the prefixed adjective *bil-* and *mil-* is attested in the O.Ir. text "Rule of Ailbe of Emly" where we find the line *Techtaire mláith, mil-tengthach* "A smooth, honey-tongued messenger" which has manuscript variants (*m*)*bláith* and (*m*)*biltengtach* (O Neill, "Rule of Ailbe," 106 § 44).

For O.Ir. *mrath* "treachery, betrayal" all manuscripts read *brath*. The later substitution of *br/bl* for original *mr/ml* (*GOI*, 128 § 211) is recorded in its transitional form *mbr/mbl* at § 6.87 *Ferr m*(*b*)*ruig m*(*b*)*lichtaib*. It is possible to read the third word as *bráth* "judgement, a legal precept". This latter word would make good sense, particularly if *bil* is to be read with a positive meaning. Such a reading would parallel § 1.54 *Ad·cota miltengae breithemnas*. Meyer translated this maxim as "Treachery has a good tongue" (*Contributions*, 216). Gwynn translated it as "A smooth tongue begets (leads to) treachery" ("Senbriathra Fithail," 268). I have interpreted it as standing in contrast to § 1.54. For another example of *mrath*, see § 4.17 *Descad mraith sanas*.

1.30 This maxim is not found in Rec. L. It is contained in a gloss from O'Clery: *sothnge .i. soitheangach .i. breitheamh .i. adcoda sothnge siodhughadh .i. dligidh an breitheamh sith do dhénamh* "eloquence i.e. one who is eloquent i.e. a judge i.e. persuasion brings conciliation i.e. the judge should make peace" (Miller, "O'Clery's Glossary," 49). The gloss makes it clear that "eloquence" was expected of every judge, and should be used to produce peace or accord. The *Aibidil* contains the line *saí cach suthngai* "Every well-spoken person is a sage" (Smith, "Alphabet of Cuigne," 67 § 66). *Audacht Morainn* contains the advice *bad ṡuthnge* "be well-spoken" (Kelly, *Audacht*, 16 § 55 line 134). Other compounds of *tengae* are found at §§ 1.29, 1.54, 3.32; *soithnge* occurs at § 6.16a (see discussion).

1.31 Binchy noted that "*airlabrae* (occasionally *airlabrad*) invariably means 'representation' of others by acting as spokesman on their behalf before king or brehon" ("*Féchem, fethem, aigne*," 22). The following entry from O'Davoren links this and the preceding maxim: *suithnge .i. sothengaidh .i. maith a erlabra* "eloquence i.e. a well-spoken person i.e. his *airlabrae* is good" (Stokes, "O'Davoren's Glossary", 458 § 1467). Other maxims which use *áine* in this sense of "mental brightness, perspicacity" are §§ 6.47, 6.96. Other examples of compounds of *labrae*, some of which are not certain, are found at §§ 1.38, 1.67, 4.9.

1.32 *Apgitir Chrábaid* lists *dochraite* as one of the "four hells of mankind in this world" (Hull, "Alphabet of Piety," 74 § 28 line 136). It is opposed to *sochraite*, for which see §§ 3.9, 6.17. *Daidbre* can be contrasted with *saidbre(s)* at § 1.1. In a gnomic poem we find the line *eochair dograing daidbre* "poverty is the key to affliction" (Meyer, "Mitteilungen [1908]," 270 § 10).

1.33 In the *Aibidil* a similar saying reads *measam ugra imnead* "Anxiety is the worst of strife" (Smith, "Alphabet of Cuigne," 69 § 11).

1.34 I follow Smith's translation for this maxim. He compared the modern English proverb "Necessity is the mother of invention" ("*Senbriathra Fithail*," 15).

1.35 The manuscripts vary widely as to the reading of the third word of this maxim. The forms in $L_{1,3,4}$ suggest *saigthige* "aggressive in pursuing claims, litigious". The reading in L_2 suggests *soichlige* "liberality, generosity". N_2 reads *soaite* "a good teacher(?)". But the readings from N_1 and Rec. Y suggest a reading based on *sáith* "sufficiency, fill", or an abstract noun formed from the adjective *sáithech*. This latter reading is given support when contrasted with the following maxim.

1.36 *Cumgae* < *cumung* "narrow, constrained" is listed in *Apgitir Chrábaid* as one of three things "that is worst for the mind" (Hull, "Alphabet of Piety," 74 § 33 lines 153–54).

1.37 Rec. L consistently has the reading *gnímcha* which, according to *DIL*, is attested only in this context. Rec. N and Y both agree in reading *gnímrad*. *DIL* lists this word as ā.f, but Thurneysen described it as originally o.n (*GOI*, 169 § 263). In an O.Ir. homily *gnímrada* is used to translate Latin *opera* (Strachan, "Old-Irish Homily," 3).

1.38 This reading is not found in Rec. L. *TC* § 14.7 reads *folabra gúach* "false muttering", and in the same text, *folabra(d) n-indsci* "a muttering speech" (*TC* § 22.9 = *CIH* vi, 2342.4 = § 9.8 in Appendix 2). In *Audacht Morainn* two types of rulers are mentioned who had to contend with discontent among their subjects (Kelly, *Audacht*, 18 §§ 58–62, esp. §§ 61–62, and discussion at p. xviii). See § 1.67 *Ad·cota (f)laith labrai/lobrai* for a maxim which may be a variant of this one.

1.39 This maxim is not found in Rec. L. In *Audacht Morainn* the good ruler is encouraged to be *fírián* "just" in a long list of exemplary traits (Kelly, *Audacht*, 16 § 55 line 131). See § 3.3 *Dligid fír fortacht*.

1.40 This maxim is not found in Rec. L. The substantivized adj. *maith* is often used to designate the moral "good" (see T. F. O'Rahilly's arguments that the abstract noun *maithe* iā.f, listed in *DIL*, is a ghost-word; "Varia II," 335–37). Many of the witnesses have the possessive pronoun *a* before the third word. Compare § 3.14 *Dligid maith mórad.*

1.41 This maxim is not found in Rec. L. I am not aware of any other example of *crodlesc*; it is not listed in *DIL*. I take it to be a compound of *crod* "cattle, herd, property" and *lesc* "lazy, reluctant", with a proposed meaning "careless with one's own property". Compare similar compounds like *traiglesc* "slow-footed" (*DIL* T 272.7); or *céimlesc*, as in *céimleasg i gcath* "cool in conflict, slow to flee" (*DIL* C 101.68) This maxim stands in contrast to the following maxim.

1.42 This maxim is not found in Rec. L. It should be contrasted with the preceding maxim. Compare § 5.7 *Tosach tocaid trebaire.*

1.43 Rec. N and Y both have *fúasnad* "disturbance", Rec. L has *frithorcun* "offence, annoyance". Both words make good sense and are attested in early sources.

1.44 This maxim is not found in Rec. L.

1.45 This maxim is not found in Rec. L. Plummer discussed a line from the commentary to the *Senchas Már* (*AL* i, 300.14–15 = *CIH* ii, 420.32, 421.9–11) which he reconstructed and translated as follows: *in gertbruthcan .i. ag bruith in neich is cain do losaib 7 do eolusaib do neoch bis i ngalur* "The milk-pottage, i.e. boiling what is good in the way of herbs together with charms for a sick man" ("Notes on Passages [1916]," 130 § 5). He pointed out that the commentator had etymologized *brothchán* as *bruth caín* "fair boiling". In the law-tract *Di Astud Chirt 7 Dligid*, the line *losa brochain cacha muige* "the pottage-herbs of every field" is glossed by *do leiges* "for medicine" (*AL* v, 486.12–13, 488.9–10 = *CIH* i, 242.17– 18, 34). A similar line is found in a commentary on the *Heptads* (*AL* v, 260.12–13 = *CIH* i, 38.27–28). From *Bretha Crólige*, Binchy translated "no [person on] sick-maintenance is entitled in Irish law to any condiment except garden herbs; for it is for this purpose that gardens have been made" ("*Bretha Crólige*," 22–23 § 27). Two anecdotes from a religious text relate improvement in the health of those consuming pottage to which special ingredients had been added. In the first anecdote the pottage is called *tiuglagin*, in the second, *menadach* (Gwynn and Purton, "Monastery of Tallaght," 146–47 § 52, 157–58 §§ 73–74).

1.46 This maxim is not found in Rec. L. *Fúachtain* is a later vb.n. of *fo·fich* "trespasses, commits an offence, does injury"; the older vb.n. was *fogal*. There is no discrepancy in meaning between the two, and it is possible that the later form was substituted for the earlier one since it did not affect the meaning or alliteration.

1.47 This maxim is not found in Rec. L. In *TC* § 31.10 we have the line *fénnid cách co trebad* "everyone is a *fénnid* till he takes up husbandry", which implies that until a *fénnid* inherits an estate he is landless (McCone, "Werewolves, Cyclopes," 10–11; Nagy, *Wisdom of the Outlaw*, 41–79 *et passim*; Patterson, *Cattle-Lords*, 122–24 *et passim*). In *Críth Gablach* a *fénnid* is listed as part of a king's household (Binchy, *Críth Gablach*, 23.591). Smith noted the similar Welsh proverb *Yn mhob gwlad y megir glew* "In each country a warrior is nurtured" ("*Senbriathra Fithail*," 66). I take the present maxim to express the same notion. See also the discussion of *láechdacht* at § 7.12.

1.48 This maxim is not found in Rec. L. Readings from Rec. Y support the form *léignid* "learned man, scholar".

1.49 This maxim is not found in Rec. L. *Menmnach* must be seen here in a pejorative sense. *DIL* suggests the meaning "self-assertive, swaggering". The *Aibidil* contains the saying *mórda cach menmnach* "every high-spirited person is proud" (Smith, "Alphabet of Cuigne," 64 § 40). *Triads* no. 233 lists *trí as mó menma bís* "three whose spirits are highest". The three are: (1) a young scholar after reading his psalms, (2) a youth who has donned a man's clothing, (3) and a young girl who has just been made a woman. *DIL* lists *miscais* as a fem. n-stem, but its nasal inflexion is only attested from Mid.Ir. sources. It may be inflected here by analogy with such acc. sg. n.f words as *aisndís* (see under *aisnéis* in *DIL* A 248.29–30). *Cais*, of which *miscais* is a compound, never has nasal inflexion.

1.51 This maxim is found in all three recensions. For sentiment, compare §§ 1.6 *Ad·cota fáiscre rof·áiscre*, 6.58 *Ferr síd sochocad*, 6.77 *Ferr gáes gaisciud*, which are also found in all recensions.

1.52 *Cocorus* is glossed by O'Clery as *siothcáin* "peace". He quoted this maxim and commented: *dlighidh an duine ar a mbí clú siothchain d'fagháil* "A man who has fame ought to find peace" (Miller, "O'Clery's Glossary," 387). *TC* § 31.8 reads *sochlu cách co áir* "Everyone is fair-famed till he is satirized". Contrast Dinneen who cited the saying *Dlighidh gach s[ochlach] sluagh-réim* which he translated as "He who would have fame must fight for it" (s.v. *sochlach*).

1.53 This maxim is not found in Rec. Y. Smith assumed that *dícháelad* was a compound formed from the privative *dí-* and the verbal noun *cáelad* [u.m?] "act of growing slender" ("*Senbriathra Fithail*," 15; *GOI*, 446–47 § 723). This example is the only attestation of which I am aware (*DIL* D 79.14, s.v. *díchoélad*). All witnesses point to such a word. L₁ has a clear accent over the *i* in the first syllable. In the second syllable, the *oi* of L₁, *æ* of L₂,₃,₄, and the Mod.Ir. *ao* of N₁,₂, all support an original *áe* diphthong.

1.54 N₁ and L₂ both read *brithemnas* for the third word, whereas L$_{1,3,4}$ and Y$_{1,2}$ all have *brithemnacht*. Binchy made no distinction between these two abstract nouns (*Críth Gablach*, 44). I have opted for the ending *-as* (see Greene, "Varia IV," 155–61). Contrast this maxim with § 1.29. Other compounds of *tengae* are found at §§ 1.30, 3.32, 6.16.

1.55 This maxim is not found in Rec. L. In Würzburg *fáilte* glosses *gaudium* (Wb. 14ᵈ12, *Thes.* i, 596) and *beatitudo* (Wb. 19ᵈ22, *Thes.* i, 626) and implies spiritual joy or bliss. Likewise in Würzburg, *féle* "liberality, modesty, propriety", is coupled with *genas* "purity, chastity" (Wb. 28ᵇ11, *Thes.* i, 681). This maxim could be rendered "Spiritual joy engenders a sense of modesty". Another gnomic text contains the saying *eochair ferta féile* "modesty opens up to virtue" (Meyer, "Mitteilungen [1908]," 270 § 7).

1.56 This maxim is not found in Rec. L. It reflects the notion, expressed in *Uraicecht Becc*, that a man can elevate his status through his skills and talents (see Introduction, pp. 17–18).

1.57 This maxim is found only in Rec. N. For the third word, N₁ has *digge* and N₂ has *dinge*. O'Brien noted the use of *gg* for *ng* in older texts ("Life of Brigit," 351). I read the third word as *dinge*, vb.n. of *dingid* "crushes, quells" as in *TC* § 16.112 *ferr a ndinge a ngrádugud* "better to quell them than to love them". This maxim is an alliterating counterpart of § 1.36 *Ad·cota doíre cumgai*.

1.58 This maxim is not found in Rec. L. In Broccán's *Hymn*, which praises St Brigit, we find the line *ní cair in domuin cathim* which is translated "She loved not to enjoy the world" (*Thes.* ii, 328.2). This line has the gloss *.i. caithem in domuin di fein* "i.e. the comsumption of the world by herself" (*Thes.* ii, 328.23–24). *Apgitir Chrábaid* cautions against confusing certain vices with similar virtues, *malartchae ₇ caithmige i fail eslabrae* "prodigality and wastefulness beside generosity" (Hull, "Alphabet of Piety," 64 § 11 line 54). Compare § 1.26 *Ad·cota briugas bronnud*.

1.59 This maxim is not found in Rec. L. In the Homilies from Lebor Brecc, included among the sinners to be found on the left hand of the Creator on the day of judgement, are *lucht na snímche ₇ na toirsi sægulda* "people of sorrow and world weariness" (Hogan, *Irish Nennius*, 34 § 52). Compare § 5.17 *Tosach tróge toirsige*, and notes for § 6.33 *Ferr techt allatróg*.

1.60 This maxim is not found in Rec. L. It is difficult to know if it should be read with the sense that a *drochben* "gets" or "obtains" *díbe* "refusal, denial" from others, that is, that she deserves it; or if what is meant is that *díbe* "niggardliness, parsimony" is a characteristic of the *drochben*, as stated in the list *cúic airdena déc drochmná* "fifteen signs of a bad woman" (Smith, "*Senbriathra Fithail*," 61). *Triads* no. 181 lists the "three strayings of bad womanhood (*drochbanas*)". In *Triads* no. 72 one of the "three unfortunate things for a householder" is *tarcud do drochmnái* "proposing to a bad woman". *TC* § 16.113 proclaims *ní bí enech ná anim ná cloth ac neoch contúasi fri drochmná* "he who listens to bad women will have neither honour nor life nor fame".

1.61 This maxim is not found in Rec. L. For the proper qualities of a chief *TC* § 6.8 says *rop becda* "let him be humble". Speaking of the learned man *TC* § 15.36 says *sái cech sochoisc* "every tractable person is sage". But there is also a cautionary note in *TC* § 29.13 which says *diamba robecda, bid dígraid* "if you are too humble, you will be without status". *Apgitir Chrábaid* has the line *nibi fíriōn, nādbi fir-umal* "he is not just, who is not truly humble" (Hull, "Alphabet of Piety," 66 § 16 line 76). In a secular context *Bríatharthecosc Con Culaind* uses the word *umal*: *bát umal múnta ó gáethaib* "be humble when instructed by the wise" (Smith, "Briatharthecosc Conculaind," 188–89 § 25).

1.62 This maxim is not found in Rec. L. In the law-tracts *lobar* "weak, infirm" may refer to a person who is incapable of attending to his own affairs. We find the contrast between *lobar* in the legal sense and *galar* "sick, ill" in the O.Ir. "Rule of Ailbe of Emly": *dénad adlaicc cech lobair / la cobair cech fir galair* "let him perform the need of each incapable person, together with the assistance of every sick person" (O Neill, "Rule of Ailbe," 96 § 2). O'Clery glossed *lubhra* [= *lobrae*]: *adcoda lubhra luinne .i. do gheibh an duine easlán fearg ré a denamh* "incapacity results in vehemence (from others) i.e., the incapable person received anger for what was done" (Miller, "O'Clery's Glossary," 18). The maxim as preserved in O'Clery used the abstract of *lobar*, in contrast to the maxim as preserved in Rec. N and Y. *TC* § 15.8 reads *báeglach cech labor* "every arrogant person [*labor*] runs a risk", but two variants read *lobor* [*lobar*] and the legal sense may apply here. In a religious text *lobar* can mean "weak in faith". *Apgitir Chrábaid* says *ar it sochaidi ata étaidi immin firinni, acht it ferg-luindig occai* ... "for there are many who are zealots concerning the truth, but they are fierce and angry when engaged therein ..." (Hull, "Alphabet of Piety," 66 § 15 line 70). The "weak in faith" suffer the "vehemence" of those who are zealous.

1.63 This maxim is not found in Rec. L.

1.64 This maxim is not found in Rec. L.

1.65 Bíathad is a legal term which means the supplying of hospitality to all persons, particularly when they are on a journey (Binchy, *Críth Gablach*, 76–77). Providing refection for the poor suggests the Church's practice of giving alms. Broccán's *Hymn*, in a section praising St Brigit's hospitality, has the line *níbu brónach int oscur* "the outsider was not sorrowful", and is glossed *.i. do biathad bocht* "i.e. from feeding the poor" (*Thes.* ii, 334.2, 14). See the variants at § 1.1 for finite verbal forms of *bíathaid*.

1.66 This maxim is not found in Rec. L. *Briugaid* is the Mid.Ir. form of O.Ir. *briugu* "hospitaller" (for a discussion of his functions, see Binchy, *Críth Gablach*, 79; Patterson, *Cattle-Lords*, 96, 201–2). Oblique forms of consonantal stems were used for nom. sg. as early as the Milan glosses (McCone, "Würzburg and Milan Glosses," 91). Rec. Y supports the variant based on *mug* "slave", Rec. N supports the reading with *mag* "field". Compare the primary reading with the *Uraicecht Becc* line which reads *nibi briugu nadbi cedach* "he is not a hospitaller who has not a hundredfold" (*AL* v, 76.10 = *CIH* v, 1608.14). The commentaries state that among his hundredfold possessions should be men in the capacity of slaves (*mug*) or servants (*AL* v, 76.15 = *CIH* v, 1608.15).

In both $N_{1,2}$ the second word is *brug-*, with a suspension mark over the *g*, which suggests O.Ir. *mruig*, perhaps as *brugach* <*mruigech* "one possessed of lands", or the abstract *brugas* <*mruiges*. Maxims with *briugas* are found at §§ 1.26, 6.19.

1.67 This maxim is not found in Rec. N. Were it not for the fact that Rec. Y clearly distinguishes two separate maxims, this one might be treated as a variant of § 1.38 *Ad·cota flaith folabra(d)*. All manuscripts read *flaith* for the second word, which in Mid.Ir. was often confused with *laith* "liquor" (*DIL* F 161.20–35). I have restored *laith* here for reasons of sense and alliteration. The ambiguities do not end here, however. Rec. Y readings suggest the abstract noun *lobrae* [< *lobar*] "infirmity, incapability", and Rec. L readings are based on *labrae* [< *labor*] "talkativeness". Compare *TC* § 15.8 *báeglach cech labor* "every talkative person runs a risk" which has the variant *lobor* [= *lobar*] "incapable person".

If we read *flaith* as *laith* "liquor" then it stresses two of liquor's negative results: "incapacity" and "talkativeness". The sentiments of both variants contradict the statement about the responsibilities of the *flaith* "lord" which says: *ar ní flaith téchta[e] nád ingella laith ar cach ndomnach* "for he is not a proper lord who does not assure liquor for every Sunday" (Binchy, *Críth Gablach*, 21.543–44). For some maxims which might shed light here, see examples with *cuirm* "ale" at §§ 1.20, 1.69, 6.61; and examples with compounds of *mescae* "intoxication" at §§ 4.25, 5.13, 5.14. For other maxims with *flaith* see §§ 1.38, 6.36. For examples with compounds of, or forms derived from, *labrae* see §§ 1.31, 1.38, 4.9. For maxims with *lobar* or *lobrae* see §§ 1.62, 5.18, 6.81.

1.68 Rec. N does not contain this maxim. Rec. Y distinguishes this one from § 1.21 *Ad·cota echlach utmailli* thus preventing their treatment as variants. Based on the meaning of *étlae* "evading, taking by stealth" as used in "*Cáin Lánamna*," (*AL* ii, 360.17–19 = *CIH* ii, 507.1–3; Thurneysen, "*Cáin Lánamna*," 24–25), we might interpret this maxim more fully as "removal (by stealth, of articles held in common by a couple) results in a change (in the terms of their contract)". *Utmaille* is used in this legal sense (see discussion at § 1.21). To interpret this maxim in a religious sense, translating *etlae* as "renunciation, self-denial, purity", seems possible, but not as likely, since *utmaille* means not only "change" but implies "uncertainty".

1.69 This maxim is found only in Rec. L. *TC* § 1.44 lists among those things which are "best for a king" *imbed fína sceo meda* "an abundance of wine and mead". It seems probable that this maxim is derived from § 1.20 *Ad·cota cuirm carna / cornu* (which see). Contrast § 1.15 *Ad·cota gáes clotha* (found in Rec. N and Y).

§ 2 Ba Faitech

§ 2 This short section, found in all recensions, never contains more than seven lines. In five manuscripts, $Y_{3,4,5}$ and $L_{1,3}$, this section has only six lines. The missing line is always § 2.3. The style of this section is different from the three-word maxims, with two sentence-types represented. The first type (§§ 2.1, 2.2) takes the form "be (...) so that you may not be (...)"; and the second type (§§ 2.3–7) "be (...) so that you may be (...)". These preceptual sentences, which contain an imperative of the copula followed by a consecutive clause in the subjunctive, are stylistically more akin to *speculum* texts proper than anything else in this text. However, the sentiments expressed agree with the maxims as a whole.

2.1 These first two lines of § 2 are parallel in construction to a string of lines in *Tecosca Cormaic* which begin with a negative command, *ní ba* (...) *arnába* (...) (*TC* §§ 19.23–35). The first of these reads *ní ba choibchech ar ná ba fiachach* "do not be fond of bargaining so that you may not be burdened with debts" (*TC* § 19.23). *Fíach* may mean "penalty, obligation". A person who is *fiachach* may owe a financial debt or may have incurred fines as a penalty. *TC* § 31.4 reads *cara cách co fíachu* "everyone is a friend until it comes to debts / fines".

2.2 The semantics of *trebar* and its abstract *trebaire* are discussed at § 4.8 *Descad trebaire túae. TC* § 15.10 reads *trebar cech trebthach* "every farmer is prudent". A short text entitled "The Duties of a Husbandman" begins *dia mba trebthach, ba trebor* "If you would be a husbandman, be prudent" (Meyer, "Duties of a Husbandman," 172). It advises the husbandman to treat all visitors as Christ and ends with the exhortation *ba ar Dia gacha ndéne* "Whatsoever you do, let it be for God" (172). *Gabálach* is the adjective formed from *gabál*, vb.n. of *gaibid* "lays hold of, grasps". N_1 reads *arnabatur gabalach*, with the *ur* as an abbreviation over the *t*. N_2 reads *turghbhal-*. These readings suggest influence from an adjective formed from *targabál* "transgression, sin".

2.3 This is the line omitted by those manuscripts that have six lines for this section. I have restored the first adjective as *éimid*, following Rec. Y and L_4 (= *emidh*). L_2 reads *hemich*, but *éimid* and *éimech* overlap in the sense "swift, prompt", which I have expressed in translation as "obliging". The Rec. N manuscripts have readings based on *enech* "honour, respect". *Sercach* is ambiguous because it could mean "loved, lovable, loving"; but the first meaning seems best here. This ambiguity is evident at *TC* § 15.4 which reads *torsech cech sercach* and is translated as "every lover is melancholy". In the *Aibidil* we find the entry *tormaidid* (read *tormaigid*) *cech sercach* which Smith translated as "Every loving person is increasing (in love)" ("Alphabet of Cuigne," 61 § 21).

2.4 The primary reading with *airdirc* is supported by L_1. The secondary reading is supported by N_1 *dercach*, interpreted as the adjective formed from *dérc(c)* (*deercc*) "charity", a compound of *Dia* "God" and *serc* "love". This latter reading makes good sense and echoes *sercach* of § 2.3. Thurneysen noted that the Y_1 reading *bat eslabar coroterderc-* suggested an original which read *corot·erdercthar* "that you may be extolled", the pres. pass. sg. subj. of *airdircid* ("Zu irischen Handschriften," 21 note 4). The various readings from manuscripts of all three recensions suggest that some such form once existed. L_1 reads *corbot erdairc*, L_2 *coro dergthar*, L_3 *coro* [illegible], L_4 *coro dercthar*, Y_1 *coroterderc-*, Y_2 *corod terderc-*, N_1 *gurbat dercach*, N_2 *corbat derctach*. Carney discussed a similar problem with a form that may be *airderc* or *atairderc* (*Blathmac*, 118–19 note to line 101).

2.5 In a section enumerating the proper qualities of a lord, *TC* §§ 6.15–16 states *rop gartaid, rop sochraid* "let him be generous, let him be decorous". However, *TC* § 19.31 warns *ní ba rogartaid ar ná ba aithbe* "do not be too generous so that you do not suffer decline". The noun *gart* "generosity" is found at § 6.55. *Sochraid* (*so* + *cruth*) can be compared to the maxims containing *caínchruth* at §§ 1.3, 6.63.

2.6 The noun *buide*, or its compounds, can be found at §§ 1.11, 6.67. The word *airech* I take to be an adjective derived from the abstract noun *aire* "increase", formed from the preposition *air* "before, in front" (Russell, "Varia I," 164–46). The word *aire* "increase" is admittedly rare. Attention was called to these abstract nouns formed from prepositions by Breatnach who cited an example of *aire* from the *Bretha Nemed* ("On Abstract Nouns," 18–19). In the meaning "increase" *aire* would seem to be related to the entry which *DIL* translates as "load, burden", given as a masc. io-stem. Compare an example from a poem in the law-tracts, *trom n-aire* "a heavy burden" (*CIH* vi, 2128.1 = O'Keeffe, "Cuchulinn and Conlaech," 124). Another example of *aire* "increase" occurs in the *Aibidil*, in this case compounded with *án* "splendour". It reads *anairi cach n-eslabra* "every act of generosity is a splendid increase" (Smith, "Alphabet of Cuigne," 66 § 55). The proposed meaning of "increase" suits the use of *aire* and its adjective *airech* in this example. It may also apply in maxim § 6.68 *Ferr aire íarraid.*

The primary witnesses read *irach* for the last word. *DIL* cites only one instance of this word, and that in the meaning "bountiful". It is apparently derived from the equally obscure *ir* "gift". Whatever the etymology of these words, they are close semantically to *aire* "increase" and its adj. *airech*. One must note, with regard to the adj. *irach* / *airech*, that the preposition *air* is often spelt *ir* (*GOI*, 497 § 823). The adj. *írach* "wrathful", derived from Latin *íra*, does not suit here. We can dismiss the suggestion in *DIL* (under *írach*, I 297.53–55; and see *tírech*, T 189.8–9) that we read the adjective as *tírach* "possessed of lands". This suggestion follows Meyer's transcription of this line as *gurba tírach* ("Bríathra Flainn Fína," 13.15). In N₁ the *t* and *i* are run together, but the entire line is cramped in this way and no other manuscript supports such a word division.

Airech o/ā as the adjective derived from *aire* "noble, leader" (Binchy, *Críth Gablach*, 69) could apply here as well and would parallel § 2.7 *Ba umal corba uasal.* The word *aire* and its adj. *airech* "attentive, cautious" does not seem to apply in this case and would appear to be a later development of the *aire* derived from the prep. *air* (Russell, "Varia I," 166).

2.7 Compare § 1.61 *Ad·cota umal ordan.*

§ 3 Dligid

§ 3 The verb *dligid* means "is entitled to, has a right to" and may be translated as "merits, deserves" or even "should be, ought to be". Its vb.n.
dliged can mean "law, duty" and in the gen. sg. may be used adjectivally
to mean "lawful" (Binchy, *Críth Gablach*, 84).

3.1 Compare § 1.23 *Ad·cota gáes airmitin*. Notice the inherent difference
between the two maxims containing *airmitiu*: one says that *ecnae* "learning" deserves to be honoured; the other says that honour or respect is
a natural outcome of *gáes* "wisdom". This maxim is also found at *TC*
§ 15.1.

3.2 This maxim, recorded only in $N_{1,2}$, is surely intrusive. It is also found in
TC § 15.2 following immediately upon the preceding maxim. Since N_2 is
not a copy of N_1, this intrusion was in both their exemplars. *TC* §§ 15.1–
2 introduce a section which is stylistically of the pattern (...) *cech* (...),
where the words on either side of *cech* are usually substantivized adjectives.
These two lines appear to be intrusive into *TC* § 15 as well. Their source
and the reason for their association must remain in doubt.

3.3 This maxim is found in *Di Astud Chor* (McLeod, *Early Irish Contract
Law*, 186–87 § 52) and in *Bretha Nemed Déidenach* (Gwynn, "Privileges
and Responsibilities," 22.5 = *CIH* iii, 1117.14; see also *CIH* iv, 1198.1).
The importance of *fír* in early Irish ideology is highlighted by the series
in the *Audacht Morainn* beginning *is tre fír flathemon* "it is through the
justice of the ruler" (Kelly, *Audacht*, 6–8 §§ 12–28). Compare § 1.39
Ad·cota fírián fortacht.

3.4 This maxim should be taken as a pair with the preceding. *Fír* and *gó* are
linked in the line *to·léci gó do fír* "falsehood yields to truth" (Kelly, *Audacht*, 16 § 54m line 130). Rec. A of the same text contrasts *fír flathemon*
with *gó flatha* "falsehood of sovereignty" (Kelly, *Audacht*, 62 § 25 line 76–
78 = Thurneysen, "Morands Fürstenspiegel," 82 § 25). *Triads* no. 166
lists the "three ranks which ruin tribes in their falsehood": *gó ríg, gó
senchada, gó bretheman* "the falsehood of a king, of a historian, of a judge".
As a counterpart to this maxim, *TC* § 14.8 lists under the "ways of folly"
cairigud fír "rebuking truth".

3.5 This maxim is also found in *Bretha Nemed Déidenach* (Gwynn, "Privileges and Responsibilities," 22.5 = *CIH* iii, 1117.14–15). The law manuscript H.3.18, in a section headed *secht rann .xx. it friasa* [recte *triasa?*] *toet
feab ₇ ordain do duine* "twenty-seven ways through which worth and dignity come to a person" contains the line *tri chocad fri cloíne* "through batt-

ling against iniquity" (*CIH* ii, 574.17). In a poem attributed to Dubthach maccu Lugair we find the phrase *do chosc cacha claíne cuindrech* (McCone, "Dubthach maccu Lugair," 29 § ii and note page 30 = *CIH* ii, 340.29). See Bergin's comments on *cosc et cuindrech* "correction and castigation" ("Further Remarks," 2).

3.6 This maxim has a close parallel in the *Bretha Nemed Déidenach* which reads *dlighidh imreson edorgaire* "an argument merits mediation" (Gwynn, "Privileges and Responsibilities," 22.7–8 = *CIH* iii, 1117.16–17). On the other hand, *Triads* no. 135 warns one against mediating, and notes of the unfortunate mediator, *doberar béimm n-etargaire ina chinn* "the blow of mediation is dealt on his head". *Triads* no. 154 records that one of the "three bloodsheds which need not be answered for" is *fuil etargaire* "bloodshed of mediation".

3.7 A *rath* was the fief or stock-payment which a lord bestowed upon a client from whom he could expect in return certain obligations or tribute, *ríara*, pl. of *ríar* (Thurneysen, "Aus dem irischen Recht I," 368). But *rath* also means the "granting of a favour", and in a religious context it may mean "(divine) grace". The variant in Rec. N is *ríarugud*, vb.n. of *ríaraigid* "serves, ministers to, does the will of". This gives the sense that the stock-payment or bestowal from a lord should be ministered to. Contrast § 3.8 *Dligid fuidir frithfolta*. This pair (§§ 3.7, 3.8) together imply that although the client is under obligation to the lord for receiving the *rath*, nevertheless the lord is expected to reciprocate and acknowledge his obligations to his clients. See also § 6.8 *Ferr rath ríaraib / ríarugud*.

We may also read the second word as *ráth* "surety" which can refer either to the person undertaking the surety, or to the surety itself (Binchy, *Críth Gablach*, 102–4). Reading *ríara* for the third word, as in Rec. L and Y, *ráth* seems better interpreted as the person who undertakes the surety. The maxim would then mean that the person who acts as surety is entitled to do so according to certain *ríara* "demands, stipulations". Compare this interpretation to § 3.11 *Dligid ráth a imdegail*. If we read the third word as *ríarugud* with Rec. N, then *ráth* is likely to refer to the abstract sense "suretyship". The meaning would be that any "surety" undertaken should be ministered to and carried out to the best of one's ability.

3.8 *Frithfolad* is a service or obligation owed in return for another, as in the relationship between lord and tenant (see § 1.12 *Ad·cota féle frithfolta*). The *fuidir* was a low-status tenant-at-will. Binchy noted that "although his condition is semi-servile, he retains the right to abandon his holding on giving due notice to the lord . . ." (*Críth Gablach*, 93; Charles-Edwards,

Kinship, 307–36; see also Patterson, *Cattle-Lords*, 152–54). A *fuidir* is thus bound to his lord in a relationship that is less clearly defined than that of the different grades of *céle* (Binchy, *Críth Gablach*, 80; McLeod, *Contract Law*, 59, 60). Charles-Edwards stated that a *fuidir* is a "man who cannot rely upon his kindred for status and support but instead must rely on his lord" ("Social Background," 48; see discussion in Stacey, *Road to Judgment*, 121–23). The *fuidir* does not contribute to the noble status of his lord in *Críth Gablach* (Charles-Edwards, "*Críth Gablach*," 60). This maxim emphasizes the reciprocal character of their relationship, and since the *fuidir* relies more on his lord than the lord does on him for status and security, it implicitly urges a sense of responsibility from the lord toward the *fuidir*. See § 3.7 *Dligid rath ríara*.

3.9 This maxim is not found in Rec. Y. *Aite* is both "foster-father" and "tutor, teacher". The two functions must have been identical in a great many cases. Given the emphasis in this text on training and education (§§ 3.20, 3.30) and the cautious attitude toward fosterage (§§ 3.19, 6.20) it seems that "tutor, teacher" is the better translation here. *Apgitir Chrábaid* lists *sochraite* "state of having good and many friends" as one of *cethóra flaithi duini isin chentur* "four heavens of mankind in this world" (Hull, "Alphabet of Piety," 74 § 27 line 135). Contrast *dochraite* at § 1.32. Binchy cited a maxim which might be taken as the reverse of the present one, *arfeith cenn a memru* "the head (superior) looks after his members (subordinates)" ("*Féchem, fethem, aigne*," 20).

3.10 The *naidm* "enforcing surety" is someone who binds a contract by placing his honour at risk as guarantee rather than his property or person (Binchy, *Críth Gablach*, 100–1; McLeod, *Contract Law*, 16; Stacey, *Road to Judgment*, 34–38). Taking *nascar* as rel. pres. pass. sg. of *naiscid* "binds, exacts a pledge", the interpretation of the maxim is that the "enforcing surety" is entitled to full reparation should the party for whom he has gone surety fail in his obligations. As Binchy explained, "The man who attempted to evade his commitments 'in breach of the honor of his *naidm*' had to pay his surety the value of his 'honor-price' in addition to satisfying the original debt to the other party. ... On the other hand, the *naidm* had no liability whatever toward the other contracting party for default by the principal" ("Celtic Suretyship," 362). *DIL* suggests that the third word of this maxim is *nascor*, an otherwise unattested compound of *nasc* "fastening, bond" + *cor* "contract" (*DIL* N 16.18–19). If this latter suggestion is correct, compare § 3.11 *Dligid ráth a imdegail*.

3.11 According to Binchy the "*ráth* warrants with his own property the per-

formance of an obligation by the principal for whom he stands surety"
(*Críth Gablach*, 103). The same author explains elsewhere that the *ráth*
never acted independently, but always in conjunction with a *naidm*,
thus explaining his "protection" (Binchy, "Celtic Suretyship," 364–65;
McLeod, *Contract Law*, 17; Stacey, *Road to Judgment*, 37–38 *et passim*).
See notes for § 3.7.

3.12 *Fíadnaise* "evidence of an eyewitness" is distinct from a character
witness who gives testimony by compurgation which relies on the status
of the swearer for its force (Binchy, *Críth Gablach*, 90–91). *Triads* no. 174
lists among the "three doors through which truth is recognized" *sóud fri
fíadnu* "appealing to witnesses".

3.13 This maxim is not found in Rec. L. Compare § 1.19 *Ad·cota díummus
dimdai*. Rec. A of *Audacht Morainn* contains the line *dligid cach diumsach
tairniud* "every arrogant person deserves to be abased" (Kelly, *Audacht*, 65
§ 34c line 114 = Thurneysen, "Morands Fürstenspiegel," 84 § 34c).

3.14 This maxim is found in *Bretha Nemed Déidenach* (Gwynn, "Privileges
and Responsibilities," 22.6 = *CIH* iii, 1117.15). Similar examples from
later in the Irish tradition are noted by O'Rahilly (*Miscellany*, 88–89
§ 285).

3.15 Compare § 1.13 *Ad·cota díbe dimmolad*. Rec. Y offers a variant which
replaces *dimmolad* with *dínsem* "spurning, despising, contempt". See this
latter word in a legal passage, *dínsem lebar* "despising books" (*TC* § 22.12
= *CIH* vi, 2342.4–5 = § 9.11 in Appendix 2).

3.16 This meaning of *díden* "lead, guide" (vb.n. of **di-fed-*) was first de-
scribed by Baumgarten ("Varia III," 189–92) and elaborated by Breatnach
(*Uraicecht na Ríar*, 118). Compare §§ 3.26 *Dligid othar a íarfaigid*, 3.27
Dligid éconn imchomét.

3.17 The primary reading is based on N_2. *Airndel* is attested as meaning a
"trap, snare" especially for birds (see T. F. O'Rahilly, "Notes, Mainly Etymological," 217; Marstrander, "Review of *Lexique*," 212; cf. Meyer, "*Sanas
Cormaic*," 8 § 75; Stokes, "O'Davoren's Glossary," 328 § 796). The early
law-tracts make it clear that anyone setting a trap large enough to harm
humans or livestock must issue a warning (Kelly, *Guide*, 107, 276 § 52).

Rec. L supports the secondary reading *airdál* (L_1 has *erdál*) vb.n. of
ar·dáili (**air-dál-*) "distributes". Other maxims that support the notion of
"distributions" or "sharings" are §§ 6.73 *Ferr rann répiund*, 6.83 *Ferr leth
lánetiug*, 6.93 *Ferr becc n-érai*.

Some witnesses can support either interpretation given above. N_1 reads
airnell and $Y_{1,2}$ read *airneal*. Both readings are acceptable variants of

airndel "trap". But they might also be read as *airnel* "share, portion, distribution" (*DIL* A 233.28–31), a word which is more commonly attested as *ernail*, vb.n. of *ar·condla* (**air-com-dál-*) "shares out, distributes" (Lewis and Pedersen, *Comparative Grammar*, 356 § 530.1; T. F. O'Rahilly, "Notes, Mainly Etymological," 183).

3.18 This maxim is found in all recensions. Compare maxims dealing with *dán*, §§ 6.1, 6.48, 6.97.

3.19 This maxim is found in all recensions. Wisdom-texts often express a cautious attitude toward fosterage (Ireland, "Fosterage," 93–96). Compare § 6.20 *Ferr beccfine móraltramm*, and the discussions of variant readings at § 6.32 and § 6.68. *Triads* no. 249 lists fosterage as one of the *trí dorcha in betha* "three dark things of the world". *TC* § 13.22 notes of the person given to fostering, *altromaid cech dochraid* "every indecorous person is a fosterer". And *TC* § 31.15 states *sobraig cách co altrom* "everyone is tranquil until it comes to fosterage". In certain cases the terms of fosterage could be altered, for example, the "mother-kin" might annul the fosterage of a son if improperly carried out by the father. The following legal maxim is stated in terms similar to our maxim: *imfochaid altruma ō maithre* "the (right of) annulment of fosterage by the 'mother-kin',", (Binchy, "Family Membership," 182; Mulchrone, "Rights and Duties of Women," 198; see also Kelly, *Guide*, 86–90).

Nevertheless, early Irish literature, from the secular sagas to the writings of the Church, consistently emphasized the importance of fosterage in Irish society. For example, several characters argue over who will be permitted to foster Cú Chulainn (van Hamel, *Compert Con Culainn*, 6–8). In the anecdotes about St Patrick collected by Tírechán, one of the daughters of Lóeguire asks if the son of God had many fosterers, a question tantamount to asking how important and esteemed he was (*si filium eius nutrierunt multi*; Bieler, *Patrician texts*, 142.20; see further Patterson, *Cattle-Lords*, 189–91).

3.20 Only Rec. Y reads *sen* which was chosen because it alliterates and because this maxim is found in the commentaries in the tract on succession (*AL* iv, 372.8 = *CIH* iv, 1289.6). The other recensions have *maigister*. Compare §§ 3.9 *Dligid aite a sochraiti* and 3.24 *Dligid aite airraim*. Two lines from the *Aibidil* read *fáid cach sen, sen cach ecnaid* "every old man is a prophet, every learned person is old" (Smith, "Alphabet of Cuigne," 59 §§ 3, 4).

3.21 The reading of this maxim is from Rec. L and Y. Rec. N provides a reading like *Dligid foíndel furfócrae*. *Furfócrae* is a Mid.Ir. development.

Foíndel "wandering, roaming" in a legal context means "evasion of responsibilities". Someone who is *foíndelach* (var. *foíndledach*) becomes "fugitive, vagrant" after proscription ((*fur*)*fócrae*) by his *fine* "kindred" (*AL* ii, 288.1–8 = Thurneysen, "Aus dem irischen Recht I," 374–75 §§ 37–38; and *AL* iii, 410.19–22 = *CIH* iv, 1157.14–16). A *foíndelach* is unable to fulfill expected social obligations. In certain contexts it is clear that he has deliberately evaded his legal responsibilities. In this sense, he is to be contrasted with someone who is *trebthach* "a good steward". However, *Triads* no. 198 offers a view of the *foíndelach* as a victim of circumstances which may be beyond his control. The triad reads: *trí foglúaiset foinledchu: ingreim, dolud, dommatu* "Three things that cause vagrants: persecution, loss, poverty". For a discussion of someone who has defaulted in a contract, see notes for § 6.49.

3.22 Rec. N and Y read *míngoire*, Rec. L reads *míne* "tenderness". *Audacht Moraínn* has the line: *ad·mestar athra sceo máthra moínib goire gorforsaide* "Let him estimate fathers and mothers with benefits of maintenance [and] dutiful constancy" (Kelly, *Audacht*, 14 § 49 line 108). Compare the discussion between Adomnán and his mother, Rónnat (Meyer, *Cáin Adamnáin*, 4–7). But see the notes for § 3.23 for a noticeable exception to this sentiment.

3.23 Smith noted that, according to the commentaries in the *Córus Béscnai*, if a son could not afford to maintain both his parents, he was to choose his father over his mother ("*Senbriathra Fithail*," 34; *AL* iii, 54.25–30). By contrast, there were circumstances where a son could withdraw maintenance from his father (see Patterson, *Cattle-Lords*, 211).

3.24 This maxim is not found in Rec. L. Compare § 3.9. O'Rahilly cited the more recent proverb *dlighidh ollamh urraim ríogh* "a man of letters deserves a king's honour" (*Miscellany*, 104 § 326).

3.25 *Coibche* "bargain, contract" has the more specific meaning "bride-price" (Thurneysen, "Heirat," 114 *et passim*; Thurneysen, "Aus dem irischen Recht III," 314, 356–60; Patterson, *Cattle-Lords*, 297–98). Other terms for "bride-price" in this text are *slabrae* (§ 6.17) and *tinnscrae* (§ 6.44). A line in the *Aibidil* states *cach coibchi a certugud* "To every contract its adjustment" (Smith, "Alphabet of Cuigne," 52 § 33).

3.26 O'Clery cited this maxim and noted .*i. dlighidh anté bhios in othras a choimhéd* "he who is in sickness should be attended" (Miller, "O'Clery's Glossary," 8). For discussions of *othrus* "sick-maintenance", see Binchy, *Críth Gablach*, 91 under *folog*; and Binchy, "Sick-Maintenance," 78–134.

3.27 The person who is *éconn* "lacking in sense" is without full legal capacity because of status, sex, age, or mental condition. Binchy cites the phrase *fo bith as conn ar econn feith* "because it is the normal person (with full legal capacity) who looks after the abnormal (the dependent, e.g., wife, son *in potestate*, *fuidir*, etc., whose capacity is restricted or non-existent)" ("*Féchem, fethem, aigne*," 20; also Gwynn, "Privileges and Responsibilities," 33.32; and Stokes, "O'Davoren's Glossary," 335 § 827). *Bretha Étgid* echoes the same principle: *faill dano do connaib cen imcomet cach ecuind* "neglect, indeed, by the legally capable in not looking after the incapable" (*AL* iii, 500.21 = *CIH* i, 331.26). Compare the line from *Di Astud Chirt 7 Dligid*: *ailid cach econd a iarfaige* "every (legally) incapable person should be looked after" (*AL* v, 490.6-7 = *CIH* i, 243.32).

3.28 This maxim is not found in Rec. L. The third word must be emended to obtain a good reading. I have chosen *aurchailliud*, an unattested masculine u-stem vb.n. formed from weak *i*-verb *ar·cuilli* (**ar-coll-*) "prohibits, forbids, inhibits" (*GOI*, 446–47 § 723). All forms in all manuscripts have only one *l* (Y_1 has *aurcailiud*). O'Clery provides the gloss *urchailte .i. toirmisgthe* "forbidden" (Miller, "O'Clery's Glossary," 65). One could also emend the third word to *érchoíliud* u.m, vb.n. of *as·rochoíli* "defines, determines", which Breatnach has argued has a similar semantic range to that postulated for *airchenn* "fixed, definite" to "limited, restrained, temperate, chaste". Breatnach cited this maxim in support of his argument (*Uraicecht na Ríar*, 123–24). However, no witness suggests a long vowel in the first syllable: $N_{1,2}$ read *ur-*, $Y_{1,2}$ read *aur-*. Emendation is therefore necessary. *Anidan* "impure" is common in legal and religious texts. For example, a tract on legal custody has the line *ainidun cach n-ecubus* "every wilful neglect is wrong [impure]" (*AL* ii, 2.4–5 = *CIH* v, 1723.13–14).

3.29 Binchy defined *comaithches* as "the legal relationship that arises from the fact of adjacent ownership of land, whether this be the result of partition between kinsmen or simply of geographical contiguity between strangers or kin. It is a quasi-contractual relationship, secured by mutual pledges and sanctioned by fixed fines." ("Archaic Legal Poem," 161; see also Charles-Edwards and Kelly, *Bechbretha*, 31–34 and notes pp. 92–93, 110–11; Charles-Edwards, *Kinship*, 415–24; and Patterson, *Cattle-Lords*, 223–32 *et passim*). *Coímchloud*, vb.n. of *con·imchloí*, has the meaning "interchanges, exchanges" in legal texts. It is used with this meaning in *Triads* no. 72 and 73. Since *comaithches* refers to the interrelationships among land-holding peers, and not to the obligations between lord and clients, I translate *coímchloud* as "reciprocal dealings".

3.30 *Mer* can be either a temporary or permanent state indicative of diminished mental or judgemental capacity (see Smith, "Advice to Doidin," 66–85; cf. *CIH* iv, 1276.18–1277.13). *TC* § 13.15 reads *tibir cech mer* "every fool is a laughing-stock". One *speculum* poem contains the line *drúth cech mer* "every madman is a buffoon" (O'Donoghue, "Advice to a Prince," 47 § 20).

3.31 This maxim, found only in Rec. N, may be a variant of § 3.17. *Aurdonál* "herald, crier" is attested in *Triads* no. 253 as among the *teora sírechta flatha* "three deprivations of a chief", the second deprivation being *buiden cen erdonail* "a troop without a herald".

3.32 *Tengae* and its compounds may be used as metaphors for legal pleading (cf. Binchy, "*Coibnes Uisci Thairidne*," 79 note for § 5). The *étnge* deserves time to state his case whenever his interests are involved. The commentaries for *Di Chetharslicht Athgabála* contain the line *ma ettenga in fer* which is translated "if the man ... be not a lawyer", but it seems better to say that he is inarticulate and incapable of effective legal pleading (*AL* i, 80.28 = *CIH* ii, 356.30). For examples of compounds of *tengae*, see §§ 1.29, 1.30, 1.54 and 6.16a.

3.33 *Tuinide* "possession, ownership" is postulated as a vb.n. of **do·neith*, discussed by Bergin as derived from **ni-sed-* ("Miscellanea," 111; "Varia II," 136). Rec. N witnesses suggest that the second word be read as *tóraic*, vb.n. of *do·fuiric* (**to-fo-air-icc-*) "finds, comes upon", and which Binchy tentatively translated as "discovery" (*Críth Gablach*, 37 note to line 530). Rec. Y and L_1 suggest that we read the second word as *tairec(c)* vb.n. of *do·airicc* (**to-air-icc-*) "comes, finds, gets". *Tairec* has been translated as "providing, supplying, preparations". Relying on this latter reading, Gwynn translated this maxim as "Provision of food deserves perpetuity of possession" and stated that this seems to mean that the tenant who entertains his lord should have his holdings secured ("Senbriathra Fithail," 270). Whether we read *tóraic* or *tairec*, the sense, derived from their finite verbal forms, seems to be that to find, use and maintain a "found" object entitles one to its possession. In the *Heptads* a "found" object is called a *frith* and elaborate principles are set down as to the proportion of its value which goes to the finder (*AL* v, 320.7–322.6 = *CIH* i, 55.18–59.30; see Mac Niocaill, "Jetsam, Treasure Trove," 105–7). As Smith noted, this maxim appears to be an early recognition of "squatter's sovereignty" ("*Senbriathra Fithail*," 35). But it is not clear if this maxim can be applied to uninhabited land. Compare O'Rahilly, *Miscellany*, 94 § 297. See § 6.34 *Ferr móin immattrub*.

3.34 When Cairpre asks what is the worst arguing before an assembly, part of the answer is *aí utmaille* "an unsteady pleading" (*TC* § 25.5). Similarly, the *Aibidil* contains the maxim *measam āi ūdmailli* "unsteadiness is the worst pleading" (Smith, "Alphabet of Cuigne," 68 § 5).

3.35 This maxim is found only in Rec. N. In *Uraicecht Becc* this notion is stated *saer cach o mainib* "everyone gains privilege through wealth" (*AL* v, 18.12 = *CIH* ii, 638.7, v, 1594.14; cf. Mac Neill, "Ancient Irish Law," 273 § 6).

3.36 This maxim is found only in Rec. N. This and the following maxim are to be taken as a pair. I translate them in the light of *Triads* no. 136 which states that the "three false sisters" are *béss, dóig, toimtiu,* translated by Meyer as "perhaps, maybe, I dare say". The implications of the maxim seem to be that if anyone expresses doubt or suspicion (*amaires*) about testimony, then the person offering that testimony must give his word (*bríathar*) on it. The doubt or suspicion thus introduces a degree of uncertainty, which is designated here as *bés* "perhaps". That, at least, seems to be the notion expressed in a gloss upon this maxim, *dligid bes breithir .i. masa aenduine ruc amarus air, is dligid .b.b.* (*CIH* ii, 656.37).

3.37 This maxim is found only in Rec. N. See the previous note (§ 3.36) for a discussion of the related maxim and *Triads* no. 136 which translates *dóig* as "maybe". According to the gloss on this maxim, it appears that if two people cast doubt on the testimony, then the person offering that testimony must swear a *díthech* "oath of denial", vb.n. of *do·toing* "swears away, denies by oath". Thus the doubt or suspicion introduced by two persons is called *dóig* "probability, maybe". A gloss on this maxim, found in conjunction with the previous one, reads: *masa dias ruc amarus air, is dligid doig dithech* (*CIH* ii, 656.37–38). In support of this reading, O'Clery glossed *dóig* as *fiadhnaise deise* "testimony of two persons" (Miller, "O'Clery's Glossary," 404).

3.38 This maxim is found only in Rec. N. Only N_2 has a full reading for the third word. The abbreviation *.F.* is found in N_1. If we take this maxim as related to the two previous ones, then its meaning is that once *fír* "truth, proof" has been established at a hearing, then *fiach* "payment due" should be paid according to the decision reached.

§ 4 DESCAD

§ 4 Descad is a noun of uncertain gender and declension. Its modern reflex, *deasca*, is masculine. In origin it was a term used in brewing and could mean "dregs, sediment" — and by extension came to have a pejorative sense of "the lowest of, the worst of" — or it could signify the nearly opposite sense of "ferment, leaven". These latter meanings suggest a sense like "catalyst, inducement", which suits many of the following maxims well. On the other hand, a more neutral sense "characteristic, symptom" is supported by its interchange with *airde* "sign, token, characteristic"; see §§ 4.1, 4.16.

4.1 This maxim is quoted in *Sanas Cormaic* under the headword *adart* "pillow", where it says that lying on a pillow *is arde codalta* "is a sign of sleep", and then adds by way of explanation, *unde dicitur descaid cotalta freslige* (Meyer, "*Sanas Cormaic*," 5 § 43; also *CIH* ii, 606.12). This is an example where *descad* is equivalent to *airde* "sign, token".

The semantic range of *freslige* is difficult to determine. It may simply mean "lying down" (Binchy, *Críth Gablach*, 9.234). However, in O'Davoren *freslige* is glossed by *firindeall* "true arrangement, true preparation" (Stokes, "O'Davoren's Glossary," 372 § 1005). *TC* § 31.24 reads *milsem codalta freislige* which Meyer translated as "the sweetest part of sleep is cohabitation", a meaning which is supported by Wb. 9ᶜ26 *ind fresligthdi* glossing *concubitores* (*Thes.* i, 554). Other examples of *freslige* from *Tecosca Cormaic* do not help clarify its meaning. *TC* § 16.12 *freslige roscéla*, which Meyer translated as "putting up with exaggeration", does not seem to relate to the present maxim. But *TC* § 16.57 *airrechtga fresligi*, which he translated as "tenacious in cohabitation", is supported by *TC* § 16.49 *étradcha lige* "lustful in bed".

With many late examples of *descad* as "dregs, the worst of" it is possible to read this maxim in two nearly contradictory ways. Firstly, following *Sanas Cormaic*, it can be read neutrally as an aphoristic statement that "lying down is a characteristic of, or an inducement to, sleep"; or, secondly, with a disparaging sense that "the dregs of sleep are cohabitation". This latter reading gains support from maxims which caution against sexual misconduct, §§ 1.4 *Ad·cota drús dígnae*, 1.60 *Ad·cota drochben díbe*, 4.7 *Descad drúise dánatus*.

4.2 *Sírecht* "longing, lamentation, deprivation" is treated here as a fem. ā-stem (Bieler and Carney, "Lambeth Commentary," 46 note to line 44). *Triads* no. 253 lists the *teora sírechta flatha* "three deprivations of a chief". Murphy noted that "Lowness of tone and monotony . . . were probably the marks of *dord*-music" (*Duanaire Finn*, 256; Matheson, "Words from Gaelic," 257–58). The form *dorda* (nom. pl.?) in Y_1 suggests that *dord* was originally neuter. Other manuscripts in Rec. Y read *dordán*.

4.3 This maxim is very obscure. *Díbe* [io.n?], is the expected vb.n. of *do·ben* "cuts away, takes away, deprives of". O'Clery glossed it with *díultad* (Miller, "O'Clery's Glossary," 399), which in Wb. 5ᵇ7 (*Thes.* i, 527) and 6ᶜ2 (*Thes.* i, 536) translates *scandalum*, and may mean "denying (the truth of), refusing (to acknowledge)". If "scandal", implying rejection by one's peers, is an appropriate translation for *díbe* then compare the lines from the following poem: *ní moc[h]in in fer gráid ibes an digh, don linn mesca cidh maith leis, is íad sin desca in dímais* "unfortunate is the man of status [ecclesiastical orders] who drinks the draught from the pool of intoxication though he like it, (for) that induces contempt" (Meyer, "Mitteilungen [1915]," 53 § 27). On the other hand, *díbe* may mean "refusal", and the interpretation that "drink induces one to refuse others" may apply here. *Triads* no. 64 lists among the "unfortunate things for a man" *deog therc d'uisci, ítu i cormthig* "a scant drink of water, [and] thirst in an alehouse". Compare *Triads* no. 93 which states that one of the "three fewnesses that are better than plenty" is *úathad carat im chuirm* "a fewness of friends around ale". *Díbe* is also glossed by *tart* "thirst" in O'Clery (Miller, "O'Clery's Glossary," 400). A contentious dialogue between Fíthal and Cormac stresses the connection between drink and a resulting thirst, in which Cormac says *bíd ítv iar n-ól, a Fíthail* "there is thirst after drinking, O Fíthal" (Meyer, *Hibernica minora*, 83 line 2). The foregoing makes a reading like "Drink is a catalyst for thirst" seem possible. Compare compounds of *mescae* at §§ 4.25, 5.13, 5.14.

The maxim from L₃ reads *deoghmaire* "cupbearer" for the third word. Episodes from the saga literature connect the *deogbaire*'s refusal to serve with thirst. In "The Second Battle of Moytura" Lug asks his cupbearers to help him gain victory in the coming battle. They comply by bringing a great thirst on the enemy (Stokes, "Battle of Moytura," 90–91 §§ 110–11; Gray, *Cath Maige Tuired*, 52–53 §§ 110–11). A triad in *Bretha Nemed Toísech* reads *tuile, aithbe, etla nemtiger deoghbuire* "a flowing, an ebbing, a taking away characterize a cupbearer" (*CIH* vi, 2220.14). This maxim appears to stress the characteristic of *étlae* "taking away".

4.4 This maxim also allows for the interpretation of *descad* in a pejorative sense, "hatred is the dregs of anger".

4.5 *Athargab* "weapon, arms" is not a common word, but it is used at Wb. 22ᵈ10 (*Thes.* i, 641) to gloss *armatura*. Etymologically it is made up of *aith* "re-, ex-" (*GOI*, 499 § 824) and *forgab* "blow, thrust". Compare § 1.6 *Ad·cota fáiscre rofáiscre*.

4.6 Rec. N has *ēc(c)a*, gen. sg. of *éc* "death" (Quin, "Notes on Irish Words,"

52). This is the version Smith opted for in his translation ("*Senbriathra Fithail,*" 73). I chose the form with *eclae* "fear, dread" because of the close parallel with *TC* § 13.20 *ecal cech uamnach* "every timorous person is apprehensive".

4.7 Since *drús* implies sexual appetite, we may assume that *descad* is meant to convey a negative characteristic. One wisdom text begins advice with the line *cid ben dogné drúis* "should a woman indulge in lust" (O'Donoghue, "Cert cech rīg co réil," 272 § 51). The Mid.Ir. form *dánatus* is attested in all manuscripts. The O.Ir. form *dánatu* is attested once (Sg. 90ª5, *Thes.* ii, 134).

4.8 The semantic range of *trebaire* extends from an original sense of "farming, husbandry" to "prudence, discretion". Implicit in its meaning is the notion of "good management, stewardship" (see *treb, Lexique* T 126–28). In *Apgitir Chrábaid* the *cethoir trebairi* "four discretions" are (1) the erosion of desires, (2) fear of torments, (3) love of tribulations, and (4) belief in the rewards (Hull, "Alphabet of Piety," 72 § 22 lines 120–21). Rec. A of *Audacht Morainn* lists *tua ₇ trebaire* as among those things considered best in human wisdom (Kelly, *Audacht*, 67 § 42 line 159 = Thurneysen, "Morands Fürstenspiegel," 86 § 42).

4.9 This maxim forms a pair with the preceding maxim. All manuscripts in Rec. Y read *solabra* where *s* has replaced *r*. Among the "ways of folly" listed at *TC* § 14.32 is *rolabra cen gáis* "too much talking without wisdom". For other examples of *labrae* and its compounds, see §§ 1.31, 1.38, 1.67a.

4.10 I take *cartha* as gen. sg. of an otherwise unattested *carad* u.m, vb.n. of *caraid* "loves, cherishes", which in O.Ir. normally used the suppletive noun *serc* as its vb.n. (*GOI*, 445–46 § 721 and translators' note, 683 § 157). *Carad* is the regular and predictable vb.n. formation from the weak verb *caraid* (*GOI*, 446–47 § 723). In L₃ this maxim reads *descaid carthana gnáthgaire*, using the gen. sg. of *carthain*, a late vb.n. of *caraid*. The same vb.n. is used in *TC* § 4.11 *tigerna do charthain* "to love one's lord". *Gnáthgaire* (L₃), *gnáth* "customary" + *gaire* "nearness", appears to be an expansion of *gnáthaige* in a more literal sense of "lingering about, hanging around". Compare § 4.16. *Descad serce sírsilliud.*

4.11 *Coillte* is an attested gen. sg. of *collud*, vb.n. of *coillid* "damages, violates". All manuscripts in Rec. N and Y read *caillti*, which makes *cailte* "meanness, stinginess", the abstract of *calad* "hard", a likely reading (*GOI*, 74–76 § 120 for *l(l)* before a consonant). This latter reading has a verbal parallel in a line from Broccán's *Hymn* which uses adjectives rather than abstract nouns. The poem celebrates St Brigit and states *nīrbu chalad cessachtach* "she was not hard [and] niggardly" (*Thes.* ii, 328.2). The substitution of *ai* for *oi* has been noted before in this text (*gaire* equals *goire* at § 3.20 etc.) and forms of *collud* spelt with *a(i)* are recorded (*DIL* C 328.17–23; *GOI*, 52–53 § 81). I therefore favour reading *coillte* gen. sg. of *collud*, rather then *cail(l)te*, abstract of *calad*. *Cesachtaige* "grumbling, complaining" may imply "grudging" or "niggardliness", as in *TC* § 16.52 *cessachtaige biid* "niggardly with food". See § 1.14 *Ad·cota dochell cesacht*.

4.12 This maxim in L₃ has the order reversed from that in Rec. N and Y and reads *d[escad] dímaisi genus*. The fact that *genus* is nom. sg. and not gen. sg. (*gensa*) shows that this is not an inadvertent scribal transposition. The maxim as preserved in L₃ might be translated as "Chastity is an inducement to unadornedness". In *Triads* no. 180 *fosta gensa* "a steady chastity" is one of the "three steadinesses of good womanhood". *Triads* no. 207, on the other hand, lists *genas* among the "three aged sisters".

4.13 The etymology of *cobrae* "speech, conversation" is not known (*Lexique* C 136–37) although its meaning is clear from the example *cobre domunde* glossing *profanas uocum nouitates* (Wb. 29ᶜ10; *Thes.* i, 689). The reading suggested in L₃, *comrád*, also supports this meaning. This text does not single out women for censure. Contrast the misogynistic series in *TC* § 16.

A different interpretation from that given in the translation deserves mention. Watkins discussed various compound formations of nouns with *cobur* "desiring" (<*ad·cobra* "desires", vb.n. *accobur*), e.g., *milchobur* "honey-desiring" and *ólchobar* "drink-desiring" ("Varia II," 115–16). *Cobrae* may be seen as an abstract formation of *cobur* with the feminine abstract ending *-e* (*GOI*, 165 § 257; but see also 169 § 262.4; and cf. *ólchobra, ólchobrach, DIL* O 136.37–43). The prefix *ban-* is used to create feminine nouns from corresponding masculine nouns and has an adjectival force (*GOI*, 164 § 254). There are times, however, when *ban-* seems as well translated by the gen. pl. For example, O'Davoren interpreted *banbrethaib* as *bretha ban*, that is, not "female-judgements", but "judgements of [for] women" (Stokes, "O'Davoren's Glossary," 369 § 994). This suggests the possibility of reading *banchobrae* as "desire for women" and allows a translation of this maxim as "Desire for women is an inducement to folly". Compare maxims which stress sexual morality, §§ 1.4 *Ad·cota drús dígnae*, 1.60 *Ad·cota drochben díbe*, 4.7 *Descad drúise dánatus*.

4.14 Compare *mire* "madness, recklessness" with *báes* (§§ 1.5, 1.25, 4.13) and *burbae* (§§ 1.5, 1.63, 4.21, 4.29, 6.18). Compare *eochair mire mellgal* "reckless fury is the key to madness" (Meyer, "Mitteilungen [1908]," 270 § 4). See *mer* at § 3.30.

4.15 All manuscripts have the oblique form *imcaisin* for nom. sg. *imcaisiu*, but such changes are already attested in the Glosses (McCone, "Würzburg and Milan Glosses," 91). From the *Aibidil* compare *imchisneach cach santach* "every greedy person is watchful" (Smith, "Alphabet of Cuigne," 66 § 58). See § 4.16 for another example of watchfulness.

4.16 This maxim is found in *Tochmarc Étaíne* (see also § 6.58 for another maxim found in early narrative). In the version published by Windisch from MS Egerton 1782 the maxim reads (*iss*) *airdhenu sercci sírsilliuth* ("*Tochmarc Étaíne*," 121.11), whereas the version from Lebor na hUidre reads *descaid serci sírsilliud* (121.28). In a verson bound with the Yellow Book of Lecan the form is (*is*) *deascaidh seirci sirsillidh* (Bergin and Best, "*Tochmarc Étaíne*," 164 § 3). This is another example of *descad* used interchangeably with *airde*, and therefore to be read in the neutral sense of "token, symptom, characteristic" although the sense of "inducement" is not ruled out. O'Rahilly cited this maxim from the Egerton version. He said it might be modernized as *comharthaí grádha sír-fhéachaint* (*Miscellany*, 94 § 295). Compare § 4.10 *Descad cartha gnáthaige*.

4.17 For the two maxims in this text which contain *mrath* "treachery", all manuscript versions have the later spelling *brath*; see also § 1.29 *Ad·cota biltengae mrath*. One wisdom-text warns against *bōegal braith* "risk of betrayal" (O'Donoghue, "Cert cech rīg co réil", 270 § 44). *Triads* no. 243 lists *brath* "treachery" as one of the three things that are worst for a lord.

4.19 All manuscripts have a form which suggests Mid.Ir. *sláinte*, rather than O.Ir. *sláine* or *slántu* (*GOI*, 165 § 258).

4.20 I have read this maxim, with Rec. Y, as *bithgubae* "constant mourning". Rec. N reads *bithdubae* "constant gloom". Either reading makes sense. This maxim forms a pair with the previous one. Compare *to·léci brón do fáilti* "Sorrow yields to joy" (Kelly, *Audacht*, 14 § 54b line 119).

4.21 In *Triads* no. 197 *serbae* is "one of the three things which show a bad man". The adjectives from *serbae* and *burbae* are associated at *TC* § 13.13 *serb cech borb* "every boor is bitter", and at *TC* § 28.3 in a description of the worst type of person which begins, *fer garb serb borb* ... "a rough, bitter, rude man ...".

4.22 A similar maxim is found at *TC* § 13.18, *imresnaid cech n-aneólach* "every uninformed person is quarrelsome". The same maxim also appears in *Bretha Nemed Déidenach* in the form *imresnaigh gach aineolach* (Gwynn, "Privileges and Responsibilities," 20.14–15).

4.23 *Anbal cech anecnaid* "every ignoramus is shameless" (*TC* § 13.19) is a closely parallel maxim formed from adjectives rather than abstract nouns.

4.24 This maxim is found only in Rec. Y. It expresses the same sentiment as the biblical *Contritionem praecedit superbia, et ante ruinam exaltatur spiritus* "Pride goes before destruction, and a proud spirit before a fall" (Proverbs 16:18). See § 5.11 *Tosach uilc úabarbríathar*.

4.25 These last five maxims in the *descad* series are found only in L₃. Other maxims with *mescae* or its compounds are found only in Rec. N; see §§ 5.13. 5.14.

4.26 *Aithigid* as a vb.n. means "frequenting, visiting" and hence by extension "practice". *Éolas* is knowledge gained through practice or experience. For other maxims which discuss familiarity or frequenting, compare §§ 4.10 *Descad cartha gnáthaige* and 1.17 *Ad·cota aithgne augrae*.

4.27 The regular nom. pl. ending of *bés* u.m "custom, habit" would have been *-e* in O.Ir., but already by the time of the Würzburg glosses the ending *-a*, as in our text, is attested (*GOI*, 198 § 312).

4.28 In a gloss on *udar* (= O.Ir. *áugtor* < Lat. *auctor*) O'Davoren states *u[g]dar in dána is e is coir dia freagra* "it is right that the expert in the craft answer for it" (Stokes, "O'Davoren's Glossary," 484 § 1612 = *CIH* iv, 1531.15–16). That is to say, the one who is trained, the one who has *fis* "knowledge", is responsible for explaining the intricacies of a skill. Compare the modern proverb *doras feasa fiafruighe* "Questioning is the door of knowledge" (O'Rahilly, *Miscellany*, 85–86 § 281). *Fis* and its compounds are found at §§ 6.14, 6.76, 6.92.

§ 5 TOSACH

§ 5 The *tosach* series is the most consistently uniform from recension to recension, even to the point that the last line of this section in every manuscript is *Arailiu maith mesrugud*, showing that all recensions had a common exemplar. In Rec. L this series comes first in every manuscript. The basic meaning of tosach is "beginning" but for the purposes of this text one must often consider the senses of "first principle, basis". In O.Ir. *tosach* is a neuter o-stem which one would expect to nasalize the following dependent genitive. This never happens in any of our manuscripts. Thurneysen noted that "nasalization of a following dependent genitive or an adverbial is not consistently shown; it is, however, more frequent in Ml.

than in Wb." (*GOI*, 148 § 237). We must deem this lack of nasalization
to be inconclusive for purposes of dating.

5.1 The saga *Cath Maige Roth* contains the maxim *ferrdi fis fiarfaigid*
"Knowledge is the better for inquiry" (O'Donovan, *Dun na n-Gedh*, 160).
O'Rahilly cited the modern equivalent *doras feasa fiafruighe* "Questioning
is the door of knowledge" (*Miscellany*, 85–86 § 281).

5.2 Compare § 4.18 *Descad debtha athchomsán*. In *Triads* no. 213 *augrae* is
one of the "three angry sisters". TC § 16.20 says women are *airrechtga
ugrai* "augmenters of strife". *TC* § 19.19 reads *ní ba chond ugra* "do not be
a leader in strife", and *TC* § 31.16 reads *rúnaid cách co ugra* "everyone
keeps secrets till it comes to a quarrel".

5.3 Only the manuscripts of Rec. N clearly show a gen. sg. form of *etech* o.n
"refusal, refusing". Most manuscripts in Rec. Y and L appear to have the
gen. sg. of *éthech* o.n "a false oath, lying, perjury". But this latter word
seems too strong for the context. For an example of a compound of *etech*,
see § 6.83. Numbered among the "ways of folly" at *TC* § 14.29 is *airlicud
il* "much lending". On the other hand, *TC* § 3.33 lists among "what is
best for the good of the tribe" *airlicud éim* "ready lending", and *TC* § 3.35
reads *íasacht follán* "lending without stint". Binchy noted that *airlicud*, like
íasacht, may be used in the general sense of "borrowing" (*Críth Gablach*,
74). This latter meaning lends support to a variant with *éthech*.

5.4 In *Triads* no. 213 one of the "three angry sisters" is *écndach*. Cormac
advises Cairpre at *TC* § 19.11, *ní dlútha écnach* "do not join in slander".
At *TC* § 16.18 women are said to be *cundamna écnaig* "accustomed to
slander", and at *TC* § 16.34 they are *écnaig míadamla* "slanderers of dignity". In *Apgitir Chrábaid* one of the four things which does not happen
to someone who loves God is *ní [m]ben écndach* which Hull translated as
"defamation does not touch him" ("Alphabet of Piety," 72 § 21 line 118).

5.5 Binchy discussed "honour-price" and the words used to denote it (*Críth
Gablach*, 84–86). This maxim appears to support the rigid hierarchical
organization of early Irish society as outlined in the law-tracts, but contrast §§ 1.61 and 2.2.

5.6 Compare *TC* § 15.36 *sái cech sochoisc* "every tractable person is sage".
Triads no. 251 lists the "four elements of wisdom" with an explanatory
phrase for each element. Two of the phrases relate to this maxim: *sái cach
somnath* "every teachable person is sage" and *sochoisc cach sothengtha* "every
well-spoken person is tractable". *Somnath* (*so* + *múnad*) and *sochoisc* (*so* +
cosc) both mean "teachable, tractable". *Apgitir Chrábaid* states that the
person who converts his own soul can convert the people of the whole

world *acht betis sochoisci* "provided they were tractable" (Hull, "Alphabet of Piety," 68 § 18 line 93). See Bergin's discussion of *cosc* ("Further Remarks," 1–3).

5.7 *Trebaire* has a basic meaning of "good husbandry, management, steward-ship" and extends that meaning to "prudence, discretion, security". See also § 4.8. *Tocad* has an original sense of "fortune, chance, destiny" but its semantic range favoured the positive sense of "good fortune, wealth, prosperity" (*Lexique* T 84–85).

5.8 This maxim begins a fifteenth-century bardic poem where it is attributed to Fíthal (Mac Cionnaith, *Dioghluim Dána*, 415 § 120).

5.9 The use of *crábud* "piety, devotion" lends itself to a religious interpre-tation. Another gnomic text has the line *eochair chundla crābud* "piety leads to prudence" (Meyer, "Mitteilungen [1908]," 270 § 1).

5.11 Compare § 4.24 *Descad uilc úabar*, found only in Rec. Y.

5.12 In *Apgitir Chrábaid* two of the "four hells of mankind in this world" are *galar ⁊ sentu* "disease and old age" (Hull, "Alphabet of Piety," 74 § 28 line 136). *TC* § 15.5 reads *crimnach cech galrach* "every sickly person is wasted" (this translation is based on taking *crimnach* < *creimm* vb.n. of *creinnid* "gnaws, corrodes, devours").

5.13 This maxim is found in Rec. N only. *Mescae* means "drunkenness, intoxication, confusion". The prefix *so* + *mescae* here cannot mean "good drunkenness". Elsewhere, the term clearly means "intoxication". For example, only water is drunk to quench thirst *uair cech lind soomescthea is descaid dermait Dé* "for every intoxicating draught is an inducement to forget God" (Meyer, "Alexander and Dindimus," 3 § 64 line 16–17). See McLeod's comments about drunkenness and legal capability (*Contract Law*, 56–58).

5.14 This maxim is found in Rec. N only. The prefix *do* + *mescae* "intoxi-cation" cannot mean literally "bad drunkenness" since it constitutes the "beginning of good fortune". Contrast § 5.13.

5.15 This maxim complements § 5.11 *Tosach uilc úabarbríathar*. Compare § 1.30 *Ad·cota soithnge sídugud*.

5.16 Greene explained the etymology of *lepaid* as "*leth* 'side' in its prepositional sense 'with' and the verbal noun of the substantive verb *buith*", i.e., "being with" ("Miscellanea," 337–39; this etymology was chal-lenged by R. A. Breatnach, "Semantics," 260–61). Gwynn pointed out that *leptha* < *lepaid* denoted responsibility for sheltering a tribeless man who was guilty of offence and for which the shelterer might be liable for heavy fines ("Privileges and Responsibilities," 230 note for p. 41.31).

Binchy noted that "*lepaid* is a very common metaphor for 'protection'"
(*Críth Gablach*, 71). I therefore take this maxim as a warning that harbouring or associating with guilty or undesirable persons will lead to a
diminution of one's own status.

It seems less likely that *lepaid* means "bed", although this maxim might
appear to be a statement about the status of offspring from illicit affairs
or about marrying down the social scale. For example, *Triads* no. 167,
which reads *Trí sóir dogníat dóeru díb féin* "Three privileged ones who
lower their own status", lists a *rígan téite co haithech* "a queen who goes to
a peasant". A maxim from *Aibidil* addresses itself to that situation (if we
accept the proposed emendation), *measam laidi* (lege *ligi*) *lethard* "the
worst bed is an unequal one" (Smith, "Alphabet of Cuigne," 69 § 9; and
see *leth*, *DIL* L 131.32–35).

5.17 *Triads* no. 133 lists the "two sisters" *tlás ₇ trúaige* "weariness and
wretchedness". Compare § 1.59 *Ad·cota sáegul snímchi*.

5.18 All witnesses read *lubra(i)* for the second word, a well attested variant
of *lobrae*, the abstract of *lobar* "weak, sick, (legally) incapable" (see § 1.62).
DIL defines *lén* with meanings ranging from "defeat, misfortune" to
"sloth, idleness". I follow a meaning like "impairment, reversal, setback"
which conveys the idea of "defeat, misfortune" and the resultant "idleness,
inertia". *Lén* conveys that sense of pessimism and helplessness which an
otherwise fortunate person feels after a setback, and which the poor con-
tinually live with because of the constraints of their low status. Thus
Triads no. 243 can include *lén* among the "three worst things for a chieftain" because, as the leader, a chieftain must be confident and decisive.
This maxim seems to echo a line from *Audacht Morainn* admonishing the
monarch not to let gifts and treasures blind him ... *for lobru lén* "to the
legally incapable in their impairment" (Kelly, *Audacht*, 10–11 § 31 line 83
and note p. 42 and p. xviii). See § 6.81a for another maxim with *lén*.

Despite the agreement of all manuscripts in reading *lubra(i)*, this word
cannot be read as the gen. sg. of *lubair* i.f < Lat. *labor(em)*. In Dinneen's
dictionary this maxim, under the headword *léan*, is explained as *tosach
lubhra l[éan]* "one is slow or loth at the beginning of labour".

5.19 In a triad in the law-tract *Di Astud Chirt ₇ Dligid* one of the three
remedies for plagues is *nemfoirgeal gūa* "not to testify falsehood" (*AL* v,
452.3 = *CIH* i, 231.30). *Gúforcell* is listed in an O.Ir. penitential as a
transgression worthy of three and a half years' penance (Gwynn, "Irish
Penitential," 156–58 §§ 9, 16 = Bieler, *Penitentials*, 267–68 §§ 9, 16).

5.20 N₁ reads *soben* for the third word. All other witnesses (including N₂) read *dagben*. In *Triads* no. 73 the first of the *trí búada trebairi* "three excellent things for a land-holder" is *tarcud do degmnái* "proposing to a good woman". O'Rahilly notes Diarmaid's words of self-reproach from "The Pursuit of Diarmait and Gráinne", *Mairg ná deineann cómhairle deaghmhná* "Woe to him who does not follow the advice of a good wife" (*Miscellany*, 33–34 § 119).

DIL states that the inflexion of *sothcad* and *dothcad* (*so-* / *do-* + *tocad*) fluctuates between o-stem and u-stem, but the argument for a u-stem inflexion is based on ghost forms taken from Meyer's edition where, for this and the following maxims, he has the forms *sodcha* and *dotcha* ("Bríathra Flainn Fína," 16 lines 20–21, where both words must be gen. sg.). He clearly based his readings on N_1 which has *sodch-* (with an expansion stroke) and *dotcha* (without expansion stroke) respectively. For these forms N_2 has *sotch-* and *dotch-*. Meyer apparently treated *sodch-* of N_1 as *sodcha* (rather than *sodchaid*) based on the reading *dotcha*. But this latter form must be considered a scribal oversight of a type found elsewhere in N_1. Although the omission of final *d* is a permissible variant in many contemporary manuscripts it is not typical of this text. We may assume the scribe of N_1 has simply neglected to include the last letters, *dotcha*[*id*]. Such oversights are repeated in N_1 at §§ 1.40 *at- maith a mola*[*d*], 5.9 *.t. crabuid cosma*[*ilius*], 6.72 *.f. asda*[*d*] *aimiris*. For each of these examples, N_2 has readings which enable us to supply the missing letters from N_1. These readings must also be compared with §§ 5.13, 5.14, two maxims unique to Rec. N, but also found in the *tosach* series. The N_1 readings are §§ 5.13 *.t. dotchaid somesci*, 5.14 *.t. sotchaid domesci*, forms which demonstrate o-stem inflexion of *sothcad* / *dothcad* in agreement with forms in other manuscripts.

5.21 As in the previous maxim N_1 reads *doben*. All other witnesses (including N_2) read *drochben*. *Triads* no. 72 lists among the "three unfortunate things for a householder" *tarcud do drochmnái* "proposing to a bad woman". There are several triads which begin *trí dotchaid* . . . "the three misfortunes of . . ."; see *Triads* no. 44, 64, 65, 71, 132.

5.22 *Triads* no. 243 lists the "three worst things for a chief" as *lén* (discussed at § 5.18), *brath*, *míairle*. This maxim cautions against the traditional picture, painted in the sagas, of obligatory generosity required of anyone seeking honour and power (cf. O'Leary, "Contention at Feasts," 115–27). The advice in this maxim is repeated in *TC* § 19.31, *ní ba rogartaid ar ná ba aithbe* "Do not be too generous so that you will not suffer decline". *Apgitir Chrábaid* offers the warning not to confuse certain vices and virtues, *malartche ⁊ caithmige i fail eslabrae* "prodigality and wastefulness beside generosity" (Hull, "Alphabet of Piety," 64 § 11 line 54).

5.23 This is the last line of the *tosach* series in every manuscript in every recension, and reads something like *araile maith mesrugud*. The first word must be *arailiu*, dat. sg., used adverbially in the meaning "conversely, alternatively, on the other hand" (*GOI*, 239 § 379; see Bergin, "Varia I," 29; Pedersen, "*Di chosscc alailiu*," 188–92; Quin, "*Alailiu, arailiu*," 91–95). The unexpressed copula would follow *arailiu* (*GOI*, 494 § 818). A line which warns against over-eating reads *is maith māin mesrugud* "moderation is a good benefit" (Meyer, "Mitteilungen [1910]," 297). This last line in the series is meant to be contrasted with the preceding maxim and may originally have been a gloss on it later incorporated into the text.

Meyer's note for this maxim reads "i.e. another copy has instead: *tosach maith mesrugud*" ("Bríathra Flainn Fína," 16 note 11). It is tempting to agree with Meyer and supply the missing *tosach* as understood. *Maith* is attested as the gen. sg. of the adjective used substantivally (*GOI*, 226 § 357). However, I prefer to normalize the text. *DIL* suggests reading the first word as the verb *ar·áili* "induces" (*DIL* A 377.13–15), but such a break in the pattern of a series is unprecedented in this text except in Rec. N at § 3.2.

§ 6 FERR

§ 6 *Ferr* "better" expresses the comparative degree of *maith, dag-* "good" (*GOI*, 235 § 373). That which is being compared appears in the dative without a preposition (*GOI*, 160 § 251.1; 232 § 366.2), or may be expressed in a phrase or clause with *ol* or *in* (*GOI*, 232 § 366.2). For example, in an O.Ir. homily, the homilist, using the dative without preposition, says of the Lord, *is ardu nimib, is ísliu talmanaib, is letha muirib* "he is higher than the heavens, lower than the earth, wider than the seas" (Strachan, "Old-Irish Homily," 3). The following is an O.Ir. example from *Apgitir Chrábaid* of a comparsion using a form of *ol*: *Is ferr ecnæ cen suíthe oldās suíthe cen ecnæ* "Wisdom without learning is better than learning without wisdom" (Hull, "Alphabet of Piety," 76 § 36 line 165). The Mid.Ir. form *inā* [= Mod.Ir. *ná*] is used before the thing being compared (rather than O.Ir. *in*) in the examples with *ferr* found in X$_{1,2}$. All forms of comparison of adjectives are uninflected and show no difference in number or gender (*GOI*, 232 § 367).

6.1 The importance of *dán* is stressed at *TC* § 15.38 *innmusach cech dán maith* "every good art is wealth-producing". *Indmas* means "wealth, (movable) goods" as opposed to "(wealth in) land" which is implicit in *orbae*. The "Caldron of Poesy" states of the acquisition of poetry *is ferr cach orbu* "it is better than any patrimony" (Breatnach, "Caldron of Poesy," 72.112; Henry, "Caldron of Poesy," 127). In the *Aibidil* we find the line *cach dán a dūil(g)ine* [= *dúlchinne*] "every art has its rewards" (Smith, "Alphabet of Cuigne," 51 § 29). *Triads* no. 196 lists *dán* as one of the "three things which show every good man (*dagferas*)". Compare §§ 1.56 *Ad·cota ségonn soíri* and 3.18 *Dligid óc elathain*. Other maxims that contain *orbae* are problematical, see §§ 6.23, 6.24.

6.2 This ambiguous maxim appears in all recensions. The best attested meaning for *lugae* (*luige*) "oath" is as the vb.n. of *tongaid* "swears, takes an oath" (Binchy, *Críth Gablach*, 99). The second meaning for *lugae* is "yearning, want, deficiency" as in the phrase from *Bretha Crólige* which reads *aragair luge ndige* "which inhibits desire for a drink" (Binchy, "Bretha Crólige," 36–37 § 45; cf. van Hamel, *Compert Con Culainn*, 5 § 5). Of the two entries for *lugae* in O'Clery the second is glossed *.i. tart no iota* "i.e. thirst or yearning" (Miller, "O'Clery's Glossary," 18). *Ledb* "a strip of skin, leather or cloth" also seems to mean "weal, welt" on the skin raised by a "stroke, blow". This latter meaning is better attested in the later language (see Dinneen and Ó Dónaill s.v. *leadhb*). The meaning "strip of leather or cloth" is emphasized in an etymological gloss which reads *ledb .i. leth an faidb í* "*ledb*, i.e. it is half the spoils", implying a "strip" or "rag" (Meyer, "*Sanas Cormaic*," 71 § 832). *Fodb* "spoils" often refers to clothing taken from the dead. O'Brien compared the personal name Ledbán with the Welsh adj. *lleddf* "plaintive" ("Irish Proper Names," 212). If our word *ledb* is cognate with Welsh *lleddf* it is not clear how that meaning would apply to this maxim.

The primary reading assigned to this maxim is based on *ledb* as "strip, rags, remnant, a small amount". For *lugae* I apply the sense "yearning". The maxim thus stresses moderation of the appetites and satisfaction with a small quantity. Compare §§ 6.73 *Ferr rann répiund*, 6.83 *Ferr leth lánetiug*, 6.93 *Ferr becc n-érai*. A more radical interpretation applies if we use the meaning of *ledb* as "welt, weal". It would portray mortification of the body to drive out carnal desire. However, that sentiment is extreme for this text. But see § 6.4 *Ferr slán sásad* which is also compared with penitential practices.

Gwynn translated and commented on this maxim as follows: " 'A weal is better evidence than an oath': i.e. marks of violence are the best evidence of an assault" ("Senbriathra Fithail," 268). If we are to take *lugae* as "oath, act of swearing" and *ledb* as either "weal, welt" or the actual "stroke, blow, lashing", then we may have an oblique reference to methods used to obtain a confession. It might be translated as "Better the lash than an oath". However, nothing in the literature on ordeals confirms this view (Stokes, "Irish Ordeals," 183–229, esp. §§ 1–55; on ordeals, see further Kelly, *Guide*, 209–13; Stacey, *Road to Judgment*, 118–19). The "Penitential of Finnian" says of anyone who swears a false oath that the scourge (*plaga*) shall not depart from his house (Bieler, *Penitentials*, 80–81 § 22; this entry contains a paraphrase of Ecclesiasticus 23:12). The practice of flogging, often to impose discipline (*cosc*), is common (Bergin, "Further Remarks," 1–3; Kelly, *Guide*, 221–22). Many examples can be quoted from the Bible, for example, *et virga in dorso imprudentium* "and a rod for the fools' back" (Proverbs 26:3; see also 10:13 and 19:29). The misogynist section of *Tecosca Cormaic* says of women, "better to whip (*flescad*) them than to humour them, better to scourge (*sroigled*) them than to gladden them, better to beat (*túargain*) them than to coddle them, better to smite (*búalad*) them than to please them" (*TC* § 16.106–9). But none of these latter examples uses *ledb*, or a word derived from it.

6.3 This maxim is found in all recensions. One could imagine it being applied in the context of a case of self-defence. Another possible interpretation for this maxim is to read *airm* f, "place, location", and to translate "Better a bad place than to be without a place". Given the latter interpretation, compare §§ 6.34, 6.84.

6.4 No variant for this maxim is found in Rec. L. *Slán* "wholeness, soundness, health" in a legal context implies "freedom from liability, immunity". *Sásad*, vb.n. of *sásaid* "satisfies, assuages", implies satisfaction derived from food. *DIL* translates this maxim as "it is better to be healthy than glutted" (*DIL* S 261.12–13). The maxim seems to emphasize combating gluttony with moderate fasting as found in the penitentials (Gwynn, "Irish Penitential," 136–37 = Bieler, *Penitentials*, 259 § 1c). For sentiment, compare §§ 1.26 *Ad·cota briugas bronnad*, 1.58 *Ad·cota crod a chaithim*. I do not understand the variant in Rec. Y. Y₁ reads *f. liechslansasai* without a clear break between words. Y₂ reads *f. liech slansasai*.

6.5 This maxim is not found in Rec. L. No manuscript offers an example of a dat. pl. for *sét*, a word which is often used in the plural. In Y₁ this maxim has the gloss *.i. a hithiar a rec* which is obscure to me.

6.6 This maxim is not found in Rec. L.

6.7 This maxim is not found in Rec. L. It is the only example cited in *DIL*
for *angbus*. No explanation is offered beyond Smith's translation "dignity
is better than gluttony". I treat it here as an abstract noun formed from
the adj. *angbaid* "fierce, ruthless" (Meyer, *Contributions*, 103; O'Brien,
"Varia IV," 157). I postulate its formation from *angbaid* + the masc. abstract ending *-us* = *angbdus*, created on analogy with *cubaid* "harmonious"+
-us > *cuibdius* (*GOI*, 166 § 259.3). Another possible interpretation is to
see *angbus* as having been created through a scribal error for *angbocht*
"great poverty", a word found in legal commentaries (Stokes, "O'Davoren's Glossary," 214 § 112). If the word is the result of a scribal error, it
represents a failure to note the common abbreviation consisting of a line
over an *s* = *-(a)cht*.

6.8 This maxim has a different variant in every recension. Contrast § 3.7
Dligid rath ríara / ríarugud. Note that, whereas Rec. N has the variant
ríarugud at § 3.7a, it is Rec. L which has that word here. I translate this
maxim based on the primary interpretation at § 3.7, that is, taking *rath* as
"fief" or "stock-payment" from a lord, and *ríar / ríarugud* as obligations
or tribute owed in return by the client. Note also that at § 3.7a variant
interpretation reading *ráth* "surety, suretyship" made sense, but it does not
seem to apply here. The variant in Rec. Y, *ferr road rer(aib)*, is obscure.
Road (? = *ro* + *ád*) "prosperity, luck" duplicates a meaning of *rath* as "fortune, prosperity", but *DIL* cites only one example of it from the *Dindshenchas* (*DIL* R 80.33–34). Y_1 contains the Latin gloss *.i. expectare*.

6.9 This maxim is not found in Rec. L. This and the following maxim
make a pair which must be interpreted together. *Éolas* is knowledge
gained through experience or practice. *Ilar* means "many, an abundance,
a multiplicity". In the context of this and the following maxim, that "multiplicity" must refer to skills or abilities. *Ilar* is, therefore, translated as
"many [talents]". Note the example of Lug Samildánach, in the "Second
Battle of Moytura", whose prestige was based on mastery of many arts
(Stokes, "Battle of Moytura," 74–79 §§ 53–71; Gray, *Cath Maige Tuired*,
38–41 §§ 53–71).

6.10 This maxim must be read in conjunction with the preceding one. *Ilar*
is a neuter o-stem and will nasalize the following noun. I take the third
word to be the abstract noun *oscrae* io.n, formed from *oscar* o.m "an outsider, unskilled or ignorant person". The neuter suffix *-e* was evidently no
longer productive by the time of the Glosses (*GOI*, 169 § 262.4). I can
find no other example of the abstract *oscrae*. But many examples can be
cited for *oscar*. *Bretha Nemed Toísech* has the line *oscar cach i ceird araili*

"everyone is unskilled in the trade of another" (Breatnach, *Uraicecht na Ríar*, 23.80 and note p. 28 = Stokes, "O'Davoren's Glossary," 431 § 1326 = *CIH* iv, 1519.20 = Smith, "*Cach* Formulas," 275). O'Davoren offers the explanation *oscor .i. aineolach* "unskilled, i.e. ignorant" (Stokes, "O'Davoren's Glossary," 431 § 1326). The form *oscrae* in all manuscripts shows a palatalized consonant cluster. (N_1 has *naiscre*, N_2 has *noiscre*, Y_1 has *noiscri*). The phenomenon of palatalization was an ongoing process which was active from the O.Ir. period into modern times (Greene, "Growth of Palatalization," 127–36).

6.11 This maxim is found in all recensions. Prisoners of war were often made slaves (Kelly, *Guide*, 95–98). Compare the biblical *melior est canis vivus leone mortuo* "A living dog is better than a dead lion" (Ecclesiastes 9:4). Also compare § 7 in this text, particularly the last half beginning § 7.12 *doilig dán láechdacht*. Contrast the opposite sentiment *is ferr trú iná truagán truag* "better to be fey [i.e., fated to die] than a pitiable wretch" (O'Donoghue, "Advice to a Prince," 45 § 6).

6.12 This maxim is not found in Rec. Y. *Airbire* is declined here as an iā-stem based on the readings from N_1, Y_1.

6.13 Rec. Y and L read *de(i)bech*. N_2 reads *deabhuith*. N_1 reads *deb-*, which may be expanded as either *debech* or *debuith*. Both words have the same meaning.

6.14 This maxim is not found in Rec. L. *Sét* is well attested in the metaphorical sense as a "way of doing" or "manner of living" in both legal and religious contexts. This maxim emphasizes the notion that knowledge is not to be sought as an end in itself. See §§ 6.57 *Ferr sobarthu suíthiu*, 6.75 *Ferr réide rogaís*, 6.92 *Ferr grés sous*.

　　The use of *sét* as "chattel, wealth" in these maxims tends to be found in disapproving contexts: §§ 1.18 *Ad·cota santach séotu*, 6.5 *Ferr sonaide séta[ib]*, 6.15 *Ferr suthaine séta[ib]*.

6.15 This maxim is not found in Rec. L. None of the manuscripts shows the dat. pl. form which has been restored here. Compare § 6.96 *Ferr búaine áini* and § 6.43 *Ferr tiugbae torud*.

6.16 This maxim is not found in Rec. L. The primary reading is based on Rec. Y. The secondary reading is clearly attested only in $N_{3,4}$ which have *soitnge*. N_1 reads *soitch-* and N_2 reads *soitce*; both could conceivably be expanded as either *sothced* or *soithnge*. The N_2 reading, *soitce*, also suggests *so + itche* "a good request".

6.17 This maxim is not found in Rec. L. *Slabrae* "stock, wealth in cattle" may also mean "marriage portion, dowry". *Tinnscrae* (§ 6.44) and *coibche*

(§ 3.25) are other terms which may mean "bride-price". Contrast the use of *dochraite* at § 1.32.

6.18 This maxim is not found in Rec. L. *Bréo* "flame" is found in Rec. Y, *brab* "superiority, superlativeness" is attested in Rec. N. Contrast the frequent use of *burbae* elsewhere in this text.

6.19 This maxim is not found in Rec. L. *DIL* lists *brugas* as a variant of *briugas*, which is the reading of N_3 (*DIL* B 210.55). The variant readings at § 1.26 support *DIL*. N_2 reads *brugachus*, a word which may derive from either *briugu* or *bruig* (*DIL* B 210.41–42). Since both N_1 and Y_1 read *brugas*, it is possible to explain *brugas* (= *mruiges*) as the abstract of *mruig* "cultivated land, holding" (see Greene on abstract suffixes -*as*, -*us*: "Varia IV," 155–61). Such a maxim would be translated as "Landholding is better than (having) cattle". However, the abstract *mruiges* does not seem to be attested (but see § 1.66).

Briugas "function of a *briugu*, hospitality" (Kelly, *Guide*, 36–38, 139–40; Binchy, *Críth Gablach*, 79) may also mean "abundance, excess". *Búar*, in the primary interpretation, is "cattle, herds" (but see McLeod's comments on *bóár* "cow-killing": *Contract Law*, 316). For another example of *búar* in this sense, see § 6.91. The phrase *brugas búar* has been noted as a possible *dvanda* compound (Stokes, "Buchet's House," 227; Greene, *Fingal Rónáin*, 42 note to line 489). There is no reason to see *brugas búar* as a *dvanda* compound here, for if it is, we have lost the third element of our maxim.

6.20 This maxim is not found in Rec. L. The reading as given here follows Rec. N. Readings in Rec. Y follow the form *f[err] becc fine ⁊ mor n-altrama*, which may represent the incorporation of a gloss attempting to explain the original maxim. The phrase *mór n-altrama* is Old Irish. For a discussion of *altramm*, see § 3.19; and for possible variants which deal with fosterage, see the notes for §§ 6.32, 6.68.

6.21 Rec. L. does not contain this maxim. Both prefixes, *re^n*- or *ria^n*- (*GOI*, 527–28 § 851) and *íar^n*- (*GOI*, 515–16 § 840), are attested in compounds where evidence of nasalization is never shown, for example, *recomrac* "disyllable" and *íarcomrac* "trisyllable" (*Lexique* R 12).

6.22 This maxim is not found in Rec. L and is preserved imperfectly in Rec. N. N_1 omits the third word altogether. N_2 reads *namuib*, and N_3 has *namha*.

6.23 This maxim and the following one must be taken as a pair. They are not found in Rec. L. Such "two-way" maxims occur elsewhere in wisdom-texts. An example from the *Aibidil* states: *Cach urrudus co deoraidecht, cach deoraidecht co hurradus* "Everyone is subject to native law until he becomes an outcast, everyone is considered an outcast until subject to native law" (Smith, "Alphabet of Cuigne," 56 §§ 56–57).

The Latin word *urbs, urbis* "city" would take the form *uirb* in Old Irish, and that word would fit both maxims formally, but the meaning would still be obscure. There is a word *foirb* "landed property, an estate" whose nom. sg. and dat. sg. forms would suit both maxims, but which makes little sense. Nor does the (probably) related word *orb(b)* "landed estate, heir, scion" fit well in both maxims. A similar maxim, *ferr fer orbu* "A man is better than an inheritance of land" (*AL* iv, 246.15 = *CIH* vi, 2012.32), suggests that *uirb* (*orb?*) implies a person, if this is a parallel maxim. For example, *dí-uirb* seems to mean a "landless" or perhaps a "disinherited person" (*CIH* v, 1555.8; cf. Gwynn, "Privileges and Responsibilities," 28.29). Other possible examples include the entry in *Sanas Cormaic* which reads: *orb nomen uiri a quo Orbraige nominatur* (Meyer, "Sanas Cormaic," 86 § 1006); the compound *ballorb* = "partial heir(?)" (Breatnach, *Uraicecht na Ríar*, 36); and the entry in O'Mulconry (this may be merely an etymological gloss) which reads: *luchorp .i. oirb locha* "a *luchorp*, i.e. a being from a lake" (Stokes, "O'Mulconry's Glossary," 270 § 795). Substantives derived from the Latin adjective *orbus* "childless, parentless" might also apply. Following these suggestions, and applying the meaning of *orb* "heir, scion" listed above, one might suggest translating this maxim as "Better heirs than an inheritance". But that reading is formally and semantically inadequate to explain the second maxim in the pair. Compare § 6.43 *Ferr tiugbae torud*.

6.24 This maxim must be taken as the second member of a pair (see § 6.23). It is not found in Rec. L. *Orbae* "patrimony, inheritance" is neuter and should nasalize the following vowel-initial word. We can explain the lack of nasalization by taking *orbae* as nom. pl., but we are still left with the problem of the maxim's meaning.

6.25 This maxim and the two which follow should be taken as a group. None of the three is found in Rec. L. *Drúb* is glossed by O'Clery as *tairisiomh nó comhnaidhe* "remaining or staying" (Miller, "O'Clery's Glossary," 405). *Fodrúb* o.m, with the same basic meaning, is attested at Ml. 22ᵃ6 (*Thes.* i, 34) and the verb *fo·drúba* is attested at Ml. 49ᵇ10 (*Thes.* i, 151). In the commentaries on *Amra Choluim Chille* the 3sg. pret. dep. of a verb *drúbaid* is attested: *ara fat ro drubastar fo recht noeb* "because of the time he remained under the holy law" (Stokes, "*Amra Choluimb Chille*," 274 § 100). *Déine* is used again at § 6.26. Contrast § 6.45 *Ferr teiched tairisem*.

6.26 This maxim should be taken as the second of a group of three. It is not found in Rec. L. *Dobele* is not listed in *DIL*. I treat it as an iā.f noun (*GOI*, 165 § 257) formed from the adjective *dobail* "unlucky, unpropitious" (compare *sobail*), which is itself formed from the noun *bal* ā.f "condition, situation" (cf. *GOI*, 219 § 345.2). *Dobail* is glossed *cen bail* by O'Mulconry (Stokes, "O'Mulconry's Glossary," 249 § 322). Lack of syncope may be due to the conscious reformation of the word. See *DIL* under *doible* and *duible*, both of which have proposed meanings which might apply here. Examples of the alternation between -*a*(*i*)- and -*e*(*i*)- occur irregularly but are attested (*GOI*, 53–54 § 83a; 308 § 487d).

6.27 This maxim, which is the third in a group of three (see §§ 6.25, 6.26), is not found in Rec. L. *Dochor* "is a contract ... in which the purchase-price ... does not represent the value of the purchase so that one of the parties suffers a loss" (Thurneysen, "Sochor," 158; see McLeod, *Contract Law*, 34–35, 69, 77). Outside a legal context *dochor* might be translated as "misfortune, harm". Thurneysen explains further that *dochor* was not necessarily an invalid or illicit contract, for which see *míchor*, but was considered as "*morally* bad" ("Sochor," 159). The sense of this maxim is "Better (to act in) an unfavourable situation than (submit to) disadvantage (i.e. an unfair contract)". For other compounds of *cor*, see §§ 3.10 (notes only), 6.42.

6.28 This maxim is not found in Rec. L. *Búaid* "victory, triumph (in battle)" may specify a special "virtue, excellence" which an individual possesses. In this latter sense it is often translated as "gift". The following maxim, which also contains *búaid*, seems to form a couplet with this one, but its interpretation is very problematical.

6.29 This maxim is not found in Rec. L. The form of the third word in N_1 is *blipecht* which *DIL* cites (with a question mark) as "warfare", relying on Smith's translation ("*Senbriathra Fithail*," 82 § 31). I have chosen the Rec. Y reading, *pliptecht*, because it is the word for which I can make the best suggestion. In Mod.Ir. we have the word *leibideacht* "carelessness, slovenliness", and in certain modern Irish dialects we find words with a *pl* and *l* alternation in word-initial position, for example, (*p*)*leib* "simpleton, listless fool" (de Bhaldraithe, *Irish of Cois Fhairrge*, 114). This suggests the possibility of a word like **pleibideacht*, with the same meaning as *leibideacht*, which looks very much like our word *pliptecht*. Thus we can postulate an O.Ir. word like **pleip*(*i*)*techt* (both with and without syncope), with a meaning "carelessness, slovenliness", from which descended a Mod.Ir. word **(p)leibideacht* with the same meaning (cf. Mod.Ir. *pleibeach* "plebeian"). Such a word could be derived from Latin *plebitas* (*plepitas*) "commonness, vulgarity", with loss of the final Latin syllable *-as* (*GOI*, 568 § 916) and the addition of the fem. abstract suffix *-acht* (*GOI*, 167 § 260). The alternation of initial *p*/*b*, as in *pliptecht* / *blip*[*t*]*echt*, is often attested in early Irish words borrowed from Latin, for example, *péist* / *béist* <Latin *bestia* (see further Greene, "In momento," 25–31). Thus, we may have had a maxim with a meaning like "Excellence is better than commonness". For other examples of *búaid*, see § 6.28 and note for § 6.50a.

6.30 This maxim is found in all recensions. I follow Gwynn's translation ("Senbriathra Fithail," 269). Compare §§ 6.70 *Ferr bás bithbiniu* and 6.79 *Ferr greimm grefiul*. See *bríg* at § 1.27, and *bág* at § 1.25a.

6.31 This maxim is not found in Rec. L. *Dúil* may mean "element, being", and in the plural "created universe, Creation". We may read this maxim as a statement implying that mankind stands at the center of the Creation. *Dúil* may also mean "book, codex" particularly of lists such as genealogies, glossaries, rules for poetics, etc. *Dúil* may be intended to translate Latin *elementa* and *abgitorium* (See Márkus, "Patrick's Alphabets," 1–15).

6.32 This maxim is not found in Rec. L. I interpret it by relying on the sense of *trebaire* as "farmer's requisites", that is, all of the implements and structures which are necessary for the successful homestead. Following this interpretation, the maxim appears to favour the potential to perform work as opposed to the finished product itself.

It is possible that the third word is a compound of *aic*(*c*)*e* "fosterage". This text maintains a cautious attitude toward fosterage (see §§ 3.19, 6.20, 6.68).

6.33 This problematical maxim is not found in Rec. L. Thurneysen suggested that *techt* is a shortened form of *techtad* "having, possessing, taking possession" ("*Cáin Lánamna*," 12 note 1). The third word I take as formed from the adj. *trúag* (*tróg*) o/ā which, when used as a substantive, would be inflected as a neuter o-stem. It has a well-attested variant *at-trúag* (*DIL* s.v.). The prefix *ala-* "second, another" (*GOI*, 248 § 394) has a common variant *all-* (*GOI*, 309 § 488). Although formally these explanations suit this maxim as preserved in Rec. Y, it is not clear how we are to treat it semantically. A religious interpretation seems appropriate: "Better possession (of heaven) than (suffer) another state of wretchedness (i.e. hell, after this wretched life)". We must also consider the possibility that we are dealing with the prefix *al*(*l*)-, *ol*- "beyond" (*GOI*, 500 § 825; cf. *alltar*, *allmuir*). In this sense, compare §§ 1.59 *Ad·cota sáegul snímchi*, 5.17 *Tosach tróge toirsige*.

On the other hand, a nearly opposite interpretation can be given for this maxim if we read *techt* ā.f (var. *techta*), vb.n. of *téit* "goes, departs". We then have a maxim which could be translated as "Better depart than (suffer) another state of wretchedness".

Gwynn suggested reading the maxim as *ferr téchtai allaitrebad* and translated it as "Better dues than migration" ("Senbriathra Fithail," 271). He offered the explanation, "better to pay one's lord his dues than to be evicted and leave the country" ("Senbriathra Fithal," 271). However, *allaitrebad* is not attested in any manuscript, although it is now listed in *DIL* with this example cited. The closest readings are found in $N_{1,2}$ which have *allaitr-*, but *allaitrebad* is not the best expansion of that abbreviation. *Téchtae* "legal rightness, what is due by law" is a neuter io-stem. Gwynn got around the lack of following nasalization by treating it as plural, a solution which could be applied to this maxim as *Ferr téchtae allatróg* "better proper dues than another state of wretchedness" (or "wretchedness beyond").

6.34 This maxim is found in all recensions. The translation follows Gwynn's interpretation of the maxim ("Senbriathra Fithail," 268). I treat the third word as a compound of *imm-* "circum-, around" + *attrab* o.n "dwelling in, inhabiting". In the glosses on the Carlsruhe Beda dat. sg. *imatrebdidiu* glosses *circumhabitato* (*Thes.* ii, 25.40). From the early saga "Expulsion of the Déisi", *DIL* cites forms which may derive from the verb *imm·attrebea* (Meyer, "Expulsion of the Dessi [1901]," 114 § 14; Meyer, "Expulsion of the Déssi [1907]," 138 line 85). The context in the saga supports the notion of being hemmed in by potentially hostile neighbours. Binchy suggested that *attrab*, in an archaic legal poem, may mean "squatting, illegally possessing another's land" ("Archaic Legal Poem," 165 note to line 74). This sense applies to the examples in the "Expulsion of the Déisi". For a maxim that complements this "political" interpretation, see § 6.84 *Ferr fróech forbbu*. On the other hand, settlement patterns in Ireland tend to display scattered farmsteads and tend not to have dwellings crowded together. Note also the eremitical tradition of deliberate isolation.

6.35 This maxim, as presented in the edition, is found in Rec. Y and L. The form in Rec. N reads *ferr senfíacha senfala* (= N_1). *Éc(c)raite* "enmity" and *fola* (*fala*) "resentment" have similar meanings; the latter word is more common in later texts. Torna used this maxim in the form *is fearr sean-fhiacha 'ná sean-fhala* when he told how the poet Seán na Ráithí-neach had to wait seven years to receive payment for a poem which he had written for Seán Ó Briain, bishop of Cloyne (Ó Donnchadha, *Dánta na Ráithíneach*, 75). The maxim with *fola*, as found in Rec. N, has been discussed by others (O'Rahilly, *Miscellany*, 1 § 3; Henry, *Saoithiúlacht*, 96–97).

6.36 This maxim is not found in Rec. L. Binchy showed that *folad* "property, wealth", in legal contexts, means "the 'values' which one side grants to or gets from the other as a result of their mutual relationship" ("Irish History and Law," 28). If *foltaib* here means the materials by which a person sustains himself in his functions, then this maxim might be compared with maxims which favour specific qualities over possessions: §§ 6.15 *Ferr suthaine séta[ib]*, 6.22 *Ferr ecnae n-anaib*, 6.78 *Ferr goire imbiud*.

6.37 This maxim is not found in Rec. L. Compare §§ 6.30, 6.70, 6.79.

6.38 This maxim is not found in Rec. L.

6.39 This maxim is not found in Rec. L. After Cú Chulainn's victory over Fer Diad, he is made to say *ro marbus dom garbchluchi* "I slew by my rough play" (C. O'Rahilly, *Book of Leinster Táin*, 99.3591).

6.40 This maxim is not found in Rec. L. The primary reading is from Rec. Y. The meanings of the two variants are, apparently, that it is better to be embarrassed, or to accept a slight, rather than to allow one's passions to erupt into a confrontation. I take *grúad* "cheek" of Rec. N to mean figuratively a "blush on the cheek". Compare §§ 1.61 *Ad·cota umal ordan*, 6.6 *Ferr dígde dígail*. For another example of *grís(ad)*, see § 6.55.

6.41 This maxim is not found in Rec. L. The two readings do not split evenly between recensions. Rec. Y and $N_{3,4}$ read *cáemnae*. $N_{1,2}$ have *gnímrad*. The semantic range of *cáemnae* extends from "protecting, safeguarding" to "entertainment, pleasure". *TC* §§ 16.58–59 says women are *frithberta[cha] cóemnai, cuimnige díchoemnai* "opposed to being maintained, [but] mindful of not being maintained". *Carthain cáemna* "love of good cheer" reflects the sense of "entertainment, pleasure" (Meyer, *Aislinge*, 93.26; Jackson, *Aislinge*, 36 § 66 line 1133). Contrast § 6.50 *Ferr cloth cach biud*. For *gnímrad*, see § 1.37 *Ad·cota borb gnímrad* where it means "work, labour".

6.42 This maxim is not found in Rec. L. *Mac(c)* is a "surety" or "security" (Plummer, "Passages in the Brehon Laws," 113–14). Its meaning overlaps with *naidm* (Kelly, *Guide*, 172; McLeod, *Contract Law*, 15–17). *Míchor* is an "invalid or illicit contract" undertaken by someone without the clear legal right to do so and, therefore, is liable to be impugned (Thurneysen, "Sochor," 159). For compounds of *cor* (Binchy, *Críth Gablach*, 81), see §§ 3.10 (notes only), 6.27.

6.43 This maxim is found in all recensions. I can make no better suggestion than to follow Gwynn's translation. He noted that *tiugbae* apparently refers to "a surviving representative of the family" ("Senbriathra Fithail," 269). In L₁ this word has a mark of reference with a note at the bottom of the page which, unfortunately, is itself unintelligible because key words are illegible (A. O'Sullivan, *Book of Leinster*, 1517). This maxim seems to contradict our expectations that one would want to be survived by family members who would be able to take care of one in old age. Contrast maxims containing *goire*, §§ 3.20, 3.22, 3.23, 6.78.

6.44 This maxim is found in all recensions. The flexion of *tinnscrae* (< *to-ind-ess-cren-*) is almost certainly io.n, like *tochrae*, vb.n. of *do·cren*, which is similar in meaning. I follow Thurneysen who translated it as *besser (ist) Stamm als t[innscra]* and commented *dass eine Frau besser im eigenen Stamm bleibt statt für ein "tindscra" nach auswärts verheiratet zu werden* "that it is better that a woman stays with her own family rather than be given out in marriage for a bride-price" ("Heirat," 121; and see Patterson, *Cattle-Lords*, 289). Contrast the line in the *Aibidil* which reads *cach tua(i)th a tindscra* "to each tribe belongs its bride-price" (Smith, "Alphabet of Cuigne," 50 § 18). A woman was often married off so that her family could receive payment for her. In an episode from *Bethu Brigte* Brigit prevented herself from being given in marriage. The text explains: *ba sæth lia brathrea gait di-si in tinscrae erru* "her brothers were sorry that she kept the bride-price [*tinnscrae*] from them" (Ó hAodha, *Bethu Brigte*, 5.145 and note p. 46). Other words which may be translated as "bride-price" are *slabrae* (§ 6.17), *coibche* (§ 3.25) and *íarraid* (§ 6.68).

6.45 This maxim is found in all recensions. It is quoted in the seventeenth-century "Contention of the Bards", where it is described as a *sean-fhocal gnáthach ár sean* "a common proverb of our ancestors". I follow McKenna's translation (*Iomarbhágh na bhFileadh*, 152 § 44a).

6.46 This maxim is found in all recensions. *Trummae* is listed among the "three qualities which bespeak good fortune (*caíntocad*)" in *Triads* no.131 where it is translated as "self-importance". *Dínnime* is the abstract noun formed from *dínnim* "careless", which is itself formed from the privative prefix *dí* + *sním* "care" (*GOI*, 544 § 873). Among the "three things which tell every humble person (*cach n-umal*)" *Triads* no.191 lists *dínnime*, which is translated "homeliness", but in the context might more accurately be rendered "indolence, carelessness".

6.47 In a poem said to have been composed by Fothad na Canóine at the inauguration of Áed Oirdnide (ca. 797) we find the line *crábad, ecna óg /*

lubar lōr rit lind "piety, perfect wisdom, ample labour during your reign" (O'Donoghue, "Cert cech rīg co réil," 274 § 63). In a monastic context *laubair* means "manual labour". Gwynn translated this maxim as "Labour is better than fasting" ("Senbriathra Fithail," 269) and stated that it reflected the monastic life. However, in this text *áine* is used to mean "mental brightness".

6.48 This maxim is not found in Rec. L. All manuscripts in Rec. N read *dam(h)* which makes no sense here. The word *déinmiche* (*déinmige*), which is not listed in *DIL*, is the fem. iā-stem abstract noun (*GOI*, 165 § 257) formed from the adj. *déinmech* "lazy, inactive". The adjective is itself derived from the privative prefix *di-*, *de-* + *gnímach* (Meyer, "Zur keltischen Wortkunde," 187 § 239). This maxim complements the two previous ones (§§ 6.46, 6.47). Compare § 6.97 *Ferr drochdán dílmaini.*

6.49 This maxim is found in all recensions. It is very obscure. Gwynn suggested translating as "A cow is better than a year('s work)", and included the comment, "this seems to refer to the scale of wages" ("Senbriathra Fithail," 269). In support he cited these lines from the metrical *Dindshenchas*: *bói i faichill ri bliadain mbuic / ac tuilliud óen-bó is óen-bruit* "he was on hire for an easy year, / earning one cow and one cloak" (Gwynn, *Dindshenchas* iii, 310–11 lines 91–92). Refer also to a note by Gwynn on the same topic in the "Teaching of Máel Ruain" (*Rule of Tallaght*, 91 note to c. 40).

On the other hand, this maxim may refer to the compensation due to a *ráth* "paying surety" when the person he has gone surety for has defaulted. Robin Stacey has argued that when a debtor defaulted and the *naidm* "enforcing surety" had been unable to collect on the debt then the *ráth* took over. If, at this stage, the *ráth* was able to collect the debt from the debtor he also received a cow as compensation for his trouble. If, however, the debtor continued to default interest accrued on his debt at the rate of one fifth per month for a year (*Road to Judgment*, 39–42). This maxim appears to be telling a defaulting debtor that it is better to pay up on the defaulted debt as soon as possible (and pay an additional cow), before the penalties move into the interest-bearing period of a year. If this interpretation is correct, it is interesting for taking the point of view of an "underdog", the person who has defaulted and failed to meet his payments in the terms of a contract. See *naidm* at § 3.10 and *ráth* at §§ 3.11, 6.95. See discussion at § 6.27. For what can happen to someone who defaults in a contract, see § 3.21 and notes.

6.50 This maxim is not found in Rec. L. There is a clear split in readings between Rec. N and Y. N₁,₃,₄ all read *f[err] cloth gach biudh.* N₂ reads *f[err] cloth biudh.* Most Rec. Y readings (Y₂,₃,₄,₅,₆,₇) have *ferr cloith canbuaid.* Y₁ has the reading *cā* before *buaid,* which can be expanded as *can,* as found in the other manuscripts of Rec. Y, or as *cach,* that is, *ferr cloth cach búaid,* which creates a pattern parallel to that found in N₁,₃,₄. All manuscripts in Rec. Y read *cloith* which suggests a masc. o-stem nom. pl. (*cluith;* see *GOI,* 47 § 75) rather than a neuter o-stem; the same reading is found again in Y₁ at § 6.64 (cf. Carney, *Blathmac,* 151 note to line 993). The primary reading is well supported by readings from other wisdom-texts. Rec. A of *Audacht Morainn* has the lines *ní ria clotha ar bíad* [L₁ *ar is ferr dín cloth oldás din bíd*] "do not sell honour for food [for it is better to defend honour than shelter food]" (Kelly, *Audacht,* 68 § 43 lines 163–64 = Thurneysen, "Morands Fürstenspiegel," 86 § 43). *TC* § 11.2–3 paraphrases the lines just quoted: *ma contúaisi frim thecosc, nír tharta th'enech ar choirm ná ar biad, ar is ferr dín cloth oldás dín mbiid* "If you listen to my teaching, do not give your honour [*enech*] for ale nor for food, for it is better to defend one's honour [*cloth*] than to shelter one's food". O'Rahilly discussed a modern proverb *ní fearr biadh ná ciall* "food is not better than sense" (*Miscellany,* 110 § 339).

6.51 This maxim is not found in Rec. L. *Adbar* "material, matter" may be used in much the same sense as *damna* which denotes the "potential to become" inherent in a person or thing. Compare the modern proverb *fearr amhail ná dóith* "Better 'it is so' than 'it may be so'" (O'Rahilly, *Miscellany,* 44 § 154).

6.52 This maxim is not found in Rec. L. As preserved in Rec. N and Y it is very obscure. For the second word, Rec. N manuscripts read *luchair* "sheen, splendour"(?). Y₁ has *laurchauri* and Y₂ has *laurchuari* which I take to be *lurchaire* "foal". For the third word both recensions have *trenri(o)th,* except for N₁ which reads *tindrith.* If the first element of the latter word is *tind* "bright, dazzling", then it forms a compound similar to *trénrith.* The N₁ reading may also be taken as *tinnriud* "damage, injury" (vb.n. of **to-ind-reth-*), with a meaning like "Splendour is better than injury". The maxim as interpreted here seems to stress the notion of potential over accomplishment. For example, that it is better to have a mare which produces a foal rather than one which is particularly fast (*trénrith*).

6.53 This maxim is not found in Rec. L. The exact form and inflexion of the third word is uncertain. The vb.n. of *con·clich* "starts, precipitates" is attested in later texts as *cuclaige* iā.f "shaking, tottering, collision". The word is attested in *Audacht Morainn* as *cuicilche* (Kelly, *Audacht,* 10 § 28 line 69), and in our text as N₁ has *cucilche*, N₂ has *cucailce*, Y₁,₂ have *cucuilgu*. All examples from Rec. N end in *-e*, and are uncertain as to declension. All examples from Rec. Y end in *-u* (compare Rec. Y readings at §§ 6.70 *bithbiniu* and 6.84 *forbbu*) which suggest that it be treated as a neuter io-stem (*GOI*, 448–49 § 725).

6.54 This maxim is found in all recensions. *Gíallnae* "submission" is a term used for "base clientship". Binchy noted that the person who enters a relationship of *gíallnae* with a lord is not "unfree" but that their relation-ship is "essentially contractual and is terminable by either party on certain conditions" (*Críth Gablach*, 97). Binchy also suggested that *gíallnae* (<*gíall* "hostage") may originally have involved the handing over of an actual hostage to secure the contract (*Críth Gablach*, 95–98; see discussion in Stacey, *Road to Judgment*, "Hostage-Sureties," 82–111). Rec. B of *Audacht Morainn* has an example of *gíallnae* in the broader sense of submission: *to·léci doféth do gíallni* "turbulence yields to submission" (Kelly, *Audacht*, 16 § 54j line 127; see Carney, *Blathmac*, 34–35 § 99 line 394, where *gíallnae* is translated as "[justly imposed] subjection"; and *Blathmac*, 131 note for line 394). Hostage-taking helped to ensure the submission of vassals. Among those things best for a king in *Tecosca Cormaic* was *géill i nglassaib* "hostages in shackles" (*TC* § 1.8), and among those things best for the good of the tribe was *géill do inchaib* "hostages for status" (*TC* § 3.34).

DIL cites the variant from L₁, *ferr cride gialla*, as an example of *cride* in the sense of "valour" (*DIL* C 528.45), but the meaning in this maxim is more likely to be "affection, loyalty".

6.55 There are three reasonable readings given for this maxim which all express broadly the same view. Rec. L and N₂,₃,₄ have readings which favour the vb.n. *grísad* "inciting, injuring (with satire)". Rec. Y favours *gres(s)* "attack, insult". N₁ shows clearly the dat. pl. of *grís* "heat, ardour". See § 6.40 for examples of *grís(ad)*.

6.56 Rec. L and Y agree in favouring *tairisiu* "confidence, faithfulness, trustworthiness". Rec. N readings support *taircsiu* "attempt, effort". Both variants agree in stressing the importance of "reliability" as opposed to a person who makes empty promises.

6.57 None of the manuscripts reads *sobarthu* n.f "well-being, blessing, prosperity". N₁ Y₁,₂ have *soburthan*, L₁ has *sobarthain*, but the occurrence of oblique forms for nominative has been noted elsewhere in this text. Rec. L and Y readings favour *suíthe* "learning, knowledge", which I have treated as an io-stem. The version in X₁ *ferr sobarthan ina imad* suggests that its redactor understood Rec. N variants, $N_{1,2}$ have *saithe*, N_3 has *saoithe*, to mean "sufficiency, fill". Compare §§ 6.14, 6.31, 6.75, 6.92.

6.58 This maxim, which is found in all recensions, is also found in a saga (Stokes, "*Togail Troí,*" 46.1454; see § 4.16). The prefix *so-* links the second and third words through alliteration but it is not semantically empty. In one *speculum* poem the line is embellished to *is ferr síd sochocad sruith* and translated "Better is peace than prudent goodly warfare" (O'Donoghue, "Advice to a Prince," 47 § 18). In a footnote O'Donoghue pointed out that the phrase is used in the *Annals of the Four Masters*: ... *an ffearr síth iná sochoccadh* "who preferred peace to war" ("Advice to a Prince," 52 note 5; O'Donovan, *Four Masters* v, 1724 sub anno 1580). The poem edited by O'Donoghue also states *is maith cech dál dia tic síd* "good is every meeting from which peace comes" ("Advice to a Prince," 46 § 13; Best and O'Brien, *Book of Leinster* iii, 609 line 18718 = *is ferr cech dal dia tic síd*). Compare § 6.13 *Ferr dál debiuch.*

6.59 This maxim is found in all recensions. It is not clear which partner's family is the *sochenél*. It seems probable that it means that a man is better off marrying a good woman than simply marrying into a good family; but it could mean that a man who marries a good woman is better off than the man whose only asset is that he comes from a good family. Either interpretation compliments the good wife. Compare § 5.20 *Tosach sothcaid dagben.*

6.60 This maxim is found in all recensions, although it is omitted from L_1. *Súan* is usually translated "sleep", but a meaning more like "repose, tranquillity, indifference" is called for here. An instance where the latter sense applies is found in a line from Broccán's *Hymn* which reads *ní bu sanct-Brigit súanach / ní bu úarach im seirc Dé* (*Thes.* ii, 332.2). The editors translated *súanach* as "drowsy" but this word, and *úarach* (<*úar* "cold"), should be taken figuratively and translated as "indifferent, apathetic, uninterested". That is, "Saint Brigit was not indifferent, she was not apathetic about loving God". *Triads* no. 197 lists *serbae* "bitterness" as one of the three things which reveals bad manhood (*drochferas*).

6.61 All recensions have this maxim, but only Rec. N and Y have witnesses which show earlier n-stem inflexion of the dat. sg. *cormaim* (*GOI*, 192 § 302.3). Contrast the sentiments of this maxim with *Triads* no. 93 which lists among the "fewnesses that are better than plenty" *úathad carat im chuirm* "a fewness of friends around ale".

6.62 This maxim is not found in Rec. L. Cormac told Cairpre that among the things which are "worst for a person's body" is *rosáith* "over-eating" (*TC* § 21.7). Compare § 6.4 *Ferr slán sásad.* In a figurative use of the word, Máel Díthruib told Máel Ruain that among his four wishes was *mo saith for tacaldaimsiu* "my fill of conversation with you" (Gwynn and Purton, "Monastery of Tallaght," 136 § 25 line 26–27). See § 1.35 for a word derived from *sáith*.

6.63 This maxim is found in all recensions. Contrast § 1.3 *Ad·cota cíall caínchruth*.

6.64 The form of this maxim is based on the readings from Rec. N and Y. Readings from Rec. L treated at § 6.94 seem likely to be variants of this maxim. But Rec. Y contains two separate maxims, one of which requires treatment here with the Rec. N variants, and the other with Rec. L readings at § 6.94, which see. The variants of the third word, Y_1 has *cubaidh* and Y_2 has *cubuidh*, should be seen as spelling variants of *cumaid* with lenited *b* replacing lenited *m*, rather than as *cubaid* "harmonious, fitting", which does not make good sense here.

6.65 This maxim is found in all recensions. The form *comaid* in N_1 reflects an attested dental inflexion of *comae* "payment, terms" which according to Thurneysen was original ("Aus dem irischen Recht III," 337 § 28; *Lexique* C 161). But an example from "An Old-Irish Metrical Rule" of the gen. sg. bound by rhyme proves that by ca. 800 it could be inflected as an iā-stem (Strachan, "Metrical Rule," 202 § 29). L. Breatnach has identified *coimded* u.m "confiscation, custody" as the vb.n. of an otherwise unattested verb *con·íada* ("*Bretha Nemed Toísech*," 30). The simple verb *íadaid* means "encloses, encompasses, seals up".

6.66 I translate this maxim following Gwynn's suggestion of reading *áithe* figuratively as "sharp words" ("Senbriathra Fithail," 269). Gwynn's interpretation is supported by examples such as §§ 6.83 *Ferr leth lánetiug* and 6.93 *Ferr becc n-érai*; and by the notion of supplication implicit in §§ 1.11 *Ad·cota becdatu caínbuidi, 6.67 Ferr buide dígbáil*.

This maxim is attested in all recensions, but no clear division between the recensions is to be found in the variant readings. *Aithe* "recompense, requital", vb.n. of *ad·fen*, was a neuter noun, but no trace of following nazalization has been preserved. For difficulties in choosing between *aithe* and *áithe* see the note in "Esnada Tige Buchet" (Greene, *Fingal Rónáin*, 43 note to line 505).

The *a* in the form *aopudh*, found in Rec. Y, may be explained as the use of a possessive pronoun to express the objective genitive of the verbal noun of a transitive verb. Since some witnesses read *ithe* ($N_{1,2}$ L_3) for the second word, it seems possible to read this maxim as *Ferr a ithe a opud* "Better to eat it than to refuse it".

6.67 This maxim is found in all recensions. The semantics of *buide* is discussed at § 1.11.

6.68 This ambiguous maxim is found in all recensions. I translate *aire* as "increase" derived from the preposition *air*, as set out by Russell ("Varia I," 164–66; see § 2.6). I take this maxim to mean that to prosper (increase) through one's own efforts is better than relying on the proceeds from a fosterage-fee (Patterson, *Cattle-Lords*, 169; cf. Kelly, *Guide*, 87–88, 117). This text maintains a cautious attitude towards fosterage. See §§ 3.19 *Dligid altramm imfochaid*, 6.20 *Ferr beccfine móraltramm*. *Íarraid* could also apply to a dowry, and this text is unenthusiastic about making gains through marriage contracts. Compare §6.44 *Ferr túath tinnscru*.

The following interpretation is based on meanings of these two words which are well attested only in a later period. *Aire* may mean "heed, watch out", and *íarraid* is the vb.n. of a verb meaning "seek, search for". This maxim could therefore mean something like "Better to care for something (now) than to have to seek for it (later)".

6.69 All recensions have this maxim, but there is a clear division between Rec. N and Y, on the one hand, and Rec. L, which reverses the word order of the other two recensions. Both *aicsiu* and *aititiu* have nasal inflexion which is accurately reflected in the transpositions, proving that they are not due simply to scribal error. *Aititiu*, vb.n. of *ad·daim* "acknowledges, concedes, consents to", has the legal meaning "acknowledgement" of a contract or transaction (Stacey, *Road to Judgment*, 67–68). The primary reading is found in Rec. N and Y. It seems to mean that before one consents to the terms of a contract, one should confirm or verify ("see") any property dealt with by the contract. If this interpretation is valid then it contravenes the secondary reading represented by Rec. L.

6.70 Only Rec. Y contains the variant given as the primary reading here. Both Rec. N and L have the variant with *bithainim*. The reading in Rec. Y offers evidence that many of these maxims are intended to be interpreted from the Church's point of view. In a discussion of the death penalty in early Irish law, Kelly has noted that "In general, Irish canon law places more emphasis on the death penalty than the secular law-texts" (*Guide*, 216, and discussion pp. 216–21). An O.Ir. poem from the introduction to the *Senchas Már*, attributed to Dubthach maccu Lugair, emphasizes the Church's support, through St Patrick, for the death penalty. The poem reads: *Bibdu cách léices bibdada. Biru bás bibdada* "Everyone who lets criminals off is a criminal. I condemn criminals to death" (McCone, "Dubthach maccu Lugair," 8, 29). An O.Ir. poem ascribed to

St Mo-ling praises a king for putting criminals to death (Meyer, *Miscellanea Hibernica*, 17–18). A poem in the *Dindshenchas* attributes Benén (= Benignus, a companion of St Patrick) with promoting the death penalty. The translation of the quatrain is: "Whoever transgresses the law of the kings / Benén prescribed firmly for ever / that he should not thrive in his tribe, / but should die in his mortal sin". The final line reads *acht a bás 'n-a bith-bine* (Gwynn, *Dindshenchas* iii, 18–19). The *Annals of Ulster* for the year 746 note that six captives were hanged for violating sanctuary at Domnach Pátraic (Mac Airt and Mac Niocaill, *Annals of Ulster*, 200–1).

Wisdom-texts also support the death penalty. *Tecosca Cormaic* includes among the things best for a king *báded bidbadu* "let him extinguish criminals" (*TC* § 1.37), and among the true rights of a king *marbad ulcu* "let him slay evildoers" (*TC* § 2.5). *Triads* no. 92 includes among "the three deaths which are better than life" *bás foglada* "the death of a robber", but the variant in the Book of Ballymote reads *bás bithbenaig* "death of a criminal". Compare *cech merlech borb bōeth / a erlech collūath* "Let every violent wanton rebel be put to death at once" (O'Donoghue, "Cert cech ríg co réil," 270–71 § 45). From the *tecosc* in the "Battle of Airtech" we find among the things incumbent upon Cuscraid, *díth bithbinech* "destruction of criminals" (Best, "Battle of Airtech," 173, 180 § 3).

The concern with *ainim* "blemish", found in Rec. N and L, is well represented in *Bretha Déin Chécht* (Binchy, "*Bretha Déin Chécht*," 40–41 §§ 30–31). However, preferring death to a lasting blemish seems extreme for the sentiments of this text. *Bretha Étgid* states that Cormac mac Airt was removed from the kingship of Tara because of a blemish (*AL* iii, 82.16–84.7 = *CIH* i, 250.10–16). In the Old Irish saga of Fergus mac Léti, the protagonist's death was indirectly brought about as the result of a blemish (Binchy, "Fergus mac Léti," 33–48).

6.71 This maxim, with its variants, is found in all recensions. The form as given in the edition is found in Rec. L. Rec. N manuscripts suggest the compound *airfognam* "service". Rec. Y manuscripts read *auognam* which perhaps represents *fognam* preceded by a possessive pronoun expressing the objective genitive (see discussion at § 6.66), or a corruption of *aurgnam* "household work, service" (Kelly, *Guide*, 73; Thurneysen, "*Cáin Lánamna*," 29).

6.72 This maxim is found in all recensions. *TC* § 16.53 says that women are *amairsi erlabra* which Meyer translated as "incredulous of speech".

6.73 N_1 Y_1 L_1 all support an otherwise unattested form *répend* o.n, vb.n. of *répaid* "rends, tears", for the third word. Compare *scríbend* o.n, vb.n. of *scríbaid* "writes", and *légend* o.n, vb.n. of *légaid* "reads" (*GOI*, 455 § 737). The vb.n. *répad* u.m is attested in $L_{2,3}$ which have *rebad*. Both *scríbaid* and *légaid* also have later attested verbal nouns that take the forms *scríbad* and *légad* respectively.

6.74 This maxim is not found in Rec. L. I treat the third word as made up of the intensive prefix *ro-* + *logud* u.m, vb.n. of *logaid* "concedes, remits". If this reading is correct then all manuscripts show syncope, N_1 has *rolgad*, Y_1 has *rolgud*; except for N_2 which has *rolag-*. In the Milan glosses *logaid* means "obtains, acquires" and is equivalent to *ad·cota*. It glosses the Latin verbs *obtinere* and *impetrare* (*DIL* L 185.34–36). In the laws it means "permit, concede" (Thurneysen, "*Cáin Lánamna*," 54 § 26). In this case the broadest possible sense of *rath*, as vb.n. of *ernaid* "bestows, grants", seems best. This maxim seems to mean that it is better to be granted something given willingly, than to obtain it only after it has been conceded (perhaps unwillingly).

6.75 This maxim is missing from L_1 but is found in all other manuscripts in Rec. L. The phrase *réde fri doíni* "evenness" or "mildness towards men" is used in "Riagail Comgaill" (Strachan, "Metrical Rule," 193 § 2) and *Apgitir Chrábaid* (Hull, "Alphabet of Piety," 72 § 20 line 115). For other maxims which point out that wisdom or knowledge is not the greatest gift, see §§ 6.14, 6.57, 6.92.

6.76 This maxim is found in all recensions. Other examples of *fís* and its compounds are found at §§ 4.28, 6.14, 6.92.

6.77 This maxim is found in all recensions. It is an O.Ir. equivalent of the biblical *Melior est sapientia quam arma bellica* (Ecclesiastes 9:18).

6.78 This maxim is found in all recensions. Attendance to parents, elders and those less fortunate than oneself was stressed in § 3 *dligid*. Several maxims value personal relationships over possessions: §§ 6.17 *Ferr sochraite slabrai*, 6.44 *Ferr túath tinnscru*, 6.61 *Ferr carae cormaim*.

6.79 This maxim is found in all recensions. The exact derivation of *grefel* is problematical, but its meaning "disorder, confusion, chaos" is clear enough (see Gwynn, "Some Irish Words," 63–64; Carney, *Blathmac*, 129 note to line 347). The variety of forms for this word, *grefel* N_1 and L_1, *crephul* Y_1, displays the difficulties in establishing its etymology. Marstrander rejected Meyer's proposal, **gre(g)-suel*, on phonetic grounds (Marstrander, "Remarques," 384; Meyer, *Wortkunde* v, 633–34 § 83; ix, 399 § 235). The examples cited by Meyer and Gwynn suggest *grefel*. Carney favoured *crephel* which he printed in his edition of *Blathmac*. *Crapul* is the reading in Rec. Y (except Y$_1$) suggesting that later scribes were confusing the Old Norse borrowing *crapall* "fetter, bond". I favour the form *grefel* and treat it as an o-stem. Compare §§ 6.30 *Ferr bríg bágaib*, 6.37 *Ferr caíntórmach cintaib*, 6.70 *Ferr bás bithbiniu*.

6.80 This maxim is found in all recensions.

6.81 This maxim is not found in Rec. L. N$_1$ reads *lin* with ⱡ *e* written above the line, N$_{2,3}$ read *lin*, Y$_1$ reads *lín* for the second word. All manuscripts have readings for the third word which are acceptable variants of *lobrae* "infirmity, weakness (in faith), legal incapacity". For the primary reading I follow the majority of manuscripts and read *lín* "full complement, number necessary to complete a task", which makes good sense here. In his edition, Meyer chose *lén* for the second word ("Bríathra Flainn Fína," 20.2). For a discussion of the semantics of *lén*, see § 5.18 *Tosach lobrae lén*, for which this variant seems to be a corollary. The other Rec. Y manuscripts do not make sense here. (Y$_2$ has *ferr leghenn liubhra*. Compare the variants at § 1.48 *Ad·cota léigend libru*).

6.82 This maxim is found in all recensions. The manuscript readings, especially N$_2$ which has *laimtnighe*, suggest a feminine abstract noun formed from *laimthenach* "daring", which shows syncopation of the second rather than the third syllable, as in *laimthinche* "audacity, daring". An example of the adjective is found at *TC* § 7.21 *nírba laimthenach ciarba lúath* "I was not impetuous although I was swift".

6.83 This maxim is not found in Rec. L. Compare §§ 6.53 *Ferr coimsetu cucilchiu*, 6.93 *Ferr becc n-érai*. O'Rahilly noted the modern proverb *fearr leath-bhairghean ná bheith gan arán* "Better half a loaf than to be without bread" (*Miscellany*, 41 § 143).

6.84 This maxim is not found in Rec. L. I take the third word to be *forbbae* io.n, vb.n. of *for·ben* "smites, strikes, cuts". It is close in sentiment to the "political" interpretation given for § 6.34 *Ferr móin immattrub*. The meanings "fury, fierceness" or "roughness" for *fróech* (*fráech*) do not seem to apply here.

6.85 This maxim is not found in Rec. L. *Dúthracht* is also found at § 1.2.

6.86 This maxim is found in all recensions. All witnesses agree in the form *mórsliab* for the third word. None has the expected dat. sg. *-sléib*, which has been restored in the edition.

6.87 This maxim is not found in Rec. L. For the second and third words, all witnesses record forms with the transitional spellings *mbr-*or *mbl-* for words that in O.Ir. began with *mr-* or *ml-*. Land was always considered more valuable than movable property.

6.88 This problematical maxim is not found in Rec. L. The primary reading is based on Rec. Y. *Frithoíb* is taken to be a compound of *frith-* "against, counter" + *oíb*, f "semblance, appearance". Compare the compound *anáeb* (< *oíb*) "that which is unpleasant, distress". Formally the third word could be a dat. pl. of *frith* "a find, estray, a waif". Its meaning might be "Better proof (of ownership) than found objects". Another possible interpretation is to read the third word as dat. pl. of *frithaí* "counter-suit", a legal term attested only once in *DIL*. The flexion of *aí* "legal suit" is uncertain, and its relationship to *áui* "poetic art" is unclear (*Lexique* A 19). If it is derived from the latter word then we would expect dental inflexion.

The secondary reading is from Rec. N, but note that N_1 does not contain this maxim, or any of those remaining in the *ferr* section. I base this interpretation on the idea that a *fert* (*fertae*) "grave mound, tumulus" was used as a boundary marker and that an ancestor's grave marked the boundary and was felt to help protect the tribal territory. The graves might be marked by *ogam* inscribed standing stones and could serve as legal evidence for claim to land (Kelly, *Guide*, 204). Charles-Edwards describes rituals used to lay claim to land involving crossing over these ancestral graves. As he says, this legal procedure "depends upon a belief that the dead do not merely survive but may take an active part in the affairs of the living" ("Boundaries," 85).

It is also possible to take *fertaib* as dat. pl. of *fiurt* "miracle, wonder" and give an interpretation that reflects an analytical mode of thought, that is, "Better proof than wonders".

6.89 This maxim is found only in Rec. Y. It seems to have a misogynistic ring which is usually absent from this text, particularly when compared with *TC* § 16.

6.90 This maxim is not found in Rec. L. It is missing from N_1. In the other manuscripts of Rec. N, the third word is the vb.n. *suidiugud* "putting, placing, arranging". The form preserved in Rec. Y is one of the few examples of a finite verbal form used for the third word in the maxims. (Y_1 has *suidigthir*, Y_2 has *suidigtir*). I have restored *suidigther*, the relative 3sg. pres. pass. of *suidigidir* (*GOI*, 459 § 750). All manuscripts in Rec. Y include the Latin gloss *ut congruum fiant*. A possible analogue found in the Anglo-Saxon gnomic collection from MS Cotton Tiberius B ("Maxims II") reads *fyrd sceal ætsomne, tirfæstra getrum* "an army must act together, a band set on glory" (Dobbie, *Minor Poems*, 56.31–32).

6.91 This maxim is found only in Rec. Y. All manuscripts read *briat(h)ar* for the third word; the dat. sg. *bréithir* has been restored in the text. This maxim perhaps means "Better (a payment of) cattle than a promise". For another example of *búar*, but one which is problematical, see § 6.19.

6.92 This maxim is not found in Rec. N. The translation follows Gwynn ("Senbriathra Fithail," 269). Compare §§ 6.14 *Ferr sét sous*, 6.57 *Ferr sobarthu suíthiu*, 6.75 *Ferr réide rogaís.*

6.93 This maxim is found in all recensions, but only Rec. Y shows nasalization after the adjective *becc* o/ā when used as a neuter substantive. Based on the readings of $Y_{1,2}$ I have treated *érae* "refusal" as a fem. iā-stem. Compare §§ 6.53 *Ferr coimsetu cucilchiu*, 6.66 *Ferr áithe opud*, 6.83 *Ferr leth lánetiug.*

6.94 This maxim is not found in Rec. N. Y_1 and L_3 preserve the older disyllabic *cloud* as opposed to the later long vowel of *clód* "turn, convert, change, alter". *Cummae* is vb.n. of *con·ben* "smites, cuts off, destroys". For sentiment, compare § 6.84 *Ferr fróech forbbu.*

The reading at L_2 (= *f*[*err*] *cloth cumma*) raises the possibility that the redactor was influenced by the maxim at § 6.64 *Ferr cloth cumaid*. But all Rec. Y manuscripts make a clear distinction between the two maxims. If we read the third word as *cumae* "grief" then we have a maxim that reads "Better change than grief". However, no manuscript shows the dental inflexion of this word, but this could reflect the modern form *cumha*.

6.95 This maxim is not found in Rec. N. *Ré* may mean a "period of time, interval". Binchy noted that in legal procedure *ré* refers to the time fixed for a hearing ("*Féchem, fethem, aigne*," 31). I follow the translation offered by Gwynn who explained, "This seems to mean that it is better to ask for time to pay a debt than to offer securities, which may lead to further difficulties" ("Senbriathra Fithail," 269). For other examples of *ráth*, see §§ 3.11, and discussion at 3.7, 6.8.

6.96 This maxim is not found in Rec. N. The quality of *búaine* "permanence, constancy" can be compared to *astud* "steadiness" in §§ 3.34, 6.72.

6.97 This maxim is not found in Rec. N. *Dílmaine* can mean both "idleness" and "exemption (from responsibility), being unrestricted". *Drochdán* also presents ambiguities for it might suggest a craft which is poorly practised or a craft which is of low prestige. This maxim seems best interpreted using the latter sense and suggests that any work is better than none. Compare §§ 6.47 *Ferr laubair áini* and 6.48 *Ferr dán déinmichi*. O'Rahilly cited the following modern proverb, *Námha ceard muna cleachttar* "A trade that is not practiced is an enemy" (*Miscellany*, 117 § 354).

6.98 The remaining five maxims are found only in L_2. *Engnam* and *enech* are often found in association. One gnomic poem reads *eochair engnam enech* "Honour opens out to prowess" (Meyer, "Mitteilungen [1908]," 270 § 4). O'Clery equates the two, *eangnamh .i. eineach*, but he also glosses *eangnamh* with *gliocas* "cleverness, shrewdness" (Miller, "O'Clery's Glossary," 407).

6.99 The manuscript reads *degnurm* which I take to be for *degmuirn* "ardour, exuberance". When Cairpre asked Cormac "by what means sovereignty was taken upon tribes and families and peoples" part of the answer was *a feib dúthchusa ⁊ airlabra* "by virtue of inherent abilities and eloquence" (*TC* § 5.4).

6.100 Contrast Cormac's answer when Cairpre asked him "what was the sweetest thing he had heard", part of which was *ilach íar mbúaid* "exultation after victory" (*TC* § 10.4).

6.101 The semantic range of *múcnae* and its derivatives is not clear. The form *múcnaid* appears to be an agent noun (*GOI*, 170–71 § 267) rather than an abstract noun. Dinneen gives *múchnaid* as a variant of *múchna*. In *Apgitir Chrábaid* the abstract nominal form *múcnatu* is used in a section distinguishing vices from virtues, *múcnatu i fail fírinne* "repression beside justice" (Hull, "Alphabet of Piety," 64 § 11 line 51). *TC* § 13.16 says *múcna cech mog* "every slave is repressed". In the *Aibidil* the same form as found in this maxim is used. It suggests an agent noun, and reads *múcnaid cach borb-chrāideach* "Every harsh-tormenter is a repressor" (Smith, "Alphabet of Cuigne," 67 § 62).

The second word of this maxim has several plausible interpretations. I have translated the maxim using *gres* in the sense "attack, attempt, effort", but there is also a word *grés* "continuance, practice" and *grés* "handicraft, workmanship".

6.102 The meaning of *rosc* here is not clear. It later developed a specialized meaning in the verb *roscaid* "excites, incites". As interpreted, this maxim is similar in sentiment to the preceding one. *Dígbad* is an alternative vb.n. for *do·gaib* "takes away, diminishes", for the other vb.n., *dígbál*, see § 6.67.

§ 7 MAITH DÁN ECNAE

§ 7 This section is stylistically unlike any other section yet the sentiments agree with those in the maxims. It contrasts the benefits of *ecnae* "learning" with the deficiencies of *láechdacht* "the martial life". This section is difficult to describe stylistically. It is not straightforward prose, nor is it poetry. Lines are not rhymed, nor is there any consistent pattern of alliteration, either internal or linking. When broken into sense groups most lines contain two or three stressed syllables. As in much early poetry, adjectives may precede the nouns they modify. Parallelism is used to good effect throughout.

7.1 This line is parallel in structure to § 7.12. Each line introduces one of the two distinct halves of this section. Both lines are best treated as copular sentences with the first element, *dán*, being preceded by its adjective, a syntactic feature usually restricted to poetry and assumed to be indicative of age (*GOI*, 229 § 362; cf. Stokes, *Félire Óengusso*, p. xxxviii; Kelly, "Poem in Praise," 6–7; Carney, "*A maccucáin*," 30, 37). *Ecnae* refers to "learning" acquired through study and often implies study of Christian doctrine (L. Mac Mathúna, "Wordfield 'Knowledge'," 155). This section has the most overtly Christian message in the text, yet the concerns of this section are as much with this world as with the next. The benefits to be derived from *ecnae* offer explicit rewards in both worlds. In *Immacallam in dá Thuarad*, Néde tells Ferchertne that he is son of *Ecna mac na trí nDea nDána* "Learning, son of the three gods of *dán*" (Stokes, *Colloquy of Sages*, 30.139; see also T. F. O'Rahilly, *Ir. Hist. & Myth.*, 315). Comparing ecclesiastical scholars and the *filid*, the law-tract *Míadślechta* states: *is ecna mathair cacha dana dib* "wisdom [*ecnae*] is the mother of each learned profession amongst them" (*AL* iv, 356.26 = *CIH* ii, 586.28–29; Breatnach, *Uraicecht na Ríar*, 99 note 44). For other examples of *ecnae* or its compounds, see §§ 3.1, 4.23, 5.10, 6.22. But see also *éolas* (§§ 4.22, 4.26, 5.1, 6.9), *fís* (§§ 4.28, 6.14, 6.76, 6.92), *gáes* (§§ 1.15, 1.23, 3.2, 6.75, 6.77). For other examples of *dán* or its compounds, see §§ 6.1, 6.48, 6.97. For associations with teaching and learning, see *aite* (§§ 3.9, 3.24), *elathu* (§ 3.18), *maigister* (§ 3.20a), *múnad* (§ 3.30).

7.2–5 These four lines are all parallel in structure, the formula being *do·gní* [*ecnae*] *X di Y* "[learning] makes an X of a Y". All witnesses have substituted *do* for the original preposition *di / de*, a well-attested process in the O.Ir. period (*GOI*, 505 § 831.C). Our text does not emphasize the hierarchical structure of early Irish society, and although it mentions the *rí* "king" and *ánsruth* "poet of the second rank, noble", the emphasis is more on accomplishment attained through *ecnae* than on inherited rank and privilege.

Ánsruth denotes the rank of a poet immediately below the top ranked *ollam filed*. The latter has the same honour-price as a king (cf. Breatnach, "Bretha Nemed Toísech," 16–17 § 19 and note p. 38). *Ánsruth* may refer to someone with the necessary talent — and who has followed the appro-

priate course of study — to be equal to an *ollam*, but who lacks the required family background to claim the title. In the context of the benefits
of *ecnae*, *ánsruth* is an appropriate term since it represents the attempt to
raise one's social status through one's own efforts and skills (see Breatnach, *Uraicecht na Ríar*, 93–94, 97 and 106–9 §§ 10–12, 114–15 § 22).
An *esert* is "one who neglects his holding, a tramp, a vagrant", etymologically *ess + fert* "one who leaves his land" (*GOI*, 508 § 834; see also Kelly,
Guide, 100; Charles-Edwards, *Kinship*, 419–20).

The notion of raising a *dochenél* to a *sochenél* is related to the individual's efforts to raise his own status (note the three-generation requirement
in Breatnach, *Uraicecht na Ríar*, 94–98; cf. increasing one's honour-price
by increasing one's qualifications in *Bretha Nemed Toísech*: Breatnach,
"*Bretha Nemed Toísech*," 16–17 §§ 17–20; even the slave may elevate his
status, particularly through association with the Church: Kelly, *Guide*, 95–
97). Contrast the *sóerthúatha* and *dóerthúatha*, that is, free and unfree
tribes. Note *soíre* at §§ 1.35, 1.56, 3.35 and *doíre* at §§ 1.36, 1.57, 5.16.

The contrast between *gáeth* "wise" and *báeth* "foolish" may distinguish
the "legally capable person" (*gáeth*) from the "legally incapable person"
(*báeth*) (McLeod, *Contract Law*, 59). See *gáes* §§ 1.15, 1.23, 3.2, 6.75,
6.77, 9.9 and *báes* §§ 1.5, 1.25, 4.13.

§ 7.6–7 These lines, along with § 7.8–10, continue the description of *ecnae*.
Note that the *deired* "end, result" of *ecnae* is better than its commencement.

§ 7.8–9 These two lines indicate the Christian milieu of this text which, at
the same time, avoids promoting any specific theological message. Compare the use of *cenntar* and *alltar* in an Old Irish penitential: *miscais in
chenntuir, serc ind altair* "hatred of this world, love of the world to come"
(Gwynn, "Irish Penitential," 138–39 § d). Note the echo of § 7.8 at § 3.1
Dligid ecnae airmitin.

§ 7.10–11 *Derchoíntech* is appropriate to a religious context as shown by the
gloss *derchoíntea de·rochoínet a n-ícc* "of the despair wherewith they despair
of their salvation" (Wb. 21ᵇ1; *Thes.* i, 633). § 7.11 has the appearance of
a gloss incorporated into the main text. Compare the use of *nem* "heaven"
to *alltar* at § 7.9, and contrast *ifernach* "damned, hell-bound" at § 7.17.
N_3 and L_3 expand *dó* to *don anmain* "(bestowing heaven) upon the soul",
and L_2 reads *fri foglaim nimi* "for learning of heaven".

§ 7.12 This line is parallel in structure to § 7.1 with the adjective *doilig*
preceding its noun *dán*. I translate *láechdacht < láech* as "the martial life".
However, this translation does not represent its full semantic range and it
must be thought of as incorporating both sexual licence and blood-letting,

particularly as seen from the perspective of the early Irish Church. Mac Cana argued that the term *láech*, in its narrower meaning "warrior", cannot be attested before the middle of the eighth century, at least not in heroic literature ("Two Notes," 125–28). *Láech* is generally assumed to be derived from Latin *laicus* which is supported by certain glossary entries (Meyer, "*Sanas Cormaic*," 66 § 794; Stokes, "O'Mulconry's Glossary," 269 § 777). Watkins, on the other hand, proposed a native etymology for *láech* from **lāw-iko-* ("Indo-European Metrics," 241 note 1).

The Latin word *laicus* is well attested in the broad meaning "layman" associated with a monastic community. In the early Latin penitentials the clerical preoccupations with their *laici* centred on both blood-letting and sexual license (cf. Bieler, *Penitentials*, "Finnian" 86–89 §§ 35, 36, 37, 39s; "Bigotian" 220–21 § 4; note the textual variants at § 7.16). These concerns are represented for clerics in the O.Ir. "Rule of Ailbe of Emly" which states that neither "a warrior nor a woman" *fénid ná banscál* should be found in association with the monks (O Neill, "Rule of Ailbe," 104–5 § 37a).

Glossarial entries consistently show a *láech* associated with sexual licence. The entry in *Sanas Cormaic* for *laíches* "laywoman" derives the word from *láech* and *fess* "cohabiting with" or "feast" (Meyer, "*Sanas Cormaic*," 66 § 795; see also *coitreb*, Stokes, "O'Davoren's Glossary," 284 § 542; and *fessa*, Stokes, "O'Mulconry's Glossary," 259 § 526). Many Irish marriage practices, including acceptance of temporary sexual liaisons and polygyny, were not sanctioned by the Church (cf. Ó Corráin, "Women," 6–7; Ó Corráin, "Marriage," 5–24). The *aithech baitside* "baptized commoner" in *Críth Gablach* was expected to observe proper marriage laws, fasts, Sundays, and Lent (Binchy, *Críth Gablach*, 6.144–45).

Sharpe stated that *laicus* in the seventh- and eighth-century hagiographical texts "may mean someone outside the Christian fold and hateful to it, practicing a more or less organized form of brigandage" ("The Devil's Men," 76). In other words, the early usage of Latin *laicus* may be associated with the activities of *fíanas* "the profession of a roving warrior" (Nagy, *Wisdom of the Outlaw*, 41–79 *et passim*) and *díberg* "marauding, pillaging". McCone described a *fían*, from which is derived the abstract *fíanas*, as "an independent organization of predominantly landless, unmarried, unsettled, and young men given to hunting, warfare, and sexual license in the wilds outside the *túath* . . ." ("Werewolves, Cyclopes," 13). *Apgitir Chrábaid* disapproved of *fíanas* (Hull, "Alphabet of Piety," 72–73 § 25). The O'Mulconry entry for *díberg* equates it with *fíanas* and contrasts it with *láechdacht*, associating *díberg* and *fíanas* with pagan practices (Stokes, "O'Mulconry's Glossary," 248 § 309). The O.Ir. penitential commutations offer a clear example of the concern about blood-letting among the laity in the statement "for there is hardly a single layman or laywoman who has not some part in manslaughter" (Binchy, "Penitential Commutations," 60 § 8 = Bieler, *Penitentials*, 279 § 8).

As in other societies of the early Middle Ages, each member of a *túath* was a potential warrior. We need only recall that the *Cáin Adamnáin*, in addition to protecting clerics and women, was promulgated on behalf of innocent children *co mbat ingníma fri guin duine* "until they are capable of slaying a man" (Meyer, *Cáin Adamnáin*, 24–25 § 34). *Críth Gablach* describes the *aithech baitside* "baptized commoner" as someone who avoids killing people — except on a day of battle or when someone is seeking his head (Binchy, *Críth Gablach*, 6.142–44; see also *slógad*, *Críth Gablach*, 106). Furthermore, compulsory military service was an obligation for both individuals and communities in base clientship (Mac Neill, *Celtic Ireland*, 87; Kelly, *Guide*, 31; Patterson, *Cattle-Lords*, 168, 225–26).

The specific meaning of "warrior" for *láech*, attested from the eighth century onward, is likely to be a result of the greater control exerted by the Church in attempting to curb the effects of the endemic warfare of early Irish society, an effort which is recorded in the promulgation of *Cáin Adamnáin* in 697 and *Lex Patricii* ca. 737. Nevertheless, by the late eighth and early ninth centuries, when the monastic communities themselves began to wage war openly with one another, it was their lay tenants who bore the brunt of the fighting (Hughes, "Church and the World," 101–5).

The use of *dán* to describe *láechdacht* is intended to contrast with § 7.1, that is, *ecnae* vs. *láechdacht*. *Ecnae* "learning (in Latin and in Irish)" implies attendance at a monastic school and acceptance of the Church's strictures. *Láechdacht* implies full participation in the secular practices of the *túath*, including blood-letting and sexual license (at least in the Church's view). An example of forms of violence described as *dán* can be found in *Togail Bruidne Da Derga* where Conaire's foster-brothers complain: *im gabáil dána a n-athar 7 a seanathar díb, .i. gat 7 brat 7 guin daíne 7 díberg* "about the taking of the occupation (*dán*) of their father and their grandfather from them, i.e. theft and plunder and manslaughter and marauding" (Stokes, "Dá Derga's Hostel," 28 §18; Knott, *Togail Bruidne*, 6 § 18 lines 192–94). This example from a saga meets the three-generation requirement for Conaire's fosterbrothers to become hereditary experts in their chosen *dán* (Breatnach, *Uraicecht na Ríar*, 94–98) and suggests that *díberg* "marauding" might be an elected profession for some members of a *túath*.

7.13–15 The use of *dérgnae* "undistinguished" continues the contrast with *ecnae*. *Dérgnae* is derived from the privative *dí-* + *érgnae* "understanding, discernment, the exhibition of wisdom". In *Immacallam in dá Thuarad*, in that section where Néde presumes to tell Ferchertne his background, he states that he is son of *Rochond mac Ergnai, Ergna mac Ecnai* "Great intelligence son of discernment, discernment son of learning" (Stokes, *Colloquy of Sages*, 30.137–38). *TC* § 29.14 reads *dia mba rolabar, bid dérgna*, which Meyer translated as "if you be too talkative, you will not be heeded". But *labar* implies arrogance and *dérgnae* conveys a lack of discernment. The deliberate contrast between *duí* "simpleton, unskilled practitioner" and *suí* "expert, skilled practitioner" sustains the metaphor based on learning and the application of *dán*. An ironic note is struck by the fact that a *suí* [*láechdachtae*] is *duthain* "transitory, short-lived", reminding us that *láechdacht* implies participation in warfare.

7.16–17 The two variants at § 7.16, *tregtach* "pierced through, pained" (Rec. N, Y) and *étradach* "lustful, vicious" (Rec. L), reflect the Church's concern with violence and sex. For example, in the O.Ir. penitentials it says that anger kills the soul of man *amal tregtas foebar corp nduini* "like the edge of a weapon pierces a man's body" (Gwynn, "Irish Penitential," 164 § 1a; see *GOI*, 534 § 856; T. F. O'Rahilly, "Notes, Mainly Etymological," 168–69). *Pecad étraid* "a sin of lust" is noted in a religious text (Gwynn and Purton, "Monastery of Tallaght," 143 § 41) and a married couple from the *áos tuati* "laity" are referred to as *áos étraich* "lustful people" (Gwynn and Purton, "Monastery of Tallaght," 154–55 § 67). The fact that the dead from among the practitioners of *láechdacht* are *ifernach* "damned, hell-bound" equates with Sharpe's description of a *laicus* as "someone outside of the Christian fold and hateful to it" ("The Devil's Men," 76). $X_{1,2,4}$ have conflated and slightly altered §§ 7.12–17 as follows: *doilig dán láechdacht, ní suthain a mbí (sic), ifernaig a mairb*. The middle line reads "Its living are not long-lived" (cf. Baumgarten, "Syntax," 108–9).

7.18 The two variants of this line distinguish between the subjunctive, best represented in Rec. L, and the indicative, best represented in Rec. Y. *Do·im(m)na (do)* is attested in two meanings which both suit here, the first "bequeaths, commits to, entrusts", and the second, "enjoins, commands". All manuscripts in Rec. N and L, except for L_1, have a verbal form equivalent to [*ní*] *timain*. This form is listed by Lewis and Pedersen as 3sg. pres. indic. citing the example from X_1, an unreliable authority (*Comparative Grammar*, 385 § 598).

7.19 The form given in the primary reading is found in Rec. N. *Mairg* seems to be used as an attributive adjective parallel in structure to §§ 7.1 and 7.12. The second reading is found in Rec. Y and L. *Mairg* is often followed by *do* of person. The genitive of the relative particle a^n has no specialized form (*GOI*, 322 § 507d).

7.20 This last line is found only in Rec. N. The form ·*tair* is 3sg. pres. subj. of *do·airicc* "comes, finds, gets", which may function as a future perfect hypothetical, particularly in law-texts (*DIL* D 187.47). It might thus be translated as "is accomplished, is completed, is effected" (cf. Strachan, "Old-Irish Metrical Rule," 203; *AL* vi, 685).

Appendix 1

§ 8 Cía féGam ránac

The section edited here, referred to as § 8, is found in Rec. Y and in N_2. Meyer edited and translated it in the preface to *Tecosca Cormaic* from N_2 where it has the heading *Flann Fína beos* (*TC*, vi–vii). The contents do not vary between N_2 and the Rec. Y manuscripts except in sequence. There is, however, a significant difference in the age of the language. The text of Rec. Y is Old Irish as shown by the superlative of the adjectives; the verbal form *ránac*, 1 or 2sg. pret./perf. prototonic of *ro·icc* "comes (upon)"; forms of the copula, and the agreement in number of predicative adjectives with them. All corresponding forms in N_2 are late. This section shows how texts can be modernized through transmission, thus obscuring the period of their origin.

This section is unlike any of the others presented in this edition. It names several groups found in the south of Ireland, specifically in Munster. It cites a characteristic in the superlative in the form "Who are the (...)est you have met?", and then, usually, makes an unfavourable comparison.

Síl nÁedo Sláine, an Uí Néill sept located in Mag Breg, receive unequivocal praise. They dominated the high-kingship of Tara through-out the latter half of the seventh century. Their king, Fínsnechta Fledach, ruled from ca. 675–95, a reign that overlaps for ten years with that of Flann Fína / Aldfrith, ca. 685–705. Aldfrith succeeded to the throne of Northumbria after the death of his half-brother Ecgfrith who had sent an Anglo-Saxon army into Ireland in 684 which devastated Mag Breg (Mac

Airt and Mac Niocaill, *Annals of Ulster*, 148–49; Binchy, *Críth Gablach*, xiv). This English campaign in Ireland would have been during the reign of Fínsnechta.

The Glasraige seem never to have been very important. They are associated with regions in Munster, Co. Meath, and Co. Louth (Hogan, *Onomasticon*, 439). There is no clear reason why they should be singled out for scorn, but *Triads* no. 45 includes them among the Crecraige and Benntraige as *trí huilc Hérenn* "the three evil ones of Ireland".

The variant readings are from $Y_{1,2}$, N_2.

§ 8.1   Cía fégam ránac?
8.2   Fir Maige Féne $_7$ gáeth.
8.3   Cía ansam ránac?
8.4   Araid Cliach $_7$ árchoin.
8.5   Cía dánam ránac?
8.6   Corcu Loígde $_7$ mucca.
8.7   Cía tétem ránac?
8.8   In Déisi $_7$ mílchoin.
8.9   Cía solmam ránac?
8.10 Osraige $_7$ demnai.
8.11 Cía eclam ránac?
8.12 Uí Liatháin $_7$ caírig.
8.13 Cía mescam ránac?
8.14 Ciarraige $_7$ minntáin.
8.15 Cía úallcham ránac?
8.16 Múscraige $_7$ cailig cerc.
8.17 Cía gairbem ránac?
8.18 Orbraige $_7$ aittenn.
8.19 Cía dech ránac?
8.20 A n-as mesam Síl Áedo Sláine,
8.21 $_7$ a n-as dech di ṡuidib
8.22 is fri aingliu it cosmaili.

8.1 fegain Y_2 : feighe N_2 || rangais N_2
8.2 m(h)uig(h)i $Y_{1,2}$ N_2 || .F. $Y_{1,2}$: feine N_2 || et N_2 || gæth $Y_{1,2}$: gaoth N_2
8.3 ansom $Y_{1,2}$: hannsa N_2 || ranacc Y_2 : rangais N_2
8.4 aruidh Y_2 || et N_2
8.5 dana N_2 || ranacc $Y_{1,2}$: rangais N_2
8.6 corco laig- Y_1 : corclaighi Y_2 : corco læighdhe N_2 || et N_2 || [. . .] N_2
8.7 tetheom Y_1 : teteom Y_2 || ranacc $Y_{1,2}$: rangais N_2
8.8 an deissi Y_1 : an deisi Y_2 : na deisi N_2 || et N_2 || miolchoin N_2
8.9 solmha N_2 || rangais N_2
8.10 oisraighi Y_1 : osr-e N_2 || et N_2 || deamhnæ N_2
8.11 heclam $Y_{1,2}$: hegl-e N_2 || ranacc Y_2 : rangais N_2

§ 8.1 Who are the keenest you have met?

8.2 The Men of Mag Féne and wind.

8.3 Who are the most troublesome you have met?

8.4 Araid Cliach and guard dogs.

8.5 Who are the boldest you have met?

8.6 Corcu Loígde and pigs.

8.7 Who are the most fervent you have met?

8.8 The Déisi and hunting dogs.

8.9 Who are the quickest you have met?

8.10 Osraige and demons.

8.11 Who are the most timorous you have met?

8.12 Uí Liatháin and sheep.

8.13 Who are the most befuddled you have met?

8.14 Ciarraige and titmice.

8.15 Who are the proudest you have met?

8.16 Múscraige and cocks.

8.17 Who are the coarsest you have met?

8.18 Orbraige and gorse.

8.19 Who are the best you have met?

8.20 The worst of the race of Áed Sláine,

8.21 and the best of them

8.22 are like angels.

8.12 .h. liathain Y_1 : ua liathain Y_2 : hui liathain N_2 || et N_2 || caoirigh N_2

8.13 mesam Y_1 : mesgamla N_2 || ranacc Y_2 : rangais N_2

8.14 ciarraig- Y_1 : ciarr-e N_2 || et N_2 || mintain $Y_{1,2}$: menntain N_2

8.15 huallchum Y_1 : huaillcum Y_2 : huallcha N_2 || ranacc Y_2 : .R. N_2

8.16 muscraighi Y_1 : musccr-e N_2 || et N_2 || coil- fedha N_2

8.17 gairbium $Y_{1,2}$: airbe N_2 || ranuc Y_2 : ragais N_2

8.18 orbraighi Y_1 : orbr-e N_2 || et N_2 || aittend Y_2 : aitend N_2

8.19 caite as N_2 || deach $Y_{1,2}$ || rangais N_2

8.20 in as N_2 || mesum $Y_{1,2}$: mesa N_2 || sil æd(h)a sl-i $Y_{1,2}$: do siol aodha slaine N_2

8.21 et in as ferr N_2 || do suid(h)i $Y_{1,2}$: dibsein N_2

8.22 is fri haingliu Y_1 : as fri haincclib nimhe N_2 || it cossmaile Y_1 : it cosm-e Y_2 : ata cosmaile N_2

8.23 Cía mesam ránac?
8.24 A n-as dech Glasraigi,
8.25 ⁊ a n-as mesam di ṡuidib
8.26 is fri demnai it cosmaili.

8.23 mesom $Y_{1,2}$: mesamh N_2 || rangais N_2
8.24 an us dech Y_2 : an as deach N_2 || glasrighe Y_2 : glasr-e N_2

8.23 Who are the worst you have met?
8.24 The best of Glasraige,
8.25 and the worst of them
8.26 are like demons.

8.25 $_7$ an as messum Y_1 : et inas mesa N_2 || do suid(h)ib(h) $Y_{1,2}$: dibsein N_2
8.26 as fri demn- N_2 || it cossmaili iat sidhe Y_1 : is cosm-e iat Y_2 : at cosm-e N_2

Notes

§ 8.1 The superlative ending of adjectives is usually *-em* with a tendency to palatalize the preceding consonant (*GOI*, 234 § 370). However, all Rec. Y manuscripts agree in making the *g* of the superlative of *féig* non-palatal. Rec. Y, as opposed to N$_2$, consistently preserves the *-m* of the O.Ir. superl. endings. The verbal form *ránac* is found throughout Rec. Y (*GOI*, 529–30 § 852.B). N$_2$ consistently reads *rangais*. One would expect, in Late Mid. or Classical Irish, the 2sg. pret. of *ro·icc* to take the form *ránacais / ránagais* (Dottin, *Manuel* i, 190 § 288). However, the syncopation of 2sg. pret. is also attested for *do·icc* in Classical Irish. Despite ambiguity as to person in the form *ránac*, it is best treated as 2sg. following the testimony of N$_2$ and supported by the question-and-answer format found in O.Ir. texts of various genres.

8.7 Thurneysen pointed out that *té* "hot" was a consonantal stem adj. with a nom. pl. f. *téit* (*GOI*, 228 § 360; *Lexique* T 38). But *tét* "wanton, mighty", although it may derive formally from the oblique form of *té*, must be kept semantically distinct from it (Murphy, "*Té; tét; téith*," 317–19; *Lexique* T 55). Murphy cited some early examples of *tét* as "wanton", but it is not clear from the example in our text that sexual misconduct is implicit and so I translate with a less specific word.

8.22 After the preposition *fri* Rec. Y readings clearly show acc. pl. forms as opposed to the dat. pl. of N$_2$. In O.Ir. relative clauses non-relative forms of the copula are commonly used (*GOI*, 319–20 § 505). Note the contrast between the non-relative form *it* of Rec. Y in a relative context and the specifically relative form *ata* of N$_2$.

Appendix 2

§ 9 SECHT COMARTHAI DÉC

The section edited here, referred to as § 9, is found in Rec. Y and L, but not in Rec. N. Binchy's *Corpus iuris hibernici* includes, from TCD MS 1432 (E.3.3), the same list as is found in Rec. L (*CIH* vi, 2342.1–6). It is also found in § 22 of Meyer's edition of *Tecosca Cormaic*, with some additions (§§ 9.18–21) and omissions (§§ 9.5–7, 9.15). *TC* §§ 23, 24, 25, 26 also list characteristics called either *mesam tacrai* "the worst pleading" or *mesam aí* "the worst arguing". The section edited here is usually headed *secht comarthai déc drochthacrai* "The seventeen signs of bad pleading". However, L_1 and the copy in MS E.3.3 are both headed *sé comarthai déc* "the sixteen signs" (see further Kelly, *Guide*, 195). Despite the headings, only Rec. Y and *TC* § 22 contain seventeen entries. Rec. L manuscripts and MS E.3.3 each contain the same eighteen entries. The text as edited here is based on Rec. Y (see Appendix 3). The extra entry found in Rec. L witnesses and MS E.3.3, along with three entries found only in *TC* § 22, are included at the end of the seventeen *comarthai* found in Rec. Y, bringing the total number of entries to twenty-one. The variant readings are from $Y_{1,2}$, $L_{1,2,3}$.

Secht comarthai déc drochthacrai

§ 9.1   Frithchathugud fis,
9.2   attach ndrochbérlai,
9.3   ilar n-aithise,
9.4   cathugud cen chomarthae,
9.5   a molad fadesin,
9.6   fáilte fri tuisel tacrai,
9.7   tomus fri arddu,
9.8   folabrad n-insce,
9.9   imtholtu ngaíse,
9.10   derbad n-indeirb,
9.11   dínsem lebor,
9.12   soud fri nósu,
9.13   airde ngotha,
9.14   utmaille tacrai,
9.15   tacrae fergach,
9.16   sprecad sochaide,
9.17   cathugud cáich,
9.18   rigne labartha, (Rec. L, E.3.3, *TC* § 22.8)
9.19   a adbchlos fadéin, (*TC* § 22.18)
9.20   grécha cinn, (*TC* § 22.19)
9.21   lugae íar mbreith. (*TC* § 22.20)

---

§ 9.1 frithcathiugudh Y_1 : frithcatugud Y_2 || fessa L_1
9.2 atach $Y_{1,2}$ L_3 : achor L_2 || drochberla $L_{1,2}$
9.3 ilor Y_2 : hilar L_2 || nathaisi $Y_{1,2}$ L_3 : nathise L_1 : nathaise L_2
9.4 caithiughud $Y_{1,2}$: cathigud L_1 || can L_2 : gan L_3 || c(h)omartha Y_1 $L_{1,2,3}$: comurth[. . .] Y_2
9.5 bodheissin $Y_{1,2}$: fodesin L_2 : badesin L_3
9.6 failti Y_1 : failti re L_2 || tusel Y_1 $L_{1,2}$: tuisil L_3 || tacra Y_2 L_2 : tagra L_3
9.7 tomus re L_2 || harddu Y_1 : hardu Y_1 : harda L_2 : hard L_3
9.8 folabrdh Y_1 : folabra L_2 || nindsce Y_1 : nidsce Y_2 : ninsci L_1 : nindsci L_2 : nindscne L_3
9.9 imt(h)olta Y_1 $L_{1,3}$: imolta Y_2 L_2 || ngaisse $Y_{1,2}$: ngaisi $L_{1,2}$

The Seventeen Signs of Bad Pleading

§ 9.1 Disputing what is known,
9.2 taking refuge in bad language,
9.3 frequent recourse to abusive language,
9.4 contending without proof,
9.5 praising oneself,
9.6 welcoming [another's] mistake in pleading,
9.7 reckoning [oneself] among distinguished persons,
9.8 muttering during delivery,
9.9 exulting in cleverness,
9.10 affirming what is uncertain,
9.11 spurning books,
9.12 turning against legal precedents,
9.13 loudness of voice,
9.14 unsteadiness in pleading,
9.15 an angry pleading,
9.16 inciting the crowd,
9.17 contending with everyone,
9.18 tedium in speech,
9.19 blatant self-promotion,
9.20 loud outbursts,
9.21 swearing after judgement.

9.10 dearbad L_3 || ninderb L_1 : nindearb L_2 : ndindearbh L_3
9.11 dinseamad L_2 : dinsium L_3 || leabor $Y_{1,2}$: lebar L_2 : leabar L_3
9.12 soad fri L_2 || noise Y_1 $L_{1,2}$: noisse Y_2 : noisi L_3
9.13 airdde $Y_{1,2}$ L_1 : ardi L_2
9.14 udmaille L_3 || tacra Y_2 L_2 : tagra L_3
9.15 tacrai $Y_{1,2}$: tacra $L_{1,2}$: tagra L_3 || feargach L_3
9.16 sp-adh $Y_{1,2}$: spcad L_1 : spreagadh L_3
9.17 caithiugadh $Y_{1,2}$: catingud L_1 : cathad L_3
9.18 rigni L_2 : *om.* Y || <labartha> *om.* Y

Notes

§ 9.1 As early as the Würzburg glosses the flexion of *fis* fluctuated between o-stem and u-stem (*DIL* F 152.39–40). But only L_1 shows u-stem inflexion.

9.2 It was noted at § 5 *tosach* that nasalization of a following dependent genitive is not consistently shown in Old Irish (*GOI*, 148 § 237). In this case all witnesses show nasalization except for $L_{1,2}$. In line § 9.3 all witnesses show nasalization. All witnesses have the metathesized form *-bérlae* which is attested as early as Würzburg (*GOI*, 113 § 181). The prefix *droch-* is ambiguous here. It might imply profane or abusive language as in § 9.3, or, since *bérlae* entails specialized technical language, it may imply resorting to lapses in precise usage thus obscuring the arguments.

9.5 $Y_{1,2}$ and L_3 have *bodeisin* or some similar form. No forms beginning with *b* are listed by Thurneysen (*GOI*, 306–7 § 485).

9.6 *Tuisel* is vb.n. of *do·fuisli* "slips, stumbles, falls". This line implies that one should not show joy at the collapse of an opponent's argument and stresses court decorum and orderly procedure.

9.7 *Tomus* is vb.n. of *do·midethar* "weighs, measures, estimates" which uses the preposition *fri* to denote what is being measured against as a standard. I have implied in the translation that the person pleading should not compare himself with famous people, a sentiment reflecting humility which agrees with §§ 9.5, 9.9 and 9.19.

9.8–10 These three maxims, in all witnesses, show nasalization of the following dependent genitive, but none of the initial nouns is attested as neuter (see also § 9.13). Both *folabrad* and *derbad* are masc. u-stems. *Imtholtu* is a fem. n-stem. We should not expect them to nasalize a following dependent genitive, but even when quoted in other contexts these phrases show nasalization.

The commentary in O'Clery for *folabrad n-insce* reads as follows: *folabhra ninnsci .i. duine ag labhairt an fad do bheith duine eile ag tagra* "i.e. one person talking while another person is pleading" (Miller, "O'Clery's Glossary," 422). The gloss in MS E.3.3 reads *do buaidhreath tacra an fechamhan* "to disturb the pleading of the litigant" (*CIH* vi, 2342.8–9).

For *imtholtu ngaíse*, *Tecosca Cormaic* has the variant *imscoltad ngáise* which Meyer translated as "hair-splitting" (*TC* § 22.10). Although *imscoltad* would be declined as a masc. u-stem or o-stem, the following dependent genitive nevertheless shows nasalization.

9.11 This line leaves no doubt that we are dealing with a literate cultural milieu, as one might expect to find at a monastic school. Compare the first half of § 7 which stresses the benefits of *ecnae*. *Lebor* also occurs at § 1.48, and *dínsem* at § 3.15a.

9.12 I take the last word in this line to be *nós* (<*noës*) "legal science, law, custom" (Thurneysen, "Aus dem irischen Recht V," 398–99) which in *Sanas Cormaic* is listed as *nōs .i. nóe-fis .i. fios nōnbuir* "*nōs*, i.e. nine-knowledge, i.e. knowledge of nine men" (Meyer, "*Sanas Cormaic*," 82 § 970). If it is a compound of *fis* then it should be treated as a masc. u-stem or o-stem. It is not likely to be the British loan-word *nós* with the less specific meaning "custom, precedent" (*DIL* s.v.).

Soud fri is ambiguous here. I have translated it word for word, in agreement with Meyer, as "turning against" (*TC* § 22.13). However, *soid* (*fri*) is attested with the meaning "turns towards, returns to" in *Críth Gablach* (Binchy, *Críth Gablach*, 12.311) and in the *Heptads* (*AL* v, 202.7 = *CIH* i, 22.10, ii, 547.23 etc.). *Triads* no. 174 lists one of the "three doors through which truth is recognized" as *sóud fri fíadnu* "appealing to witnesses".

9.13 The interpretation of *airde* as "highness, loudness" seems well attested, for example, *roairde ngotha* (*TC* § 22.14), and the entry in O'Clery's Glossary *bo i roairde ngotha no i roisli ngotha* (*CIH* ii, 662.32, iii, 1041.4). However, the formation of an abstract noun from the adj. *ard* and the suffix -*e* (*ardae/airde*) results in a fem. noun (*GOI*, 165 § 257). We should not, therefore, expect nasalization of the following dependent genitive (see §§ 9.8–10). There is, however, a neuter noun *airde* meaning "sign, token, portent, quality". If *airde* "loudness" is meant here, then the nasalization may be by analogy to the neuter *airde*.

9.15 *Tacrae fergach* is listed as one of the *trí doruis gúa* "three doors of falsehood" (*Triads* no. 173).

9.18 This line is found in all manuscripts of Rec. L as well as in MS E.3.3 (*CIH* vi, 2342.2) and *TC* § 22.8. *Triads* no. 177 lists the *trí búada insci* "three glories of speech" as *fosta, gáis, gairde* "steadiness, wisdom, brevity".

Appendix 3

Y₁: DIPLOMATIC EDITION

The following is a diplomatic edition of the text as found in Y₁, the best surviving representative of Rec. Y (see discussion pp. 24–25).

Roscada Flainn Fina maic Ossa rig Sacsan insso sis

(§ 1 *Ad·cota*)

atchota socheall saidbre
atcota duthracht dorta
atcota ciall cruth
a. druis digna
a. sercc briatra
a. misais airbire
a. lesci faistine
a. feile fritholta
a. dibi dimlad
a. doichell ceisacht
a. gais clotha
a. hiumli ailgine
a. aichni augra
a. santach seotu
a. dimus dímda
a. cuirm carna

a. echlach utmailli

a. accobur feidle

a. gæs airmitin

a. æis all—

a. baes bagh ł bægul

a. brugaid bronnad

a. brigh barann

a. barann bibdu

a. biltenga brath

a. soithgne sighug—

a. áine aurlabra

a. daidbre docraiti

a. ímresin ímned

a. terce leire

a. saire saithchi

a. daire cuimge

a. borb gnimrudh

a. flaith folabrad

a. beccdatu cainbuide

a. firian fortacht

a. maith a moladh

a. crodhleisc legad

a. trebadh toradh

a. fergach fuasnad

a. troda— tuargain

a. brochan bithnert

a. frithbert fuachtain

a. ferann feinnid

a. leignigh libra

a. me*n*mnach miscais

a. failti feile

a. segunn saeire

a. crodh a caithim

a. sæg— snimche

a. drochbhean dibi

a. humal ordan

a. sognim soalaigh

a. lobur luínne

a. builli borbla—

a. bocht a biathadh
a. briugaid mughu
a. fascre rofascre
a. flaith lubrai
a. etlai utmaille
a. miltenga braithemnacht
a. bron debtaighi
a. cath cainíud
a. sochlach cocoruss

(§ 5 *Tosach*)

Tosach aigrai athcusan
tosach eithigh airliugudh
t. ecnaigh airbiri
t. eolais imcomarc
t. ordain enecclann
t. suithi socoisci
t. tocaidh trebaire
t. feili fairsingi
t. uilc uaborbriathar
t. crabuid cosmailius
t. eaccnai alghíne
t. corai cainepert
t. daire drochlepaidh
t. crine gallraighi
t. troighe toirrsighi
t. lubrai lén
t. cutma guforcell
t. sothocaid dagbén
t. dotacaidh drochben
t. miarli malartacha
araili maith mesrug—

(§ 2 *Ba faitech*)

bat faitech arnarbat fiachach
bat treabar arnarbat gabaltach

bat emidh corbat sercach
bat eslabar corot erder—c
bat gartaig corop sochraigh
bat buideach corbo irach
bat humal corbo huassal

(§ 8 *Cía fégam ránac*)

cia fegam ranac
fír muighi .F. ₇ gæth
cia ansom ranacc
araid cliach ₇ arcoín
cia danam ranacc
corco laig— ₇ mucca
cia tetheom ranacc
an deissi ₇ milcoín
cia solmam ranac
oisraighi ₇ demnai
cia heclam ranac
.h. liathain ₇ cairigh
cia mesam ranac
ciarraig— ₇ míntain
cia huallchum ranac
muscraighi ₇ cailig cerc
cia gairbium ranac
orbraighi ₇ aittenn
cia deach ranac
an as mesum sil
æda sl*ain*i ₇ an as dech do suidi
is fri haingliu it cossmaile
cia mesom ranac
an as deach glasraighi
₇ an as messum do siudhib
is fri demnai
it cossmaili iat sidhe

(§ 3 *Dligid*)

Dligidh eacnai airmideín
dlighid fir fortacht
dligid gó cairiug—
d. cloeíne cuindrech
d. augra etargaire
d. rath ríara
d. fuidir fritholta
dligidh maith moradh
d. dimmus dermat
d. dibi dinsem
d. airneal airfocra
d. óc elathain
d. altram imfochíd
d. sen sogaire
d. ath*air* ogreir
d. m*athai*r mingaire
d. aiti erraím
d. foendela— fuacra
d. coibchi certug—
d. econn himcoimed
d. anidhan aurcailiud
d. comathches cloemclod
d. mer munadh
d. maidm nascara
d. rath a imdegail
d. fiadnaisi a fuigell
d. dall ditin
d. othur iarfaighidh
d. eitgi amsir
d. tairic tuínídhe
d. ai astud

(§ 6 *Ferr*)

ferr dán orbbai
ferr ledp luga
f. doairm diairm

f. dail debech

f. moin immatreab

f. mogh marbadh

f. mag mórsliabh

f. tighba toradh

f. tuath tinscra

f. teithedh tairisim

f. truma dinnímí

f. tairisiu tarrngere

f. liechslansasai

f. sonaidi seoita .i. a hithiar a rec

f. digdi dighu ꝉ digail

f. ordan angbas

f. road reraib .i. expectare

f. fir frithaib

f. eolas ilur

f. ilar noiscri

f. esomna air*b*iri

f. set sous

f. suthaine seotu

f. sothced slogh

f. sothced seitchi

f. slog suidigthir ut congruum fiant

f. socraiti slabhrai

f. breo borbbai

f. brugas buar

ferr buar briathar

f. recond iarconn

f. eccna nanaib

f. beccfine ꝉ mor naltrama

f. uirb orbbai

f. orba uirb

f. gress souss

f. drub deíne

f. deíne dobele

f. dobele dochur

f. bethu buadhaib

f. buaid pliptecht

f. brig bagaib

f. duini duilib

f. drochtreabaire degaici

f. techt allathrugh

f. senfiach senecraiti

f. flaith foltaib

f. caintormaig caintaib

f. gním gallraithi

f. cluichi garbai

f. goradh grisaib

f. clu caemna

f. mac michoraib

f. laubar aíne

f. dan deínmichi

f. bo bliadhaín

f. cloith ca—buaidh

f. aurlam nadbur

f. laurchauri trenrith

f. caimsetu cucuilgu

f. cridhi giallnai

f. gart gressaib

f. soburthan suithi

f. sidh sococodh

f. sob— sochiniul

f. suan serbae

f. cara cormaim

f. ciall caincruth

f. cloith cubaidh

f. coma coemdíud

f. ai[c]hi aopudh

f. aire iaraidh

f. aicsi aititin

f. anæ auognam

f. astudh aímíris

f. rann repínn

f. rath rolgud

f. redhe rogæs

f. ruus ruathur

f. gæs gascudh

f. gaire immudh

f. greim crephul
f. luaithi díghairsi
f. lín lobræ
f. lere laimníthi
f. leth lanethiug
f. bas bithbiníu
f. buidi dighbail
f. becc nerai
f. airmidíu saith
f. froech forbbu
f. duthracht dlig—
f. mbruig mbli[cht]aib
f. cloudh cuma
f. ré rathaib
f. buáne áne
f. drochdan dilmaine

(§ 4 *Descad*)

Descaidh cotulta freislighi
d. sirechta sirdorda
d. dibi deog
d. ferge miscaiss
d. athargaib esarcon
d. ecla huamun
d. druisi danatus
d. trebaire tuæ
d. edtreabaire solabra
d. cartha gnathaide
d. caillti cessachtge
d. gensa dímaisi
d. bæsi bancobra
d. mire rogairi
d. sainti imcaisin
d. seirci sírsellad
d. braith sanas
d. debtha athcosán
d. fælti slaínti

d. broin bithguba
d. searba burba
d. aneolais imrisaín
d. aínble aneacna
d. uilcc uabar

(§ 9 *Secht comarthai déc*)

seacht comarta da decc drochtacrai
.i. frithcathiugudh fis
atach ndrochberlai
ilar nathaisi
caithiughud cen comartha
a moladh bodheissin
failti fri tusel tacri
tomus fri harddu
folabradh níndsce
imtolta ngaisse
derbadh níndeírb
dínsem leabor
soud fri noise
airdde ngotha
utmaille tacrai
tacrai fergach
sprecadh sochaidhe
caithiugadh caich

(§ 7 *Maith dán ecnae*)

Dán eccna
doni righ do bocht
doní anadh do esseirt
dogní socenel do doceniul
dogní gæth do bæth
maith a tossach
fearr a deiredh
airmitnech hisin cenntur
loghmar isin alltur

ni dercaintech fri deireadh
.i. fri tabairt nime dó
Doiligh dan læchdacht
ni herdaircc
₇ is dergna a duí
gnimach duthain a súi
it tregtaidh a bí
it ifernnaigh a mairb
ni timnai ath*air* dia mac
mairg dianid dan læchdacht

Appendix 4

L₁: DIPLOMATIC EDITION

The following is a diplomatic edition of the text as found in L₁, the best surviving representative of Rec. L (see discussion pp. 28–30).

Senbri*athr*a Fithail inso sis

(§ 5 *Tosach*)

tossach augrai athchosan
t. ethig arlicud
t. écnaig airbire
t. eolais imchomarc
t. ordain enecland
t. súthi sochoisce
t. tocaid trebaire
t. féli forsinge
t. crabaid cosmailius
t. ecnai algine
t. uilc uaborbriathar
t. córai cáinep*er*t
t. doíre drochlepaid
t. crine gallraige
t. tróge toirsige
t. lubra lén

t. cutma guforgell
t. sodchaid dagben
t. dodchaid drochben
t. miarli malartcha
árrali maith mesrug—

(§ 1 *Ad·cota*)

atchota sochell rodabiatha
a. duthracht dorota
a. ciall cáinchruth
a. báes burba
a. fascre rofascre
a. miscais airbire
a. druis digna
a. lesci fatsine
a. becdatu cáinbude
a. diummus dimda
a. coirm clotha
a. fergach frithorgain
a. flaith labrai
a. etla utmailli
a. accobur feidli
a. gaís airmitiu
a. báis bága
a. brugas bronnud
a. bríg baraind
a. biltenga brath
a. miltenga brithemnacht
a. áne erlabra
a. daidbre dochraite
a. brón debthaige
a. cath cóiniud
a. sochlach cocorus
a. imresain imned
a. immad díchoilad
a. terca leire
a. soíre soigthige

a. doíre cumga
a. borb gnimcha

(§ 2 *Ba faitech*)

bat fattech arnabat fiachach
b. trebar arnabat gabalach
b. eslabar corbot erdairc
b. gartaid corbat sochraid
b. buidech *corbat* irách
b. umal corbot uasal

(§ 6 *Ferr*)

ferr dán orbba
f. ledb luge
f. dál debech
f. doairm diairm
f. moín immatreb
f. mog marbad
f. mag mórsliab
f. tigba torud
f. tuath tinnscra
f. teiched tairisem
f. trumma dinnimi
f. tairisiu tairngire
f. sobarthain suithe
f. senfíach senécraite
f. síd sochocad
f. soben sochen*iu*l
f. cride gialla
f. cara coirm
f. ciall cáinchruth
f. colud cuma
f. coma coimtid
f. athe opad
f. aire iarraid
f. atitiu acsin

f. ana fognam
f. astud amaires
f. rand repind
f. rath riarugud
f. ré rathaib
f. rous ruathur
f. gart grísad
f. grés soos
f. gáis gasced
f. gaire immad
f. gremm *gre*fel
f. luathi digairsi
f. lubair áine
f. leíre lamide
f. bó bliadain
f. búane ane
f. bríg bágaib
f. bás bithanim
f. bude digbail
f. bec éra
f. drochdán dilmaine

(§ 3 *Dligid*)

dligid ecna airmitin
d. fír fortacht
d. gó cairigud
d. clóine cundrech
d. ugra etargaire
d. rath riara
d. aite a sochraite
d. naidm nascar
d. rath a imdegail
d. fiadnaise a fugell
d. fudir fritholta
d. maith mórad
d. díbe dimmolud
d. dall dítin

d. erdál erfócra
d. óc eladain
d. altram imfochaid
d. magist— sogaire
d. foindelach fuacra
d. coibche certugud
d. athair sogaire
d. *mathai*r míne
d. mer múnud
d. othur iarfaigid
d. eitge amsir
d. tairec tunide
d. aí astud

(*TC* § 31)

Gaeth cach co rreic a forbbai
baeth cach co lluaig[i] tíri
rectaid cách co lenbo
ferach ca— co crésíni
sochla .c. co áir
brugaid .c. co éthech
fénnid .c. co trebar
amus .c. co forus
sochond .c. co mesca
codnach .c. co feirg
sognaid .c. co fuacht
sobraig .c. co haltram
rúnid .c. co ugra
fálid .c. co dona
dana .c. co ethech
erra .c. co fogail
traigthech .c. co cairpdech
caíd ca— ceól co cruit
sochraid .c. sona
dochraid ce— ndona
milsem ca— lochta a airgid

milsem ce— céol ceól ind orcín
milsem ce*ch*a corma a cétdeog

(§ 9 *Secht comarthai déc*)

sé comartha déc drochthacrai
.i. frithchathugud fessa
attach drochb*er*la
ilar nathise
cathigud cen chomartha
rigne labartha
a molad fadesin
failte fri tusel tacrai
tomus fri arddu
folabrad ninsci
imtholta ngáisi
derbad ninderb
dínsem lebor
soud fri noise
airdde ngotha
utmaille tacrai
tacra fergach
spcad sochaide
cátingud cáich

(*TC* § 29)

is aíl damsa co fessur cinnas beo
et*er* bæthu 7 gæthu
7 gnathchib 7 ingnathchib
et*er* sénaib 7 ocaib
7 ecnaidib 7 anecnai—
ar a mac fri Fithal
ni *hannsa* ar Fithal
nirbat rogáeth
nirbat robaeth
n. rouallach
n. dimbrigach

n. romorda
n. robecda
n. rolabar
n. rothó
n. rochrúaid
n. rothim
diambat rogaeth
frithotsailfid*er*
diambat robaeth
nottogaidfaid*er*
d. rouallach
notdimdaigfaid*er*
d. robecda
bat digraid
d. rolabar
bat dergna
d. rothó
nitsuilfither
d. rochuaid
forditbrisfid*er*
d. rothim
notdr[. . .]fider

(*TC* § 30)

c*eist* cinas rombeo
ni *hannsa*
bat gaeth fri gáis arna rottogaitha nech i ngáis
bat uallach fri uaill arna tucthar crich fort
bat becda fri becdataid indentar do thol
bat labor fri labra inotagar cath
bat tó fri tó inétsider aisneis
bat cruaid fri cruas arnachat tarda [. . .]ech in eísleis
bat moeth fri mæthi arnadot rocra cach

(*Senbríathra* § 10)

Cid immangéb trebad
ol a mac fri Fithal
ni *hannsa* ol Fithal
im indeoin
Cade ind indeoin trebtha ol in mac
ni *hannsa*
ben maith ol Fi*thal*
Cinnas atgniusa in degmnai ar in mac
ni *hannsa*
asa deilb ₇ asa costud ar Fi*thal*
.i. ni thuca in cail ngarit ossí chamfinnach
ni thuca in remair ngarit
ni thuca in faind fatai
ni thuca in dupai ndochoisc
ni thuca in nudir nabbuidi
ni thuca in duib temlidi
ni thuca in cenaind ngairectaig
n. in cáil clandmair is i druthethaind
n. in miarlig miep*er*taig ce*ch*a tuca
c*eist* cia ben dobér ol in mac
ni *hannsa* ol Fi*thal*
matchotai na finna forsiunga
na bána gela cenduba

(*Senbríathra* § 11)

Cid as dech ban
ni *hannsa*
ben nad fetatar fir remut acht matcheathar
iarmothá sin ni gabtha friu ara naicenta
et nidat follaigthe ar richtain a lessa
cid dogen friu ol in mac
a ngab— dara nanmi cipsi chruth beithi ol Fi*thal*
ar noco derglastar et*er* díb meni gabtar dara naínme

(*Senbríathra* § 12)
Cid as messo ban
ni *hannsa*
bé chairn
Cid as messom andas*id*e
ni *hannsa*
fer dodabeir i cormthech coa chen[. . .]
cid as messo andate diblínaib
ni *hannsa*
mac berar etarru
ninaile
ninturcaba
ní mora ar ni bia cen nethig ₇ cen mebail

(§ 7 *Maith dán ecnae*)
Dán ecna
dogni rig do bocht
dogní anrath do essirt
d. sochen*e*l do dochen*iu*l
d. gæth do bæth
maith a thossach
ferr a dered
airmitnech isin chentur
logmar issind altur
ni dercointech fri dered
.i. fri tabairt nime dó
dolig dán læchdacht
ni erdairc
₇ is dergna a dúi
gnimuch duthain a súi
it etradaig a bí
it iff*e*rnaig a mmairb
nir thimna athair da mac
mairg dianid dan læchdacht

Appendix 5

N₁: DIPLOMATIC EDITION AND COLLATION
WITH Y₁ AND L₁

The following is a collation of Y_1 (p. 25 and Appendix 3) and L_1 (pp. 29–30 and Appendix 4) with N_1 (pp. 22–23), the manuscript upon which this edition is based. Maxims not found in these manuscripts have been supplied from other manuscripts as appropriate. Only the second and third words of each maxim are given. The numbers to the left of each entry represent the sequence of maxims in their respective manuscripts.

N_1	Y_1	L_1
(§·1 *Ad·cota*)		
1.1 socell saidbres	1 socheall saidbre	1 sochell rodabiatha
1.2 dutracht dorata	2 duthracht dorta	2 duthracht dorota
1.3 ciall caincruth	3 ciall cruth	3 ciall cáinchruth
1.4 druis digna	4 druis digna	7 druis digna
1.5 bais burba		4 báes burba
1.6 faiscre rofaiscre	58 fascre rofascre	5 fascre rofascre
1.7 maiscais airbiri	6 misais airbire	6 miscais airbire
1.8 dergi liamna		
1.9 lesci faistine	7 lesci faistine	8 lesci fatsine
1.10 serc briathra	5 sercc briatra	
1.11 becdata cainbude	35 beccdatu cainbuide	9 becdatu cáinbude

1.12 feile fritfolta	8 feile fritholta	
1.13 dibe dimmolad	9 dibi dimlad	
1.14 docell cesacht	10 doichell ceisacht	
1.15 gais clotha	11 gais clotha	
1.16 umal algine	12 hiumli ailgine	
1.17 aichne augra	13 aichni augra	
1.18 santach seota	14 santach seotu	
1.19 dimus tornem	15 dimus dímda	10 diummus dimda
1.20 coirm corna	16 cuirm carna	
1.21 echlach utmaille	17 echlach utmailli	
1.22 acobar feidli	18 accobur feidle	15 accobur feidli
1.23 gæs airmitin	19 gæs airmitin	16 gaís airmitiu
1.24 aos allad	20 æss all—	
1.25 bais baogal	21 baes bagh ⁊ bægul	17 báis bága
1.26 briug— brondad	22 brugaid bronnad	18 brugas bronnud
1.27 brigh barann	23 brigh barann	19 bríg baraind
1.28 barann bidb—	24 barann bibdu	
1.29 biltengga brath	25 biltenga brath	20 biltenga brath
1.30 sotnge sidug—	26 soithgne sighug—	
1.31 aine irlapra	27 áine aurlabra	22 áne erlabra
1.32 daidbre dochraite	28 daidbre docraiti	23 daidbre dochraite
1.33 imrisan imned	29 ímresin ímned	27 imresain imned
1.34 terci lere	30 terce leire	29 terca leire
1.35 saíre sáithe	31 saire saithchi	30 soíre soigthige
1.36 daire cumca	32 daire cuimge	31 doíre cumga
1.37 borb gnimrad	33 borb gnimrudh	32 borb gnimcha
1.38 flaith folabrad	34 flaith folabrad	
1.39 firian fortacht	36 firian fortacht	
1.40 maith a mola	37 maith a moladh	
1.41 crodlesc leghadh	38 crodhleisc legad	
1.42 trebad torad	39 trebadh toradh	
1.43 ferg— fuasnadh	40 fergach fuasnad	12 fergach frithorgain
1.44 trodach tuarcain	41 troda— tuargain	
1.45 brothcain bithnert	42 brochan bithnert	
1.46 frithbert fuachtain	43 frithbert fuachtain	
1.47 feronn feindidh	44 ferann feinnid	
1.48 leigiunn liubr—	45 leignigh libra	
1.49 menmnach miscais	46 menmnach miscais	
1.50 bron debthuighe	62 bron debtaighi	24 brón debthaige

1.51 cath caine	63 cath cainíud	25 cath cóiniud
1.52 sochlach cogarus	64 sochlach cocoruss	26 sochlach cocorus
1.53 imed dicaol—		28 immad díchoilad
1.54 miltenga brethemnus	61 miltenga braithemnacht	21 miltenga brithemnacht
1.55 failti fele	47 failti feile	
1.56 segaind saire	48 segunn saeire	
1.57 dair digge		
1.58 crodh a caithem	49 crodh a caithim	
1.59 saog— snimce	50 sæg— snimche	
1.60 drochben dibi	51 drochbhean dibi	
1.61 umal ordan	52 humal ordan	
1.62 lobar luinde	54 lobur luínne	
1.63 buille borba	55 builli borbla—	
1.64 sogniom soalaig	53 sognim soalaigh	
1.65 bocht a biathad	56 bocht a biathadh	
1.66 brug— muige	57 briugaid mughu	
1.67	59 flaith lubrai	13 flaith labrai
1.68	60 etlai utmaille	14 etla utmailli
1.69		11 coirm clotha

(§ 2 *Ba faitech*)

2.1 ba faitech	1 bat faitech	1 bat fattech
arnaba fiachach	arnarbat fiachach	arnabat fiachach
2.2 ba trebur	2 bat treabar	2 b. trebar
arnaba*tur* gabalach	arnarbat gabaltach	arnabat gabalach
2.3 bad enigh	3 bat emidh	
gurbat sercach	corbat sercach	
2.4 ba heslabar	4 bat eslabar	3 b. eslabar
gurbat dercach	corot erder—c	corbot erdairc
2.5 ba gartait	5 bat gartaig	4 b. gartaid
gurub socraidh	corop sochraigh	corbat sochraid
2.6 badh buidach	6 bat buideach	5 b. buidech
gurbat irach	corbo irach	*corbat* irách
2.7 ba humal	7 bat humal	6 b. umal
gurab uasal	corbo huassal	corbot uasal

(§ 3 *Dligid*)

3.1 ecna armitin	1 eacnai airmideín	1 ecna airmitin

3.2 arfich gais gail		
3.3 fir fortacht	2 fir fortacht	2 fír fortacht
3.4 go a cairiug—	3 gó cairiug—	3 gó cairigud
3.5 claon condrech	4 cloeíne cuindrech	4 clóine cundrech
3.6 ugra etargaire	5 augra etargaire	5 ugra etargaire
3.7 rat riarug—	6 rath ríara	6 rath riara
3.8 fuider frithfol—	7 fuidir fritholta	11 fudir fritholta
3.9 aiti a socraidi		7 aite a sochraite
3.10 naidm nascur	24 maidm nascara	8 naidm nascar
3.11 rat a imdegail	25 rath a imdegail	9 rath a imdegail
3.12 fiadnusi fugell	26 fiadnaisi a fuigell	10 fiadnaise a fugell
3.13 dimus dermit	9 dimmus dermat	
3.14 maith morad	8 maith moradh	12 maith mórad
3.15 dibe dimolad	10 dibi dinsem	13 díbe dimmolud
3.16 dall ditin	27 dall ditin	14 dall dítin
3.17 airnell aurfocra	11 airneal airfocra	15 erdál erfócra
3.18 occ eladain	12 óc elathain	16 óc eladain
3.19 altrom imfochaid	13 altram imfochíd	17 altram imfochaid
3.20 maigister sogaire	14 sen sogaire	18 magist— sogaire
3.21 faindel furfocra	18 foendela— fuacra	19 foindelach fuacra
3.22 mathair mingaire	16 m*atha*ir mingaire	22 m*atha*ir míne
3.23 athair a oghreir	15 ath*air* ogreir	21 athair sogaire
3.24 aide urraim	17 aiti erraím	
3.25 coibche certug—	19 coibchi certug—	20 coibche c*er*tugud
3.26 othur a iarf*aig*i	28 othur iarfaighidh	24 othur iarfaigid
3.27 econd imcomet	20 econn himcoimed	
3.28 anidhan urchailedh	21 anidhan aurcailiud	
3.29 comaithches caomclod	22 comathches cloemclod	
3.30 mer munad	23 mer munadh	23 mer múnud
3.31 aurdonal erfocra		
3.32 etnge amsir	29 eitgi amsir	25 eitge amsir
3.33 toreic tuinide	30 tairic tuínídhe	26 tairec tunide
3.34 ai astud	31 ai astud	27 aí astud
3.35 sommai saire		
3.36 bes breithir		
3.37 doig dithech		
3.38 fir .F.		

(§ 4 *Descad*)

		(from L₃)
4.1 cotulta frislige	1 cotulta freislighi	1 codulta frislíge
4.2 sirrechto sirdord	2 sirechta sirdorda	2 síreacca sírord
4.3 dibe deog	3 dibi deog	3 dibe deoghmaire
4.4 feirgi miscais	4 ferge miscaiss	5 ferge romiscais
4.5 athargaib esarcoin	5 athargaib esarcon	
4.6 eca uaman	6 ecla huaman	6 eagla omhan
4.7 druisi danatus	7 druisi danatus	8 druíne danadus
4.8 trebaire tuæ	8 trebaire tuæ	9 treabhaire tuar
4.9 etrebaire rolabra	9 edtreabaire solabra	10 etreabaire rolabra
4.10 carta gnathuige	10 cartha gnathaide	11 carthana gnathgaire
4.11 caillti cesachtoige	11 caillti cessachtge	12 cailte cesar
4.12 gensa dimaisi	12 gensa dímaisi	13 dímaisi genus
4.13 baisi bancobra	13 bæsi bancobra	14 baisi banchomradh
4.14 mire rogaire	14 mire rogairi	15 míre rogaire
4.15 sainti imcaisin	15 sainti imcaisin	16 sainte imchasaid
4.16 serce sirsill—	16 seirci sírsellad	17 seirce sirsill—
4.17 braith sanuis	17 braith sanas	18 braith sanais
4.18 debtha athchosan	18 debtha athcosán	20 deabtha acmosan
4.19 failti slainti	19 fælti slaínti	24 failte slainte
4.20 broin bithduba	20 broin bithguba	26 broín bithgubha
4.21 serb— burba	21 searba burba	19 serba burba
4.22 aineoluis imrisain	22 aneolais imrisaín	27 aineolais imreasain
4.23 ainble ainecna	23 aínble aneacna	7 aínfhele aineacna
4.24	24 uilc uabar	

The following five maxims appear in L₃ *only.*

4.25		4 romesce rool
4.26		21 eolais aithigidh
4.27		22 crabaid cainbesa
4.28		23 freagra fis
4.29		25 burba bithfognam

(§ 5 *Tosach*)

5.1 eoluis imcomarc	4 eolais imcomarc	4 eolais imchomarc
5.2 ugra atchosan	1 aigrai athcusan	1 augrai athchosan
5.3 eit— airlegad	2 eithigh airliugudh	2 ethig arlicud
5.4 ecnaigh oirbire	3 ecnaigh airbiri	3 écnaig airbire
5.5 ordain eneclainn	5 ordain enecclann	5 ordain enecland
5.6 saithe sochoisce	6 suithi socoisci	6 súthi sochoisce

5.7 tocuid trebaire	7 tocaidh trebaire	7 tocaid trebaire
5.8 feile fairsinge	8 feili fairsingi	8 féli forsinge
5.9 crabuid cosma	10 crabuid cosmailius	9 crabaid cosmailius
5.10 ecnai algine	11 eaccnai alghíne	10 ecnai algine
5.11 uilc uabarbriathro	9 uilc uaborbriathar	11 uilc uaborbriathar
5.12 crine gallruighe	14 crine gallraighi	14 crine gallraige
5.13 dotchaid somesci		
5.14 sotchaid domesci		
5.15 coru cainepert	12 corai cainepert	12 córai cáinepert
5.16 daire drochlebaid	13 daire drochlepaidh	13 doíre drochlepaid
5.17 troige torrsige	15 troighe toirrsighi	15 tróge toirsige
5.18 lubra len	16 lubrai lén	16 lubra lén
5.19 cudma guforgell	17 cutma guforcell	17 cutma guforgell
5.20 sodch— soben	18 sothocaid dagbén	18 sodchaid dagben
5.21 dotcha doben	19 dotacaidh drochben	19 dodchaid drochben
5.22 miarle malarta	20 miarli malartacha	20 miarli malartcha
5.23 araile maith mesrug—	21 araili maith mesrug—	21 árrali maith mesrug—

(§ 6 *Ferr*)

6.1 dan orba	1 dán orbbai	1 dán orbba
6.2 ledb luga	2 ledp luga	2 ledb luge
6.3 doairm diairm	3 doairm diairm	4 doairm diairm
6.4 slan sasad	13 liechslansasai	
6.5 sonaighe seota	14 sonaidi seoita	
6.6 digde digail	15 digdi dighu ɫ digail	
6.7 ordan angbus	16 ordan angbas	
6.8 rath riaruib	17 road reraib	28 rath riarugud
6.9 eolus ilar	19 eolas ilur	
6.10 ilar naiscre	20 ilar noiscri	
6.11 mug marb—	6 mogh marbadh	6 mog marbad
6.12 essomnai orbiri	21 esomna airbiri	
6.13 dail deb—	4 dail debech	3 dál debech
6.14 set sofis	22 set sous	
6.15 suithaine seota	23 suthaine seotu	
6.16 soitch— slog	24 sothced slogh	
6.17 sochraide slaibre	27 socraiti slabhrai	
6.18 brab burba	28 breo borbbai	
6.19 brugas buar	29 brugas buar	
6.20 beccfine moraltrom	33 beccfine ɫ mor naltrama	

6.21 recond iarconn	31 recond iarconn	
6.22 eccna [omitted]	32 eccna nanaib	
6.23 uirb orba	34 uirb orbbai	
6.24 orba uirb	35 orba uirb	
6.25 drub dene	37 drub deíne	
6.26 dene dobele	38 deíne dobele	
6.27 dobele dochar	39 dobele dochur	
6.28 beatha buaduib	40 bethu buadhaib	
6.29 buaidh blipecht	41 buaid pliptecht	
6.30 brigh baghuidh	42 brig bagaib	41 bríg bágaib
6.31 duine duilib	43 duini duilib	
6.32 drochtrebaire dagaicde	44 drochtreabaire degaici	
6.33 techta allaitr—	45 techt allathrugh	
6.34 moín imaitreb	5 moin immatreab	5 moín immatreb
6.35 senfiacha senfala	46 senfiach senecraiti	14 senfíach senécraite
6.36 flaith foltuib	47 flaith foltaib	
6.37 caintormaig cintoib	48 caintormaig caintaib	
6.38 gnim gallruige	49 gním gallraithi	
6.39 cluiche gairbe	50 cluichi garbai	
6.40 gruad grisadh	51 goradh grisaib	
6.41 clu gnimrad	52 clu caemna	
6.42 mac midchoruib	53 mac michoraib	
6.43 tigba torad	8 tighba toradh	8 tigba torud
6.44 tuath tindscra	9 tuath tinscra	9 tuath tinnscra
6.45 teich— tairisium	10 teithedh tairisim	10 teiched tairisem
6.46 trumma dinime	11 truma dinnímí	11 trumma dinnimi
6.47 lubair aine	54 laubar áine	37 lubair áine
6.48 dam denmide	55 dan deínmichi	
6.49 bo bliaduin	56 bo bliadhaín	39 bó bliadain
6.50 cloth gach biudh	57 cloith ca—buaidh	
6.51 urlam nadbair	58 aurlam nadbur	
6.52 luchair tindrith	59 laurchauri trenrith	
6.53 caimseta cucilche	60 caimsetu cucuilgu	
6.54 cridei gialla	61 cridhi giallnai	17 cride gialla
6.55 gart grisaib	62 gart gressaib	31 gart grísad
6.56 taircsi tarngire	12 tairisiu tarrngere	12 tairisiu tairngire
6.57 soburthan saithe	63 soburthan suithi	13 sobarthain suithe
6.58 sidh sochocad	64 sidh sococodh	15 síd sochocad
6.59 soben soceneoil	65 sob— sochiniul	16 soben socheniul

6.60 suan serba	66 suan serbae	(L₂₋₈) = suan serba
6.61 cara cormaim	67 cara cormaim	18 cara coirm
6.62 armiti saite	90 airmidíu saith	
6.63 ciall caincruth	68 ciall caincruth	19 ciall cáinchruth
6.64 cloth cumaid	69 cloith cubaidh	
6.65 comaid coimdiud	70 coma coemdíud	21 coma coimtid
6.66 ithe obad	71 ai[c]hi aopudh	22 athe opad
6.67 buide dibail	88 buidi dighbail	43 bude digbail
6.68 aire iarraid	72 aire iaraidh	23 aire iarraid
6.69 aicsi aitidin	73 aicsi aititin	24 atitiu acsin
6.70 bas bithainim	87 bas bithbiníu	42 bás bithanim
6.71 ana urfognum	74 anæ auognam	25 ana fognam
6.72 asda aimiris	75 astudh aímíris	26 astud amaires
6.73 roind rebaind	76 rann repínn	27 rand repind
6.74 rath rolgad	77 rath rolgud	
6.75 reide rogais	78 redhe rogæs	(L₂₋₈) = reide rogais
6.76 rus ruathar	79 ruus ruathur	30 rous ruathur
6.77 gais gaisced	80 gæs gascudh	33 gáis gasced
6.78 gaire imad	81 gaire immudh	34 gaire immad
6.79 greim grefel	82 greim crephul	35 gremm grefel
6.80 luithe digairsi	83 luaithi díghairsi	36 luathi digairsi
6.81 lin ꞅ e lubra	84 lín lobræ	
6.82 leire laimnide	85 lere laimníthi	38 leíre lamide
6.83 leth lanetech	86 leth lanethiug	
6.84 fraech forbæ	91 froech forbbu	
6.85 dutracht dliged	92 duthracht dlig—	
6.86 mad morsliab	7 mag mórsliabh	7 mag mórsliab
6.87 mbruithe mblichtai	93 mbruig mbli[cht]aib	
6.88 fior fertuib (N₂)	18 fir frithaib	
6.89	25 sothced seitchi	
6.90 slogh suidiugadh (N₂)	26 slog suidigthir	
6.91	30 buar briathar	
6.92	36 gress souss	32 grés soos
6.93 beg era (N₂)	89 becc nerai	44 bec éra
6.94	94 cloudh cuma	20 colud cuma
6.95	95 ré rathaib	29 ré rathaib
6.96	96 buáne áne	40 búane ane
6.97	97 drochdan dilmaine	45 drochdán dilmaine

The following five maxims appear in L₂ *only.*

6.98	48 engnum enech
6.99	49 degnurm duchas
6.100	50 ana ilach
6.101	51 gres mucnaid
6.102	52 rosc digbad

(§ 7 *Maith dán ecnae*)

7.1 maith dan ecna	dán eccna	dán ecna
7.2 doni ri do bocht	doni righ do bocht	dogni rig do bocht
7.3 doni ansruth	doní anadh	dogní anrath
do eisirt	do esseirt	do essirt
7.4 dogni sochinel	dogní socen*e*l	d. sochen*e*l
do dochinel	do docen*iu*l	do dochen*iu*l
7.5 dogni gæth do bæth	dogní gæth do bæth	d. gæth do bæth
7.6 maith a tosach	maith a tossach	maith a thossach
7.7 ferr a dered	fearr a deiredh	ferr a dered
7.8 airmitin isin cennt—	airmitnech hisin cenntur	airmitnech isin chentur
7.9 logmur isin altur	loghmar isin alltur	logmar issind altur
7.10 ni derchaintech	ni dercaintech	ni dercointech
fri deired	fri deireadh	fri dered
7.11 .i. fri tab*air*t nime do	.i. fri tabairt nime dó	.i. fri tabairt nime dó
7.12 Doil— dan læchdacht	doiligh dan læchdacht	dolig dán læchdacht
7.13 ni horrd*er*c	ni herdaircc	ni erdairc
7.14 ₇ dergna a dai	₇ is dergna a duí	₇ is dergna a dúi
7.15 gnimach duthain a sai	gnimach duthain a súi	gnimuch duthain a súi
7.16 it tregdaid a bi	it tregtaidh a bí	it etradaig a bí
7.17 it ifernaid a mairb	it ifernnaigh a mairb	it iff*er*naig a mmairb
7.18 ni timain athair	ni timnai athair	nir thimna athair
dia mac	dia mac	da mac
7.19 mairg dan laoechdacht	mairg dianid dan læchdacht	mairg dianid dan læchdacht

7.20 muna thair aithrighe moir

Bibliography

Anderson, Alan Orr, and Marjorie Ogilvie Anderson, ed. and trans. *Adomnan's Life of Columba*. Revised ed. Marjorie O. Anderson. Oxford: Clarendon Press, 1991.

Atkinson, Robert. *The Yellow Book of Lecan, a Collection of Pieces (Prose and Verse) in the Irish Language* [facsimile]. Dublin: Royal Irish Academy, 1896.

Baumgarten, Rolf. "Varia III. A Note on *Táin Bó Regamna*." *Ériu* 34 (1983): 189–93.

———. "The Syntax of Irish *ar marb, ar mbeo : ar mairb, ar mbí*." *Ériu* 40 (1989): 99–112.

Bergin, Osborn. "Miscellanea." *Ériu* 10 (1926–28): 111–12.

———. *Stories from Keating's History of Ireland*, 3rd ed. Dublin: Royal Irish Academy, 1930.

———. "Varia II." *Ériu* 11 (1932): 136–49.

———. "Varia I." *Ériu* 14 (1946): 29–30.

———. "Further Remarks on Wb. 9a23." *Ériu* 17 (1955): 1–3.

———, and Richard I. Best. "*Tochmarc Étaíne*." *Ériu* 12 (1934–38): 137–96.

Best, Richard I. "The Battle of Airtech." *Ériu* 8, no. 2 (1916): 170–90.

———. "The Yellow Book of Lecan." *Journal of Celtic Studies* 1 (1949–50): 190–92.

———, and Michael A. O'Brien, ed. *The Book of Leinster, formerly Lebar na Núachongbála*, vol. 3. Dublin: Dublin Institute for Advanced Studies, 1957.

Bieler, Ludwig, ed. *The Irish Penitentials*. Scriptores Latini Hiberniae, vol. 5. Dublin: Dublin Institute for Advanced Studies, 1963.

———, ed. and trans. *The Patrician Texts in the Book of Armagh*. Scriptores Latini Hiberniae, vol. 10. Dublin: Dublin Institute for Advanced Studies, 1979.

———, and James Carney. "The Lambeth Commentary." *Ériu* 23 (1972): 1–55.

Binchy, Daniel A. "*Bretha Crólige*." *Ériu* 12 (1934–38): 1–77.

———. "Sick-Maintenance in Irish Law." *Ériu* 12 (1934–38): 78–134.

———. "Appendix: Family Membership of Women." In *Studies in Early Irish Law*, ed. Daniel A. Binchy, 180–86. Dublin: Hodges, Figgis, 1936.

———, ed. *Críth Gablach*. Mediaeval and Modern Irish Series, vol. 11. Dublin: Dublin Institute for Advanced Studies, 1941.

———. "The Saga of Fergus mac Léti." *Ériu* 16 (1952): 33–48.

———. "*Bretha Nemed*." *Ériu* 17 (1955): 4–6.

———. "Irish Law Tracts Re-edited: I. *Coibnes Uisci Thairidne*." *Ériu* 17 (1955): 52–85.

———. "The Old-Irish Table of Penitential Commutations." *Ériu* 19 (1962): 47–72.

———. "*Bretha Déin Chécht*." *Ériu* 20 (1966): 1–66.

———. "Celtic Suretyship, a Fossilized Indo-European Institution?" In *Indo-European and Indo-Europeans, Papers Presented at the Third Indo-European Conference at the University of Pennsylvania*, ed. G. Cardona et al., 355–67. Philadelphia: Univ. of Pennsylvania Press, 1970.

———. "An Archaic Legal Poem." *Celtica* 9 (1971): 152–68.

———. "*Féchem, fethem, aigne*." *Celtica* 11 (1976): 18–33.

———. "Irish History and Irish Law: II." *Studia Hibernica* 16 (1976): 7–45.

———, ed. *Corpus Iuris Hibernici*, vols. 1–6. Dublin: Dublin Institute for Advanced Studies, 1978.

———. "Brewing in Eighth-Century Ireland." In *Studies on Early Ireland: Essays in Honour of M. V. Duignan*, ed. B. G. Scott, 3–6. Belfast: privately printed, 1981.

Bischoff, Bernhard. "Turning-Points in the History of Latin Exegesis in the Early Middle Ages: I. Introduction." In *Biblical Studies: the Medieval Irish Contribution*, ed. Martin McNamara, 74–94. Dublin: Dominican Publications, 1976.

Bitel, Lisa M. *Land of Women, Tales of Sex and Gender from Early Ireland*. Ithaca and London: Cornell Univ. Press, 1996.

Bloomfield, Morton W., and Charles W. Dunn. *The Role of the Poet in Early Societies*. Cambridge: D. S. Brewer, 1989.

Born, Lester K. "The Perfect Prince According to the Latin Panegyrists."

Transactions of the American Philological Association 63 (1932): 20–35.

Breatnach, Liam. " 'The Caldron of Poesy'." *Ériu* 32 (1981): 45–93.

———. "On Abstract Nouns from Prepositions in Irish." *Celtica* 15 (1983): 18–19.

———. "Varia IV." *Ériu* 34 (1983): 194–95.

———, ed. *Uraicecht na Ríar, the Poetic Grades in Early Irish Law.* Early Irish Law Series, vol. 2. Dublin: Dublin Institute for Advanced Studies, 1987.

———. "The First Third of Bretha Nemed Toísech." *Ériu* 40 (1989): 1–40.

———. "Poets and Poetry." In *Progress in Medieval Irish Studies*, ed. Kim McCone and Katharine Simms, 65–77. Maynooth: Saint Patrick's College, 1996.

Breatnach, Risteard A. "The Semantics of 'lepaid' < 'leth + buith'." *Éigse* 7 (1953–55): 260–61.

Bromwich, Rachel, ed. and trans. *Trioedd Ynys Prydein, the Welsh Triads*, 2nd ed. Cardiff: Univ. of Wales Press, 1978.

Byrne, Francis John. "Seventh-Century Documents." *Irish Ecclesiastical Record*, n.s., 108 (1967): 164–82.

———. *Irish Kings and High-Kings.* London: B. T. Batsford Ltd., 1973.

Carey, John. "The Testimony of the Dead." *Éigse* 26 (1992): 1–12.

Carney, James. "Nia son of Lugna Fer Trí." *Éigse* 2 (1940): 187–97.

———, ed. *The Poems of Blathmac Son of Cú Brettan, together with the Irish Gospel of Thomas and a Poem on the Virgin Mary.* Irish Texts Society, vol. 47. Dublin: Irish Texts Society, 1964.

———. "Three Old Irish Accentual Poems." *Ériu* 22 (1971): 23–80.

———. "Linking Alliteration ('Fidrad Freccomail')." *Éigse* 18 (1980–81): 251–62.

———. *"A maccucáin, sruith in tíag."* *Celtica* 15 (1983): 25–41.

Carruthers, Mary J. *The Book of Memory, a Study of Memory in Medieval Culture.* Cambridge Studies in Medieval Literature, vol. 10. Cambridge: Cambridge Univ. Press, 1990.

Chadwick, H. Munro, and Nora K. Chadwick. *The Growth of Literature.* Vol. 1, *The Ancient Literatures of Europe.* Cambridge: Cambridge Univ. Press, 1932; reprinted 1986.

Charles-Edwards, Thomas M. "Boundaries in Irish Law." In *Medieval Settlement, Continuity and Change*, ed. P. H. Sawyer, 83–87. London and New York: Edward Arnold, 1976.

———. "The Social Background to Irish *Peregrinatio*." *Celtica* 11 (1976): 43–59.

——. "*Críth Gablach* and the Law of Status." *Peritia* 5 (1986): 53–73.

——. *Early Irish and Welsh Kinship.* Oxford: Clarendon Press, 1993.

——, and Fergus Kelly, ed. *Bechbretha: an Old Irish Law-Tract on Bee-Keeping.* Early Irish Law Series, vol. 1. Dublin: Dublin Institute for Advanced Studies, 1983.

Clancy, Thomas Owen and Gilbert Márkus, OP. *Iona, the Earliest Poetry of a Celtic Monastery.* Edinburgh: Edinburgh Univ. Press, 1995.

Colgrave, Bertram, ed. and trans. *Two "Lives" of Saint Cuthbert, a Life by an Anonymous Monk of Lindisfarne and Bede's Prose Life.* Cambridge: Cambridge Univ. Press, 1940; reprinted New York: Greenwood Press, 1969.

——, and R. A. B. Mynors, ed. *Bede's Ecclesiastical History of the English People.* Oxford: Clarendon Press, 1969.

Corthals, Johan. "Early Irish *Retoirics* and their Late Antique Background." *Cambrian Medieval Celtic Studies* 31 (1996): 17–36.

Davies, Morgan Thomas. "Protocols of Reading in Early Irish Literature: Notes on Some Notes to *Orgain Denna Ríg* and *Amra Coluim Cille.*" *Cambrian Medieval Celtic Studies* 32 (1996): 1–23.

de Bhaldraithe, Tomás. *The Irish of Cois Fhairrge, Co. Galway: a Phonetic Study,* revised ed. Dublin: Dublin Institute for Advanced Studies, 1966.

de Brún, Pádraig. "Lámhscríbhinní Gaeilge sa Mhuileann gCearr." *Éigse* 19 (1982–83): 82–102.

Dinneen, Patrick S., ed. *The History of Ireland by Geoffrey Keating, D.D.,* vol. 2. Irish Texts Society, vol. 8. London: Irish Texts Society, 1908.

——, ed. and comp. *Foclóir Gaedhilge agus Béarla, an Irish-English Dictionary,* revised ed. Dublin: Irish Texts Society, 1934.

Dobbie, E. van Kirk, ed. *The Anglo-Saxon Minor Poems.* The Anglo-Saxon Poetic Records, vol. 6. New York and London: Columbia Univ. Press, 1942.

Dottin, Georges. *Manuel d'irlandais moyen,* 2 vols. Paris: Édouard Champion, 1913.

Doyle, Edward G., trans. *Sedulius Scottus, On Christian Rulers and the Poems.* Medieval & Renaissance Texts & Studies, vol. 17. Binghamton: Center for Medieval and Early Renaissance Studies, 1983.

Dumville, David N. "Two Troublesome Abbots." *Celtica* 21 (1990): 146–52.

Eliade, Mircea, editor-in-chief. *The Encyclopedia of Religion.* New York: Macmillan; London: Collier Macmillan, 1987.

Ford, Patrick K., trans. *The Poetry of Llywarch Hen.* Berkeley and Los Angeles: Univ. of California Press, 1974.

Frantzen, Allen J. *The Literature of Penance in Anglo-Saxon England.* New Brunswick, N.J.: Rutgers Univ. Press, 1983.

Goody, Jack. *The Domestication of the Savage Mind.* Cambridge: Cambridge Univ. Press, 1977.

Gray, Elizabeth A., ed. *Cath Maige Tuired, the Second Battle of Mag Tuired.* Irish Texts Society, vol. 52. Naas: Irish Texts Society, 1982.

Greene, David. "Miscellanea." *Celtica* 2 (1954): 334–40.

———, ed. *"Esnada Tige Buchet."* In *Fingal Rónáin and Other Stories,* 27–44. Mediaeval and Modern Irish Series, vol. 16. Dublin: Dublin Institute for Advanced Studies, 1955.

———. "In momento, in ictu oculi . . . ." *Ériu* 21 (1969): 25–31.

———, ed. *Duanaire Mhéig Uidhir, the Poembook of Cú Chonnacht Mág Uidhir, Lord of Fermanagh 1566–1589.* Dublin: Dublin Institute for Advanced Studies, 1972.

———. "The Growth of Palatalization in Irish." *Transactions of the Philological Society* (1973): 127–36.

———. "Varia IV." *Ériu* 28 (1977): 155–67.

Greenfield, Stanley B., and Daniel G. Calder. *A New Critical History of Old English Literature.* New York and London: New York Univ. Press, 1986.

Gwynn, Edward J., ed. *The Metrical Dindshenchas,* vol 3. Todd Lecture Series, vol. 10. Dublin: Royal Irish Academy, 1913; reprinted Dublin: Dublin Institute for Advanced Studies, 1991.

———. "An Irish Penitential." *Ériu* 7 (1914): 121–95.

———, ed. *The Rule of Tallaght.* Hermathena, no. 44, Second Supplemental Volume. Dublin: Hodges, Figgis, & Co.; London: Longmans, Green, & Co., 1927.

———. "Senbriathra Fithail." *Revue Celtique* 46 (1929): 268–71.

———. "Some Irish Words." *Hermathena* 24 (1935): 56–66.

———. "An Old-Irish Tract on the Privileges and Responsibilities of Poets." *Ériu* 13 (1942): 1–60, 220–36.

———, and W. J. Purton. "The Monastery of Tallaght." *Proceedings of the Royal Irish Academy* 29 C (1911–12): 115–79.

Hancock, W. N., Thaddeus O'Mahony, Alexander Richey and Robert Atkinson, ed. and trans. *Ancient Laws of Ireland,* 6 vols. Dublin: Thom; London: Longman, Green, 1865–1901.

Hansen, Elaine T. *The Solomon Complex, Reading Wisdom in Old English Poetry.* Toronto: Univ. of Toronto Press, 1988.

Harvey, Anthony. "Early Literacy in Ireland: the Evidence from Ogam." *Cambridge Medieval Celtic Studies* 14 (1987): 1–15.

Havelock, Eric. A. *Preface to Plato.* Cambridge, Mass. and London: Belknap Press, 1963.

Hellman, S., ed. *Sedulius Scottus. Quellen und Untersuchungen zur lateinischen Philologie des Mittelalters.* Munich: Beck'sche Verlagsbuchhandlung, 1906.

Henry, Patrick L. *The Early English and Celtic Lyric.* London: George Allen & Unwin Ltd., 1966.

———. *Saoithiúlacht na Sean-Ghaeilge, Bunú an Traidisiúin.* Baile Átha Cliath [Dublin]: Oifig an tSoláthair, 1978.

———. "The Caldron of Poesy." *Studia Celtica* 14–15 (1979–80): 114–28.

Herren, Michael W., ed. *The Hisperica Famina: II. Related Poems, a Critical Edition with English Translation and Philological Commentary.* Studies and Texts 85. Toronto: Pontifical Institute of Mediaeval Studies, 1987.

Hogan, Edmund, ed. and trans. *The Irish Nennius from L. na hUidre and Homilies and Legends from L. Brecc.* Todd Lecture Series, vol. 6. Dublin: Royal Irish Academy, 1895.

———. *Onomasticon Goedelicum Locorum et Tribuum Hiberniae et Scotiae, an Index, with Identifications, to the Gaelic Names of Places and Tribes.* Dublin: Hodges & Figgis; London: Williams and Northgate, 1910; reprinted Dublin: Four Courts Press, 1993.

Howlett, David. "Five Experiments in Textual Reconstruction and Analysis." *Peritia* 9 (1995): 1–50.

———. *The Celtic Latin Tradition of Biblical Style.* Blackrock: Four Courts Press, 1995.

Hughes, Kathleen. "The Church and the World in Early Christian Ireland." *Irish Historical Studies* 13 (1962): 99–113.

Hull, Vernam E. "The Wise Sayings of Flann Fína (Aldfrith, King of Northumbria)." *Speculum* 4 (1929): 95–102.

———. "*Apgitir Chrábaid*, the Alphabet of Piety." *Celtica* 8 (1968): 44–89.

Ireland, Colin. "Aldfrith of Northumbria and the Irish Genealogies." *Celtica* 22 (1991): 64–78.

———. "Aldfrith of Northumbria and the Learning of a *Sapiens.*" In *A Celtic Florilegium, Studies in Memory of Brendan O Hehir,* ed. Kathryn A. Klar, Eve E. Sweetser, and Claire Thomas, 63–77. Lawrence, Mass.: Celtic Studies Publications, 1996.

———. "The Ambiguous Attitude toward Fosterage in Early Irish Literature." In *Studies in Honor of Jaan Puhvel, Part One, Ancient Languages and Philology,* ed. Dorothy Disterheft, Martin E. Huld and John Greppin, 93–96. Journal of Indo-European Studies Monograph, no. 20. Washington, D.C.: Institute for the Study of Man, 1997.

Jackson, Kenneth H. *Studies in Early Celtic Nature Poetry.* Cambridge: Cambridge Univ. Press, 1935; reprinted Felinfach: Llanerch Publishers, 1995.

————, ed. *Early Welsh Gnomic Poems*. Cardiff: Univ. of Wales Press, 1935.

————, ed. *Cath Maighe Léna*. Mediaeval and Modern Irish Series, vol. 9. Dublin: Dublin Institute for Advanced Studies, 1938; repr. with corrigenda 1990.

————, ed. *Aislinge meic Con Glinne*. Dublin: Dublin Institute for Advanced Studies, 1990.

Kelly, Fergus. "A Poem in Praise of Columb Cille." *Ériu* 24 (1973): 1–34.

————, ed. *Audacht Morainn*. Dublin: Dublin Institute for Advanced Studies, 1976.

————. *A Guide to Early Irish Law*. Early Irish Law Series, vol. 3. Dublin: Dublin Institute for Advanced Studies, 1988.

Kenney, James F. *The Sources for the Early History of Ireland: Ecclesiastical, an Introduction and Guide*. New York: Columbia Univ. Press, 1929; repr. Dublin: Pádraic Ó Táilliúir, 1979.

Kirshenblatt-Gimblett, Barbara. "Toward a Theory of Proverb Meaning." *Proverbium* 22 (1973): 821–27. Reprinted in *The Wisdom of Many, Essays on the Proverb*, ed. Wolfgang Mieder and Alan Dundes, 111–21. Garland Folklore Casebooks, vol. 1. New York and London: Garland Publishing, 1981.

Knott, Eleanor, ed. *Togail Bruidne Da Derga*. Mediaeval and Modern Irish Series, vol. 8. Dublin: Dublin Institute for Advanced Studies, 1936.

Lapidge, Michael, and Michael Herren, trans. *Aldhelm, the Prose Works*. Ipswich: D.S. Brewer; and Totowa: Rowman & Littlefield, 1979.

————, and Richard Sharpe. *A Bibliography of Celtic-Latin Literature 400–1200*. Royal Irish Academy Dictionary of Medieval Latin from Celtic Sources, Ancillary Publications, volume 1. Dublin: Royal Irish Academy, 1985.

Larrington, Carolyne. *A Store of Common Sense, Gnomic Theme and Style in Old Icelandic and Old English Wisdom Poetry*. Oxford: Clarendon Press, 1993.

Lewis, Henry, and Holger Pedersen. *A Concise Comparative Celtic Grammar*, 3rd ed. Göttingen: Vandenhoeck & Ruprecht, 1974.

Mac Airt, Seán, and Gearóid Mac Niocaill, ed. *The Annals of Ulster (to A.D. 1131) Part I: Text and Translation*. Dublin: Dublin Institute for Advanced Studies, 1983.

Mac Cana, Proinsias. "The Three Languages and the Three Laws." *Studia Celtica* 5 (1970): 62–78.

————. "Two Notes." *Celtica* 11 (1976): 125–32.

————. *The Learned Tales of Medieval Ireland*. Dublin: Dublin Institute for Advanced Studies, 1980.

Mac Cionnaith, Láimhbheartach: see McKenna, Lambert

McCone, Kim. "The Würzburg and Milan Glosses: Our Earliest Sources of 'Middle Irish'." *Ériu* 36 (1985): 85–106.

———. "Dubthach maccu Lugair and a Matter of Life and Death in the Pseudo-Historical Prologue to the *Senchas Már*." *Peritia* 5 (1986): 1–35.

———. "Werewolves, Cyclopes, *Díberga*, and *Fíanna:* Juvenile Delinquency in Early Ireland." *Cambridge Medieval Celtic Studies* 12 (1986): 1–22.

———. *The Early Irish Verb*. Maynooth Monographs, vol. 1. Maynooth: An Sagart, 1987.

Mac Con Iomaire, Liam, comp. *Ireland of the Proverb*. Dublin: Town House, 1988.

McKenna, Lambert, ed. *Iomarbhágh na bhFileadh, the Contention of the Bards*, vol. 1. Irish Texts Society, vol. 20. London: Simpkin, Marshall, Hamilton, Kent & Co., Ltd., 1918.

———, ed. *Dioghluim Dána*. Baile Átha Cliath [Dublin]: Oifig an tSoláthair, 1938.

———, ed. *The Book of O'Hara, Leabhar Í Eadhra*. Dublin: Dublin Institute for Advanced Studies, 1951.

Mackinnon, Donald. *A Descriptive Catalogue of Gaelic Manuscripts in the Advocates' Library Edinburgh and Elsewhere in Scotland*. Edinburgh: Brown, 1912.

McLeod, Neil. "The Concept of Law in Ancient Irish Jurisprudence." *Irish Jurist*, n.s., 17 (1982): 356–67.

———, ed. *Early Irish Contract Law*. Sydney Series in Celtic Studies, vol. 1. Sydney: Centre for Celtic Studies, n.d. [1992].

Mac Mathúna, Liam. "An Introductory Survey of the Wordfield 'Knowledge' in Old and Middle Irish." In *Philologie und Sprachwissenschaft*, Akten der 10. Österreichischen Linguisten-Tagung, ed. Wolfgang Meid and Hans Schmeja, 149–57. Innsbruck: Innsbrucker Beiträge zur Sprachwissenschaft, 1983.

Mac Mathúna, Séamus, ed. and trans. *Immram Brain, Bran's Journey to the Land of the Women*. Tübingen: Max Niemeyer, 1985.

Mac Neill, Eoin. *Celtic Ireland*. Dublin: Martin Lester, Ltd.; London: Leonard Parsons, Ltd., 1921; revised ed., Dublin: Academy Press, 1981.

———. "A Pioneer of Nations." *Studies* 11 (1922): 13–28, 435–46.

———. "Ancient Irish Law: the Law of Status or Franchise." *Proceedings of the Royal Irish Academy* 36 C (1921–24): 265–316.

Mac Niocaill, Gearóid. "Jetsam, Treasure Trove and the Lord's Share in Medieval Ireland." *The Irish Jurist*, n.s., 6, no. 1 (1971): 103–10.

Marstrander, Carl. "Bídh Crínna." *Ériu* 5 (1911): 126–43.

———. "Remarques sur les 'Zur keltischen Wortkunde I–VI' de Kuno Meyer." *Revue Celtique* 36 (1915–16): 335–90.

———. Review of *Lexique étymologique de l'irlandais ancien*, by J. Vendryes. *Lochlann* 2 (1962): 196–226.

Márkus, Gilbert. "What Were Patrick's Alphabets?" *Cambrian Medieval Celtic Studies* 31 (1996): 1–15.

Matheson, Angus. "Some Words from Gaelic Folktales." *Éigse* 8 (1956–57): 247–58.

Meehan, Denis, ed. *Adamnan's "De Locis Sanctis"*. Scriptores Latini Hiberniae, vol. 3. Dublin: Dublin Institute for Advanced Studies, 1958.

Meyer, Kuno. "Die Geschichte von Philipp und Alexander von Macedonien aus dem Lebar Brecc." In *Irische Texte*, vol. 2, no. 2, ed. Whitley Stokes and Ernst Windisch, 1–108. Leipzig: Hirzel, 1887.

———, ed. and trans. *Aislinge meic Conglinne, the Vision of MacConglinne, a Middle-Irish Wonder Tale*. London: David Nutt, 1892.

———, ed. *Hibernica Minora, Being a Fragment of an Old-Irish Treatise on the Psalter*. Anecdota Oxoniensia. Oxford: Clarendon Press, 1894.

———. "The Expulsion of the Dessi." *Y Cymmrodor* 14 (1901): 101–35.

———, ed. and trans. *Cáin Adamnáin, an Old-Irish Treatise on the Law of Adamnan*. Anecdota Oxoniensia. Oxford: Clarendon Press, 1905.

———. "The Duties of a Husbandman." *Ériu* 2 (1905): 172.

———. *Contributions to Irish Lexicography*, A–C, vol. 1, no. 1. Halle: Max Niemeyer, 1906.

———. *The Triads of Ireland*. Todd Lecture Series, vol. 13. Dublin: Hodges, Figgis, & Co.; London: Williams & Norgate, 1906.

———. "The Expulsion of the Déssi." *Ériu* 3 (1907): 135–42.

———. "Mitteilungen aus irischen Handschriften." *Zeitschrift für celtische Philologie* 6 (1908): 257–72.

———. *The Instructions of King Cormac mac Airt*. Todd Lecture Series, vol. 15. Dublin: Hodges, Figgis, & Co.; London: Williams & Norgate, 1909.

———. "Bríathra Flainn Fína maic Ossu." *Anecdota from Irish Manuscripts*, vol. 3, ed. O. J. Bergin, R. I. Best, K. Meyer, J. G. O'Keeffe, 10–20. Halle: Max Niemeyer; and Dublin: Hodges, Figgis, & Co., 1910.

———. "Mitteilungen aus irischen Handschriften." *Zeitschrift für celtische Philologie* 7 (1910): 297–312.

———. *Zur keltischen Wortkunde*, vol. 1–9. Berlin: Verlag der Königlichen Akademie der Wissenschaft, 1912–19.

———, ed. "*Sanas Cormaic*, an Old-Irish Glossary Compiled by Cormac úa

Cuilennáin, King-Bishop of Cashel in the Tenth Century." *Anecdota from Irish Manuscripts*, vol. 4, ed. O. J. Bergin, R. I. Best, K. Meyer, J. G. O'Keeffe. Halle: Max Niemeyer; and Dublin: Hodges, Figgis & Co., 1912.

———. "The Correspondence between Alexander and Dindimus." *Anecdota from Irish Manuscripts*, vol. 5, ed. O J. Bergin, R. I. Best, K. Meyer, J. G. O'Keeffe, 1–8. Halle: Max Niemeyer; and Dublin: Hodges, Figgis, & Co., 1913.

———. "Mitteilungen aus irischen Handschriften." *Zeitschrift für celtische Philologie* 10 (1915): 37–54.

———. *Miscellanea Hibernica*. University of Illinois Studies in Language and Literature, vol. 2, no. 4. Urbana, Ill.: Univ. of Illinois, [1916] 1917.

———. "Zur keltischen Wortkunde X." *Zeitschrift für celtische Philologie* 13 (1921): 184–93.

Mieder, Wolfgang. *International Bibliography of Explanatory Essays on Individual Proverbs and Proverbial Expressions*. Bern: Peter Lang, 1977.

———. *Proverbs in Literature: An International Bibliography*. Bern: Peter Lang, 1978.

———. *International Proverb Scholarship: An Annotated Bibliography*. New York: Garland Press, 1982.

Miller, Arthur W. K. "O'Clery's Irish Glossary." *Revue Celtique* 4 (1879–80): 349–428; 5 (1881–83): 1–69.

Moisl, Hermann. "The Bernician Royal Dynasty and the Irish in the Seventh Century." *Peritia* 2 (1983): 103–26.

Mulchrone, Kathleen. "The Rights and Duties of Women with Regard to the Education of Their Children." In *Studies in Early Irish Law*, ed. Daniel A. Binchy, 187–205. Dublin: Hodges, Figgis, 1936.

Murphy, Gerard, ed. *Duanaire Finn, the Book of the Lays of Fionn*, vol. 3. Irish Texts Society, vol. 43. Dublin: Educational Company of Ireland, [1941] 1953.

———. "Te; tét; téith." *Celtica* 3 (1956): 317–19.

Ní Chróinín, Áine: see O'Sullivan, Anne

Nagy, Joseph Falaky. *The Wisdom of the Outlaw, the Boyhood Deeds of Finn in Gaelic Narrative Tradition*. Berkeley, Los Angeles, London: Univ. of California Press, 1985.

———. "Sword as Audacht." In *Celtic Language, Celtic Culture: A Festschrift for Eric P. Hamp*, ed. A. T. E. Matonis and Daniel F. Melia, 131–36. Van Nuys, Calif.: Ford & Bailie, Publishers, 1990.

Ní Dhonnchadha, Máirín. "An Address to a Student of Law." In *Sages,*

Saints and Storytellers: Celtic Studies in Honour of Professor James Carney, ed. Donnchadh Ó Corráin, Liam Breatnach, and Kim McCone, 159–77. Maynooth Monographs, vol. 2. Maynooth: An Sagart, 1989.

O'Brien, Michael A. "Varia IV." *Ériu* 11 (1932): 154–71.

————. "The Old Irish Life of St Brigit, Part II. Introduction and Notes." *Irish Historical Studies* 1, no. 4 (1939): 343–53.

————, ed. *Corpus Genealogiarum Hiberniae*, vol. 1. Dublin: Dublin Institute for Advanced Studies, 1962.

————. "Notes on Irish Proper Names." *Celtica* 9 (1971): 212.

Ó Cathasaigh, Tomás. "Curse and Satire." *Éigse* 21 (1986): 10–15.

Ó Concheanainn, Tomás. "The Book of Ballymote." *Celtica* 14 (1981): 15–25.

————. "Scríobhaithe Leacáin Mhic Fhir Bhisigh." *Celtica* 19 (1987): 141–75.

Ó Conchúir, Breandán. *Scríobhaithe Chorcaí 1700–1850*. Baile Átha Cliath [Dublin]: An Clóchomhar, 1982.

Ó Corráin, Donncha(dh). *Ireland before the Normans*. The Gill History of Ireland, volume 2. Dublin: Gill and Macmillan Ltd., 1972.

————. "Women in Early Irish Society." In *Women in Irish Society, the Historical Dimension*, ed. Margaret Mac Curtain and Donncha Ó Corráin, 1–13. Dublin: Arlen House, [1978] 1979.

————. "Marriage in Early Ireland." In *Marriage in Ireland*, ed. Art Cosgrove, 5–24. Dublin: College Press, 1985.

————, Liam Breatnach, and Aidan Breen. "The Laws of the Irish." *Peritia* 3 (1984): 382–438.

Ó Donnchadha, Tadhg, ed. *Dánta Sheáin Uí Mhurchadha na Ráithíneach*. Baile Átha Cliath [Dublin]: Connradh na Gaedhilge, 1907.

————. "*Cert cech ríg co réil.*" In *Miscellany Presented to Kuno Meyer*, ed. Osborn Bergin and Carl Marstrander, 258–77. Halle: Max Niemeyer, 1912.

————. "Advice to a Prince." *Ériu* 9 (1921–23): 43–54.

O'Donoghue, Tadhg: see Ó Donnchadha, Tadhg

O'Donovan, John, trans. *The Banquet of Dun na n-Gedh and the Battle of Magh Rath, an Ancient Historical Tale*. Dublin: Irish Archaeological Society, 1842; reprinted Felinfach: Llanerch Publishers, 1995.

————, ed. *Annals of the Kingdom of Ireland, by the Four Masters*, vol. 5. Dublin: Hodges and Smith, 1851.

Ó hAodha, Donncha, ed. *Bethu Brigte*. Dublin: Dublin Institute for Advanced Studies, 1978.

O'Keeffe, J. G. "Cuchulinn and Conlaech." *Ériu* 1 (1904): 123–27.

O'Leary, Philip. "Contention at Feasts in Early Irish Literature." *Éigse* 20 (1984): 115–27.

Ó Muraíle, Nollaig. "Leabhar Ua Maine *alias* Leabhar Uí Dhubhagáin." *Éigse* 23 (1989): 167–95.

O Neill, Joseph. "The Rule of Ailbe of Emly." *Ériu* 3 (1907): 92–115.

Ong, Walter J. *Orality and Literacy, the Technologizing of the Word.* London and New York: Methuen, 1982.

O'Rahilly, Cecile. "Marcach = 'messenger'?" *Celtica* 7 (1966): 32.

———, ed. *Táin Bó Cúalnge from the Book of Leinster.* Dublin: Dublin Institute for Advanced Studies, 1967.

———, ed. *Táin Bó Cúailnge, Recension I.* Dublin: Dublin Institute for Advanced Studies, 1976.

O'Rahilly, Thomas F., ed. *A Miscellany of Irish Proverbs.* Dublin: Talbot Press, 1922.

———. "Tuillim buide." *Zeitschrift für celtische Philologie* 17 (1928): 206–12.

———. "Notes, Mainly Etymological." *Ériu* 13 (1942): 144–219.

———. *Early Irish History and Mythology.* Dublin: Dublin Institute for Advanced Studies, 1946.

———. "Varia II." *Celtica* 1 (1950): 328–86.

Orchard, Andy. *The Poetic Art of Aldhelm.* Cambridge Studies in Anglo-Saxon England, volume 8. Cambridge: Cambridge Univ. Press, 1994.

Ó Riain, Pádraig, ed. *Corpus Genealogiarum Sanctorum Hiberniae.* Dublin: Dublin Institute for Advanced Studies, 1985.

Oskamp, H. P. A. " 'The Yellow Book of Lecan Proper'." *Ériu* 26 (1975): 102–21.

O'Sullivan, Anne. "The Four Counsels." *Éigse* 3 (1941–43): 67–68.

———. *The Book of Leinster, formerly Lebar na Núachongbála*, vol. 6. Dublin: Dublin Institute for Advanced Studies, 1983.

O'Sullivan, William. "Notes on the Scripts and Make-up of the Book of Leinster." *Celtica* 7 (1966): 1–31.

———. "Ciothruadh's Yellow Book of Lecan." *Éigse* 18 (1981): 177–81.

———. "The Book of Uí Maine formerly the Book of Ó Dubhagáin: Scripts & Structure." *Éigse* 23 (1989): 151–66.

The Oxford English Dictionary. 2nd edition. Oxford: Clarendon Press, 1989.

Patterson, Nerys Thomas. *Cattle-Lords and Clansmen, the Social Structure of Early Ireland*, 2nd ed. Notre Dame and London: Univ. of Notre Dame Press, 1994.

Pearson, A. I. "A Medieval Glossary." *Ériu* 13 (1942): 61–87.

Pedersen, Holger. "O.Ir. *di chosscc alailiu.*" *Ériu* 15 (1948): 188–92.

Pender, James. "K. Meyers Nachträge zu Pedersens Verbalverzeichnis." *Zeitschrift für celtische Philologie* 18 (1930): 305–52.

Plummer, Charles, ed. *Venerabilis Baedae Opera Historica*, vol. 2. Oxford: Clarendon Press, 1896; repr. 1975.

———. "Notes on Some Passages in the Brehon Laws." *Ériu* 8, no. 2 (1916): 127–32.

———. "Notes on Some Passages in the Brehon Laws III." *Ériu* 9 (1921–23): 109–17.

Power, Nancy. "Classes of Women Described in the *Senchas Már*." In *Studies in Early Irish Law*, ed. Daniel A. Binchy, 81–108. Dublin: Hodges, Figgis, 1936.

Quin, E. Gordon. "Notes on Irish Words." *Hermathena* 99 (1964): 49–54.

———, et al., ed. and comp. (*Contributions to a*) *Dictionary of the Irish Language Based Mainly on Old and Middle Irish Materials*. Dublin: Royal Irish Academy, 1913–75.

———. "Old-Irish *alailiu, arailiu.*" *Studia Celtica* 2 (1967): 91–95.

Radner, Joan N., ed. *Fragmentary Annals of Ireland*. Dublin: Dublin Institute for Advanced Studies, 1978.

Robinson, F. N. "Irish Proverbs and Irish National Character." *Modern Philology* 43, no. 1 (1945): 1–10. Reprinted in *The Wisdom of Many, Essays on the Proverb*, ed. Wolfgang Mieder and Alan Dundes, 284–99. Garland Folklore Casebooks, vol. 1. New York and London: Garland Publishing, 1981.

Röhrich, Lutz and Wolfgang Mieder. *Sprichwort*. Stuttgart: Metzler, 1977.

Rowland, Jenny. *Early Welsh Saga Poetry, a Study and Edition of the Englynion*. Cambridge: D. S. Brewer, 1990.

Russell, Paul. "Varia I." *Ériu* 36 (1985): 163–68.

Scott, R. B. Y., trans. *The Anchor Bible, Proverbs and Ecclesiastes*. Garden City, N.Y.: Doubleday & Company, Inc., 1965.

Sharpe, Richard. "Hiberno-Latin *laicus*, Irish *láech* and the Devil's Men." *Ériu* 30 (1979): 75–92.

Shippey, T. A., ed. and trans. *Poems of Wisdom and Learning in Old English*. Cambridge: D. S. Brewer; Totowa, N. J.: Rowman and Littlefield, 1976.

Simpson, Dean. "The '*Proverbia Grecorum*'." *Traditio* 43 (1987): 1–22.

———. *Sedulii Scotti Collectaneum Miscellaneum*. Corpus Christianorum, Continuatio Medievalis, vol. 67. Turnhout: Brepols, 1988.

Sims-Williams, Patrick. "Thought, Word and Deed: an Irish Triad." *Ériu* 29 (1978): 78–111.

———. *Religion and Literature in Western England 600–800*. Cambridge Studies in Anglo-Saxon England, vol. 3. Cambridge: Cambridge Univ. Press, 1990.

Sjoestedt(-Jonval), Marie-Louise. "Études sur le temps et l'aspect en vieil irlandais." *Études Celtiques* 3 (1938): 219–73.

Smith, Peter. "Aimirgein Glúngel Tuir Tend: a Middle-Irish Poem on the Authors and Laws of Ireland." *Peritia* 8 (1994): 120–50.

Smith, Roland. "On the Briatharthecosc Conculaind." *Zeitschrift für celtische Philologie* 15 (1925): 187–92.

———. "The *Speculum Principum* in Early Irish Literature." *Speculum* 2 (1927): 411–45.

———. "The Alphabet of Cuigne mac Emoin." *Zeitschrift für celtische Philologie* 17 (1928): 45–72.

———. "The *Senbriathra Fithail* and Related Texts." *Revue Celtique* 45 (1928): 1–92.

———. "Fithal and Flann Fína." *Revue Celtique* 47 (1930): 30–38.

———. "Further Light on the *Finnsruth Fithail*." *Revue Celtique* 48 (1931): 325–31.

———. "The Advice to Doidin." *Ériu* 11 (1932): 66–85.

———. "The *Cach* Formulas in the Irish Laws." *Zeitschrift für celtische Philologie* 20 (1936): 262–77.

Stacey, Robin Chapman. *The Road to Judgment, from Custom to Court in Medieval Ireland and Wales*. Philadelphia: Univ. of Pennsylvania Press, 1994.

Stancliffe, Clare. "Oswald, 'Most Holy and Most Victorious King of the Northumbrians'." In *Oswald, Northumbrian King to European Saint*, ed. Clare Stancliffe and Eric Cambridge, 33–83. Stamford: Paul Watkins, 1995.

Stevenson, Jane. "The Beginnings of Literacy in Ireland." *Proceedings of the Royal Irish Academy* 89 C (1989): 127–65.

———. "Literacy and Orality in Early Medieval Ireland." In *Cultural Identity and Cultural Integration, Ireland and Europe in the Early Middle Ages*, ed. Doris Edel, 11–22. Blackrock: Four Courts Press, 1995.

Stokes, Whitley. "*Togail Troí* aus H.2.17." In *Irische Texte*, vol. 2, no. 1, ed. Whitley Stokes and Ernst Windisch, 1–142. Leipzig: Hirzel, 1884.

———. "The Irish Ordeals, Cormac's Adventure in the Land of Promise, and the Decision as to Cormac's Sword." In *Irische Texte*, vol. 3, no. 1, ed. Whitley Stokes and Ernst Windisch, 183–229. Leipzig: Hirzel, 1891.

———. "The Second Battle of Moytura." *Revue Celtique* 12 (1891): 52–130, 306–8.

———. "The Annals of Tigernach: Third Fragment." *Revue Celtique* 17 (1896): 119–263.

———. "The Bodleian *Amra Choluimb Chille.*" *Revue Celtique* 20 (1899): 30–55, 132–83, 248–87, 400–37.

———. "O'Mulconry's Glossary." *Archiv für celtische Lexikographie*, vol. 1, ed. Whitley Stokes and Kuno Meyer, 232–324, 473–81. Halle: Max Niemeyer, 1900.

———. "The Destruction of Dá Derga's Hostel." *Revue Celtique* 22 (1901): 9–61, 165–215, 282–329, 390–437.

———. "A List of Ancient Irish Authors." *Zeitschrift für celtische Philologie* 3 (1901): 15–16.

———. "O'Davoren's Glossary." *Archiv für celtische Lexikographie*, vol. 2, ed. Whitley Stokes and Kuno Meyer, 197–504. Halle: Max Niemeyer, 1904.

———. "The Songs of Buchet's House." *Revue Celtique* 25 (1904): 18–39, 225–27.

———, ed. and trans. *Félire Óengusso Céli Dé, the Martyrology of Oengus the Culdee.* London: Henry Bradshaw Society, 1905; repr. Dublin: Dublin Institute for Advanced Studies, 1984.

———. *The Colloquy of the Two Sages*, 2nd ed. Paris: Librarie Émile Bouillon, 1905; also in *Revue Celtique* 26 (1905): 4–64.

———, and John Strachan, ed. *Thesaurus Palaeohibernicus: a Collection of Old-Irish Glosses, Scholia, Prose, and Verse*, 2 vols. Cambridge: Cambridge Univ. Press, 1901–3; repr. Dublin: Dublin Institute for Advanced Studies, 1975.

Strachan, John. "An Old-Irish Metrical Rule." *Ériu* 1 (1904): 191–208.

———. "An Old-Irish Homily." *Ériu* 3 (1907): 1–10.

Taylor, Archer. *The Proverb.* Cambridge, Mass.: Harvard Univ. Press, 1931.

Thurneysen, Rudolf. "Zu irischen Handschriften und Litteraturdenkmälern." In *Abhandlungen der Königlichen Gesellschaft der Wissenschaften zu Göttingen*, Philologisch-Historische Klasse n.F., vol. 14, no. 3. Berlin: Weidmannsche Buchhandlung, 1912–13.

———. "Morands Fürstenspiegel." *Zeitschrift für celtische Philologie* 11 (1917): 56–106.

———. *Die irische Helden- und Königsage bis zum siebzehnten Jahrhundert.* Halle: Max Niemeyer, 1921; repr. Hildesheim and New York: Georg Olms, 1980.

———. "Aus dem irischen Recht I. Das Unfrei-Lehen." *Zeitschrift für celtische Philologie* 14 (1923): 335–94.

———. "Aus dem irischen Recht III." *Zeitschrift für celtische Philologie* 15 (1925): 302–76.

————. "Aus dem irischen Recht IV." *Zeitschrift für celtische Philologie* 16 (1927): 167–230.

————. "Aus dem irischen Recht V." *Zeitschrift für celtische Philologie* 18 (1930): 353–408.

————, ed. *Scéla Mucce Meic Dathó.* Mediaeval and Modern Irish Series, vol. 6. Dublin: Dublin Institute for Advanced Studies, 1935.

————. "*Cáin Lánamna.*" In *Studies in Early Irish Law,* ed. Daniel A. Binchy, 1–80. Dublin: Hodges, Figgis, 1936.

————. "Heirat." In *Studies in Early Irish Law,* ed. Daniel A. Binchy, 109–28. Dublin: Hodges, Figgis, 1936.

————. "Sochor." In *Féil-Sgríbhinn Eóin Mhic Néill,* ed. Eóin Ua Riain [John Ryan], 158–59. Dublin: At the Sign of the Three Candles, 1940; repr. Dublin: Four Courts Press, 1995.

————. *A Grammar of Old Irish.* Translated by D. A. Binchy and Osborn Bergin. Dublin: Dublin Institute for Advanced Studies, 1946; revised and enlarged edition with supplement, 1975.

van Hamel, A. G., ed. *Compert Con Culainn and Other Stories.* Mediaeval and Modern Irish Series, vol. 3. Dublin: Dublin Institute for Advanced Studies, 1933.

Vendryes, J., E. Bachellery and P.-Y. Lambert, comp. *Lexique étymologique de l'irlandais ancien.* Dublin: Dublin Institute for Advanced Studies, 1959–[ongoing].

Walsh, Paul. "A Poem on Ireland." *Ériu* 8, no. 1 (1915): 64–74.

Watkins, Calvert. "Varia II." *Ériu* 19 (1962): 114–18.

————. "Indo-European Metrics and Archaic Irish Verse." *Celtica* 6 (1963): 194–249.

West, Martin L. *Textual Criticism and Editorial Technique, Applicable to Greek and Latin Texts.* Stuttgart: B. G. Teubner, 1973.

————, ed. *Hesiod, Works & Days.* Oxford: Clarendon Press, 1978.

Williams, James G. "Proverbs and Ecclesiastes." In *The Literary Guide to the Bible,* ed. Robert Alter and Frank Kermode, 263–82. Glasgow: William Collins Sons & Co., 1987; repr. London: Fontana Press, 1989.

Windisch, Ernst. "*Tochmarc Étaíne*: Das Freien um Etain." In *Irische Texte mit Wörterbuch,* vol. 1, ed. Ernst Windisch, 113–33. Leipzig: Hirzel, 1880.

Wright, Charles D. "The Irish 'Enumerative Style' in Old English Homiletic Literature, Especially Vercelli Homily IX." *Cambridge Medieval Celtic Studies* 18 (1989): 27–74.

————. *The Irish Tradition in Old English Literature.* Cambridge Studies in Anglo-Saxon England, vol. 6. Cambridge: Cambridge Univ. Press, 1993.

Glossarial Index

Headwords in regular type refer to vocabulary found in the edited texts, that is, §§ 1–9. Headwords in *bold italic* type refer to significant variants not incorporated in the text. Entries are cited by section and line numbers. A small "n" after the number means the word is discussed in the textual notes.

a: poss. pron. 3sg. m. 1.58, 1.65, 3.9, 3.11, 3.26, 9.5, 9.19; 3sg. f. 3.4, 7.14, 7.15, 7.16, 7.17; 3sg. n. 1.40, 3.12, 7.6, 7.7

a^n: relative particle 8.20, 8.21, 8.24, 8.25

adbar n. "matter, material; potential"; dat. sg. *adbur* 6.51

adbchlos m.? "pomp, vainglory; self-importance"; nom. sg. 9.19

accobur n. "desire, wish"; nom. sg. 1.22

ad·cota "gets, obtains"; 3sg. pres. indic. § 1n

áes n. "age, years; stage (of life)"; nom. sg. 1.24

aí m.? "lawsuit, case; litigation"; nom. sg. 3.34

aicde f. "material, substance; structure; manufactured article"; compd. dat. sg. *dagaicdi* 6.32

aicsiu f. "act of seeing"; nom. sg. 6.69; dat. sg. *aicsin* 6.69a

áilgine f. "gentleness"; nom. sg. 5.10; acc. sg. *áilgini* 1.16

aimires f. "lack of faith; doubt, disbelief, incredulity"; dat. sg. *aimiris* 6.72

aimser f. "time, period of time"; acc. sg. *aimsir* 3.32

ainble f. "shamelessness, indecorousness; excess"; gen. sg. 4.23

áine f. "perspicacity, wit; splendour"; nom. sg. 1.31; dat. sg. *áini* 6.47, 6.96

aín(e) f. "fasting, period of fasting"; 6.47

aingel m. "angel"; acc. pl. *aingliu* 8.22

ainim f. "blemish, defect"; compd. dat. sg. *bithainim* 6.70a

ainim(m) f. "soul, life"; 7.11

airbire f. "reproach, taunt"; nom. sg. 5.4; acc. sg. *airbiri* 1.7; dat. sg. *airbiri* 6.12

airdál vb.n. of *ar·dáili* "distributes, shares out"; nom. sg. 3.17a

airde f. "loudness; height"; nom. sg. 9.13

airde n. "sign, token, symbol; quality, characteristic"; § 4n

airdirc "renowned, famous"; 2.4, 7.13

aire "increase, gain"; nom. sg. 6.68n

airech "prone to increase"; 2.6n

airfócrae n. "proclamation, announcement; warning"; acc. sg. 3.17, 3.31: *see* fócrae

airfognam m. "service"; 6.71

airlabrae f. "right to act as spokesman; eloquence"; acc. sg. *airlabrai* 1.31: *see* labrae

airle f. "management; counsel, deliberation"; compd. gen. sg. *míairle* 5.22

airliciud m. "act of lending, loan; borrowing"; nom. sg. 5.3

-airm : *see* arm

airmitiu f. "honour, respect"; nom. sg. 6.62; acc. sg. *airmitin* 1.23, 3.1

airmitnech "respected, honoured, renowned"; 7.8

airndel n. "trap, snare"; nom. sg. 3.17

airnel "part, share; division"; vb.n. of *ar·condla* 3.17a

airraim "deference, respect"; acc. sg. 3.24

aite m. "tutor, teacher; foster-father"; nom. sg. 3.9, 3.24

aithe n. "requital, recompense; payment; retaliation"; 6.66

áithe f. "sharpness (lit. and fig.)"; nom. sg. 6.66

aithgne n. "act of knowing, recognition; familiarity"; nom. sg. 1.17

aithigid "visiting, frequenting"; nom. sg. 4.26

aithis f. "reproach, reviling; abuse, insult"; gen. sg. *aithise* 9.3

aithne n. "entrusting (for safekeeping), depositing"; 1.17

aithrige f. "penance, repentance"; nom. sg. 7.20

aititiu f. "act of acknowledging, conceding; recognition, concession, submission; consent"; nom. sg. 6.69a; dat. sg. *aititin* 6.69

aittenn m. "furze, gorse"; nom. sg. 8.18

álaig f. "habit, behaviour"; compd. acc. sg. *soálaig* 1.64

all-: composition form of *aile* "second; another"; *allatróg* 6.33n

allaitrebad "migration?"; 6.33n

allatrúag n. "another state of wretchedness; wretchedness beyond"; dat. sg. *allatróg* 6.33n: *see* trúag alltar m.? "the next world, the hereafter"; dat. sg. *alltur* 7.9

allud m. "fame, renown"; acc. sg. 1.24

altramm n. "fosterage; act of nurturing"; nom. sg. 3.19; compd. dat. sg. *móraltramm* 6.20

an-: neg. prefix

anae m. "wealth, riches; prosperity"; nom. sg. 6.71, 6.100; dat. pl. *anaib* 6.22

anecnae n. "ignorance, lack of information"; nom. sg. 4.23: *see* ecnae

anéolas m. "ignorance, lack of experience"; gen. sg. *anéolais* 4.22: *see* éolas

angbocht "great poverty"?; 6.7

angbus m.? "fierceness, ruthlessness"?; dat. sg. 6.7n

anidan "impure, faithless, insincere"; as subst. nom. sg. 3.28: *see* idan

ansae "hard, difficult; troublesome; formidable"; superl. *ansam* 8.3

ánsruth m. "noble; an accomplished person; a poet of the second rank"; acc. sg. 7.3

araⁿ: conj. (+ subj.) "so that, in order that" + neg. *arná-*; 2.1, 2.2

araile "other, another"; adverbial use of dat. sg. *arailiu* 5.23

árchú m.? "guard dog; war-hound"; nom. pl. *árchoin* 8.4

ard(d) "high, elevated, lofty"; as subst. acc. pl. *arddu* 9.7

ar·fich "fights; overcomes, vanquishes"; 3sg. pres. indic. 3.2

arm n. "weapon, arms"; in adj. with prefix *doairm* 6.3; *diairm* 6.3

arnába: *see* is

as: *see* is

astud m. "act of fixing, establishing; certainty, steadiness"; nom. sg. 6.72; acc. sg. 3.34

athair m. "father"; nom. sg. 3.23, 7.18

athargab m. "arms, weapons; attack" gen. sg. *athargaib* 4.5

athchomsán "reproach, rebuke; attack"; nom. sg. 4.18, 5.2

attach n. "refuge"; nom. sg. 9.2

attrab n. "taking possession, occupying; inhabiting; squatting"; compd. dat. sg. *immattrub* 6.34

attrúag "pitiable, wretched, sad"; 6.33

augrae n.? "strife, contention; conflict, quarrel"; nom. sg. 3.6; acc. sg. 1.17; gen. sg. *augrai* 5.2

aurchailliud m. vb.n. of *ar·cuilli* "prohibits, forbids, inhibits"; acc. sg. 3.28

aurdonál "a herald, crier"; nom. sg. 3.31

aurgnam m. "household work, service"; 6.71

aurlam "ready, prepared"; as subst. nom. sg. 6.51

ba: *see* is

báegul n. "risk, hazard; legal liability"; acc. sg. 1.25

báes f. "folly, foolishness; lack of judgement"; nom. sg. 1.5, 1.25, gen. sg. *baíse* 4.13

báeth "foolish, stupid; legally incapable"; as subst. dat. sg. 7.5

bág f. "boast, threat; contention"; acc. pl. *bága* 1.25a; dat. pl. *bágaib* 6.30

ban-: adj. prefix "female, women's"

banchobrae "conversation of women"; nom. sg. 4.13n: *see* cobrae

barae f. "hostility, vehemence"; nom. sg. 1.28; acc. sg. *barainn* 1.27

bás n. "death"; nom. sg. 6.70

bec(c) "little, small"; as subst. nom. sg. 6.93; prefix in compd. nom. sg. *beccfine* 6.20

beccfine f. "a small kindred"; nom. sg. 6.20: *see* fine

becdatu m. "humility, lowliness"; nom. sg. 1.11

ben f. "woman, wife"; compds. nom. sg. *dagben* 5.20, *drochben* 1.60, 5.21, *soben* 6.59

béo "living, alive"; as subst. nom. pl. *bí* 7.16

bérlae n. "speech, (technical) language"; compd. gen. sg. *drochbérlai* 9.2

1 bés "perhaps"; as subst. nom. sg. 3.36

2 bés m. "habit, custom; practice"; compd. nom. pl. *caínbésa* 4.27

bethu m. "life, existence"; nom. sg. 6.28

biad n. "food; refection"; dat. sg. *biud* 6.50

bíathad m. "act of feeding, maintaining; refection"; acc. sg. 1.65

bíathaid "feeds, nourishes; supports"; 3sg. pres. subj. *·bíatha* 1.1a

bibdu m. "one who is guilty of offence, culprit"; acc. sg. *bibdaid* 1.28

bil-: adj. prefix, ambiguous in meaning, "good" or "evil"

biltengae f. "an evil tongue"?; nom. sg. 1.29n: *see* tengae

bine n.? "crime, wrongdoing"; compd. dat. sg. *bithbiniu* 6.70

bith-: adj. prefix "lasting, permanent, perpetual"

bithainim f. "a lasting blemish, a perpetual defect"; dat. sg. 6.70a: *see* ainim

bithbine n.? "persistent crime; constant wrongdoing"; dat. sg. *bithbiniu* 6.70: *see* bine

bithdudae: *see* dudae

bithfognam m. "continuous servitude"; nom. sg. 4.29: *see* fognam

bithgubae m. "constant mourning, lamenting"; nom. sg. 4.20: *see* gubae

bithnert n. "lasting strength"; acc. sg. 1.45: *see* nert

bliadain f. "a year"; dat. sg. 6.49

blipecht: *see* pliptecht

bó f. "cow"; nom. sg. 6.49

bocht "poor"; as subst. nom. sg. 1.65; dat. sg. 7.2

bodeisin: *see* fadéin

borb "ignorant; uncouth; violent"; as subst. nom. sg. 1.37

brab m. "supremacy; superlativeness"; 6.18

brath: *see* mrath

bráth m. "judgement, legal precept"; 1.29

breithemnacht f. "adjudication, judgement"; 1.54

breithemnas m. "adjudication, judgement"; acc. sg. 1.54

bréo f. "flame, spark (lit. and fig.); excellence"; nom. sg. 6.18

breth f. "judgement, legal ruling"; dat. sg. *breith* 9.21

bríathar f. "word, utterance; promise"; acc. sg. *bréithir* 3.36; dat. sg. *bréithir* 6.91; acc. pl. *bríathra* 1.10; compd. nom. sg. *úabarbríathar* 5.11

bríg f. "authority; strength, force"; nom. sg. 1.27, 6.30

briugas m. "function of a *briugu*; hospitality; abundance"; nom. sg. 1.26, 6.19

briugu m. "hospitaller"; nom. sg. 1.66

brón m. "sorrow, grief; distress"; nom. sg. 1.50; gen. sg. *bróin* 4.20

bronnad m. "bestowing, giving; consuming; destroying; profligacy"; acc. sg. 1.26n

brothchán m. "broth, pottage, gruel"; nom. sg. 1.45

brugas "possession of lands"; 6.19n

búaid n. "triumph; virtue, excellence"; nom. sg. 6.29; dat. sg. 6.50a; dat. pl. *búadaib* 6.28

búaine f. "lastingness, permanence, constancy"; nom. sg. 6.96

búar n. "cows, cattle, herds"; nom. sg. 6.91; dat. sg. 6.19

buide f. "favour; gratitude"; nom. sg. 6.67; compd. acc. sg. *caínbuidi* 1.11

buidech "grateful, thankful; well-disposed"; 2.6

buille f. "blow, stroke"; nom. sg. 1.63

burbae f. "boorishness, crudity, ignorance"; nom. sg. 4.21; acc. sg. *burbai* 1.5, 1.63; gen. sg. 4.29; dat. sg. *burbai* 6.18

cach "each, every; any"; 6.50

cách "each one, everyone"; gen. sg. *cáich* 9.17

cáemnae n.? "act of protecting, providing for; entertainment"; dat. sg. *cáemnu* 6.41

cáera f. "sheep"; nom. pl. caírig 8.12

cailech m. "cock, male of various birds"; nom. pl. *cailig* 8.16

cailte f. "meanness, stinginess"; gen. sg. 4.11a

caín-: adj. prefix "fair, good"

caínbés m. "good habit"; nom. pl. *caínbésa* 4.27: *see* 2 bés

caínbuide f. "good favour"; acc. sg. *caínbuidi* 1.11: *see* buide caínchruth m. "fair form"; acc. sg. 1.3; dat. sg. 6.63: *see* cruth

caínepert f. "gentle speech, a good utterance"; nom. sg. 5.15: *see* epert

caíniud m. "weeping, lamentation; keening"; acc. sg. 1.51

caíntórmach n. "fair increase"; nom. sg. 6.37: *see* tórmach

cairiugud m. "act of rebuking; accusation"; acc. sg. 3.4

caithem f. "act of spending, consuming"; acc. sg. *caithim* 1.58

carad m. vb.n. of *caraid* "loves, cherishes"; gen. sg. *cartha* 4.10n

carae m. "friend; relative"; nom. sg. 6.61

carna "lechery, lust; meat, flesh"; acc. sg. 1.20n

cartha: *see* carad

carthain vb.n. of *caraid* "loves"; 4.10

cath m. "battle, fight"; nom. sg. 1.51

cathugud m. "act of fighting, doing battle"; nom. sg. 9.4, 9.17; compd. nom. sg. *frithchathugud* 9.1

cen: prep. (+ acc.) "without"; 9.4

cenél n. "kindred; tribe; nation"; compds. acc. sg. *sochenél* 7.4; dat. sg. *socheníul* 6.59, *docheníul* 7.4

cenn n. "head; end; mouth"; gen. sg. *cinn* 9.20

cenntar m.? "this world (as opposed to hereafter)"; dat. sg. *cenntur* 7.8

cerc f. "hen"; gen. pl. 8.16

certugud m. "putting to rights, arrangement; adjustment"; acc. sg. 3.25

cesacht m. "complaint, murmuring; niggardliness"; acc. sg. 1.14

cesachtaige f. "complaint, grumbling; niggardliness"; nom. sg. 4.11

cía: interrog. pron. "who"; 8.1, 8.3, 8.5, 8.7, 8.9, 8.11, 8.13, 8.15, 8.17, 8.19, 8.23

cíall f. "(good) sense, intelligence"; nom. sg. 1.3, 6.63, compds. nom. sg. *sochell* 1.1, *dochell* 1.14

cin m. "crime, offence; guilt, liability"; dat. pl. *cintaib* 6.37

cloíne f. "iniquity, deception; injustice"; nom. sg. 3.5

cloth n.? "reputation, fame, honour"; nom. sg. 6.50, 6.64; acc. pl. *clotha* 1.15, 1.69

cloud m. "turning; converting; change"; nom. sg. 6.94

clú n. "reputation, fame, good name"; nom. sg. 6.41

cluiche n.? "game, play; sport"; nom. sg. 6.39

co^n: conj. (+ subj.) "so that, in order that"+ *ro*, *cor-* 2.3, 2.4, 2.5, 2.6, 2.7

cobrae "speech, conversation"; compd. nom. sg. *banchobrae* 4.13n

cocad m. "war, conflict"; compd. dat. sg. *sochocad* 6.58

cocorus m. "proper arrangement; harmony, concord"; acc. sg. 1.52

coibche f. "bride-price; bargain, contract"; nom. sg. 3.25

coillte: *see* collud

coímchloud m.? vb.n. of *con·imchloí* "interchanges, exchanges"; acc. sg. 3.29

coimded m. "custody; confiscation"; dat. sg. *coimdiud* 6.65

coimsetu m. "that which is suitable, appropriate, fitting"; nom. sg. 6.53

collud vb.n. of *coillid* "damages, violates, mistreats"; gen. sg. *coillte* 4.11

comae f.? "gift, offer; bribe, ransom; terms"; nom. sg. 6.65

comaithches m. "law of neighbourhood; neighbourly relationships"; nom. sg. 3.29

comarthae n.? "sign, mark, token"; acc. sg. 9.4; nom. pl. *comarthai* § 9

conn m. "intelligence, reason; legally responsible person"; compds. nom. sg. *éconn* 3.27, *reconn* 6.21; dat. sg. *íarcunn* 6.21

cor m. "(legal) contract, agreement"; compds. dat. sg. *dochur* 6.27; dat. pl. *míchoraib* 6.42

córae f. "correctness, properness; concord"; gen. sg. 5.15

corba: *see* is

cormaim: *see* cuirm

corn m. "drinking horn, goblet"; acc. pl. *cornu* 1.20a

cosmail "like, similar"; nom. pl. *cosmaili* 8.22, 8.26

cosmailius m. "likeness, resemblance; imitation; analogy"; nom. sg. 5.9

cotlud m. "act of sleeping, sleep"; gen. sg. *cotulta* 4.1

cotulta: *see* cotlud

crábud m.? "piety, devotion"; gen. sg. *crábuid* 4.27, 5.9

cride n. "heart; affection; loyalty"; nom. sg. 6.54

críne f. "senility, old age; decay"; gen. sg. 5.12

crod m. "cattle, herd; property; wealth"; nom. sg. 1.58

crodlesc "careless as regards property, indifferent to possessions; indolent"; as subst. nom. sg. 1.41: *see* crod, lesc

cruth m. "appearance, form"; compds. acc. sg. *caínchruth* 1.3; dat. sg. *caínchruth* 6.63

cubaid "harmonious, proper, fitting"; 6.64

cucilche n.? "disturbance, turbulence; chaos"; dat. sg. *cucilchiu* 6.53n

cuindrech n. "act of correcting, chastising, controlling"; acc. sg. 3.5

cuirm n. "ale, beer"; nom. sg. 1.20, 1.69; dat. sg. *cormaim* 6.61

cumae f. "grief, sorrow"; dat. sg. *cumaid* 6.64

cumgae f. "narrowness; difficulty, distress; constraint"; acc. sg. *cumgai* 1.36

cummae n. vb.n. of *con·ben* "smites, hacks, destroys"; dat. sg. *cummu* 6.94

cutaim n. "act of collapsing, falling down"; gen. sg. *cutmae* 5.19

cutmae: *see* cutaim

dag-, deg-: adj. prefix "good"

dagaicde f. "fine structures?"; dat. sg. *dagaicdi* 6.32: *see* aicde

dagben f. "a good woman, a good wife"; nom. sg. 5.20: *see* ben

daidbre f. "poverty"; nom. sg. 1.32

dál f. "conference, assembly; consensus"; nom. sg. 6.13

dall "blind"; as subst. nom. sg. 3.16

dán m. "skill, art, craft; occupation"; nom. sg. 6.1, 6.48, 7.1, 7.12, 7.19; compd. nom. sg. *drochdán* 6.97

dánae "bold, audacious"; superl. *dánam* 8.5

dánatus m. "boldness, impudence, audacity"; nom. sg. 4.7

debech m. "strife, contention, discord"; dat. sg. *debiuch* 6.13

debtha: *see* debuith

debthaige f. "contentiousness, strife, discord"; acc. sg. *debthaigi* 1.50

debuith f. "strife, contention"; gen. sg. *debtha* 4.18

déc "ten; -teen"; § 9

dech: *see* maith

degmuirn f. "courage; high spirits; ardour, enthusiasm"; nom. sg. 6.99: *see* muirn

déine f. "swiftness, speed; haste"; nom. sg. 6.26; dat. sg. *déini* 6.25

déinmiche f. "idleness, inactivity"; dat. sg. *déinmichi* 6.48

deired n. "end, result; residue, what remains"; nom. sg. 7.7; acc. sg. 7.10

déirge n. "forsaking, abandonment"; nom. sg. 1.8; acc. sg. 1.4a

demon m. "demon, devil"; nom./acc. pl. *demnai* 8.10, 8.26

deog f. "drink, draught"; nom. sg. 4.3

deogmaire (var. *deogbaire*) m. "cupbearer"; 4.3

derbad m. "proving, certifying, affirming"; nom. sg. 9.10

dércach "charitable, benevolent; benign"; 2.4a

derchoíntech "despairing; tearful, sorrowful"; 7.10

derge f. "redness, flushing"; 1.4a

dérgnae "undiscerning; undistinguished, insignificant, common"; 7.14

dermat n.? "forgetfulness, oblivion"; acc. sg. 3.13

descad "characteristic, symptom; catalyst, inducement"; § 4

di, de: prep. (+ dat.) "of, from"; 7.2, 7.3, 7.4, 7.5, 8.21, 8.25

dí-: privative prefix

diairm "unarmed, weaponless"; as subst. dat. sg. 6.3: *see* arm

dianid: *see* do, is

díbe n. "stinginess; rejection, refusal"; nom. sg. 1.13, 3.15; acc. sg. 1.60; gen. sg. *díbi* 4.3

díchóelad m.? privative *dí-* + *cóelad* i.e. "act of not growing slender"; acc. sg. 1.53

díden f. "act of leading, guiding"; acc. sg. *dídin* 3.16

dígáirse f. "impetuosity, hurry, zealousness"; dat. sg. *dígáirsi* 6.80

dígal f. "act of avenging; vengeance, punishment"; dat. sg. *dígail* 6.6

dígbad m. "act of diminishing, growing less, failing; stifling"; dat. sg. *dígbud* 6.102

dígbál f. "lessening, diminution; privation"; dat. sg. *dígbáil* 6.67

dígde f. "deprecating (anger); seeking pardon or forgiveness"; nom. sg. 6.6

dígnae n.? "reproach, contempt, disgrace"; acc. sg. 1.4

dílmaine f. "licence; liberty; detachment, exemption; idleness"; dat. sg. *dílmaini* 6.97

dímaise f. "uncomeliness, plainness; lack of adornment"; nom. sg. 4.12

dimdae f.? "disfavour, displeasure"; acc. sg. *dimdai* 1.19

dimmolad m. "disparagement, censure"; acc. sg. 1.13, 3.15

dinge vb.n. of *dingid* "crushes, quells"; acc. sg. 1.57

dínnime f. "carelessness, shabbiness; indolence"; dat. sg. *dínnimi* 6.46

dínsem "spurning, despising; contempt, insult"; nom. sg. 9.11; acc. sg. 3.15a

díthech n. "oath of denial"; acc. sg. 3.37

dítiu f. "covering, shelter; protection"; 3.16

díummus m. "arrogance, pride"; nom. sg. 1.19, 3.13

dliged n. "what is incumbent; duty, obligation"; dat. sg. *dligiud* 6.85

dligid "is entitled to, has a right to; deserves, merits"; 3sg. pres. indic. § 3

do-: adj. prefix "bad; invalid; deficient, lacking"

do: prep. (+ dat.) "to, for"; prep. + 3sg. m. *dó* 7.11; prep. + 3sg. poss. pron. *dia* 7.18; prep. + rel. part. + 3sg. pres. indic. conjunct of copula *dianid* 7.19a

do·airicc "comes; finds, gets"; 3sg. pres. subj. prototonic ·*tair* 7.20

doairm "poorly armed, badly equipped"; as subst. nom. sg. 6.3: *see* arm

do·beir "gives"; 3sg. pres. subj. (of suppl. *ro*-form **to·rat*) *do·rata* 1.2

dobele f. "unfavourable situation, unpropitious circumstance"; nom. sg. 6.27; dat. sg. *dobeli* 6.26n

doben f. "a bad woman, a bad wife"; 5.21: *see* ben

dochell f. "inhospitality, sullenness"; nom. sg. 1.14: *see* cíall

dochenél n. "a bad kindred; a lowly family"; dat. sg. *docheníul* 7.4: *see* cenél

dochor m. "disadvantage, loss; unfair contract"; dat. sg. *dochur* 6.27: *see* cor

dochraite f. "want of friends; hardship, indignity"; acc. sg. *dochraiti* 1.32

do·gní (di) "makes (of), turns (into)"; 3 sg. pres. ind. 7.2, 7.3, 7.4, 7.5

dóig "probability, maybe"; as subst. nom. sg. 3.37

doilig "troublesome; grievous, distressful"; 7.12

do·im(m)na (do) "bequeathes, commits to, entrusts; enjoins, commands";

3sg. pres. indic. prototonic ·*timnai* 7.18; 3sg. pres. subj. prototonic ·*thimna* 7.18a

doíre f. "low (social) status; unfree status; captivity"; nom. sg. 1.36, 1.57; gen. sg. 5.16

domescae f. "sobriety, soberness"; nom. sg. 5.14: *see* mescae

do·rata: *see* do·beir

dord n.? "humming; droning, buzzing; plaint"; compd. nom. sg. *sírdord* 4.2

dothcad m. "ill-luck, misfortune"; gen. sg. *dothcaid* 5.13, 5.21: *see* tocad

droch-: adj. prefix "bad, evil; inferior"

drochben f. "a bad woman, a bad wife"; nom. sg. 1.60, 5.21: *see* ben

drochbérlae n. "bad, inappropriate language"; gen. sg. *drochbérlai* 9.2: *see* bérlae

drochdán m. "a poor skill, a lowly craft"; nom. sg. 6.97: *see* dán

drochlepaid f. "bad assocation, illegal harbourage of a proscribed person"; nom. sg. 5.16: *see* lepaid

drochthacrae n. "bad pleading, inferior arguing"; § 9: *see* tacrae

drochthrebaire f. "poor implements?"; nom. sg. 6.32: *see* trebaire

drúb f.? "delay; staying, abiding"; nom. sg. 6.25

drús f. "lust, lechery"; nom. sg. 1.4; gen. sg. *drúise* 4.7

dudae n.? "gloom"; compd. *bithdudae* 4.20

duí m. "ignoramus, simpleton; unlearned or unskilled person"; nom. sg. 7.14

dúil f. "element, being; (pl.) Creation; book, codex"; dat. pl. *dúilib* 6.31

duine m. "human being, person; mankind"; nom. sg. 6.31

duthain "transitory, short-lived"; 7.15

dúthchas m. "inherent ability; hereditary right, privilege; patrimony"; dat. sg. *dúthchus* 6.99

dúthracht "willingness, good-will"; nom. sg. 1.2, 6.85

éc m. "death"; gen. sg. *éca* 4.6a

ecal "fearful, timorous"; superl. *eclam* 8.11

echlach f. "prostitute, concubine"; nom. sg. 1.21n

eclach "timorous, fearful"; as subst. nom. sg. 1.21a

eclae f. "fear, dread"; gen. sg. 4.6

ecnae n. "wisdom, enlightenment; acquired knowledge, learning"; nom. sg. 3.1, 6.22, 7.1; gen. sg. *ecnai* 5.10; compd. nom. sg. *anecnae* 4.23

écndach n. "reviling, slander; accusation"; gen. sg. *écndaig* 5.4

éconn "wanting in sense"; as subst. "one legally incapable"; nom. sg. 3.27: *see* conn

écraite f. "enmity, grudge"; compd. dat. sg. *senécraiti* 6.35

éimech "swift, prompt; opportune"; 2.3

éimid "swift, prompt; obliging"; 2.3

elathu f. "art, science; craft, skill"; acc. sg. *elathain* 3.18

enech n. "honour, repute; dignity"; dat. sg. *eniuch* 6.98

eneclann n. "compensation (for insult, etc.), satisfaction; honour-price"; nom. sg. 5.5

engnam m. "skill (at arms); dexterity, prowess"; nom. sg. 6.98

éolas m. "knowledge, wisdom; experience; familiarity; expertise"; nom. sg. 6.9; gen. sg. *éolais* 4.26, 5.1; compd. gen. sg. *anéolais* 4.22

epert f. "saying, utterance; dictum, word"; compd. nom. sg. *caínepert* 5.15

érae f. "refusing, a refusal"; dat. sg. *érai* 6.93

érchoíliud m. vb.n. of *as·rochoíli* "defines, determines; enjoins"; 3.28

ernail "part, share; division"; vb.n. of *ar·condla* 3.17a

esarcon f. "smiting, striking; attack"; nom. sg. 4.5

esert f. "landless person; one who neglects his holdings; vagrant"; dat. sg. *esirt* 7.3

eslabar "liberal, generous; ample"; 2.4

essomnae f. "confidence, lack of fear"; nom. sg. 6.12

etargaire n. "interfering, intervention, mediation"; acc. sg. 3.6

etech n. "refusal, refusing"; gen. sg. *etig* 5.3; compd. dat. sg. *lánetiug* 6.83

éthech n. "false oath, perjury; lying"; gen. sg. *éthig* 5.3a

etlae f. "self-denial, renunciation; holiness"; nom. sg. 1.68a

étlae vb.n. of *étlaid* "evades, escapes; takes by stealth"; nom. sg. 1.68

étnge "dumb, unfit to plead; inarticulate"; as subst. nom. sg. 3.32: *see* tengae

étradach "lustful, vicious"; nom. pl. *étradaig* 7.16a

étrebaire f. "indiscretion; imprudence"; gen. sg. 4.9: *see* trebaire

fadéin: pronominal "self"; 9.19

fadesin: pronominal "self"; 9.5

fáilte f. "joy, happiness; welcome"; nom. sg. 1.55, 9.6; gen. sg. 4.19

fairsinge f. "amplitude, extent; lavishness"; nom. sg. 5.8

fáiscre m.? "coercion, repression"; nom. sg. 1.6n; compd. acc. sg. *rofáiscre* 1.6n

faitech "cautious, wary"; 2.1

fáitsine f. "conjecture, calculation; prophesying, augury"; acc. sg. *fáitsini* 1.9n

feidle f. "perseverance, constancy"; acc. sg. *feidli* 1.22

féig "keen, penetrating, acute"; superl. *fégam* 8.1

féle f. "sense of decorum, propriety; liberality"; nom. sg. 1.12; acc. sg. *féli* 1.55; gen. sg. 5.8

fénnid m. "warrior, champion"; acc. sg. 1.47

ferann n. "domain, territory"; nom. sg. 1.47

ferg f. "anger, wrath"; gen. sg. *ferge* 4.4

fergach "angry, wrathful"; 9.15; as subst. nom. sg. 1.43

ferr: *see* maith

fert f. "(grave) mound, tumulus; boundary marker"; dat. pl. *fertaib* 6.88a

fíach m. "payment, debt; legal due; fine"; acc. pl. *fiachu* 3.38; compd. nom. sg. *senfíach* 6.35

fíachach "under obligation or debt"; 2.1

fíadnaise n. "eye-witness testimony, evidence"; nom. sg. 3.12

fine f. "kindred, kin-group; family"; compd. nom. sg. *beccfine* 6.20

fír "true, genuine"; as subst. "truth, proof"; nom. sg. 3.3, 3.38, 6.88

fírián "just, righteous"; as subst. nom. sg. 1.39

fis n. "knowledge, information"; nom. sg. 4.28; gen. sg. 9.1; compds. nom. sg. *rous* 6.76; dat. sg. *sous* 6.14, 6.92

fiurt m. "miracle, wonder"; 6.88a

flaith f. "lordship, sovereignty; realm; a ruler"; nom. sg. 1.38, 1.67, 6.36

fócrae n. "act of proclaiming, announcing"; acc. sg. 3.21: *see* airfócrae

fogal vb.n. of *fo·fich* "trespasses; offends, attacks"; 1.46

fognam m. "act of rendering service; servitude"; dat. sg. 6.71; compd. nom. sg. *bithfognam* 4.29

foíndel m. "evasion of responsibility"; 3.21

foíndelach "vagrant, wandering; evading responsibilities"; as subst. "fugitive"; nom. sg. 3.21

foistine f. "state of rest, sojourning; composure; inertia"; acc. sg. *foistini* 1.9a

fola f. "grievance, resentment"; 6.35, 6.36

folabrad m. "whispering, murmuring"; nom. sg. 9.8; acc. sg. 1.38

folad n. "benefit; liability, duty; clientship obligation"; dat. pl. *foltaib* 6.36; compd. acc. pl. *frithfolta* 1.12, 3.8

foltaib: *see* folad

forbbae n. vb.n. of *for·ben* "smites, strikes, cuts"; dat. sg. *forbbu* 6.84

forcell n. "bearing witness, testifying; testimony"; compd. nom. sg. *gúforcell* 5.19

fortacht f. "help, aid; support"; acc. sg. 1.39, 3.3

frecrae n. "act of answering; response, an answer"; gen. sg. *frecrai* 4.28

freslige n. "lying down; lying with or beside"; nom. sg. 4.1: *see* lige

fri: prep. (+ acc.) "towards, against"; 7.10, 7.11, 9.6, 9.7, 9.12

frith-: prep. prefix "against, counter-"

frithaí m.? "counter-suit"; 6.88n: *see* aí

frithbert f. "act of opposing, resistance, confrontation"; nom. sg. 1.46

frithchathugud m. "fighting against; opposition"; nom. sg. 9.1

frithfolad n. "counter-obligation, reciprocal service"; acc. pl. *frithfolta* 1.12,
    3.8: *see* folad

frithfolta: *see* frithfolad

frithoíb f. "opposite appearance, antithesis"; dat. sg. 6.88: *see* oíb

frithorcun f. "harrassment; injury; offence"; acc. sg. *frithorcuin* 1.43a

fróech m. "heather, scrub; a heath, moor"; nom. sg. 6.84

fúachtain f. "molestation; offense, injury"; acc. sg. 1.46

fúasnad m. "disturbance, perturbation"; acc. sg. 1.43

fuidir f. "member of low-status class; tenant-at-will"; nom. sg. 3.8

fuigell m. vb.n. of *fo·gella* "appeals to the judgment of; pronounces a verdict,
    gives judgement concerning"; acc. sg. 3.12

furfócrae n. "act of proclaiming, proscribing; warning"; 3.21: *see* fócrae

gabálach "grasping, rapacious"; 2.2

gabáltach "grasping, rapacious"; 2.2

gáes f.? "intelligence, mental acuteness; wisdom"; nom. sg. 1.15, 1.23, 3.2,
    6.77; gen. sg. *gaíse* 9.9; compd. dat. sg. *rogaís* 6.75

1 gáeth "wise, intelligent; skillful; legally capable"; as subst. acc. sg. 7.5

2 gáeth f. "wind"; nom. sg. 8.2

gáire m. "laughter, a laugh"; compd. nom. sg. *rogáire* 4.14

gaisced m. "weapons, arms; prowess, skill-at-arms"; dat. sg. *gaisciud* 6.77

gal f. "warlike ardour, fury; steam"; acc. sg. *gail* 3.2

galraige f. "sickliness, disease"; nom. sg. 5.12; dat. sg. *galraigi* 6.38

garb "rough, coarse; rude, harsh"; superl. *gairbem* 8.17

garbae f. "roughness, asperity, fierceness"; dat. sg. *garbai* 6.39

gart "generosity, hospitality; cordiality"; nom. sg. 6.55

gartaid "generous, hospitable"; 2.5

genas m. "purity, chastity"; gen. sg. *gensa* 4.12

gíall m. "hostage, human pledge"; 6.54

gíallnae f. "submission, obeisance; hostageship"; dat. sg. *gíallnai* 6.54

gnáthaige f. "frequency, wont"; nom. sg. 4.10

gnáthgaire f. "lingering about, hanging around"; 4.10

gním m. "act of doing; activity, action"; nom. sg. 6.38; compd. nom. sg.
    sogním 1.64

gnímach "active, busy; toiling"; 7.15

gnímchae f. "activity"; 1.37

gnímrad n. "acts, deeds; labour"; acc. sg. 1.37; dat. sg. *gnímrud* 6.41a

gó f. "falsehood, lie; false judgement"; nom. sg. 3.4; compd. nom. sg.
    gúforcell 5.19

goire f. "dutifulness; filial maintenance (of relatives, etc.)"; nom. sg. 6.78;
    compds. acc. sg. *sogoiri* 3.20, 3.20a, 3.23a, *míngoiri* 3.22

gorad m. "act of heating, warming; blushing"; nom. sg. 6.40

gotha: *see* guth

gréch f. "scream, outcry"; nom. pl. *grécha* 9.20

grefel m.? "disorder, confusion; chaos"; dat. sg. *grefiul* 6.79

greimm n. "hold, grip; authority, control"; nom. sg. 6.79

gres f. "attack, insult; attempt, effort"; nom. sg. 6.101

grés m. "handicraft, workmanship; craft"; nom. sg. 6.92

grís f. "heat, fire; ardour, passion"; dat. pl. *grísaib* 6.40

grísad m. "act of blistering (by satire); causing to blush; inciting to passion,
    fomenting; affront"; dat. sg. 6.40a, 6.55

grúad n.? "cheek (with reference to shame or honour)"; nom. sg. 6.40a

gubae m. "mourning, lamenting"; compd. nom. sg. *bithgubae* 4.20

gúforcell n. "false-witness"; nom. sg. 5.19: *see* gó, forcell

guth m. "voice"; gen. sg. *gotha* 9.13

i^n: prep. (+ dat. and acc.) "in, into" + def. art. *isin* 7.8, 7.9

íar^n: prep. (+ dat.) "after"; 9.21

íarconn m. "after-thought"; dat. sg. *íarcunn* 6.21: *see* conn

íarfaigid f. "guarding, tending, looking after"; acc. sg. 3.26

íarraid f.? "fosterage-fee; dowry"; dat. sg. 6.68

idan "pure, faithful, sincere"; compd. as subst. nom. sg. *anidan* 3.28

ifern(n)ach "damned, hell-bound"; nom. pl. *ifernaig* 7.17

ilach m. "cry of exultation, shout of victory"; dat. sg. *iluch* 6.100

ilar n. "multitude, abundance; multiplicity"; nom. sg. 6.10, 9.3; dat. sg. *ilur*
    6.9

imbed n. "abundance, excess"; nom. sg. 1.53; dat. sg. *imbiud* 6.78

imcaisiu f. "looking about, surveying; gazing"; nom. sg. 4.15

imchomarc n. "inquiry, questioning"; nom. sg. 5.1

imchomét m. "act of guarding, watching over"; acc. sg. 3.27

imdegal f. "act of protecting, defending"; acc. sg. *imdegail* 3.11

imfochaid f. "act of impugning, annulling, abrogating"; acc. sg. 3.19

immattrab n.? "living hemmed in; being surrounded"; dat. sg. *immattrub*
    6.34n: *see* attrab

imned n. "anxiety, tribulation, sorrow"; acc. sg. 1.33

imresan n. "strife, contention"; nom. sg. 1.33, 4.22

imtholtu f. "willfulness, eagerness; great pleasure, delight"; nom. sg. 9.9

inderb "uncertain, unproven"; as subst. gen. sg. *indeirb* 9.10

insce f. "saying, speech, statement"; gen. sg. 9.8

irach "bountiful"?; 2.6

írach "wrathful, angry"; 2.6

is: copula; 2 sg. pres. subj. conjunct *-ba* (*arnába*) 2.1, 2.2, (*corba*) 2.3, 2.4, 2.5, 2.6, 2.7; 2sg. ipv. *ba* 2.1, 2.2, 2.3, 2.4, 2.5, 2.6, 2.7; 3sg. pres. indic. *is* 7.14, 8.22, 8.26; 3sg. pres. indic. neg. *ní* 7.10, 7.13; 3sg. pres. indic. conjunct *-id* (*dianid*) 7.19a; 3sg. rel. *as* 8.20, 8.21, 8.24, 8.25; 3pl. pres. indic. *it* 7.16, 7.17, 8.22, 8.26

it: *see* is

itche m. "request, petition"; 6.16

ithe f. "act of eating; devouring"; 6.66

labartha: *see* labrad

labrad m. "utterance, act of speaking"; gen. sg. *labartha* 9.18

labrae f. "gift of speech, talkativeness"; acc. sg. *labrai* 1.67a; compd. nom. sg. *rolabrae* 4.9

láechdacht f. "the lay state; martial life"; nom. sg. 7.12n, 7.19

laimthinche f. "daring, audacity; confidence"; dat. sg. *laimthinchi* 6.82

laith f. "liquor; ale, beer"; nom. sg. 1.67

lán-: adj. prefix "full, complete"

lánetech n. "a complete refusal, a full rejection"; dat. sg. *lánetiug* 6.83: *see* etech

laubair f. "labour, work; manual labour"; nom. sg. 6.47

lebor m. "book"; acc. pl. *libru* 1.48; gen. pl. 9.11

ledb f. "strip of skin, leather or cloth; remnant; weal, welt; stroke, blow"; nom. sg. 6.2n

legad m. "decay, perishing; running out; waste"; acc. sg. 1.41

léigend n. "reading, studying; instruction, learning"; nom. sg. 1.48

léignid m. "learned person, scholar"; nom. sg. 1.48a

léire f. "devotion, diligence; industry"; nom. sg. 6.82; acc. sg. *léiri* 1.34

lén m. "impairment, impediment, incapacity; misfortune, setback"; nom. sg. 5.18n, 6.81a

lepaid f. "protection, harbouring; bed, sleeping cubicle"; compd. nom. sg. *drochlepaid* 5.16

lesc "lazy; reluctant, unwilling"; compd. as subst. nom. sg. *crodlesc* 1.41

lescae f. "laziness, sloth; reluctance"; nom. sg. 1.9

leth n. "half"; nom. sg. 6.83

líamain f. "reproach, slander"; acc. sg. *líamnai* 1.8

liech ? 6.4

lige n. "act of lying down, reclining; bed, couch; grave"; compd. nom. sg.
    freslige 4.1

lín n.? "great number, full complement"; nom. sg. 6.81

lobar "weak, infirm; legally incapable"; as subst. nom. sg. 1.62

lobrae f. "weakness, infirmity; legal incapacity"; acc. sg. *lobrai* 1.67; gen. sg.
    5.18; dat. sg. *lobrai* 6.81

logad m. "act of conceding; concession; forgiveness, pardon"; compd. dat. sg.
    rolgad 6.74

lógmar "precious, valuable; rich, beautiful"; 7.9

lúaithe f. "swiftness, speed, promptness"; nom. sg. 6.80

luchair "bright, resplendent"; as subst. "brilliance, sheen"; 6.52

1 lugae n. "act of swearing; oath"; nom. sg. 9.21

2 lugae m.? "yearning; want, deficiency"; dat. sg. *lugu* 6.2

luinde f. "fierceness, anger, vehemence"; acc. sg. *luindi* 1.62

lurchaire "foal, colt"; nom. sg. 6.52

1 mac m. "a bond, surety"; nom. sg. 6.42

2 mac m. "son"; dat. sg. 7.18

mag n. "a plain, an open stretch of (arable) land; pasture"; nom. sg. 6.86;
    acc. pl. *muige* 1.66a

maidm n. "act of bursting forth, breaking out"; 3.10

maigister m. "teacher, master"; nom. sg. 3.20a

mairg "woe, sorrow"; followed by noun in acc. or *do* + noun; 7.19

maith "good, beneficial"; 7.1, 7.6; compar. *ferr* § 6, 7.7; superl. *dech* 8.19,
    8.21, 8.24; as subst. nom. sg. 1.40, 3.14, 5.23

malartchae f. "destructiveness, wastefulness; prodigality"; nom. sg. 5.22

mani·: preverbal part. "unless, if not"; 7.20

marb "dead, slain"; as subst. nom. pl. *mairb* 7.17

marbad m. "act of killing, slaying"; dat. sg. 6.11

máthair f. "mother"; nom. sg. 3.22

menmnach "spirited, self-assertive"; as subst. nom. sg. 1.49

mer "demented, crazy; foolish"; as subst. nom. sg. 3.30

mesam: *see* olc

mescae f. "drunkenness, intoxication"; compds. nom. sg. *somescae* 5.13,
    domescae 5.14; gen. sg. *romescae* 4.25

mesc "drunken, intoxicated; confused, befuddled"; superl. *mescam* 8.13

mesrugud m. "moderation; act of tempering, regulating"; nom. sg. 5.23

mí-: adj. prefix "bad; invalid"

míairle f. "bad management, mismanagement"; gen. sg. 5.22: *see* airle

míchor m. "an invalid contract"; dat. pl. *míchoraib* 6.42: *see* cor

mil f. "honey"; as adj. prefix "sweet, honeyed"; compd. nom. sg. *miltengae* 1.54

mílchú m. "hunting hound, greyhound"; nom. pl. *mílchoin* 8.8

miltengae f. "a sweet tongue; persuasive eloquence"; nom. sg. 1.54: *see* mil, tengae

mín "gentle, mild"; compd. acc. sg. *míngoiri* 3.22

míne f. "gentleness, mildness"; 3.22

míngoire f. "gentle maintenance"; acc. sg. *míngoiri* 3.22: *see* goire

minntán m. "a small bird; titmouse"; nom. pl. *minntáin* 8.14

mire f. "madness, frenzy"; gen. sg. 4.14

miscais f. "hatred, dislike"; nom. sg. 1.7, 4.4; acc. sg. 1.49

mlicht "milking, yield of milk"; dat. pl. *mlichtaib* 6.87

móin f. "bog; moor, waste"; nom. sg. 6.34

molad m. "act of praising; approval"; nom. sg. 9.5; acc. sg. 1.40

mór "big, large, great"; 7.20; as prefix in compds. dat. sg. *móraltramm* 6.20, *mórsléib* 6.86

mórad m. "act of making great; magnifying, exalting"; acc. sg. 3.14

móraltramm n. "much fosterage"; dat. sg. 6.20: *see* altramm

mórslíab n. "big mountain, large moorland"; dat. sg. *mórsléib* 6.86: *see* slíab

mrath "treachery, betrayal"; acc. sg. 1.29; gen. sg. *mraith* 4.17

mruig m. "inhabited or cultivated land; farmland; country-side"; nom. sg. 6.87

mruiges "possession of lands"; 6.19

mucc f. "pig, sow"; nom. pl. *mucca* 8.6

múcnaid m.? "repression, suppression"; dat. sg. 6.101

mug m. "male slave, servant"; nom. sg. 6.11; acc. pl. *mugu* 1.66

muirn f. "exuberance; mirth, clamour"; compd. nom. sg. *degmuirn* 6.99

múnad m. "teaching, instructing"; acc. sg. 3.30

naidm n. "act of binding; pledge, contract; one who acts as an enforcing surety"; nom. sg. 3.10

naiscid "binds, makes fast (a pledge or contract)"; pres. pass. sg. rel. *nascar* 3.10

námae m. "enemy"; 6.22

nascar: *see* naiscid

nem n. "heaven"; gen. sg. *nime* 7.11

nert n. "strength, might, power"; compd. acc. sg. *bithnert* 1.45

ní: neg. part. 7.18: *see* is

nós m.? "legal science, law, custom"; acc. pl. *nósu* 9.12

óc "young"; as subst. nom. sg. 3.18

ocus: conj. "and", always written ₇ in this text; 7.14, 8.2, 8.4, 8.6, 8.8, 8.10, 8.12, 8.14, 8.16, 8.18, 8.21, 8.25

óg-: adj. prefix "full, complete"

ógríar f. "complete desire, full satisfaction"; acc. sg. *ógréir* 3.23: *see* ríar

oíb f. "semblance, appearance"; compd. dat. sg. *frithoíb* 6.88

ól m. "act of drinking; carousing"; compd. nom. sg. *roól* 4.25

olc "evil, bad, wrong"; superl. *mesam* 8.20, 8.23, 8.25; as subst. gen. sg. *uilc* 4.24, 5.11

ómun m. "fear, state of being afraid, timidity"; nom. sg. 4.6

opad m. "act of refusing, rejecting, refusal"; dat. sg. *opud* 6.66

orbae n. "patrimony, inheritance (of land)"; nom. sg. 6.24; dat. sg. *orbu* 6.1, 6.23

ordan m. "dignity, honour; nobility"; nom. sg. 6.7; acc. sg. 1.61; gen. sg. *ordain* 5.5

oscrae n. "state of being unskilled; ignorance; being an outsider"; dat. sg. *oscru* 6.10n

othar m. "sick-maintenance, nursing; a sick person, a patient"; nom. sg. 3.26

pleibideacht: *see* pliptecht

pliptecht f. "commonness, vulgarity?"; dat. sg. 6.29n

ránac: *see* ro·icc

rann f. "act of sharing, dividing; portion"; nom. sg. 6.73

rath n. "fief-payment; boon; grace; prosperity"; nom. sg. 3.7, 6.8, 6.74

ráth "surety, pledge; security; guarantor"; nom. sg. 3.11; dat. pl. *ráthaib* 6.95

ré n.? "space (of time and of distance), interval; respite"; nom. sg. 6.95

reconn m. "fore-thought"; nom. sg. 6.21: *see* conn

réide f. "levelness, smoothness; steadiness"; nom. sg. 6.75

répend n. vb.n. of *répaid* "rends, tears"; dat. sg. *répiund* 6.73n

rér: *see* ríar

rí m. "a king, a chief"; acc. sg. *ríg* 7.2

ríar (earlier rér) f. "will, wish; stipulation; service (which is owed); claim"; acc. pl. *ríara* 3.7; dat. pl. *ríaraib* 6.8, *réraib* 6.8b; compd. acc. sg. *ógréir* 3.23

ríarugud m.? "act of ministering to, doing the will of, serving"; acc. sg. 3.7a; dat. sg. 6.8a

rigne f. "tenacity, toughness; slowness, prolixity; tedium"; nom. sg. 9.18

rith m. "act of running; course; career, life"; compd. dat. sg. *trénriuth* 6.52

ro-: intensive prefix

road "prosperity, luck"; nom. sg. 6.8b

ro·bíatha: *see* bíathaid

roda·bíatha: *see* bíathaid

rofáiscre m.? "great repression"; acc. sg. 1.6: *see* fáiscre

rogáes f. "much intelligence, acuteness; great wisdom"; dat. sg. *rogaís* 6.75: *see* gáes

rogáire m. "excess laughter"; nom. sg. 4.14: *see* gáire

ro·icc "comes (upon)"; 2sg. pret./perf. prototonic *ránac* 8.1, 8.3, 8.5, 8.7, 8.9, 8.11, 8.13, 8.15, 8.17, 8.19, 8.23

rolabrae f. "excess talking"; nom. sg. 4.9: *see* labrae

rolgad m. "great concession; great forgiveness"; dat. sg. 6.74: *see* logad

romescae f. "much drunkeness"; gen. sg. 4.25: *see* mescae

roól m. "much drinking"; nom. sg. 4.25: *see* ól

rosc n.? "poem, chant; maxim; an inflammatory speech, a poem used to incite"; nom. sg. 6.102

rous n. "(great) knowledge"; nom. sg. 6.76: *see* fis

rúathar m. "an onrush; attack; aggressiveness"; dat. sg. *rúathur* 6.76

sáegul m. "life, the world"; nom. sg. 1.59

saidbre f. "wealth"; acc. sg. 1.1

saidbres m. "wealth"; acc. sg. 1.1

saigthige f. "aggressiveness in pursuing claims, litigiousness"; acc. sg. *saigthigi* 1.35a

sáith f. "sufficiency, fill"; dat. sg. 6.62

sáithche f. "fulfillment, satisfaction"; acc. sg. *sáithchi* 1.35

sanas f. "whisper; secrecy"; nom. sg. 4.17

sant f. "strong desire; greed, avarice, covetousness; lust"; gen. sg. *sainte* 4.15

santach "covetous, greedy"; as subst. nom. sg. 1.18

sásad m. "act of satisfying; satisfaction; satiety"; dat. sg. 6.4

secht "seven"; § 9

ségonn "skilled, accomplished, proficient person"; nom. sg. 1.56

séitchi: *see* séitig

séitig f. "wife, consort; companion"; dat. sg. *séitchi* 6.89

sen "old, ancient"; as subst. nom. sg. 3.20; as prefix *senécraite, senfíach* 6.35

senécraite f. "old enmity; old grudge"; dat. sg. *senécraiti* 6.35: *see* écraite

senfíach m. "old obligation, old debt, old fine"; nom. sg. 6.35: *see* fíach

senfola "old grievance, old resentment"; 6.35

serbae f. "bitterness, asperity"; gen. sg. 4.21; dat. sg. *serbai* 6.60

serc f. "love"; nom. sg. 1.10; gen. sg. *serce* 4.16

sercach "beloved, lovable; loving"; 2.3

1 sét m. "unit of value; wealth, riches, possessions"; acc. pl. *séotu* 1.18; dat. pl. *sétaib* 6.5, 6.15

2 sét m. "way, path; way (of life)"; nom. sg. 6.14

síd n. "peace, good-will"; nom. sg. 6.58

sídugud m. "conciliation, making peace"; acc. sg. 1.30

silliud m. "act of gazing upon; watching"; compd. nom. sg. *sírsilliud* 4.16

sír-: adj. prefix "long-lasting, enduring"

sírdord n.? "long-lasting plaint"; nom. sg. 4.2: *see* dord

sírecht f. "longing, yearning; deprivation"; gen. sg. *sírechtae* 4.2

sírsilliud m. "constant gazing; continuous watching"; nom. sg. 4.16: *see* silliud

slabrae f. "stock (usually of cattle); a marriage portion, dowry; wealth"; dat. sg. *slabrai* 6.17

sláinte f. "wholeness, healthiness; freedom (from illness or legal liability); (spiritual) salvation"; nom. sg. 4.19

slán "whole, sound, healthy"; as subst. nom. sg. 6.4

slíab n. "mountain, moor"; compd. dat. sg. *mórsléib* 6.86

slóg m. "host, army; throng, crowd; force of numbers"; nom. sg. 6.90; dat. sg. 6.16

snímche f. "grief, sorrow, anxiety"; acc. sg. *snímchi* 1.59

so-: adj. prefix "good, excellent"

soálaig f. "good habit, good behaviour"; acc. sg. 1.64: *see* álaig

sobarthu f. "well-being; blessing, prosperity"; nom. sg. 6.57

soben f. "a good woman, a good wife"; nom. sg. 6.59: *see* ben

sochaide f. "multitude, crowd"; gen. sg. 9.16

sochell f. "liberality, generosity"; nom. sg. 1.1: *see* cíall

sochenél n. "a good kindred; exalted family"; acc. sg. 7.4; dat. sg. *socheníul* 6.59: *see* cenél

sochlach "famous, renowned, eminent"; as subst. nom. sg. 1.52

sochocad m. "a successful war; a just conflict"; dat. sg. 6.58: *see* cocad

sochoisce "tractability, instructability"; nom. sg. 5.6

sochraid "seemly, decorous; handsome"; 2.5

sochraite f. "state of having good friends; retinue, followers"; nom. sg. 6.17; acc. sg. *sochraiti* 3.9

sogním m. "good action, good deed"; nom. sg. 1.64: *see* gním

sogoire f. "dutiful maintenance; pious attendance"; acc. sg. *sogoiri* 3.20, 3.23a: *see* goire

soichlige f. "liberality, generosity"; 1.35

soíre f. "privileged (social) status; freedom"; nom. sg. 1.35; acc. sg. *soíri* 1.56, 3.35

soithnge "eloquent, persuasive"; as subst. nom. sg. 1.30, 6.16a: *see* tengae

solam "quick, speedy, prompt"; superl. *solmam* 8.9

somescae f. "drunkenness"; nom. sg. 5.13: *see* mescae

sommae f. "wealth"; nom. sg. 3.35

sonaide f. "good fortune, prosperity"; nom. sg. 6.5

sonaige f. "good fortune, prosperity"; 6.5

sothced, sothcad m. "good fortune, happiness"; nom. sg. 6.16, 6.89; gen. sg. *sothcaid* 5.14, 5.20n: *see* tocad

soud m. vb.n. of *soid* "turns, returns"; nom. sg. 9.12

sous n. "knowledge, science; learning"; dat. sg. 6.14, 6.92: *see* fis

sprecad m. "rebuking; inciting, urging on"; nom. sg. 9.16

súan m. "repose, tranquility; sleep"; nom. sg. 6.60

suí m. "man of learning, sage; expert, master"; nom. sg. 7.15

suide: anaphoric pron. "this, that"; dat. pl. *suidib* 8.21, 8.25

suidigidir "puts, places; arranges, establishes"; 3sg. pres. rel. pass. *suidigther* 6.90

suidigther: *see* suidigidir

suidiugud m. vb.n. of suidigidir 6.90

suíthe n.? "learning, knowledge; mastery, expertise"; gen. sg. *suíthi* 5.6; dat. sg. *suíthiu* 6.57

suthaine f. "lastingness, continuity; long life"; nom. sg. 6.15

tabart f. "giving, bestowing"; acc. sg. *tabairt* 7.11

tacrae n. "pleading (a law-suit), arguing, disputing"; nom. sg. 9.15; gen. sg. *tacrai* 9.6, 9.14; compd. gen. sg. *drochthacrai* § 9

·tair: *see* do·airicc

taircsiu f. "attempt, effort; an undertaking"; nom. sg. 6.56a

tairecc n. vb.n. of *do·airicc* "comes; finds, gets"; 3.33

tairisem m. "remaining, staying"; dat. sg. 6.45

tairisiu f.? "trust, confidence; faithfulness, loyalty, trustworthiness"; nom. sg. 6.56

tairngire n. "act of promising, a promise; act of prophesying"; dat. sg. *tairngiriu* 6.56

tét "fervent, wanton; mighty"; superl. *tétem* 8.7

techt m.? "possession; having legal right to"; nom. sg. 6.33

téchtae n. "legal rightness; proper dues"; 6.33

teiched m. "fleeing, flight; avoidance"; nom. sg. 6.45

tengae f. "tongue; language, speech"; compds. nom. sg. *biltengae* 1.29, *étnge*
    3.32, *miltengae* 1.54, *soithnge* 1.30, 6.16a

tercae f. "scarcity, lack; want"; nom. sg. 1.34

tinnriud m. "damage, injury"; 6.52

tinnscrae n. "dowry; bride-price"; dat. sg. *tinnscru* 6.44

tiugbae "surviving"; as subst. nom. sg. 6.43

tocad m. "fortune, chance; good fortune, prosperity"; gen. sg. *tocaid* 5.7;
    compds. nom. sg. *sothced* 6.16, 6.89; gen. sg. *dothcaid* 5.13, 5.21, *sothcaid*
    5.14, 5.20

toirnem m.? "lowering, abating"; 1.19

toirsige f. "grievousness, weariness; fatigue"; nom. sg. 5.17

tomus m. vb.n. of *do·midethar* "weighs, measures, estimates"; nom. sg. 9.7

torad n. "produce; result, profit, increase"; acc. sg. 1.42; dat. sg. *torud* 6.43

tóraic vb.n. of *do·fuiric* "finds, comes upon"; nom. sg. 3.33

tórmach n. "act of increasing; increment, addition"; compd. nom. sg.
    caíntórmach 6.37

tosach n. "beginning; first principle; basis"; nom. sg. § 5, 7.6

trebad m. "cultivating; husbandry; residence"; nom. sg. 1.42

trebaire f. "farming, husbandry; prudence, discretion"; nom. sg. 5.7; gen. sg.
    4.8; compds. nom. sg. *drochthrebaire* 6.32; gen. sg. *étrebaire* 4.9

trebar "careful, prudent, thrifty, secure"; nom. sg. 2.2

tregtach "pierced, wounded; pained"; nom. pl. *tregtaig* 7.16

trén- "strong"

trénrith m. "a strong run"; dat. sg. *trénriuth* 6.52: *see* rith

tróge f. "misery, wretchedness, affliction"; gen. sg. 5.17

trotach "pugnacious, quarrelsome"; as subst. nom. sg. 1.44

trúag (tróg) "pitiable, wretched, sad"; as subst. compd. dat. sg. *allatróg* 6.33n

trummae f. "heaviness, weight; severity, rigour"; nom. sg. 6.46

túae f. "silence"; nom. sg. 4.8

túarcun f. vb.n. of *do·fúairc* "grinds, crushes; pounds"; acc. sg. *túarcuin* 1.44

túath f. "a people, tribe; territory"; nom. sg. 6.44

tuinide n. "(entitlement of) possession, ownership"; acc. sg. 3.33

tuisel m. vb.n. of *do·fuisli* "stumbles, falls"; acc. sg. 9.6

úabar m. "pride, arrogance, vanity"; nom. sg. 4.24; in compd. *úabarbríathar*
    5.11

úabarbríathar f. "a proud word, vain speech"; nom. sg. 5.11: *see* úabar, bríathar

úallach "proud, arrogant"; superl. *úallcham* 8.15

úasal "high, lofty, exalted; noble"; 2.7

uilc: *see* olc

uirb: nom. sg./pl.? 6.23n; dat. sg. 6.24

umal "humble, obedient"; 2.7; as subst. nom. sg. 1.61

umlae f. "humility, obedience"; nom. sg. 1.16

utmaille f. "uncertainty, instability; unsteadiness, change"; nom. sg. 9.14; acc. sg. *utmailli* 1.21, 1.68

Index of Proper Names

Headwords in *italic* type refer to names found in the edited texts, that is, §§ 1–9. Headwords in regular type refer to names discussed in introductory material (where they are cited by page number) or in textual notes (where they are cited by section and line numbers).

MRTS

MEDIEVAL AND RENAISSANCE TEXTS AND STUDIES
is the major publishing program of the
Arizona Center for Medieval and Renaissance Studies
at Arizona State University, Tempe, Arizona.

MRTS emphasizes books that are needed —
texts, translations, and major research tools.

MRTS aims to publish the highest quality scholarship
in attractive and durable format at modest cost.